The Limits to Scarcity

Science in Society Series

Series Editor: Steve Rayner
Institute for Science, Innovation and Society, University of Oxford

Editorial Board: Gary Kass, Anne Kerr, Melissa Leach, Angela Liberatore,
Stan Metcalfe, Paul Nightingale, Timothy O'Riordan, Nick Pidgeon, Ortwin Renn,
Dan Sarewitz, Andrew Webster, James Wilsdon, Steve Yearley

Animals as Biotechnology
Ethics, Sustainability and Critical Animal Studies
Richard Twine

Business Planning for Turbulent Times
New Methods for Applying Scenarios
Edited by Rafael Ramírez, John W. Selsky and Kees van der Heijden

Debating Climate Change
Pathways through Argument to Agreement
Elizabeth L. Malone

Democratizing Technology
Risk, Responsibility and the Regulation of Chemicals
Anne Chapman

Genomics and Society
Legal, Ethical and Social Dimensions
Edited by George Gaskell and Martin W. Bauer

Influenza and Public Health
Learning from Past Pandemics
Edited by Tamara Giles-Vernick and Susan Craddock, with Jennifer Gunn

Marginalized Reproduction
Ethnicity, Infertility and Reproductive Technologies
Lorraine Culley, Nicky Hudson and Floor van Rooij

Nanotechnology
Risk, Ethics and Law
Edited by Geoffrey Hunt and Michael Mehta

Resolving Messy Policy Problems
Handling Conflict in Environmental, Transport, Health and Ageing Policy
Steven Ney

Rationality and Ritual
Participation and Exalusion in Nuclear Decision-making
Brian Wynne

The Limits to Scarcity
Contesting the Politics of Allocation
Edited by Lyla Mehta

Uncertainty in Policy Making
Values and Evidence in Complex Decisions
Michael Heazle

Unnatural Selection
The Challenges of Engineering Tomorrow's People
Edited by Peter Healey and Steve Rayner

Vaccine Anxieties
Global Science, Child Health and Society
Melissa Leach and James Fairhead

A Web of Prevention
Biological Weapons, Life Sciences and the Governance of Research
Edited by Brian Rappert and Caitrìona McLeish

The Limits to Scarcity

Contesting the Politics of Allocation

Edited by Lyla Mehta

publishing for a sustainable future

London • Washington, DC

First published in 2010 by Earthscan

Earthscan Ltd, Dunstan House, 14a St Cross Street, London EC1N 8XA, UK
Earthscan LLC, 1616 P Street, NW, Washington, DC 20036, USA
Earthscan publishes in association with the International Institute for Environment and Development

For more information on Earthscan publications, see www.earthscan.co.uk or write to earthinfo@earthscan.co.uk

ISBN: 978-1-84407-457-0 hardback
ISBN: 978-1-84407-542-3 paperback

Typeset by Composition and Design Services
Cover design by Susanne Harris

A catalogue record for this book is available from the British Library

Library of Congress Cataloging-in-Publication Data

The limits to scarcity : contesting the politics of allocation / edited by Lyla Mehta.
      p. cm.
   Includes bibliographical references and index.
   ISBN 978-1-84407-457-0 (hbk.) — ISBN 978-1-84407-542-3 (pbk.) 1. Scarcity. 2. Welfare economics. 3. Supply and demand. 4. Resource allocation. I. Mehta, Lyla.
   HB846.L56 2010
   338.5'21—dc22   2010019662

At Earthscan we strive to minimize our environmental impacts and carbon footprint through reducing waste, recycling and offsetting our CO_2 emissions, including those created through publication of this book. For more details of our environmental policy, see www.earthscan.co.uk.

Printed and bound in the UK by MPG Books, an ISO 14001 accredited company. The paper used is FSC certified.

For Wolfgang Sachs

Contents

List of Figures and Tables

Figures

Tables

List of Contributors

Ajaya Dixit

Executive Director
Institute for Social and Environmental Transition – Nepal (ISET-N)
GPO Box 3971
Kathmandu
Nepal

adbaluwatar@ntc.net.np

Ajaya Dixit is an analyst of water resources and environment themes in Nepal and South Asia. He is the founder of Nepal Water Conservation Foundation (NWCF) and editor of *Water Nepal*, a journal addressing interdisciplinary water and development issues. He taught hydraulics and water resources engineering at Tribhuvan University's Institute of Engineering until 1989. He was educated at Regional Engineering College Rourkela, India (1977) and University of Strathclyde, Glasgow (1981).

He serves as chairman of the board of directors of Nepal Water for Health (NEWAH), a Nepali NGO that that has helped develop drinking water supply, sanitation and hygiene services to about 1 million people. He has written extensively on water resources, trans-boundary cooperation, flood management, environment and developmental issues and is the author of *Basic Water Science*. He teaches interdisciplinary water resource management and climate change adaption at Nepal Engineering College Kathmandu and is currently directing regional research looking at climate changes impacts on flood, drought and food system adaptation in South Asia. He also is the research director of the Institute of Social and Environmental Transition (ISET) which is engaged in climate adaptation research.

Ben Fine

School of Oriental and African Studies
University of London
Thornhaugh Street
Russell Square
London WC1H 0XG
UK

bf@soas.ac.uk

Ben Fine is a professor of economics at the School of Oriental and African Studies (SOAS), and the author of numerous books, including *Theories of Social Capital: Researchers Behaving Badly*, 2010; *From Economics Imperialism to Freakonomics: The Shifting Boundaries between Economics and Other Social Sciences*, 2009, co-authored with Dimitris Milonakis and awarded the Deutscher Memorial Prize; and *From Political Economy to Economics: Method, the Social and the Historical in the Evolution of Economic Theory*, also with Milonakis, 2009, awarded the Gunnar Myrdal Prize. He took his doctorate in economics at the London School of Economics, under the supervision of Amartya Sen. His interests lie in the minerals-energy complex in South Africa; the political economy of consumption, particularly food; privatization and industrial policy; political economy, history of economic thought and economic theory and economic imperialism especially social capital.

Dipak Gyawali

Nepal Water Conservation Foundation
PO Box 2221
Kathmandu
Nepal

dipakgyawali@ntc.net.np

Dipak Gyawali, *Pragya* (Academician) of the Nepal Academy of Science and Technology and Research Director of the Nepal Water Conservation Foundation, is a hydroelectric power engineer (Moskovsky Energetichesky Institute, USSR, 1979) and a political economist focusing on natural resources (University of California, Berkeley, 1986). His interdisciplinary research agenda focuses on society-technology-resource base interface, with water and energy as entry points. He has chaired the EU's review of its international water resource research from FP4 to FP6; been a member of the international advisory boards of Coca Cola as well as Oxford University's James Martin Institute for Science and Civilization; and served as Nepal's Minister of Water Resources (responsible for power, irrigation and flood control) in 2002/2003. He chairs the recently founded first liberal arts college of Nepal, the Nepā School of Social Sciences and Humanities. He is also the Vice-Chair of the Technical Advisory Committee of United Nations' World Water Assessment Program and advisor to the National Association of Community Electricity Users' Nepal as well as the Nepal Biogas Support Program.

Betsy Hartmann

Betsy Hartmann
Director, Population and Development Program
Professor of Development Studies
CLPP
Hampshire College
Amherst, MA 01002
USA

bhartmann@hampshire.edu

Betsy Hartmann is the Director of the Population and Development Program and Professor of development studies at Hampshire College in Amherst, MA, USA. A longstanding activist in the international women's health movement, she writes and speaks frequently on the intersections between reproductive rights, population, immigration, environment and security concerns in activist, policy and scholarly venues. Her non-fiction books include *Reproductive Rights and Wrongs: The Global Politics of Population Control*, *A Quiet Violence: View from a Bangladesh Village* (co-authored with James Boyce) and the co-edited anthology *Making Threats: Biofears and Environmental Anxieties*. She is also the author of two political thrillers, *The Truth about Fire* and *Deadly Election*.

To find out more about Betsy, visit www.BetsyHartmann.com. To find out more about the Population and Development Program, visit http://popdev. hampshire.edu

Nicholas Hildyard

The Corner House
Station Road
Sturminster Nerwton
Dorset DT10 1YJ
UK

nick@fifehead.demon.co.uk

Nicholas Hildyard works with The Corner House, a research and solidarity group focusing on human rights, environment and development.

Jasveen Jairath

Society for Participatory Development (SPD)
F-1, Eden Banjara
Ave-8, St.7, Aurora Colony
Banjara Hills
Hyderabad 500034
A.P., India

capnet_southasia@spdindia.org

Jasveen Jairath graduated in electrical engineering and later moved to economics with a Masters in political economy from New School for Social Research, New York and a PhD from the Centre for Economics Studies and Planning, JNU, Delhi. She has been engaged with research, advocacy, networking and capacity building in the water sector through her tenures at government and non-government organizations. Through her specific field studies in Punjab, Maharashtra and Andhra Pradesh she has highlighted the social context of water to question technocratic and reductionist interpretations of mainstream water discourse. Critical interventions in the policy debates on large dams, droughts and institutional reforms have been followed by design and implementation of hands-on experimental water projects on governance of urban water and sanitation systems in Madhya Pradesh. She is the current Regional Coordinator of Capnet South Asia and has been on the Board of Governor of World Water Council. At present she operates as an independent consultant and researcher-advocate with a focus on the *politics* of water practice and policy.

Bruce Alistair Lankford

Senior Lecturer
School of International Development
The University of East Anglia
Norwich NR4 7TJ
UK

b.lankford@uea.ac.uk

At the time of writing, Bruce Lankford was Head of School at the School of International Development at the University of East Anglia. Bruce has been working in water management since 1983, initially at the irrigation system level in sub-Saharan Africa but more recently on livelihood, institutional and basin approaches to the management and governance of river basins and water resources. His research interests cover: water allocation decision-making including the use of games and gaming; polycentric governance models for IWRM (Integrated Water Resources Management); water productivity theory; socio-technical reform of irrigation performance; and irrigation policy in Africa.

Fred Luks

Fred.Luks@gmx.de

Fred Luks has studied in Hamburg and Honolulu, with research stays in Kuala Lumpur, New York and Berkeley. He has held several jobs in sustainability research, among them as visiting professor for ecological economics at the University of Hamburg. Luks was chairman of the German Association for Ecological Economics. He lives in Vienna and works as a sustainability manager for UniCredit Bank Austria. His latest book *Endlich im Endlichen* (2010) is on the relevance of irony and generosity for sustainable development.

Lyla Mehta

Institute of Development Studies
University of Sussex
Brighton BN1 9RE
UK

L.Mehta@ids.ac.uk

Lyla Mehta is a sociologist and research fellow with the Institute of Development Studies at the University of Sussex and a professor II at the Department of International Environment and Development (Noragric) Norwegian University of Life Sciences. She is also a member of the scientific committee of the Global Environment Change and Human Security Project, International Human Dimensions Project. She has worked extensively on issues concerning scarcity, access and rights to resources addressed through the case of water. Other interests include rights and the gendered dimensions of forced displacement and resistance and the cultural politics of sanitation, environment and development. She is the author of *The Politics and Poetics of Water: Naturalising Scarcity in Western India*, editor of *Displaced by Development: Confronting Marginalisation and Gender Injustice* and the co-editor of *Forced Displacement: Why Rights Matter*.

Erik Millstone

SPRU (Science and Technology Policy Research)
University of Sussex
Freeman Centre
Falmer
Brighton
East Sussex BN1 9QE
UK

E.P.Millstone@sussex.ac.uk

Erik Millstone is a professor of science policy at the University of Sussex, in SPRU – Science and Technology Policy Research. His first degree was in physics, followed by three in philosophy. Since 1974 he has been researching into the causes, consequences and regulation of technological change in the food and chemical industries. Since 1988 he has been researching the role of scientific experts, evidence and advice in public policy-making. His recent books include *BSE: Risk Science and Governance* (Oxford University Press, 2005) and *The Atlas of Food: Who Eats What, Where and Why* (Earthscan and University of California Press, 2008). Much of his current research focuses on the conditions under which poor maize farmers in Africa can respond to the challenge of climate change, as part of the STEPS (or Social and Technological Pathways to Sustainability) programme – see www.steps-centre.org/.

Jean Robert

jeanrobert37@gmail.com

Jean Robert is a freelance essayist who would like to think of himself as 'intelligent' rather than as 'an intellectual' or, if that's too pretentious, at least as a 'deprofessionalized intellectual'. He is presently preparing a 'manifesto of the resisters to the war on subsistance', a theme that he has treated in several books and articles, approaching it from the view of the material culture rather than from a formal economic perspective. He is a promoter of the untranslatable idea of 'la Décroissance' in Mexico and has been involved in co-organizing a seminar on 'Ivan Illich and the archaeology of modern certainties' which was held at the Paris XXI university in 2010.

Sajay Samuel

Clinical Professor of Accounting, and Science, Technology and Society
379, BB
Smeal: College of Business
Pennsylvania State University
University Park, PA 16802
USA

sajay@psu.edu

Sajay Samuel teaches at the Business School at Pennsylvania State University. His research is directed at uncovering thought-styles that bury or ignore vernacular forms-of-life. His current work focuses on exposing the blind spots of modern economic science and political theory because of which they serve as foot-soldiers in the war against subsistence. His reflections on the limits of scientific rationalism have appeared, most recently, in *Ideas on the Nature of Science* (ed) David Cayley (Goose Lane Press, 2009). Samuel is part of an itinerant group of thinkers, scholars, and activists deeply influenced by the thoughts and work of Ivan Illich.

Ian Scoones

Institute of Development Studies
University of Sussex
Brighton BN1 9RE
UK

I.Scoones@ids.ac.uk

Ian Scoones is a Fellow at the Institute of Development Studies (IDS), co-director of the ESRC STEPS Centre at Sussex and joint convenor of the IDS-hosted Future Agricultures Consortium. He is an agricultural ecologist by original training whose interdisciplinary research links the natural and social sciences and focuses on the relationships between science and technology, local knowledge and livelihoods and the politics of policy processes in the context of international agricultural, environment and development issues. A social and institutional perspective is at the centre of his work, which explores the linkages between local knowledge and practices and the processes of scientific enquiry, development policy-making and field-level implementation. Over the past 25 years, he has worked on pastoralism and rangeland management, soil and water conservation, biodiversity and conservation, as well as dryland agricultural systems, largely in eastern and southern Africa.

Michael Thompson

82 Bloomfield Avenue
Bath BA2 3AD
UK

Michael.Thompson@uib.no

Michael Thompson is an Institute Scholar at the International Institute for Applied Systems Analysis, Laxenburg, Austria, also a Fellow at the Institute for Science, Innovation and Society, Said Business School, University of Oxford.

Nicholas Xenos

Department of Political Science
Thompson Hall
University of Massachusetts
200 Hicks Way
Amherst, MA 01003-9277
USA

xenos@polsci.umass.edu

Nicholas Xenos is a professor of political science at the University of Massachusetts, Amherst. He is the author of *Scarcity and Modernity* (Routledge, 1989) and *Cloaked in Virtue: Unveiling Leo Strauss and the Rhetoric of American Foreign Policy* (Routledge, 2008).

Foreword

This is a dangerous book.

'Scarcity' is a key term in contemporary human development discourse. It is deeply embedded in two competing narratives. In one of these, the 'limits-to-growth' narrative of a finite world in which a recklessly expanding human population is rapidly depleting the resources on which it depends, the idea of scarcity represents the explicit boundary conditions of discourse and policy. In the other narrative, scarcity serves a more technical role in defining neoclassical economics as the 'science of resource allocation', which places markets at the centre of ever-expanding economic growth. In both cases, the idea of scarcity is seldom interrogated. To do so is intellectually dangerous. It is to question the underlying world views upon which each of these narratives, and the policies that flow from them, depend.

Scarcity in neoclassical economics is the relative scarcity of one good in relation to another, which drives the allocation decisions of consumers. The idea of scarcity in the limits-to-growth narrative, and its technical extension in ecological economics, is not relative, but generalized. Under the neoclassical assumption of relative scarcity, there is an infinite potential to substitute abundant materials for scarce ones. So while the discourse of limits ultimately depends on the assertion that the earth is a closed system, the neoclassical vision permits humanity, as a species, to transcend the finitude of any particular resource through human creativity, leading to the cornucopian vision of infinite global economic growth.

However, infinite plenitude is not a state that can ever be attained in the neoclassical world due to the theory's non-satiety requirement, which assumes that people will always prefer a large basket of goods to a small one. When we get pig-sick of smoked salmon, we add caviar to the shopping list. We can find counter-examples where societies, from hunter-gatherers in Africa to the Pennsylvania Amish, constrain their wants and in so doing achieve affluence based on the principle that 'a wealthy person is one who is content with what he has'. However, such constraint seems to rely on very intensive levels of face-to-face monitoring of behaviour and the ability to sanction or, at least, to shame transgressors. These conditions seem politically both impractical and at odds with the contemporary ideas of universal individual rights, which sit uneasily alongside the coercive mechanisms required to sustain 'voluntary' collective frugality.

Ironically, both the discourse of limits and the idea of infinite growth end up being anti-poor. The discourse of limits is straightforwardly neo-Malthusian. If there are too many people making demands on finite resources, the solution is to reduce either the level of demand or the number of demanders. If, as I have already suggested, asking the wealthy and powerful to embrace frugality or the poor to voluntarily remain poor is a political recipe that is unlikely to succeed on a significant scale (for different reasons) in say China, India and the USA, then the alternative is to limit population. The candidate populations, to which such limits are to be applied, are not, of course, those of affluent societies which are already reproducing below replacement levels, but those of the poor.

The infinite-growth narrative is a bit more subtle but no less damaging to the poor. Its neoclassical economic paradigm is underpinned by the utilitarian principle of achieving the greatest happiness of the greatest number. This, at least in part, accounts for the depth of moral outrage on the part of economists encountering inefficiency; a smaller pie means less to go around. However, the imperative to provide for societal good at the highest level of aggregation provides no guidance for securing the happiness of the various communities or individuals that make up a society. 'The guiding criterion for policy is the greatest good for society, quantitatively defined. But contemporary utilitarians, primarily economists and theorists of public choice, like Bentham, still have no principle for distributing this social good according to manifest principles of equity' (Heineman et al, 1990). A rising tide, alas, does not lift all boats and certainly does not address the issues of those that may be holed, ill equipped or poorly provisioned for the voyage.

So scarcity takes on another dimension, independently of its role as a technical device of neoclassical economics, it becomes a rationale for inequitable allocation. As the contributors to the volume repeatedly demonstrate, there is plenty of food, water and energy on this planet to meet the requirements of a population that demographers project will peak at just below 9 billion. Famines, fuel shortages, and water stress are not the result of generalized shortages, but failures of allocation to the poor who simply cannot afford to buy what they need from elsewhere. Markets respond to the buying power of the wealthy. Goods flow to those who can afford them. But by framing scarcity as an inherent characteristic of resources, both scarcity narratives naturalize the failure of societies to provide for the needs of the poor, and elide issues of equity and social justice that are uncomfortable to the beneficiaries of current distributions of wealth and power. The failure to provide for the poor and powerless becomes nature's fault not humanity's. As Amartya Sen has consistently argued, addressing the needs of the poor requires a fundamental shift from the language of scarcity to the issues of resource allocation, access and entitlement.

Such a shift will also require an explicit focus on judgements about the appropriateness of needs and wants. Both the narratives of limits and of growth not only naturalize scarcity but also 'needs and wants'.

The usual model of the representative consumer in both ecological and neoclassical economic theory has been the hedonist whose choices are made to address private wants and provide individual satisfaction. The origin of these wants is seldom addressed explicitly, but is usually assumed to lie within the individual arising from physical urges like hunger, thirst or survival. There have been numerous attempts, such as Maslow's to derive hierarchies of basic physiological needs, which must be satisfied before the individual moves on to higher psychological needs such as 'esteem' and 'self-actualization'. However, prepotency is not clear-cut, there are no sharp demarcations at which one urge disappears and the next suddenly emerges. Many have argued that self-actualization is actually the most fundamental, and the implication that needs can be divided into lower material needs for 'survival' and higher, more abstract needs for 'self-actualization' legitimizes a distribution of power in favour of educated elites. A further observation that arises from viewing such hierarchies through the lens of scarcity narratives is that the so-called lower needs are those that are consumed in use, while the higher needs, such as love and esteem actually increase with their exercise, and thus the distinction reiterates the elite Malthusian divide between the enlightened and productive elite and the self-destructive and rapacious poor.

A radical critique of the idea of needs and wants is to be found in the claim of Mary Douglas (1986), that consumption is not the expression of well-ordered preferences driven by the need to satisfy physical urges or vaguer internal demands, but to negotiate social relations:

> *A person wants goods for fulfilling personal commitments. Commodities do not satisfy desire; they are only tools or instruments for satisfying it. Goods are not ends. Goods are for distributing, sharing consuming or destroying publicly in one way or another. To focus on how persons relate to objects can never illuminate desire. Instead research should focus on the patterns of alliance and authority that are made and marked in all human societies by the circulation of goods. Demand for objects is a chart of social commitments graded and timetabled for the year, the decade, or the lifetime ... [R]estricting consumption of goods restricts participation in the extended social conversation for which they are used.* (Douglas et al, 1998)

Recasting needs and wants alongside scarcity in an authentically social, rather than naturalized, framework transforms the policy challenge. It reinforces Sen's focus on the structure and processes of entitlements and social commitments and challenges us to reassess those arrangements. This book's comprehensive critique of the totalizing discourses of scarcity that block such alternative modes of inquiry makes an excellent start.

Steve Rayner
Oxford 2010

References

Douglas, M., Gasper, D., Ney, S. and Thompson, M. (1998) 'Human needs and wants' in S. Rayner and E. L. Malone (eds) *Human Choice and Climate Change: Volume 1 The Societal Framework*, Battelle Press, Columbus OH, pp195–264

Heineman, R. A., Bluhm, W. T., Peterson, S. A. and Kearney, E. N. (1990) *The World of the Policy Analyst: Rationality and Values in Politics*, Chatham House Publishers, Chatham NJ

Preface and Acknowledgements

The chapters in this book were originally presented at a conference on 'Scarcity and the politics of allocation', held at the Institute of Development Studies at the University of Sussex in June 2005. Funded by the 'Science and Society Programme' of the Economic and Social Research Council (ESRC), this interdisciplinary conference brought together about 50 participants from all five continents and from a range of disciplinary backgrounds (sociology, anthropology, economics, political science, theatre, soil science, engineering, philosophy, history, etc.). Despite the heterogeneity in the group, there was much epistemic consensus. Most of the participants would see themselves as politically motivated scholars and/or 'scholar activists' with a strong commitment to enhancing scholarship and promoting social justice. Consequently, the conference was rich in intellectual substance and creativity, energy and passion. It was rooted in the conviction that 'scarcity' may be acting as a totalizing discourse in the south in the same way that 'risk' does in the north. In both cases, science and technology are often expected to provide solutions, but such expectations embody a multitude of unexamined assumptions about the nature of the 'problem', about the technologies and about the so-called institutional fixes that are put forward as the 'solutions'. There were 16 paper presentations, while the concluding session included commentaries on alternative ways to look at scarcity and key lessons for future research and action. This book is the result of this conference and my own research on scarcity, in particular water scarcity.

The volume would not have been possible without the support and hard work of many individuals who contributed with their ideas, time and enthusiasm. It has been a pleasure to work with such a committed and interesting group of people and I thank all the authors for their hard work and patience, and for tolerating my editorial interventions and some delays. Unfortunately, not everybody who presented a paper at the conference could write one for this volume, but hopefully the following pages will capture some of the rich and stimulating discussions we had there.

It was a pleasure to be a part of the ESRC 'Science and Society Programme' as a researcher for the project 'Science, Technology and Water Scarcity: Investigating the "Solutions", RES – 151-25-0021'. The conference was a culmination of this project. The programme funded both the conference and my research and I thank the ESRC for this. In particular, I am very grateful to

Steve Rayner, Director of the programme, who played a key role in making both the conference and this book happen. We have shared similar interests in unpacking scarcity debates and it has been great to work with him in the context of the Science and Society Programme to develop my ideas on scarcity, where he was generous with his support and ideas. I also thank Anne Marie McBrien of the Science and Society Programme for her constant help and support. Oliver Burch was fantastic in organizing the logistical arrangements of the workshop and I thank Nurit Bodemann-Ostow and Catherine Setchell for their meticulous note-taking.

I am grateful to those who contributed actively at the conference (as chairs, discussants and speakers) and others who also contributed with ideas, guidance and their generous intellectual support. I thank Franck Amalric, Vinita Damodaran, James Fairhead, Tim Forsyth, Richard Grove, Lawrence Haddad, Sheila Jasanoff, Melissa Leach, Synne Movik, Peter Newborne, Alan Nicol, Paul Nightingale, Steve Oga Abah, Jenks Okwori, Ian Scoones, Jan Selby, John Toye, Barbara van Koppen, Shiv Visvanathan, Brian Wynne and Farhana Yamin.

I began research on water scarcity in 1994 and I have been interested in scarcity issues ever since. While researching water issues, it emerged that, as well as understanding the various contestations of water scarcity, it was even more important to subject the concept of 'scarcity' itself to scrutiny. This has been a long journey and I am particularly grateful to those whose ideas and work have inspired me over the years. I owe very special thanks to Nick Hildyard, Jean Robert and Nick Xenos, whose work helped me use my empirical research on water to engage conceptually and critically with the notion of scarcity. Paul Wright dug out the most amazing references and writings on scarcity. Many thanks! I am very grateful to the countless families in Kutch, western India, who have taken me into their homes and lives and taught me what it means to live with scarcity and uncertainty. I have written about this elsewhere and this book does not capture my own empirical work on scarcity. However, my life-changing experiences in Kutch continue to shape my work and the way I view the world. I will always be indebted to my friends in the village of Merka for their generosity and inspiration.

Much of this book was finalized when I was at the Department of International Environment and Development Studies (Noragric) at the Norwegian University of Life Sciences. I thank my Noragric colleagues for providing me with such a supportive and collegial environment. In particular, I am deeply grateful to Espen Sjaastad who provided critical comments on several draft chapters. I wish he had made it to the conference and contributed a chapter himself. Many, many thanks and hopefully we will also work together one day!

I am also grateful for the support and patience of Earthscan, in particular Nick Ascroft, Alison Kuznets, Claire Lamont and Rob West. I thank Judy Hartley for copy-editing this manuscript with both humour and patience. Naomi Vernon's help was key towards the end. Finally, I must thank my family. My parents and brother have always believed in me. Espen's help was immense in strengthening the argument of the volume. Morten pushed me to finish this volume, gave valuable comments and is always there for me.

Tara's arrival delayed the finalization of this volume but I must thank her and Morten for ensuring that I don't experience a scarcity of love or happiness. I hope that Tara and her generation grow up in a fairer world.

Finally, I thank Wolfgang Sachs. Unfortunately he could not attend the conference, and illness prevented him from contributing to the book. He has, however, followed this project closely from the beginning and has contributed generously with his ideas and intellectual support. His stimulating and critical work has inspired me and many others and it is with appreciation and gratitude that this book is dedicated to him.

List of Acronyms and Abbreviations

AGRA	Alliance for a Green Revolution in Africa
BIWMP	Bagmati Integrated Watershed Management Project
BMBF	German Federal Ministry of Education and Research
BWP	Bagmati Watershed Project
CAADP	Comprehensive African Agricultural Development Programme
CAP	Common Agricultural Policy
CGIAR	Consultative Group for International Agricultural Research
CPR	Common Property Resource
DDP	The Desert Development Program
DFID	Department for International Development (UK)
DPAP	Drought-Prone Areas Program
EA	entitlement approach
EPS	Environment, Population and Security Project
ESRC	Economic and Social Research Council
EU	European Union
FAD	food availability decline
FAO	UN Food and Agriculture Organization
GDP	Gross Domestic Product
GOI	Government of India
GWP	Global Water Partnership
ICPD	International Conference on Population and Development
ICRAF	International Centre for Research on Agroforestry
IDS	Institute for Development Studies
IFDC	International Fertilizer Development Centre
IFPRI	International Food Policy Research Institute
ISET	Institute of Social and Environmental Transition
ISRO	Indian Space Research Organisation
IWMI	International Water Management Institute
IWRM	Integrated Water Resources Management
KISS	keep it simple, stupid
MDGs	Millennium Development Goals
MNCs	multinational corporations
NIE	New Institutional Economics

NSC	National Security Council
NEP	National Energy Policy
NEPDG	National Energy Policy Development Group
NWCF	Nepal Water Conservation Foundation
OECD	Organisation for Economic Co-operation and Development
OPEC	Organization of the Petroleum Exporting Countries
PAI	Population Action International
PGSI	Pew Global Stewardship Initiative
RBMSIIP	River Basin Management and Smallholder Irrigation Improvement Project
SFI	Africa-wide Soil Fertility Initiative
Sida	Swedish International Development Agency
SIWI	Stockholm International Water Institute
SMUWC	Sustainable Management of Usangu Wetlands and its Catchment
SOAS	School of Oriental and African Studies
SÖF	Socio-Ecological Research programme
TINA	there is no alternative
UDC	underdeveloped country
UNCED	UN Conference on Environment and Development
UNCTAD	United Nations Conference on Trade and Development
UNDP	United Nations Development Programme
UNFPA	United Nations Population Fund
USAID	United States Agency for International Development
WCED	World Commission on Environment and Development
WCW	World Commission on Water
WHO	World Health Organization
WMDs	weapons of mass destruction
WPI	Water Poverty Index
WRD	Water resource development
WSSD	World Summit on Sustainable Development
WWC	World Water Council
WWF	World Water Forum

Introduction

Lyla Mehta

Conventional wisdom suggests that we live in an age of permanent scarcity. Scarcity is considered to be an inescapable and ubiquitous feature of human existence. While not denying that there are biophysical limits to natural resources and that women and men (especially the poorest and powerless among them) often encounter chronic shortages of food, water and energy, this book argues that it is now time to question universalist portrayals of scarcity and write their obituary.

Why is this important? Of late, there has been a flurry of scarcity reports and concerns. In March 2009, the UK government's chief scientific adviser, Professor John Beddington, declared that the planet faced 'a perfect storm' of food shortages, scarce water and insufficient energy resources that threatened to unleash public unrest, cross-border conflicts and mass migration leading to major upheavals in the world and coming to a head in 2030 (Sample, 2009). The years 2007–2008 saw dramatic increases in world food prices, causing much social unrest in both the south and north. Mainstream interpretations of the crisis attribute blame to an ever-increasing population and the changing diet of the growing middle-class populations in Asia. Critics, by contrast, argue that causes lie elsewhere, for example in diverting land to grow biofuels largely for consumption in the north, structural changes in trade and agricultural production, rising oil prices and perverse subsidy regimes.

The past few years have also witnessed a growing concern about water scarcity and its threat to human well-being and livelihoods, economic and agricultural production, as well as the threat of 'water wars' having both international and intranational dimensions. Does all this suggest a déjà vu perhaps of the 1970s where resource scarcity was a prominent political concern due to the oil shocks and accompanying financial crises? The 1970s raised critical questions regarding the existence of scarcity among plenty and abundance, about the need to set 'limits' to growth (see Meadows et al, 1972) and about the imperative for all humankind to coexist on 'spaceship earth', our one planet which was increasingly being viewed as fragile and vulnerable.

Almost 40 years on and in the midst of another global financial crisis, climate change poses new challenges to both human existence and resource availability. 'Water wars', famine and oil threats still appear as news stories. Resource scarcity continues to be linked with population growth and growing environmental conflicts, and science and technology or innovation are usually evoked as the appropriate 'solutions'. Scarcity remains an all-pervasive fact of our lives. But what is scarcity? Why has blame been attributed to it for many of humankind's woes, for centuries? Why is it so all-pervasive and does its all-pervasive character help or hinder us in governing the allocation and distribution of crucial resources such as water, oil, food and so on? What are the different disciplinary perspectives on scarcity? Are the economists to be blamed for creating scarcity? Are there alternative viewings of 'scarcity' and better ways to talk about finite resources? These questions are the focus of this volume.

In this book, theoretical and empirical contributions examine changing conceptions of scarcity historically and critically engage with scarcity's taken-for-granted nature across three domains (water, food and energy) and the implications for theory, institutional arrangements, policy responses and innovation systems. The authors of this volume demonstrate that scarcity is not merely a natural phenomenon that can be isolated from planning models, allocation politics, policy choices, market forces and local power, social and gender dynamics. Several authors demonstrate that *Homo economicus* is neither universal nor desirable. The scarcity postulate (in other words, that needs, wants and desires are unlimited and the means to achieve these are scarce and limited) that unpins modern economics need not be universal. Needs, wants and desires do not have to be endless and unlimited (see Leiss, 1988). The book's starting point is that 'scarcity' has emerged as a totalizing discourse in both the north and south[1] with science and technology often expected to provide solutions, but such expectations embody a multitude of unexamined assumptions about the nature of the 'problem', about the technologies and about the so-called institutional fixes that are put forward as the 'solutions'.

More often than not, the problem lies in how we see scarcity and the ways in which it is socially generated. Conventional visions of scarcity that focus on aggregate numbers and physical quantities are privileged over local knowledges and experiences of scarcity that identify problems in different ways. The 'scare' of scarcity has led to scarcity emerging as a political strategy for powerful groups, and problematic ideas of nature and society continue to get reproduced. These feed into simplistic and often inappropriate solutions that cause inaccessibility and perpetuate exclusions. Thus, the scarcity problem gets aggravated.

This volume is a significant contribution on the part of leading scholars and scholar activists to question scarcity's taken-for-granted nature and assumptions. While not denying that scarcities exist for many and that our planet is in peril (not least due to the wanton overexploitation of resources and climate change), our contention is that scarcity is not a constant variable that can be blamed for all our woes. Instead, we need to be aware of the politics of allocation and the ways in which scarcity is politicized, especially to suit the interests of powerful players.

This volume has the following overarching aims. One: it seeks to denaturalize scarcity and demonstrate that scarcity rarely takes place due to the natural order of things. Instead, it is usually the result of exclusion and unequal gender, social and power relations that legitimize skewed access to and control over finite and limited resources. As such, scarcity is a relational concept that is often the result of market forces dictating issues concerning demand and supply (see the chapters in Part II, this volume). This is why some authors in this volume argue that the finitude or finiteness of a thing does not necessarily lead to its scarcity because value may be derived from factors other than rarity (see Chapters 2 and 6, this volume). While issues concerning access are not new and have been ably theorized by political ecologists, Marxists and feminists,[2] the volume's contribution is in linking local access issues to discourses and experiences of scarcity, allocation politics alongside governance and knowledge systems.

Two: we argue that there is often a gap between universalized and global portrayals of scarcity and the nature of resources and the ways in which these are locally perceived and experienced. This means we need to discursively unpack what is meant by scarcity and for whom is what scarce. For example, several chapters in Part III demonstrate that blanket, universal and aggregate portrayals of food and water crises are preferred by policy-makers and donors rather than focusing on local-level knowledges and experiences of scarcity. The word 'scarcity' derives from the Old Northern French word *escarsete* to refer to the quality, condition or fact of being scarce. It also refers to frugality and parsimony, an insufficiency of supply in proportion to the need or demand and finally an insufficiency of supply in a community or the necessities or life connoting a time-bound dearth (Oxford English Dictionary, 1971). From being a time-bound and contextual phenomenon, several authors demonstrate how scarcity now tends to be universalized in academic and policy debates, largely because it is the raison d'être of economics (see also Xenos, 1989). This volume examines diverse ways to view scarcity that challenge the scarcity postulate. Several authors also examine specific global visions of scarcity around food, water, energy and agricultural issues and how these blank out local-level complexities, politics, uncertainties and varied responses to scarcities. Our contention also is that scarcity as promoted by multilateral and bilateral donors, government bureaucracies and think-tanks usually triumphs over local understandings and visions of the problem. It is this politics of knowledge that this volume seeks to confront while challenging and unpacking simplistic global visions.

Three: aggregate and technical assessments of resources also rarely capture their multifaceted nature and embeddedness in culture, history and politics. All this has a bearing on how resources are valued and thus rendered scarce or not. For example, water is simultaneously a natural element or H_2O, essential for the ecological cycle, a spiritual resource for millions who worship at holy river banks and oceans, a commodity which can be mined, bottled, sold and traded, and a life-giving element without which human survival is not possible. These multiple meanings of water are rarely captured in global water assessments or dominant water scarcity and 'water wars' debates (see for example, United

Nations World Water Assessment Programme, 2009). Similarly, analysts such as Homer-Dixon (2001), who make powerful links between resource scarcity, population growth and conflict, often tend to overstate the problem of scarcity and see it as a constant variable, ignoring that the problem may lie in distributional issues, ethnic rivalries, power politics and so on.

Four: this volume seeks to contest the politics of allocation and governance arrangements that support skewed resource use and abuse. Globally, the problem of chronic hunger exists, despite the fact that there is more than enough food to feed everyone (see Chapters 8 and 10, this volume). In wealthy countries, perverse subsidy regimes have led to a generation of surpluses, and strawberries – once luxury items – are staple foods available all year round. In growing economies such as India, chronic malnutrition and unequal access to food persist despite the so-called successes of the Green Revolution, economic liberalization and biotechnology. Thus, over and above unpacking what is meant by scarcity, we need to focus on governmentality (see Foucault, 1991) and how discussions of scarcity can legitimize policy. This means looking at the role of powerful actors in advancing certain agendas concerning scarcity largely to promote certain solutions (see below). The politics of allocation is rarely neutral. Thus, we need to ask: who is defining and promoting certain notions of and solutions to scarcity? Who is participating and shaping decision-making processes concerning global, national, regional and local estimates of scarcity and resource allocation?

Five: scarcity often emerges as a political strategy and is used to justify certain interventions over others. In the name of scarcity, coupled with fears of teeming numbers, controversial interventions such as large dams, nuclear energy and biotechnology are often put forward as solutions by politically powerful actors while blanking out discussions and deliberations of more suitable alternatives (see Chapters 1, 2, 8 and 12 and others in this volume).[3] Efficiency arguments mostly prevail over equity ones. The scare of scarcity remains a means of diverting attention away from the causes of poverty and inequality that may implicate the politically powerful. Scarcity is also a powerful tool to colonize the future and to shape it in certain ways (see Chapter 8, this volume). Thus, the political strategy of scarcity continues to be remodelled as a concept to justify the means and interventions of the powerful, and neo-Malthusianism arguments are given an additional explanatory power when the future is colonized through scarcity arguments.

Six: this volume consequently opposes neo-Malthusian arguments that posit simplistic linkages between soaring numbers, climate change, conflict and resource scarcity. Over two centuries have passed since Thomas Malthus falsely argued that population growth would exceed food production with checks required from deaths, disease, famine and late marriage. Malthusianism and neo-Malthusianism have had pernicious impacts on scarcity politics. Several authors in this volume engage with the reach and power of neo-Malthusianism, its problematic implications and the huge body of evidence discrediting it (see Chapters 3, 8 and 10). But neo-Malthusianism remains highly fashionable, from Hollywood stars to respected scholars such as the creator of Gaia,

James Lovelock and Washington think tanks.[4] While I do not want to deny that humanity can certainly be a burden on the planet, we argue in this volume that a fixation with overpopulation ignores focusing attention on more crucial aspects such as how power is distributed in society, unequal gender, caste and ethnic discrimination, unfair terms of trade, state planning, centralizing technologies, tenure arrangements, ecological degradation and so on.

Seven: this volume critically engages with notions of limits. It is over 40 years since the Club of Rome funded the *Limits to Growth* (Meadows et al, 1972) report which drew on now discredited doomsday predictions of resource use, production, pollution and population growth through computer simulation models. Despite all the problems with the work, the imperative to limit needs and consumption patterns cannot be denied because it is the drive for abundance that leads to never-ending needs, wants and desires. As we know from Aristotle, if you want satisfaction and happiness you need limits to acquisitiveness and growth to allow for human flourishing and the good (Aristotle, 1831). Still, as Luks (Chapter 5, this volume) argues, even constructivist trends in economics are now arguing that limits are as much social constructions as needs, wants, markets, scarcity and prices. What count as basic needs in some societies could be luxuries elsewhere (Sopher, 2006). How does the satisfaction of needs, wants and desires in the north lead to deprivation in the south (Sopher, 2006)? It is also important to avoid simplistic binaries between overpopulation and overconsumption and instead ask: who is consuming what and for whom are there limits? Who sets limits and thresholds? Four thousand people, largely babies, die daily due to poor access to safe water and this is not something that sparks outrage or anger globally. There are thus some cautionary tales around the limits discourse which are discussed by some authors in this volume.

This volume is divided into three sections. Part I discusses why scarcity matters and provides a review of diverse disciplinary understandings of scarcity. It also discusses the profound implications of scarcity politics by drawing on the energy policy and the vast reach of neo-Malthusianism in the USA. Part II engages with diverse perspectives of scarcity within economics. Modern (neo-classical) economics is premised on scarcity in many different ways. The essays in this section ask where this came from, what the impacts are and considers both mainstream and heterodox perspectives of scarcity within economics. Part III turns to empirical concerns and traces scarcity politics in the domains of food, water and energy. Short commentaries before each section will discuss the arguments of individual chapters, the overall contribution of the section and how each section relates to the overall themes of the volume. Many of the examples in this book deal with water scarcity. This is due to the overall importance of water within society and because water scarcity emerges as a key example of scarcity in popular and academic discourse. Still, the volume also focuses on scarcity debates in food and energy. The empirical concern is largely resource scarcity, not the scarcity of time, love, happiness and so on which are all very worthy lines of enquiry but not possible in this volume.

In anticipation of objections from a careful reader, here are a few caveats. It would be flawed to argue that scarcity is merely constructed and/or the result of power and politics. There are biophysical realities concerning falling groundwater levels, melting ice caps and declining soil fertility that I do not want to deny. All of humanity experiences some kind of scarcity. For example, the scarcity of time is a pressing problem in highly capitalist and industrialized societies and many people suffer due to the scarcity of love and happiness. I am also aware that scarcity narratives are often portrayed strategically in order to galvanize action. KISS (keep it simple, stupid) rather than highlighting the complexity of local issues can help NGOs and donors mobilize support and funds to tackle local-level water and food crises.[5] But in the long run, I would argue that such strategic essentialisms will end up doing more harm than good and detract attention from the real nature of the problem. Finally, economists should not believe that this volume is all about bashing neoclassical economics. While most authors (including several contributing economists) acknowledge that neoclassical economics has played a key role in creating and sustaining generalized notions of scarcity, Part II has contributions that engage with diverse interpretations of scarcity within economics while also providing heterodox economic perspectives on scarcity.

This volume builds on and acknowledges the important work of several authors who have provided critiques of and alternatives to the scarcity postulate. Amartya Sen and his entitlement analysis is the focus of Ben Fine's chapter. Jean Robert and Sajay Samuel draw their inspiration from Ivan Illich's radical critiques of basic needs and scarcity (see Illich, 1978). Karl Polanyi (1944) and Marshall Sahlins (1972) and economic anthropologists who provide compelling critiques of *Homo economicus* and the logic of the market are reviewed in Mehta's chapter. Critical authors such as Nicholas Xenos (1989 and this volume), Hans Achterhuis (1993), Marianne Gronemeyer (2002), Michael Ross (1996), Murray Bookchin (2004) and Jean Robert (1994 and this volume) have provided nuanced analyses of the nature of scarcity, and incisive critiques of its politics and the ways in which it has been naturalized over time (see also Daoud, 2007 and Schrecker, 2008). This volume builds on their thinking. It is, however, unique in its contribution to conceptual debates on needs, scarcity and allocation through its interdisciplinary focus. It engages with diverse perspectives within economics and also encourages a dialogue between economics and other disciplines, thus challenging dominant views of scarcity. It also locates scarcity issues on the map of science and technology studies by focusing on the co-production of ideas of nature and society and the role of policy, science and technology in these debates. Finally, the focus on resource politics and scarcity, with their global and local linkages, also adds to debates on access and political ecology in environment and development.

These issues are of more than just academic interest: a failure to appreciate diverse understandings of scarcity helps perpetuate flawed governance interventions, policies and programmes to mitigate scarcity conditions. In fact, as several authors argue, flawed interventions around scarcity can lead to the further impoverishment and marginalization of poor people. For too long has scarcity been used by powerful actors in compelling ways as a political strategy either to maintain the status quo, prevent redistributing limited resources or to legitimize certain solutions and interventions. This has contributed to reproducing inequalities and hindering social justice. This process must now be rolled back. Hopefully this volume is a small step in that direction.

Notes

1 The parallels with risk discourses and their critiques in the post-industralized world are striking but these are beyond the scope of this volume. See Douglas and Wildavsky, 1982; Pidgeon et al, 2003; Wynne, 2001.
2 See Yapa, 1996; Peet and Watts, 1996; Elson, 1998.
3 My own work in the water domain has focused on how scarcity politics in western India has manufactured dominant narratives of scarcity which claim that the controversial Sardar Sarovar (Narmada) dam is the solution for drought-prone regions in Gujarat, when in reality these areas do not stand to benefit from the project and more locally appropriate technological solutions are ignored. Moreover, most of the water is diverted to powerful urban and agro-industrial areas (Mehta, 2005).
4 The celebrities concerned with overpopulation could learn a lesson or two from John Lennon who said in 1970, 'We have enough food and money to feed everybody. There's enough room for us, and some of them can go to the moon anyway', (O'Neill, The Guardian, 2009).
5 I thank Martin Greeley for pointing this out to me.

References

Achterhuis, H. (1993) 'Scarcity and sustainability', in W. Sachs (ed) Global Ecology: A New Arena of Political Conflict, Zed Books, London and New Jersey
Aristotle (1831[1962]) Politics (trans. T. Sinclair), Penguin, Harmondsworth
Bookchin, M. (2004) Post-scarcity Anarchism, AK Press, Oakland
Daoud, A. (2007) '(Quasi)Scarcity and global hunger. A sociological critique of the scarcity postulate with an attempt at synthesis', Journal of Critical Realism, vol 6, no 2, pp199–225
Douglas, M. and Wildavsky, A. (1982) Risk and Culture: An Essay on the Selection of Technological and Environmental Dangers, University of California Press, Berkeley
Elson, D. (1998) 'Talking to the boys: Gender and economic growth models', in C. Jackson and R. Pearson (eds) Feminist Visions of Development: Gender Analysis and Policy, Routledge, London
Foucault, M. (1991) 'Governmentality' (trans. R. Braidotti and revised by C. Gordon), in G. Burchell, C. Gordon and P. Miller (eds) The Foucault Effect: Studies in Governmentality, University of Chicago Press, Chicago
Gronemeyer, M. (2002) Die Macht der Bedürfnisse. Überfluss und Knappheit, Primus Verlag, Darmstadt
Homer-Dixon, T.F. (2001) Environment, Scarcity and Violence, Princeton University Press, Princeton
Illich, Ivan (1978) Toward a History of Needs, Random House, New York
Leiss, W. (1988) The Limits to Satisfaction. An Essay on the Problem of Needs and Commodities, McGill-Queens University Press, Kingston and Montreal
Meadows, D., Randers, J. and Behrens, W. (1972) The Limits to Growth, Earth Island Limited, London
Mehta, L. (2005) The Politics and Poetics of Water: Naturalising Scarcity in Western India, Orient Longman, New Delhi

O'Neill, B. (2009) 'We've got all the space in the world', *The Guardian*, 13 June
Oxford English Dictionary (1971) *The Compact Edition*, Oxford University Press, New York
Peet, R. and Watts, M. (eds) (1996) *Liberation Ecologies: Environment, Development, Social Movements*, Routledge, London, New York
Pidgeon, N., Kasperson, R.E. and Slovic, P.E. (eds) (2003) *The Social Amplification of Risk*, Cambridge University Press, Cambridge
Polanyi, K. (1944) *The Great Transformation: The Political and Economic Origins of our Time*, Beacon Press, Boston
Robert, J. (1994) *Water for All: Common Right, Public Service or Commodity?* Habitat International Coalition, New York
Ross, A. (1996) 'The lonely hour of scarcity', *Capitalism, Nature, Socialism*, vol 7, no 3, pp3–26
Sahlins, M. (1972) *Stone Age Economics*, Aldine Publishing Company, New York
Sample, I. (2009) 'World faces "perfect storm" of problems by 2030, chief scientist to warn', *The Guardian*, 18 March
Sen, A. (1981) *Poverty and Famines: An Essay on Entitlement and Deprivation*, Oxford University Press, Oxford
Schrecker, T. (2008) 'Denaturalizing scarcity: A strategy of enquiry for public health ethics', *Bulletin of the World Health Organization*, vol 86, no 8, pp600–605
Sopher, K. (2006) 'Conceptualizing needs in the context of consumer politics', *Journal of Consumer Policy*, Special Issue, vol 29, no 4, pp355–372
United Nations World Water Assessment Programme (2009) *Water in a Changing World*, United Nations World Water Development Report 3, UNESCO and Earthscan, London
Wynne, B. (2001) 'Creating public alienation: Expert cultures of risks and ethics on GMOs', *Science as Culture*, vol 10, pp445–481
Xenos, N. (1989) *Scarcity and Modernity*, Routledge, New York and London
Yapa, L. (1996) 'Improved seeds and constructed scarcity', in R. Peet and M. Watts (eds) *Liberation Ecologies: Environment, Development, Social Movements*, Routledge, London, New York

Part I
Why Does Scarcity Matter?

Commentary

Lyla Mehta

This section focuses on how scarcity has been naturalized in academic, policy and popular debates. It also draws attention to the problematic implications and consequences of this naturalization, for example when scarcity emerges as a trope to legitimize particular energy and population politics or a certain way of life. In Chapter 1 Lyla Mehta discusses how notions of scarcity have shifted from being time-bound to being all-pervasive – from scarcities to scarcity. Scarcity, as the raison d'être of society, and formalist notions of the 'economic' have been challenged by Karl Polanyi, Marshall Sahlins and others who have shown how markets are embedded in social relations, highlighting the substantive meanings of the 'economic'. She argues that generalized notions of scarcity tell us nothing about what scarcity means exactly, who it affects most, who creates it and who benefits from a more or less permanent state of scarcity. Her chapter also focuses on insights from non-mainstream economics, sociology and anthropology, which offer several and more nuanced ways to see scarcity, highlighting the need to look at multiple meanings of resources, socio-political perspectives and contestations around scarcity as struggles over both meaning and access.

Nicholas Xenos (Chapter 2) asks why a universal notion of scarcity has emerged in affluent societies. Drawing on his pioneering work *Scarcity and Modernity*, he argues for the need to look at the dynamic of spiralling needs and the resultant scarcity that legitimizes markets and property with abundance as the end goal. The experience of modernity in a hyper-accumulating society is one of perpetual scarcity. But the finitude of a thing does not necessarily constitute a scarcity of that thing. Diamonds are rare but their value arises not solely from their rarity but also from the aesthetic and cultural properties assigned to them as well as demand that is boosted through advertising and the role of big corporations such as De Beers. The chapter focuses specifically on the US national energy policy that was championed by George Bush and Dick Cheney. Xenos argues that energy itself, rather than its sources and the quantity used, is made out to be scarce. The policy does not discuss the need for limits as propagated by former President Carter. It also does not mention Iraq and its oil. Instead, energy is made out to be crucial to sustain

America's expanding economy and population. Implicit is also the need to secure US national interests in the Persian Gulf as well as sustain a certain American way of life.

In Chapter 3, Betsy Hartmann also focuses on popular narratives and mobilizations of scarcity in the cultural and political context of the US with applicability far beyond. Her chapter examines why Malthusianism and neo-Malthusian ideas have a remarkable staying power, despite countervailing evidence. Powerful images of 'uncontrolled fertile women' and 'angry young men' are deployed to link the so-called population explosion to problems of environmental degradation in the global south. Scarcity is at the centre of these simplistic debates. These ideas are put forward by powerful lobbies in the US, ranging from funding agencies to political parties, and are used strategically even by those who don't believe in them, with profound consequences. There is thus a need to come up with alternative languages and ideas, both in policy and in the popular imagination, as well as to challenge the widespread use of these images.

These three chapters flag up some of the bigger themes to be handled in the rest of the volume. Scarcity is often an intensely political concept requiring us to look at the different institutions and locations through which definitions are being channelled (global, national and local) and the role of power in producing cultures of legitimization. The scare of scarcity is often all-pervasive and it manifests itself in contemporary politics by drawing on powerful narratives that are deeply entrenched. Generalized and universalized notions of scarcity also tend to evoke a standardized set of market/institutional and technological solutions as the (universal) fix blocking out context-specific socio-political and cultural factors. Whether markets, innovation, rights, institutional fixes or bits of all of the above are evoked to deal with resource scarcity, they are all socio-political choices governed by the politics of allocation and decision-making and contestations about what meanings are embodied in resources. The following chapters point to the dangers of scarcity politics and urge us to question their simplistic visions.

1

The Scare, Naturalization and Politicization of Scarcity

Lyla Mehta

... the whole human development, at least up to now, has been a bitter struggle against scarcity. (Jean-Paul Sartre)[1]

The legacy of the scarcity postulate

Leading 20th-century French philosopher, Jean-Paul Sartre, sums up nicely what is taken to be a given in dominant academic and policy thinking: scarcity is an all-pervasive fact of our lives and much of human existence has been caught up in struggles against scarcity. As several authors in this book demonstrate, the scarcity postulate (that human wants are unlimited and the means to achieve these are scarce and limited) underpins modern economics which, in turn, has helped promote a universalized notion of scarcity. In this chapter, I discuss the legacy of the scarcity postulate and demonstrate how understandings of scarcity have largely been naturalized and universalized in a range of academic disciplines and dominant policy debates.[2] I argue that the scare, naturalization and politicization of scarcity has profound implications for society/nature relations and the different ways in which science and technology, as well as the market and institutions, are evoked as the universal fix. But alternative ways to conceptualize scarcity that question this universal application exist and must be drawn on. These take into account often neglected cultural, historical, institutional and socio-political and distributional issues which help us to break away from the totalizing effects of the scarcity postulate.

Why is scarcity usually associated with economics? Many economists see scarcity as essential to the definition of economics. For example, Lionel Robbins' famous and all-encompassing definition of economics is still used to define the discipline today. He wrote in 1932: 'Economics is the science which studies human behaviour as a relationship between given ends and scarce means which have alternative uses' (Robbins, 1932, p16). As Fine and others in the next section demonstrate, this definition was misleading for its time, has been misinterpreted and Lionel Robbins himself detracted from it. Still, a quick glance at any A-level textbook makes it evident that economics is still defined as the science that studies scarcity.

Authors such as Nicholas Xenos and Hans Achterhuis (Xenos, 1987; Xenos, 1989; Achterhuis, 1993) have both played a key role in demonstrating that scarcity is a child of modernity and that prior to the 17th century it was not viewed as a ubiquitous feature of the human condition. For example, in *Scarcity and Modernity* (1989) Xenos systematically shows how certain attributes of modernity have given rise to the universal notion of scarcity and that several paradigms propounded by neoclassical economics make scarcity out to be a ubiquitous and permanent feature of the human condition. The etymological roots of the word 'scarcity' go back to the Old Northern French word *escarsete* which meant insufficiency of supply.[3] Until the late 19th century, scarcity connoted a temporally bounded period of scarcity or a dearth. Scarcity was experienced cyclically, dependent usually on poor yields. After the industrial revolution, which led to cataclysmic changes creating new needs, desires and the frustration of desires, the concept acquired a new meaning which culminated in its 'invention' in neoclassical economic thought of the 18th century (Xenos, 1989, p7). From *scarcities*, which were temporally bound and spatially differentiated, came the scourge of *scarcity*, 'a kind of open-ended myth' (Xenos, 1989, p35) from which deliverance was sought. Scarcity, not *a* scarcity or *scarcities*, was essentialized and its simplistic universalization led to the obscuring of ambiguities and regional variations. In modernity, the elusive twin of scarcity is abundance, making scarcity 'the antagonist in the human story, a story with a happy ending; vanquishing of the antagonist and a life of happiness ever after and abundance for all' (Xenos, 1989, p35).

The alleged ubiquitousness of the scarcity postulate makes economics a science applicable universally in every society (for example, debates on formalist and substantive economics plagued economic anthropology). For Xenos (1989 and this volume), the roots lie in the 18th century and in the Scottish enlightenment. For example, Adam Smith's *Wealth of Nations* was a treatise on wealth creation based on the assumption that 'needs and necessities' were constantly being refined and developed (Smith, 2003). While nature can largely satisfy the wants of animals (e.g. food/shelter), human beings are different since they constantly seek improvement. Thus gradually a condition of natural scarcity pervades because of an individual's limitless wants and necessities and the limited means available in nature to satisfy them. Scarcity emerges both as the raison d'être of society and as the basis of government since there is the need for an external arbiter of justice to establish a system of rule, property rights and so on. The scarcity postulate is subsequently formalized in the work of the marginal utility theorists such as Carl Menger and Walras. The focus on wealth shifted to the relationship between individual wants and desires and the means to satisfy them. Economizing individuals need to order their wants in order to satisfy them in the best way possible (see also Chapter 6, this volume).

The next section of this book handles in detail economic perspectives on scarcity. For the moment, it suffices to say that there are diverse readings of Adam Smith's work and the role of scarcity in economics. Some economists would even dispute that economists are the creators of scarcity (see Toye, 2005). Some authors such as Hont and Ignatieff (1983) argue that the *Wealth of Nations* was centrally concerned with the issue of justice and sought to find market mechanisms to reconcile inequality of property with provision for the excluded. Regardless of the position one takes on the above, clearly notions of scarcity legitimize the need to allocate and manage property either through the means of the market or through formalizing rights regimes (formalization of water rights, for example, has gained much currency in contemporary donor discourses, not least due to 'scarce' water resources). Economics studies only those goods that exist in quantities insufficient to satisfy the social need for them. By contrast, all goods in abundance are classified as 'non-economic'. It is thus economic goods – goods that are scarce – that are made the objects of systematic human action. Of course, whether all 'resources' can be viewed unproblematically as 'economic' goods is highly contested. The declaration of water as an 'economic good' in 1992 at the Dublin conference on water and the environment is still deeply controversial in the water domain since many still feel that this legitimizes the commodification of a life-giving resource and justifies its privatization. This is because access may depend on one's ability to pay. This definition also privileges certain material aspects of water over other cultural and public good aspects.[4]

Achterhuis goes even further back in time to the world of Francis Bacon in the 17th century who articulated the vision of New Atlantis where science and technology knew no limits, the human empire was enlarged and limits existed for the sole purpose of being transgressed (Achterhuis, 1993). It was in this *Zeitgeist* that Thomas Hobbes wrote *Leviathan* where society was seen as an arena of never-ending conflict due to power struggles arising out of competition over desires, over riches and the desire to outbid each other. Society thus is a zero sum game (a 'lifeboat' where passengers fight each other) and everything is attained at somebody else's cost. Thus the ongoing power struggle makes everything scarce. Scarcity is thus the relationship between unlimited wants and limited means to achieve them with the 'Leviathan' as a semi-absolute state arising out of fear that prevents the battle of scarcity from erupting into war. Locke, another 17th-century philosopher, argued that since nature and the earth fail to produce for all, economic growth and expansion are the 'solutions' to scarcity. Thus progress and subduing nature are necessary in order to produce more.[5]

In the 19th century, Marx responded with his own vision of needs, their satisfaction and freedom.[6] For him, like Aristotle, humans only require a sufficiency of material goods necessary for life, capable of being stored and useful for the household, community and city (Aristotle, 1831). While Marx would agree with the 18th-century thinkers that needs and desires are unlimited, he seeks to convert them to full realization of self and society. This is possible through the transformation of material desires through activities such as work. Thus while 'scarcities, their satisfaction, and their re-creation in new forms ... are recurring and necessary features of modern civilization'

(Stillman, 1983, p296), Marx does not seek abundance; instead, he seeks harmony, freedom and integrity.

Finally, Keynes follows Marx's path to discuss the possibilities for human freedom. He, unlike 18th-century thinkers, distinguishes between absolute and relative scarcity and between absolute needs (those felt whatever the situation of others may be) and relative needs (the satisfaction of which make us superior to others). It is relative scarcity that leads to 'social scarcity' (that is constructed through socio-political means). In 1930 Keynes predicted an end of scarcity and a future where basic needs would be satisfied and where the raw pursuit of money or wealth would be viewed as pathological. In this virtuous future, instead, scarcity would be overcome and traditional values would be restored (Achterhuis, 1993, pp108–9). Regardless of the differences between Marx and Keynes on the one hand, and the 18th century and marginal utility thinkers on the other, one thing is clear – scarcity is ubiquitous and traps humankind in a never-ending vortex of needs and desires.

This pervasiveness is found in disciplines and concepts outside of economics too. Take sociology. An article published in 1908 in the *American Journal of Sociology* argues that scarcity is the basis of social conflict due to the infinite expansibility of human wants that in turn gives rise to economic scarcity, which is defined as the insufficiency to satisfy wants (Carver, 1908). Thus the only way is to subdue external nature in order to make it yield more abundantly the means to satisfy unlimited human wants (Carver, 1908, p631). In this way, the problem of scarcity, while being a fundamental problem of economics, provides a raison d'être for other social sciences such as sociology, and many sociologists have been seduced by these ideas and see the combat against scarcity to be the basis of social action (e.g. Balla, 1981). Thus some strands in sociology and also economic anthropology (which I go on to explore) accept economics as the 'master science' and as a result overly focus on materialist analyses at the expense of issues concerning power, symbolic meaning and culture. What alternative perspectives and framings exist to view scarcity in different ways? How has the scarcity postulate been challenged by economists and non-economists? Different ways of seeing scarcity have been put forward by non-mainstream economists, anthropologists and others, and I now go on to explore these.

Challenges to the scarcity postulate

Economic anthropology and the legacy of Karl Polanyi and Marshall Sahlins

Karl Polanyi stands out as one of the few economists who argued that economic theory and several of its core tenets (such as scarcity) are not universally applicable. To do so he analysed modern market society and compared it with pre-market societies around the world, some of them in historical perspective (see Chapters 6 and 8, this volume, who engage with subsistence-oriented societies and markets in their contributions). In *The Great Transformation* Polanyi argues that before the 19th century, market was 'embedded' in society and was both shaped and subordinated by ideology, social relations and politics. However, the great transformation that ensued after the industrial revolution and the accompanying political and economic changes led to the emergence of the 'self-regulating' market, disembedded from social control and both unleashing negative social impacts and making market forces dominate over society. However, in non-market societies, people satisfy their wants through a different logic, including reciprocity, redistribution and exchange (Polanyi, 1944).

According to Polanyi, Adam Smith and other 18th-century thinkers, emphasis on both the universality of Economic Man and markets as society's key organizing principles was a misreading of 'primitive and non-market' societies (Polanyi, 1944). In fact, Polanyi and colleagues, in particular in *Trade and Market in the Early Empires* (1957), show that not all non-European and ancient societies had, following Adam Smith, the 'propensity to barter, truck and exchange one thing for another'. Instead, Polanyi underscores the principles of the distinction between 'real' and 'fictitious' commodities since in a self-regulating market all goods are for sale, including land and labour, which become subordinate to the laws of the market (Polanyi, 1944, p75). However, for him, land, labour and money are not obvious commodities, especially if one accepts the definition that a commodity is anything that is bought or sold and must have been produced for sale. Instead, he argues that labour or human activity goes hand in hand with human existence and is not produced for sale. Similarly, land is not produced by humans and 'is another name for nature' (Polanyi, 1944, p75). Thus, market mechanisms cannot be the sole regulators of these 'fictitious commodities'.

It was in *Trade and Market in the Early Empires* that Polanyi and his collaborators criticized the scarcity postulate. Crucial for this is the distinction between the formal and substantive meaning of 'economic'. Substantive economics is concerned with 'man's dependence for his living upon nature and his fellows. It refers to the ways in which people interact with each other and nature to satisfy their basic material wants. By contrast, the formal meaning of economics draws on the choice between the alternative uses of insufficient means' (Polanyi et al, 1957, p243). According to Polanyi, the two are quite distinct. While the formal meaning implies choice between alternate uses of scarce means, the substantive meaning need contain neither choice nor insufficiency of means. He then goes on to caution that the current concept of economic fuses the 'subsistence' and the 'scarcity' meanings of economic without a sufficient awareness of the dangers to clear thinking inherent in that merger (Polanyi, 1957, p244). These debates are very relevant for the water domain where the multiple characteristics of water (e.g. social, cultural, symbolic resource) are often negated in favour of promoting water as an economic good.

Economic anthropology of the 1960s and 1970s was dominated by the debate between the formalist and substantivist views. For example, one of the main proponents of formalism, Raymond Firth, applied economic theory most explicitly to anthropology. He held that some of the basic tenets of economics (the allocation of scarce, available resources between realizable human wants, with alternative uses) leads to questions of choice involving goods and services

(Firth, 1951). He is thus concerned with incentives, scarcity, capital, choice and so on and believes that these axioms are universally applicable even in so-called primitive societies.

By contrast, Polanyi (1944 and 1957) and Marshall Sahlins (1972) have offered a series of critiques to the use of the universalist scarcity postulate. In his *Stone Age Economics*, Sahlins questions the assumption that material wants are limitless and can never be satisfied. By looking at data from a range of hunter-gatherer economies, he argues that these economies are the 'original affluent society' where material wants are easily satisfied. Thus, he begins with the postulate that human wants can be limited and few and that people can enjoy material abundance and plenty with a low standard of living and are thus free from market obsessions with scarcity. Sahlins, like Polanyi, sees a sharp dichotomy between market society and that of hunters, with the former predicated on the scarcity postulate which is then made out to be universal. However, Sahlins seeks to demonstrate that hunter societies operate under different rationalities (for example, prodigality and an emphasis on leisure and mobility) and thus need to be viewed by yardsticks far removed from those of 'modern industrial societies'. Hunters should thus be considered the classic 'Uneconomic man' where wants are scarce and means are plentiful and there is consequently no need for institutions such as property.

While both Sahlins' and Polanyi's contributions in debunking the scarcity postulate have been immense, I should also briefly mention some of the problems with their work. For one, both Sahlins and Polanyi tend to overly romanticize 'pre-modern' societies in ancient Greece, Mesopotamia and those of tribals and hunter/gatherers. They also have downplayed issues such as internal conflict, gender imbalances, acquisitiveness and so on. For example, Polanyi's thesis that the 'self-regulating' market emerged only in the 19th century could be interpreted by critics to imply that prior to the 19th century all societies largely had local markets, focused on subsistence needs and were not touched by greed and selfishness. However, this is both a gross oversimplification and also historically flawed.

Another controversial point is the outright rejection of the concept of scarcity when comparing non-market societies. Even some proponents of the substantive interpretation of economics would maintain that scarcity is a core component of every economy and how different societies cope with scarcity is a key way to compare them (Humphreys, 1969). Finally, the thinking of Polanyi and Sahlins creates a kind of false dichotomy between the emergence of markets on the one hand and the countermovement of social protection on the other, between primitive societies and capitalist societies and between production and exchange. Indeed, as French Marxist scholars (for example, Godelier) and recent trends in anthropology have demonstrated, no society can be seen to exist in complete isolation from capitalism, globalization and history. Sahlins' emphasis on reciprocity between material flows and social relations surely should not be restricted to just so-called 'primitive societies'. All markets and societies are embedded in wider social networks and even advanced market economies could benefit from their own logic of reciprocity, redistribution, production and exchange. Even where modern market institutions emerge, elite-dominated institutions may lead to restrictions on trade and rent-seeking even in situations where 'free markets' are supposed to exist (Hewitt de Alcantara, 1993). Thus, as a critical anthropological literature shows, markets are culturally and politically specific institutions that are embedded in the history and politics of place (see Appadurai, 1988; Hewitt de Alcantara, 1993). Indeed, the differentiated responses to and effects of the global financial crisis of 2009 reveal the embedded nature of capital and markets even in highly advanced capitalist societies.

Institutional approaches

Institutional approaches in economics and political sciences have also contributed significantly to discounting the scarcity postulate. The transaction cost and the collective action approach are the two key approaches within the New Institutional Economics (NIE) literature. Both these approaches focus on the role of institutions in managing scarcity and property regimes. Institutions are either the 'rules of the game in society' (Ostrom, 1990) or the formal rules and conventions, including informal codes of behaviour or norms, which emerge to regulate human behaviour and interaction. An impressive body of work by common property theorists has successfully discredited neo-Malthusian notions concerning population growth, resource availability and environmental degradation. Many empirical studies from Europe, Africa and Asia have shown how people cooperate in times of resource pressure and scarcity (Berkes, 1989; Bromley and Cernea, 1989; Ostrom, 1990). They have also drawn attention to the importance of institutions in managing resources. Here the work of Elinor Ostrom, who was awarded the 2009 Nobel Prize in Economic Science, stands out. Ostrom and other common property scholars have also shown how Hobbesian notions of anarchy, where states, regions and people fight over scarce resources, may not be an accurate or predictable scenario. Instead, through detailed empirical studies from all around the world, they have demonstrated that local and global actors have a deep understanding of their immediate environment and cooperate with each other in times of adversity to avoid high transaction costs attached to their failure to comply (Ostrom, 1990; Ostrom and Keohane, 1995).

Common property analysts such as Ostrom (1990) tend to take their theoretical grounding from game theory, looking at collective action dilemmas and focusing on the ways in which institutions or rules can be purposively crafted to produce collective action. The now large literature on Common Property Resource (CPR) management has been central in establishing the significance of local institutions, particularly in natural resource management. Initially formulated in response to Hardin's (1968) pessimistic *The Tragedy of the Commons*, early CPR work tended to overly rely on the notion of a universal rational, self-maximizing actor, rather than looking at the embeddedness of economic action in ongoing social and personal networks, and the socially constructed nature of economic institutions. By contrast, socio-economic theorists (e.g. Etzioni, 1985) and economic sociologists (e.g. Granovetter, 1985) have argued against such methodological individualism to stress the embeddedness of economic action in ongoing social and personal networks, and the socially constructed nature of economic institutions. Moreover, anthropologists and sociologists have also shown how institutionalism often tends to be functionalist and static and ignores the rootedness in the specifics of local history and sociality (Cleaver, 1998; Mosse, 2003; Mehta, 2005). These criticisms notwithstanding, institutional analyses have played a key role in highlighting that people can cooperate to manage scarcity and that scarcity problems are more linked with institutions or the lack of them, rather than with absolute quantities and numbers.

Entitlements

Amartya Sen's work also stands out as another non-mainstream economics perspective that promotes an alternative to the scarcity postulate. His work is concerned with how to ensure the access of all to an initial basic amount of resources to ensure their survival and well-being and for a necessary level of functioning (e.g. Sen, 1981, 1999). To avoid a scramble for perceived scarce resources that involves the trampling of the poor and not-so-well-off, a framework is needed whereby all individuals that make up a population are guaranteed a modicum of well-being by ensuring their access to a basic level of resources. Such a framework is provided by Sen's entitlements approach. 'Entitlement' refers not to rights in a normative sense (what people *should* have), but rather to the range of possibilities that people *can* have. Sen sees entitlements as the 'the set of alternative commodity bundles that a person can command in a society using the totality of rights and opportunities that he or she faces' (Sen, 1983, p754).

The thinking underlying Sen's entitlements approach chimes well with the idea of scarcity as a 'constructed' concept, rather than as a 'real' fact. The idea that a famine may occur even when there is no decline in food supplies is attributed to people's lack of purchasing power, rather than a physical dearth of food. The same logic has been applied to water scarcity where it is argued that some people's lack of water does not necessarily imply that water is scarce; it may simply mean that certain parts of the population are unable to gain access to water for one reason or another, be it due to an excessively high price for water, to lack of infrastructure or to social exclusion (Anand, 2007). For example, water scarcity is most commonly assessed by the use of a national metric, such as aggregate water availability in a region, or average water consumption per capita, but this tells us little about the distribution of water within the society as a whole (Anand, 2007). Hence, while water may not be scarce in aggregate terms, water 'poverty' may prevail in certain regions due to a variety of factors, including social, economic and political. Sen outlines the manner in which such forces may play out to construct localized scarcities, in terms of people's inability to gain access to a given resource. Ben Fine (Chapter 4 in this volume) engages with Sen's work in detail. He and other commentators question whether the macro, social and the cultural have been appropriately addressed in Sen's work and whether the social and contextual specificities of resources such as food, water and so on can be captured in an individualist and formalist methodology which may not take into account the role of cultures, ideologies and practices, each with their own construction of scarcity. This is where the role of culture, meaning and politics emerges as important.

Taking an interpretive approach to scarcity

Through their focus on meaning and culture, as embedded in action, interpretative approaches in sociology and anthropology (for example, the sociology of Bourdieu, Blumer and Long), constitute quite a significant challenge to the scarcity postulate. These approaches seek to understand the different perspectives, meanings and responses that different actors assign to scarcity. Rather than seeing scarcity as a phenomenon 'out there' over which humans have no control that consequently leads to standardized responses (e.g. either conflict or cooperation), interpretive approaches would be interested in looking at local-specific contingencies in culturally specific meanings and traditions. This approach would ask: how is scarcity embedded in culturally specific meanings, beliefs and traditions? How do these change with time? How do different social actors interpret the meanings of scarcity? What social practices emerge to deal with scarcity situations and how do these change over time? Interpretive approaches often go hand in hand with actor-oriented approaches.

Actor-oriented approaches would eschew seeing an individual as a rational actor who seeks to maximize her gain out of a scarcity situation. Instead, the actor-oriented perspective to scarcity would try to understand how people actively interpret scarcity in different cultures and historical conditions based on a diverse repertoire of meanings. It would also seek to understand action and responses to action as grounded in these meanings and beliefs. Emphasis would also be on actual social practices that emerge with the contingencies of scarcity. Thus every action emerges as a meaningful practice that is historically and socially contingent on local specificities that are constantly created and recreated. Thus, diverse versions or definitions of scarcity would hold, not one universalist version or definition, because interpretivists share a belief in the contingency of social life and a rejection of the assumption that people in the same situation would act in similar ways. Instead, people's experiences of the same situation are moulded by different experiences, lifeworlds, belief systems and so on. Similarly, it would be impossible to see scarcity as posited in mainstream economics as the underlying factor that determines both society and social action. Similarities with Sahlins and Polanyi are evident – for example, the eschewing of universalist portrayals of scarcity and the need for historically and culturally rooted analysis. However, interpretivists would reject Polanyi's and Sahlins' primitive versus market society dichotomy since all 'actors', be they in 'capitalist' or 'primitive' societies, would constantly be interpreting the phenomenon of scarcity (as rooted in locally and historically specific meaning, belief systems and culture) and developing social practices and institutions accordingly. Unlike the rational and Economic man of classical economic thought, interpretivists would argue that this action could also be prompted by 'uneconomic' or symbolic or moral rationalities (e.g. going without food for religious reasons or action that stems from the motivation of benediction in the afterlife, rather than more immediate material gain, etc.).

In fact, several sociological and anthropological works on resource scarcity have almost by default achieved a middle ground between substantive and formalist approaches due to their focus on culturally defined understandings of scarcity, arising due to actual shortages of resources and land, rather than from applying monetary values to resources (see Humphreys, 1969, p202). Some examples include work on soil fertility in Ethiopia (see Scoones, Chapter 9 this volume) and work on drought in South India (see Vasavi, 1999). In addition, my work in Kutch, western India, examines cultural and historical understandings of scarcity, and how different social groups have differentiated responses to scarcity which they view as a temporally bounded phenomenon, depending on the availability of fodder, water and rain, as opposed to one that is universalized through state-sponsored policies and programmes (Mehta, 2005). Such approaches are closely aligned with socio-political approaches that examine the discursive constructions of scarcity.

Socio-political perspectives: Discourses and contestations around scarcity

Socio-political perspectives of scarcity draw on a variety of disciplinary approaches including political ecology (Blaikie and Brookfield, 1987; Bryant, 1992; Peet and Watts, 1996; Forsyth, 2003) and Foucauldian discourse analysis to raise questions concerning the interactive effects between nature and society at different levels – the individual, household, community, village, region, state and world – and call for historically nuanced perspectives. They ask questions about how environmental problems are perceived at these different levels and the extent to which the definition is context-bound, and also explore the nature of relations of power and production at global and local levels, and how access to and control over resources or property rights are defined and contested in a wide range of areas: the household, community, state and world. Within this approach, contestations take place at two levels: first, over meaning and text in the very conception of environmental problems and second, in competing claims and conflicts over resources. The former emphasizes the need to understand how environmental phenomena are constructed discursively and are perceived by a host of actors; the latter stresses the need to understand the intricate web of power and social relations governing access to and control over natural resources at the macro and micro levels.

Sociologists of knowledge have long since argued that knowledge is largely socially constructed (see Berger and Luckmann, 1966) and science studies scholars such as Brian Wynne, Sheila Jasanoff and Shiv Visvanathan have helped demystify the notion that science and technology are 'objective', universal and neutral but are instead rooted in local knowledge systems and local social and power relations. Hence, socio-political perspectives of scarcity would focus on an analysis that is both discursive *and* materialist (see Escobar, 1996) where the nexus of power, ideas and social relations is the centrepiece of enquiry. Such an analysis tries to marry an ecological phenomenon (a shortage of food/water, etc.) with political economy. For example, Yapa (1996) talks of 'discursive materialism' where the focus is not just on the social, material or discursive but on all three. In his analysis of poverty and scarcity he demonstrates how scarcity is not experienced by society at large, but instead by particular social groupings and is a 'socially specific condition'. Through the power of categorization of different social groupings, poverty itself gets reified and also the 'solutions' get to be a part of a 'metanarrative' that helps reinforce the problem. Thus, scarcity is created by both discourse and practice.

The historian Ross distinguishes between socially generated scarcity (insufficient necessities for some people and not others) versus absolute scarcity (insufficient resources, no matter how equitably distributed). For him, neoliberalism has encouraged a pro-scarcity climate distinguished, economically, by deep concessions and cutbacks and politically, by the rollback of 'excessive' rights. He argues that the two kinds of scarcity have been conflated either intentionally in order to reinforce austerity measures against the poor or inadvertently due to ignorance about how natural resources are produced and distributed (Ross, 1996).

I found it helpful to distinguish between 'lived/experienced' scarcity (something that local people experience cyclically due the biophysical shortage of food, water, fodder, etc.) and 'constructed' scarcity (something that is manufactured through socio-political processes to suit the interests of powerful players (in this case the dam-building lobby and the interests of rich irrigators and agro-industrialists) for my research (see Mehta, 2005). However, the discursive nature of manufactured scarcity often exacerbates biophysical scarcity. Clearly there is the constructivist dilemma. To cast everything as 'socially and politically constructed' could in some ways deny the existence of a 'real' ecological crisis around water, food, land and so on. Constructivists could be accused of fiddling while Rome burns (Ross, 1996). This can be overcome if the materialist basis of the analysis is maintained and if the focus remains on how resource shortages and ecological degradation are primarily a result of the uneven social measures that manufacture scarcity all over the world for the economic and political gain of powerful interests.

Scarcity as a meta-level explanation and narrative

Why does it matter? It would be fair to say that formalism largely prevails both in academic and policy discourses around scarcity. I am often struck by the scarcity definitions deployed by bilateral and multilateral agencies and even governments in understanding resource availability and scarcity issues (the chapters in Part III of this volume engage with mainstream scarcity definitions in the food, water and energy domains). Definitions of scarcity usually look at absolute population numbers and absolute quantities and talk little about the politics of distribution (see Chapter 12, this volume). Of course, when pushed, most policy-makers and commentators concede that scarcity is a multifaceted and complex phenomenon. Still, in most official discourses, scarcity is universalized and naturalized and it is convenient to stick to this simplified notion of scarcity (Chapters 8 and 9 in this volume explain why).

Scarcity is also a concept that can provide meta-level explanations for a wide range of phenomena over which humans have no control. For example, Walsh makes links between scarcity and ethics and discusses how moral philosophers draw on Kant's famous declaration that we were not morally responsible for failures due to the 'niggardliness of stepmother nature' (Walsh, 1958). Thus the notion of scarcity taken from economic theory can be used to clarify the failures for which we are not to blame. This leads large farmers in Gujarat, India, to attribute rapidly declining groundwater levels to water scarcity and dwindling rainfall, and thus to whitewash aspects of human culpability and their own bad water management practices (even though a 120-year examination of rainfall patterns shows no significant change, see Mehta, 2005). Or in the Western Cape, geography is blamed instead of looking at demand management strategies to deal with Cape Town's water scarcity. Thus when scarcity emerges as the meta-level explanation or as a trope for the justification of need, it becomes a technical term and all subjective and constructivist experiences and elements are weeded out. Moreover, the socio-political dimensions are denied. A good case in point is the scarcity and conflict literature.

In the 1990s there was a surge of literature on natural resource scarcity and violent conflict. The most well known is that of Thomas Homer-Dixon at the University of Toronto. Homer-Dixon and his colleagues hypothesized that the decreasing supply of environmental resources, such as clean water, the accompanying large-scale movements of people and resultant economic deprivation would all contribute to conflicts and resource wars (Homer-Dixon, 1994 and 2001). Homer-Dixon does somewhat acknowledge the subjective aspects of scarcity and the role of ideology and perceptions in causing scarcity, but barring a couple of examples he rarely discusses the politicized aspects of scarcity or indeed how scarcity can be the result of the politics of allocation or misappropriation (Homer-Dixon, 1994). Instead, he deploys rather causal and deterministic ways to prove that unequal resource access and population growth lead to decreases in the quantity and quality of renewable resources and subsequent increasing environmental scarcity. He does concede that adaptation to environmental scarcity is possible through social and technical ingenuity – e.g. economic incentives and taxes to encourage conservation, technological innovation and 'decoupling' from developing environmental resources by focusing on alternative means of wealth creation. But poor countries usually lack this social and technical ingenuity. Shades of this thinking are echoed in work on specific resource scarcity, e.g. water. For example, Anthony Turton and colleagues talk of 'second order scarcity' – the lack of economic resources, know-how, technology or institutions to develop water, which Africa largely suffers from (Turton, 1999).

Environmental scarcity is thus seen to play an independent role in causing conflict, even though other factors such as ideology, power relations and unequal property rights matter too; they are subordinate to environmental scarcity which is the main causal factor. Thus environmental scarcity has insidious and cumulative impacts that lead to violent conflict, conflict which is likely to rise sharply in future decades when many societies will have progressively lower capacity to adapt with social and technical ingenuity.

Examples where, despite scarcity, cooperation rather than conflict occurred are largely ignored. The focus on environmental scarcity as a causal variable tends to ignore other explanatory variables (see Peluso and Watts, 2001). Environmental scarcity is thus taken as a given. It is seen to cause powerful actors to 'increase in their own favour the inequalities in the distribution of resources' (Peluso and Watts, 2001, p35). Scarcity is not seen as the result of powerful actors getting away with resource appropriation and thus enhancing degradation. Moreover, 'the politics of distribution disappear into the environmental scarcity concept' (Hauge and Ellingsen, 1998, p302). Ecosystem variability and vulnerability are also viewed as a given and constant, not as shifting and constantly subjected to change, thus negating results from new ecology which argue for the dynamic and changing nature of the environment and caution against snapshot perspectives of environmental change and phenomena. Finally, ways in which scarcity can encourage cooperation are neglected (as previously discussed in this chapter).

Solutions to 'scarcity' and the role of innovation

When scarcity is seen as a constant rather than something originating in human relations, notions of 'expansion' and 'progress' are evoked as 'solutions' to help alleviate scarcity conditions in a particular locality. Thus John Locke at the end of the 17th century saw America as the 'empty continent' that could help alleviate scarcity conditions in Europe (Achterhuis, 1993). Cecil Rhodes openly admitted that imperialism and expansion were necessary to avoid the class war in 19th-century England. And the space voyages since the 1960s also depended, in part, on new conquests to 'overcome war, scarcity and misery on earth' (Reagan quoted in Achterhuis, 1993, p107). Much of the focus on science and technology has been around the better management of scarcity. Debates around the UN Conference on Environment and Development (UNCED) in Rio and Rio plus 10 at the World Summit on Sustainable Development (WSSD) highlight that despite the recognition from a variety of quarters about 'limits to growth', economic development cannot and should not be compromised (e.g. the highly contested notion of what constitutes sustainability, see Chapter 5, this volume).

With growth usually assumed to be the means to progress and development, the scarcity of resources that enable this growth is seen as an obstacle, and solutions need to be sought. These solutions usually lie in deploying innovation, science and technology. Technology is evoked as a means to assure long-term resource abundance (Norgaard, 1994). For the 'technological optimists', scarcity is a 'normal' reaction arising due to flawed policies and poor research and development. By contrast, the technological pessimists see scarcity as a warning that infinite growth is not possible and call for the need to set limits on consumption, reorient values and so on. The latter believe that often infinite growth cannot be supported by finite stocks (Salmon, 1977, p703) and the 1970s saw the emergence of 'scarcity politics' – largely arising out of the oil shocks – which included notions of 'spaceship economy' by Boulding (1966) and Schumacher's Buddhist economics (1973). By contrast, the focus on abundance highlights human technological inventiveness in time of need ('necessity is the mother of invention') and projects that into the future, too. Technological optimist policies include the search for the new 'blue revolution' and more irrigation systems for Africa, the biotech revolution, expansion into space and so on.

In most cases, technology is made out to be an apolitical instrument – scientific committees and experts are sought as 'arbiters' (Barry, 2001) of which scarce resources are managed and allocated. But in reality, technology and techniques are deeply political – and contestations around technological solutions (be they large dams, India's fantastical river interlinking project, the now fashionable Integrated Water Resources Management (IWRM) or privatization) are sites of politics (in both the cultural and material realms). Still, technocracies are made out to be neutral sites where decisions are made about how best to deal with and manage scarcity. Often technology is both the 'problem' and the 'solution'. For example, the Sardar Sarovar (Narmada) dam is supposed to be the 'solution' for scarcity in water-starved Kutch, but it is also a 'problem' around which India's most prominent post-Independence social movement has emerged. This presents a challenge for institutional and bureaucratic organization given its ambitious scope, as well as a site to debate how best to manage water in western India. Similarly, privatization models are purported to be the 'solution' to efficiently manage 'scarce' goods and services – but their impacts on human well-being and people's basic rights are questionable, especially in the world's poorest countries. Finally, technological responses to limits and scarcities often have as much to do with social phenomena as with 'real' constraints and limits to resources. The rise and fall of research and technological focus on solar power during the 1970s and 1980s was not merely linked to the existence of fossil hydrocarbons. Instead, it was much to do with perceptions of the environment/resources and the existing political climate. Similarly, action or inaction around climate change in the United States have much to do with the politically charged nature of the debate and the nexus with corporate power.

Conclusion

I have demonstrated in this chapter that scarcity is not necessarily natural or universal. Still, in many academic and policy debates scarcity has been universalized and naturalized. These generalized notions of scarcity tell us nothing about what exactly scarcity means, who it affects most, who creates it and who benefits from this permanent state of scarcity. They have also tended to evoke a standardized set of market/institutional and technological solutions as the (universal) fix which have blocked out context-specific socio-political and cultural factors, as well as contestations around access as a legitimate focus for academic debates as well as policies and interventions. Whether markets, innovation, rights, institutional fixes or bits of all of the above are evoked to deal with resource scarcity, they are all socio-political choices governed by the politics of allocation and decision-making and contestations about what meanings are embodied in resources. As this chapter has demonstrated, non-mainstream economics, institutional perspectives and insights from sociology and anthropology offer several and more nuanced ways to see scarcity. Similarly, problematic notions of scarcity are increasingly being challenged through local-level protest and more recently at the global policy level (see UNDP, 2006). It is now time to write the obituary for these generalized notions of scarcity.

Notes

1 Jean-Paul Sartre in Xenos, 1989.
2 There are however two caveats: one, this chapter largely focuses on a range of perspectives on scarcity and is hence empirically thin. While some examples, largely from the water domain, will be provided, the empirically rich chapters to follow in this volume will flesh out several of the issues discussed in this chapter. Two, it does not extensively deal with nuanced analyses of economics and scarcity, something which I leave to the authors in the next section of this volume.
3 Other connotations from the Old Northern French include frugality, parsimony and niggardliness as well as insufficiency of supply, in a community, or the necessities of life, a dearth as well as insufficiency of supply; smallness of available quantity, number or amount; in proportion to the need or demand (Oxford English Dictionary, 1971).
4 For a range of perspectives on water, economic goods and scarcity see Chapters 6, 7, 11 and 12 in this volume. See also Mehta, 2003.
5 As Achterhuis correctly observes, while in the 17th century colonialism and expansion to the 'New World' was a possible route to escape scarcity, today this option is not available. Instead, some thinkers talk about mining space in order to meet growing wants. The reader will also be familiar with occasional reports in the media about explorations on Mars for water as a way to cope with the present water 'crisis' on Earth.
6 For debates on whether or not Marx took 'scarcity' seriously and the impacts of this on communism and capitalism see the interesting exchange between P. Wiles and Ronald L. Meek in the 1950s (Wiles, 1956) and (Meek, 1955).

References

Achterhuis, H. (1993) 'Scarcity and sustainability', in W. Sachs (ed) *Global Ecology: A New Arena of Political Conflict*, Zed Books, London and New Jersey

Anand, P.B. (2007) *Scarcity, Entitlements and the Economics of Water in Developing Countries*, Edward Elgar, Cheltenham, UK, Northampton, MA

Appadurai, A. (ed) (1988) *The Social Life of Things: Commodities in Cultural Perspective*, Cambridge University Press, Cambridge

Aristotle (1831) *Politics* (T. Sinclair, translation), Penguin, Harmondsworth, 1962

Balla, B. (1981) 'Ressourcenknappheit und soziales Handeln', in F. Rapp (ed) *Nuturverstondnis und Soziales Handeln*, Wilhelm Fink, München

Barry, A. (2001) *Political Machines: Governing a Technological Society*, The Athlone Press, London and New York

Berger, P.L. and Luckmann, T. (1966) *The Social Construction of Reality: A Treatise in the Sociology of Knowledge*, Anchor Books, Garden City, NY

Berkes, F. (1989) *Common Property Resource: Ecology and Community-Based Sustainable Development*, Belhaven Press, London

Blaikie, P. and Brookfield, H. (1987) *Land Degradation and Society*, Routledge, London, New York

Boulding, K.E. (1966) 'The economics of the coming spaceship Earth', in H. Jarrett (ed) *Environmental Quality in a Growing Economy: Resources for the Future*, Johns Hopkins University Press, Baltimore, MD

Bromley, D. and Cernea, M. (1989) *The Management of Common Property Natural Resources: Some Conceptual and Operational Fallacies*, The World Bank, Washington, DC

Bryant, R. (1992) 'Political ecology: An emerging research agenda in third world studies', *Political Geography*, vol 11, no 1, pp12–36

Carver, T.N. (1908) 'The basis of social conflict', *The American Journal of Sociology*, vol 13, no 5, pp628–648

Cleaver, F. (1998) 'Moral ecological rationality, institutions and the management of common property resources', *Development and Change*, vol 31, pp361–383

Escobar, A. (1996) 'Constructing nature: Elements for a poststructural political ecology', in R. Peet and M. Watts (eds) *Liberation Ecologies: Environment, Development, Social Movements*, Routledge, London, New York

Etzioni, A. (1985) 'The political economy of imperfect competition', *Journal of Public Policy*, vol 5, no 2, pp169–186

Firth, R. (1951) *Elements of Social Organization*, Philosophical Library, New York

Forsyth, T. (2003) *Critical Political Ecology*, Routledge, London

Granovetter, M. (1985) 'Economic action and social structure: The problem of embeddedness', *American Journal of Sociology*, vol 91, no 3, pp481–510

Hardin, G. (1968) 'The Tragedy of the Commons', *Science*, vol 162, pp1243–1248

Hauge, W. and Ellingsen, T. (1998) 'Beyond environmental scarcity: Causal pathways to conflict', *Journal of Peace Research* (Special Issue on Environmental Conflict), vol 35, no 3, pp299–317

Hewitt de Alcantara, C. (1993) 'Introduction: Markets in principle and practice', in C. Hewitt de Alcantara (ed) *Real Markets: Social and Political Issues of Food Policy Reform*, Frank Cass/EADI/UNRISD, London

Hobbes, T. (1994 [1651]) *Leviathan*, E. Curley (ed) Hackett, Indianapolis, IN

Homer-Dixon, T.F. (1994) 'Environmental scarcities and violent conflict: Evidence from cases', *International Security*, vol 19, no 1, pp5–40

Homer-Dixon, T.F. (2001) *Environment, Scarcity and Violence*, Princeton University Press, Princeton

Hont, I. and Ignatieff, M. (eds) (1983) *Wealth and Virtue: The Shaping of Political Economy in the Scottish Enlightenment*, Cambridge University Press, Cambridge and New York

Humphreys, S.C. (1969) 'History, economics, and anthropology: The work of Karl Polanyi', *History and Theory*, vol 8, no 2, pp165–212

Locke, J. (1988 [1689]) *Two Treatises of Government*, P. Laslett (ed) Cambridge University Press, Cambridge

Meek, Ronald L. (1955) 'Some thoughts on Marxism, scarcity, and Gosplan', *Oxford Economic Papers, New Series*, vol 7, no 3, pp281–299

Mehta, L. (2003) 'Struggles around "Publicness" and the right to access: Perspectives from the water domain', in I. Kaul, P. Conceição, K. Le Goulven and R.U. Mendoza (eds) *Providing Global Goods: Managing Globalization*, Oxford University Press, New York

Mehta, L. (2005) *The Politics and Poetics of Water: Naturalising Scarcity in Western India*, Orient Longman, New Delhi

Mosse, D. (2003) *The Rule of Water: Statecraft, Ecology and Collective Action in South India*, Oxford University Press, Oxford

Norgaard, R. (1994) *Development Betrayed: The End of Progress and a Co-evolutionary Revisioning of the Future*, Routledge, London and New York

Ostrom, E. (1990) *Governing the Commons: The Evolution of Institutions for Collective Action*, Cambridge University Press, New York

Ostrom, E. and Keohane, R.O. (eds) (1995) *Local Commons and Global Interdependence: Heterogeneity and Co-operation in Two Domains*, Sage Publications, Center for International Affairs, Harvard University

Oxford English Dictionary (1971) *The Compact Edition*, Oxford University Press, New York

Peet, R. and Watts, M. (eds) (1996) *Liberation Ecologies: Environment, Development, Social Movements*, Routledge, London, New York

Peluso, N. and Watts, M. (eds) (2001) *Violent Environments*, Cornell University Press, New York

Polanyi, K. (1944) *The Great Transformation: The Political and Economic Origins of our Time*, Beacon Press, Boston

Polanyi, K., Arensenberg, C. and Pearson, H. (1957) (eds) *Trade and Market in the Early Empires: Economies in History and Theory*, The Free Press, New York

Polanyi, K. (1957) 'The economy as instituted process', in K. Polanyi, C. Arensenberg and H. Pearson (eds) *Trade and Market in the Early Empires: Economies in History and Theory*, The Free Press, New York

Robbins, L. (1932) *An Essay on the Nature and Significance of Economic Science*, Macmillan, London

Ross, A. (1996) 'The lonely hour of scarcity', *Capitalism, Nature, Socialism*, vol 7, no 3, pp3–26

Sahlins, M. (1972) *Stone Age Economics*, Aldine Publishing Company, New York

Salmon, J.D. (1977) 'Politics of scarcity versus technological optimism: A possible reconciliation?', *International Studies Quarterly*, vol 21, no 4, Special Issue on International Politics of Scarcity, pp701–720

Schumacher, E.F. (1973) *Small is Beautiful: A Study of Economics as if People Mattered*, Harper & Row, New York

Sen, A. (1981) *Poverty and Famines: An Essay on Entitlement and Deprivation*, Oxford University Press, Oxford

Sen, A. (1983) 'Development: Which way now?', *The Economic Journal*, vol 93, no 372, pp745–762

Sen, A. (1999) *Development as Freedom*, Oxford University Press, Oxford

Smith, A. (2003) *The Wealth of Nations*, Bantham Books, New York (based on the 5th edition as edited and annotated by Edwin Cannan in 1904)

Stillman, P. (1983) 'Scarcity, sufficiency, and abundance: Hegel and Marx on material needs and satisfaction', *International Political Science Review*, vol 4, no 3, pp295–310

Toye, J. (2005) 'What did economists do with scarcity?', presentation at the conference *Scarcity and the Politics of Allocation*, Institute of Development Studies, Brighton

Turton, A.R. (1999) 'Water Scarcity and Social Adaptive Capacity: Towards an Understanding of the Social Dynamics of Water Demand Management in Developing Countries', Occasional Paper, No 9, Water Issues Study Group, School of Oriental and African Studies, University of London, UK

UNDP (2006) *Human Development Report 2006: Beyond Scarcity: Power, Poverty and the Global Water Crisis*, Palgrave Macmillan, New York, available at http://hdr. undp.org/en/reports/global/hdr2006/ (last accessed 11 December 2009)

Vasavi, A.R. (1999) *Harbingers of Rain: Land and Life in South India*, Oxford University Press, Delhi

Walsh, V.C. (1958) 'Scarcity and the concepts of ethics', *Philosophy of Science*, vol 25, no 4, pp249–257

Wiles, P. (1956) 'Growth versus choice', *The Economic Journal*, vol 66, no 262, pp244–255

Xenos, N. (1987) 'Liberalism and the Postulate of Scarcity', *Political Theory*, vol 15, no 2, pp225–243

Xenos, N. (1989) *Scarcity and Modernity*, Routledge, New York and London

Yapa, L. (1996) 'What causes poverty? A postmodern view', *Annals of the Association of American Geographers*, vol 86, no 4, pp707–728

2
Everybody's Got the Fever: Scarcity and US National Energy Policy

Nicholas Xenos

In his dialogue *Euthydemus*, Plato has Socrates recount to his friend Crito a conversation he had the previous day with two sophists, Euthydemus and his brother Dionysodorus. These men boast that they have developed a technique designed to refute any argument, and that they can teach it in a very short time. After listening to them deploy it in conversation with two others, and then conversing with them himself, Socrates says to Euthydemus that they should shun public performances in front of large groups because their technique is so easily and quickly learned that:

> the listeners are likely to master it right away and give you no credit. Better just talk to each other in private, or, if you must have an audience, then let no one come unless he gives you money. And if you are sensible you will give your disciples the same advice, never to argue with anyone but yourselves and each other. For it is a rare thing, Euthydemus, which is the precious one, and water is cheapest, even though, as Pindar said, it is the best. (304a–b)[1]

When an economist reads this, it is likely to look like a statement of value; an example of 'the paradox of water and diamonds' (see Chapter 4 for a discussion of the water and diamond paradox). Things like diamonds are scarcer than water and so their value is higher. To the economist within each of us, that seems obviously right.

I would like to look at this example from a different perspective from that of the economist, and one that takes full account of Socrates' irony. There are no diamonds in Plato's example that I can see. Socrates does observe that a thing's rarity determines its value relative to other things, and that water is relatively abundant and therefore 'cheapest'. But what he counsels Euthydemus to do is to create a scarcity of the brothers' technique by restricting its dissemination and creating a market for it. It is suggested elsewhere in the dialogue (304e–305b) that the technique in question is useless, a judgement often made about philosophy by non-philosophers that Plato incorporates into his Socratic dialogues in order to counter it by demonstrating the profound use (one is tempted to say 'use value') of Socrates' mode of philosophizing for living a virtuous life. And it is a staple of Plato's dialogues that Socrates is distinguished from the sophists by the fact that he does not take money for his conversation, or restrict himself to a small group of disciples but rather will converse with anyone for free. By contrast, in Socratic terms, the philosophy of the sophists, which is up for sale, is truly useless. So Socrates is ironically reflecting on the creation of a market for a useless thing. In this example, Socrates' teaching is like water, both useful and easily available.

In principle, the technique developed by Euthydemus and his brother is capable of infinite distribution; unlike diamonds, it is not inherently 'scarce'. Socrates' suggestion for how to create value out of something of this kind may be closer to the contemporary example of intellectual property rights than to a finite resource. This correction may suffice to sustain an economic interpretation of Socrates' comment, but Plato's point seems to be rather the absurdity of the situation. A useless technique, a thing of no real value, becomes valued simply because a market has been created for it. That may say something about markets, but it is not meant as a compliment to their efficiency at allocating scarce goods. It points instead to the role markets sometimes play in experiencing scarcity.

It is this kind of experience that I had primarily in mind when I wrote *Scarcity and Modernity* (1989). The simple fact of finitude of anything does not necessarily constitute a scarcity of that thing. Diamonds, to stick with that example, are relatively rare. Their value, however, is not solely due to their rarity. As the hardest natural entity, diamonds have a use value in industrial applications. But the primary source of value for diamonds has always been their ornamental desirability which depends upon their specific aesthetic and cultural properties rather than the simple fact that they were relatively rare, at least until the late 19th and early 20th centuries when large diamond deposits were discovered in Africa. When that happened, the De Beers company began a concerted advertising campaign to boost the demand for them, resulting in the now ubiquitous engagement ring. The point is that it is the demand for diamonds that makes them scarce; if no one wanted them, we would think of the supply of them – if we thought about them at all – as finite, but not scarce.

My contention in *Scarcity and Modernity* is that the general sense that human beings exist in a condition of perpetual scarcity, and that certain consequences necessarily follow from that condition for the way we think about politics, is a product of the proliferation of desire in modernity rather than the general reality of finitude (see Chapter 6, this volume, for a discussion of finiteness and scarcity). If finitude alone were the central determinant of scarcity, political theorists would have taken it into account from the beginning, but they did not. What they did take into account was the problem of desire. In the well known example from the *Republic*, Plato has Socrates suggest that he and his interlocutors construct a city in words in order to determine what justice is. The starting point for that exercise is the notion that no one is entirely self-sufficient, and therefore the city comes into being as a creation of needs (369c). As they build this city, they develop a basic notion of what we might call a division of labour but which is actually a division by craft. Included in this construction are considerations of trade, both internally and externally, and hence the need for money and for merchants and retailers. There are also people with no craft who work for wages. The resulting model seems to come close to self-sufficiency, but one of the participants in the dialogue, Glaucon, balks at the description of a city without luxuries, implying that the described city is a city for pigs. Socrates then says:

> All right, I understand. It isn't merely the origin of a city that we're considering, it seems, but the origin of a luxurious city. And that may not be a bad idea, for by examining it, we might very well see how justice and injustice grow up in cities. Yet the true city, in my opinion, is the one we've described, the healthy one, as it were. But let's study a city with a fever, if that's what you want. (372e–373a)[2]

The problem of justice, and injustice, does not arise out of a condition of 'natural' scarcity generated by finitude in this formulation, but rather out of the proliferation of desire beyond the satisfaction of need. The solution Plato offered, at least in words, was the restriction on desire through the proper ordering of the soul and, by analogy, the proper ordering of the city. That is what is meant by justice.

This attribute of the classical conceptualization can be seen as well in the political theory of Plato's successor, Aristotle. In Aristotle's formulation, the realm of necessity is the realm of the household (*oikos*) where the art of household management (*oeconomia*) includes the art of acquisition of wealth, but only in the context of achieving self-sufficiency within a bounded set of material needs (see also Chapter 6, this volume, for a further discussion of *oikos* and Aristotle). The city is the realm of justice and self-sufficiency there means participating in justice. It is noteworthy in this context that Attica experienced a regular scarcity of grain and first established trade relations with Black Sea sources of grain and placed colonies there. After the Persian War, Athens' domination of the seas and imperial control over Aegean cities as well as colonization assured its trade routes to the Black Sea. The grain trade is the only trade that was extensively regulated and controlled in Athenian law (Austin and Vidal-Nacquet, 1977, p115–117). Managing the grain trade is one example, only briefly alluded to by Aristotle, where the city might engage the realm of necessity, but this is clearly understood to be exceptional and a consequence of being beyond the collective capacity of individual households. Even here, though, acquisition is still conceptualized in terms of limits (*Pol.* 1256b26–37). But it is perhaps telling that the realm of necessity, once politicized, eventually led Athens toward expansion and, in part, to the self-justification of imperial power. First came established trade relations and colonies, then, when opportunity and power converged, imperial domination.

The Aristotelian moral framework dominated western political thought for centuries. In the modern era, and particularly in the 18th century, it was replaced by a political and social theorizing that postulated a boundless desire that was not only not destructive of society but, when properly institutionalized, constitutive of it (see Xenos, 1989, Chapter 1). David Hume encoded the new modern notion in his *Treatise of Human Nature* (1739–1740) when he made the presence of scarcity a foundational principle of justice. The comparison with Plato is instructive. Whereas Plato's 'true city' originates in need, that need is initially considered natural and finite. For Hume, on the other hand, nature has endowed the human being with 'numberless wants and necessities' (Hume, 1978 [1739, 1740], p484). As with Plato, Hume postulates that society provides the remedy for nature's limitations on the individual through the combination of forces, but in his formulation the remedy does not completely cure the problem, because, 'tho' in that situation his wants multiply every moment upon him, yet his abilities are still more augmented, and leave him in every respect more satisfied and happy, than 'tis possible for him, in his savage and solitary condition, ever to become' (Hume, 1978 [1739, 1740], p485). The dynamic of increasing wants and increasing power to satisfy them presupposes that the former outrun the latter, so that it is new wants that spur the development of human abilities. What this means is that society does not solve the problem of scarcity but rather institutionalizes it. Hume observes that, 'There are three different species of goods, which we are possess'd of; the internal satisfaction of our mind, the external advantages of our body, and the enjoyment of such possessions as we have acquir'd by our industry and good fortune'. It is the last of these that entails and reinscribes the problem of scarcity:

> We are perfectly secure in the enjoyment of the first. The second may be ravish'd from us, but can be of no advantage to him who deprives us of them. The last only are both expos'd to the violence of others, and may be transferr'd without suffering any loss or alteration; while at the same time, there is not a sufficient quantity of them to supply everyone's desires and necessities. As the improvement, therefore, of these goods is the chief advantage of society, so the instability of their possession, along with their scarcity, is the chief impediment. (Hume, 1978 [1739, 1740], p487–488)

The remedy is a social contract in which everyone realizes it is in his or her self-interest, and thus in the common interest, to establish property laws. Those laws are what Hume calls justice. Property does not signify a natural relationship to objects, but rather a conventional one and therefore a moral one (Hume, 1978 [1739, 1740], p491). Justice is a struggle because Hume denies any natural propensity towards benevolence. Instead, he finds an 'avidity … of acquiring goods and possessions for ourselves and our nearest friends' that is 'insatiable, perpetual, universal, and directly destructive of society' (Hume, 1978 [1739, 1740], p491–492). The object of law is to constrain and channel this passion. Law, or justice, is necessary only in relation to scarce goods. Were it not for this, if, like air and water, there were sufficient amounts of everything for everyone, there would be no need for justice. Thus he concludes that, ''tis only from the selfishness and confin'd generosity of men, along with the scanty provision nature has made for his wants, that justice derives its origin' (Hume, 1978 [1739, 1740], p495). By the time we reach our own era, the most influential theorist of justice in the past 50 years, John Rawls, could simply (and explicitly) follow Hume in making central among the 'circumstances of justice' a 'moderate scarcity' without which there would be 'no occasion for the virtue of justice', which he understands as adjudicating competing claims over goods (Rawls, 1971, p128).

With Hume and Rawls we can see in the comparison of Plato and Aristotle that there is a fundamental difference in the way need is related to objects in the two instances. In what I call the modern version, need has become indistinguishable from desire, and the proliferation of desire is foundational for the maintenance of society. To talk of limits in this context becomes profoundly paradoxical (see Chapter 5, this volume for a detailed discussion of limits in the context of sustainable development). The way this paradox is articulated is in a dialectical rhetoric of abundance and scarcity. We accumulate more and more, but always against the backdrop of new, unsatisfied desires. And so the strange experience of modernity in a hyper-accumulating society is one of perpetual scarcity. Prior to the modern age, scarcities were understood as limited in time and space. They arose from specific circumstances and were addressed, when they were addressed, by a multiplicity of means. A scarcity of some food source might result from a bad harvest due to weather or to political turmoil that interrupted planting or harvest or as the consequence of pillage. Such scarcities could be anticipated in a general sense and some basic provision made to blunt their effects should they arise, such as the stockpiling of relatively non-perishable food items. In the context of established political communities, these sorts of anticipated scarcities could be protected against via alliances or other routinized relationships in order to ensure access to supplies of the same or substitute goods through trade, or through military control or conquest. Such was the situation in classical Athens, for example. For us, however, there are not periods of scarcity, or specific scarcities of specific things. For us there is simply scarcity.

Energy crises and scarcity

When I wrote *Scarcity and Modernity*, a great deal of public attention was focused, as now, on the problem of scarce resources, particularly upon scarce

sources of energy and more particularly still on oil. The twin oil crises of
the 1970s – the OPEC oil crisis of 1973 and the second crisis following the
Iranian revolution that overthrew the US-backed Shah in 1979 – still rever-
berated through the collective consciousness of western Europe and North
America. This prolonged sense of crisis demonstrated how we view scarcity
in modernity. The enduring symbol of that period is President Jimmy Carter's cardigan sweater, which he wore in a so-called fireside chat in February,
1977, during which he pronounced the energy crisis to be the 'moral equivalent of war'. After his administration first instituted price controls on oil, and
then started decontrolling them, Carter gave his now famous 'crisis of confidence' speech on 15 July 1979.[3] What most people remember of that speech
is Carter's plea to his fellow citizens to turn down their thermostats as an act
of patriotism. They also remember that Carter was subsequently drubbed by
an eternally optimistic Ronald Reagan in the 1980 presidential election. But
the speech is interesting in several respects, and particularly when compared
to another presidential statement on US energy policy, the National Energy
Policy, produced by the National Energy Policy Development Group chaired
by Vice-President Dick Cheney, in May 2001. One of the interesting aspects is
the way both documents articulate the modern paradox of scarcity and abundance. Another is the presence of war, either rhetorically inscribed in the text,
as in Carter's speech, or lurking behind it, as in the Bush energy policy.

In his speech, Carter referred to a 'crisis of confidence' in the promise of
progress in America. The progress Carter had in mind is complex and tension-
riddled. 'We've always believed in something called progress', he said. 'We've
always had a faith that the days of our children would be better than our own'.
What Carter meant by 'better' is not necessarily material in nature. Instead,
Carter invoked a continuing democratic project. 'Our people are losing that
faith, not only in government itself but in the ability as citizens to serve as the
ultimate rulers and shapers of our democracy'. And part of that weakening
faith is due to a loss of individual and collective direction, because:

> too many of us now tend to worship self-indulgence and consump-
> tion. Human identity is no longer defined by what one does, but
> by what one owns. But we've discovered that owning things and
> consuming things does not satisfy our longing for meaning. We've
> learned that piling up material goods cannot fill the emptiness of
> lives which have no confidence or purpose.

Carter invoked the 'shocks and tragedy' of the assassinations of John F.
Kennedy, Martin Luther King, Jr and Robert Kennedy, the Watergate scandal
and the Vietnam War as backdrops to a loss of respect for American institutions and self-esteem. But then he turned toward more tangible concerns:

> We remember when the phrase 'sound as a dollar' was an expres-
> sion of absolute dependability, until ten years of inflation began to
> shrink our dollar and our savings. We believed that our nation's

resources were limitless until 1973 when we had to face a growing dependence on foreign oil.

Then Carter articulated a curious set of challenges from the past and the present:

We ourselves are the same Americans who just ten years ago put a man on the moon. We are the generation that dedicated our society to the pursuit of human rights and equality. And we are the generation that will win the war on the energy problem and in that process, rebuild the unity and confidence of America.

Technology and ideals mark the first of these challenges. What is at stake in the energy 'war'? How will it lead to unity and confidence? Technology can be part of it, but what ideals are at stake?

Carter made it clear that the government had been hampered by struggles for immediate advantage between the political parties. Coming together in this new war was a way to restore unity and overcome the chaos of fragmentation. The common interest would be realized on the 'battlefield of energy'. The energy crisis constituted a 'clear and present danger to our nation', he said, and cited the transition from energy independence to reliance on high-priced imported oil from OPEC countries (Organization of the Petroleum Exporting Countries), linking this dependence to domestic unemployment and inflation. This situation 'threatens our economic independence and the very security of our nation'. To respond to this threat, Carter then made several pledges. The first of these: 'Beginning this moment, this nation will never use more foreign oil than we did in 1977 – never'. To accomplish this, he proposed cutting dependence on foreign oil by 50 per cent within the next decade and imposing import restrictions in order to accomplish it. He also asked for a huge invest-ment in 'America's own alternative sources of fuel – from coal, from oil shale, from plant products for gasohol, from unconventional gas, from the sun'. He proposed the creation of a national solar bank, aimed at achieving 20 per cent of energy from solar power by the year 2000. Sticking with the war metaphor, Carter invoked two World War II agencies as his inspirations for some of his proposals and assured his audience that the vast infusion of federal money these required would go to bolster the embattled domestic economy instead of going abroad to OPEC countries. One of these models was also intended to cut through bureaucratic red tape, and the sort of regulations he had in mind became clear when he vowed, 'We will protect our environment. But when this nation critically needs a refinery or a pipeline, we will build it'. Carter prom-ised increased funding for public transportation, and then appealed to citizens to help conserve energy:

I'm asking you for your good and for your nation's security to take no unnecessary trips, to use carpools or public transporta-tion whenever you can, to park your car one extra day per week, to obey the speed limit, and to set your thermostats to save fuel. Every act of energy conservation like this is more than just common sense, I tell you it is an act of patriotism.

He was careful to add that such actions should not be seen as sacrifices, but rather as 'the most painless and immediate way of rebuilding our nation's strength. Every gallon of oil each one of us saves is a new form of production. It gives us more freedom, more confidence, that much more control over our own lives'. And doing so would restore the missing sense of purpose to American lives.

But despite his effort to avoid the call to sacrifice in his request to conserve, Carter turned to that notion when he returned to the theme of war. First he invoked the abundance of American resources; shale oil, coal, technology, skilled labour and 'innovative genius'. And along with these resources, 'I firmly believe that we have the national will to win this war'. The rhetorical demands of war lea him to ritualistically admit, 'There is simply no way to avoid sacrifice'.

Carter's speech is a good example of the conundrums that result from the paradoxical characterization of scarcity in our time. On the one hand he recognized the role the drive to accumulate plays in this dialectic. He questioned the identification of progress with material possessions and suggested that the freedom we associate with those things may actually curtail freedom and threaten democratic practices and institutions. On the other hand, he couched his requests for scaling down in terms of sacrifices that would ultimately restore the accumulating self and society that would otherwise be seen as part of the problem. While Carter sought the high ground with his talk of sacrifice and war and national purpose, the memory of that cardigan sweater represented to his viewers a direct assault on his presupposition that a majority had come to the conclusion that material prosperity alone is meaningless. Objects signify, and what that sweater signified was stronger than anything Carter had to say about limits.

What ultimately proved more powerful in that speech was the call to war. Six months after Carter gave it, he delivered his last State of the Union message, on 23 January 1980.[4] Two events of significance occurred between the two speeches: the October seizure of American hostages at the US Embassy in Tehran, Iran, after the exiled Shah was admitted into the United States for medical treatment; and the Soviet invasion of Afghanistan in December. Carter refers to these events at the outset of his speech, in terms that have become both familiar and ironic:

> *At this time in Iran, 50 Americans are still held captive, innocent victims of terrorism and anarchy. Also at this moment, massive Soviet troops are attempting to subjugate the fiercely independent and deeply religious people of Afghanistan. These two acts – one of international terrorism and one of military aggression – present a serious challenge to the United States of America and indeed to all the nations of the world.*

While emphasizing the American desire for peace, Carter noted that Soviet military power, the dependence of western democracies on Middle Eastern oil and 'the press of social and religious and economic and political change in the many nations of the developing world, exemplified by the revolution in Iran', were the challenges to that desire.[5] The threat to Middle Eastern oil, which Carter noted is the source of 'more than two-thirds of the world's exportable oil', was framed in terms of the Soviet invasion. Carter stressed the strategic importance of Afghanistan:

> The Soviet effort to dominate Afghanistan has brought Soviet military forces to within 300 miles of the Indian Ocean and close to the Straits of Hormuz, a waterway through which most of the world's oil must flow. The Soviet Union is now attempting to consolidate a strategic position, therefore, that poses a grave threat to the free movement of Middle East oil.

Carter then articulated what has come to be known as the Carter Doctrine:

> Let our position be absolutely clear: An attempt by any outside force to gain control of the Persian Gulf region will be regarded as an assault on the vital interests of the United States of America, and such an assault will be repelled by any means necessary, including military force.

The establishment of the US military's Central Command, with operational control over the entire area from the Horn of Africa to the Caspian Sea was a strategic outcome of that doctrine.[6]

One constant between this speech and his earlier one is Carter's assertion that dependence upon foreign oil was an issue of US national security. The war on the energy problem had now been redirected from a rhetorical war to the threat of a real one in order to secure that foreign oil, but Carter nevertheless returned to the necessity of a national energy policy. The proposals in the State of the Union address are essentially similar to those he put forward in the 'malaise' speech: conservation, price regulation, synthetic fuels, increased incentives for domestic coal and oil production and import restrictions on oil. He added the threat of gas rationing if necessary. But the national security justification for these moves was quickly followed by the claim that they would also curtail inflation, which was said to have been primarily the result of OPEC oil pricing. And Carter concluded his address by reiterating the call to sacrifice and the hope that 'this national commitment will be an exciting enterprise that will unify our people'.

As compared with the boost to military spending and the expansion of US military presence in the Persian Gulf region, not much came of Carter's call for a comprehensive energy policy. Nor his call to sacrifice. His defeat at the polls came at the hands of the ever-cheerful Ronald Reagan, who cut to the chase in his debate with Carter and asked, 'Are you better off now than you were four years ago?'

The US national energy policy

One of the first sustained actions of the George W. Bush presidency was the formulation of a National Energy Policy (NEP), produced by the National Energy Policy Development Group (NEPDG), chaired by Vice-President Dick Cheney, in May 2001.[7] The policy was completed in the last months of rolling blackouts and steeply rising electricity prices in California that started in the summer of 2000, before the Enron scandal began to emerge in August and, of course, before a group consisting mostly of Saudi citizens flew hijacked airliners into the World Trade Center and the Pentagon on 11 September. All of these surrounding events are either reflected in or illuminated by the National Energy Policy.

In the 'Overview' that prefaces the report, after citing the California experience, the NEPDG frames the problem in classic market terms: 'A fundamental imbalance between supply and demand defines our nation's energy crisis' (pviii). Given its opening formulation in the conceptual structure of the grim science, what is immediately interesting in the report's language is the upbeat message the NEPDG conveys in response to the situation thus defined. 'This imbalance, if allowed to continue, will inevitably undermine our economy, our standard of living, and our national security', the report warns. 'But it is not beyond our power to correct. America leads the world in scientific achievement, technical skill, and entrepreneurial drive. Within our country are abundant natural resources, unrivaled technology, and unlimited human creativity' (pviii). What has been added here to Jimmy Carter's litany of resources, technology and American ingenuity, significantly, is entrepreneurship. Where an apparently conflicted Carter problematically thought he saw dissatisfaction with a life centred on material possessions, and a lack of meaning in such a life, at the same time that he wanted to spur economic growth, the NEPDG is not of two minds. The national purpose here is indistinguishable from a standard of living that has come to be seen as a right, and the mechanism for ensuring that purpose is not a liberal model of wartime government planning, but rather turning loose the entrepreneurial dogs of neoliberal economic warfare.

The linguistic manoeuvring in the NEPDG's report is illustrative of the construction and reconstruction of scarcity situations. The so-called crisis is at once 'fundamental' and resolvable. Rather than frame the discussion in terms of limits, the report unexpectedly refers to 'abundant natural resources' and 'unlimited human creativity,' which, together with entrepreneurship and science and technology, can save 'our' standard of living. The report goes on to note that, 'America's energy challenge begins with our expanding economy, growing population, and rising standard of living. Our prosperity and way of life are sustained by energy use' (pix). It comes as no surprise that the report then asserts that the 'challenge' is not merely to sustain the status quo, but to allow for continued economic expansion and rising living standards (pix). And so the crisis articulated by the NEPDG is typical of the dynamic of scarcity engendered in modernity by the dual, and contradictory, market mentalities of generating new needs and the economizing rationality of market behaviour.

Although the report describes a situation of expanding needs, it frames the crisis as an 'imbalance' between those needs and a supply that is supposedly abundant. The clear implication is that the crux of the problem is the application of science, technology and market incentives to bring sufficient energy supplies into accord with expanding demand. The document's abstract articulation of energy scarcity is formulated, in part, with indifference with regard to specific energy sources. The claim of America's abundant energy resources is principally a claim relating to coal, which the NEPDG says is 'America's most abundant fuel source'. (Of lesser importance, in terms of emphasis within the report, are hydropower and nuclear power, which account for a combined 27 per cent of electricity sources [pxiii].) According to the report, 'the United States has a 250-year supply of coal' (chapter 1, p6). Coal accounts for 52 per cent of the resources generating electricity in the United States and 90 per cent of the coal mined in the country is devoted to this use (chapter 1, p6).[8] The California experience that is central to the report's framing of the energy crisis was about disruptions in the flow of electricity and the principal primary source for electricity is coal. The reasons for the crisis thus come down to insufficient utilization of the primary, abundant resource and inefficient distribution. In the schema developed within the report, these problems result from government regulation of coal mining and burning due to environmental concerns, on the one hand, and government regulation of electricity prices, on the other. While the oil crises of the 1970s provided the impetus to Carter's rhetoric of wartime sacrifice, the California electricity crisis becomes the lynchpin for the NEP's main emphasis on the introduction of free market incentives to resolve the crisis at both levels (production and distribution/consumption).

The NEPDG stresses the use of advanced technologies, principally flue scrubbers and high-efficiency turbines, to reduce pollution from coal-burning electrical plants and to increase efficiency.[9] The report emphasizes that, 'besides reducing pollution, environmental technologies account for about $21.3 billion in U.S. exports, and support approximately 136,000 U.S. jobs' (chapter 3, p4). So setting some environmental standards will not violate market principles as long as profits can be made in the environmental technology sector. At the same time, these standards themselves are increasingly negotiated in market terms. The report cites the Environmental Protection Agency's Acid Rain Program, which has deployed 'flexible market-based incentives instead of technology-forcing standards', as an example to be followed and proposes the development of more such legislation. These include 'market-based incentives, such as emissions-trading credits to help achieve the required reductions' in air pollution (chapter 3, p3).

In addition to the Acid Rain Program:

> *other emerging market-based environmental protection mechanisms include effluent trading, wetland mitigation banks, tradable development rights, easement purchases, off-site mitigation, and leasing or purchase of water rights. These programs can reduce mitigation or pollution control costs, increase business flexibility,*

and provide transparency and environmental protection for the public. (chapter 3, p3)

The report thus proposes to solve the problem of episodic insufficiencies of electricity, such as occurred in California, through the wholesale introduction of market mechanisms. But California had recently deregulated its electricity market. Anticipating criticisms to its proposals based on this experience, the report claims that:

> *The California electricity crisis is not a test of the merits of competition in electricity markets. Instead, it demonstrates that a poorly designed state retail competition plan can have disastrous results if electricity supply does not keep pace with increased demand. At heart, the California electricity crisis is a supply crisis.* (chapter 5, p12)

So the problem in California was not market-based deregulation but a deregulation that did not go far enough in its reliance on unrestricted supply and demand markets.

There is some merit to the report's criticism of California's stumble into deregulated electricity markets. But we now know that the blackouts were at least exacerbated, if not produced, by market manipulation on the part of the Enron Corporation. This manipulation took several forms, including using its technical expertise to send electricity purchased at capped prices within California out of the state and then resell it in the state at much higher wholesale prices (so-called ricochet deals, otherwise known as 'megawatt laundering'), creating real or phoney power line delivery congestion and then receiving bonus payments to relieve it, and shutting down at least one power plant in order to create an artificial shortage. Evidence has emerged that shows that Enron had deployed some of the same tactics to create artificial shortages in Ontario, Canada as long ago as 1998 (Coile, 2004; Egan, 2005).

In January 2001, an Enron trader had a Nevada power plant shut down during peak afternoon demand, at least contributing to a rolling blackout experienced at that time. Two months later, in March, Enron CEO Kenneth L. Lay publicly called claims that the company had manipulated the market through any such shutdown 'conspiracy theories' (Coile, 2004; Egan, 2005). At the same time, Lay was meeting with Vice-President Cheney and contributing a memo advising the NEPDG on energy policy. The intimations of a conspiracy are less significant than the fact that the very instruments advocated to resolve what is postulated as a general condition of scarcity with respect to energy resources – technology and market rationality – showed themselves in this instance to be functionally integral to exacerbating and perpetuating a condition of scarcity.

The National Energy Policy thus establishes an aura of generalized scarcity with respect to energy, in the form of a 'crisis' that is demonstrated by reference to California's rolling blackouts. But the primary energy resource for electricity is coal, a resource said to be present in an abundant supply. The problem is thus logically one of increasing supply, and that entails weakening government regulation and replacing environmental regulations with market-based incentives, which is, in a not trivial sense, creating scarcities with respect to environmental concerns. It also entails encouraging the development of new technology through market incentives to enable more efficient extraction and burning of coal. But the entire edifice is based on the tainted experience of California, where market manipulation created the very setting for which the market and technology are promoted as the solution.

Oil, US interests and the American way of life

Using the California electricity crisis as the hook for its proposals also obscures the most fundamental energy problem, which is oil. Oil had nothing to do with the California energy crisis (oil accounts for only 3 per cent of electricity generation), but it has a great deal to do with the visible living standards of Americans. The report only begins to address this issue when it notes, practically in passing, that almost all the increasing energy demand over the previous decade had been met with increased imports, and that these imports were primarily oil imports to offset declining US oil production (chapter 1, p1). Oil represents 40 per cent of US energy needs: two-thirds of that is for transportation and 25 per cent for industry, with most of the rest going to heating oil, principally in the Northeast and Midwest (chapter 1, p10). The report emphasizes recent oil price volatility, which it attributes to 'intermittent market power exerted by cartel behavior in a global petroleum market. Moreover, prices are set in a market where supply is geographically concentrated. Almost two-thirds of world proven reserves are in the Middle East' (chapter 1, p12). The report sees a threat to US security in a continued pattern of this sort, due to dependence on foreign oil. So 22 years after Jimmy Carter's call to liberate the United States from dependence upon foreign oil supplies, framed in terms of national security, we are back on the same ground. Only this time, technology, changes in regulatory policy and markets are the proposed solutions.

The technological fix proposed with regard to oil (and, to a lesser extent, natural gas) is domestically directed. The report cites advances in exploratory and drilling techniques that it claims lessen environmental impact, making some regulatory restrictions obsolete, and enabling the production of oil from 'geologically challenged areas while protecting the environment' (chapter 5, p5). Indeed, the recommendations that provoked the greatest concern among environmentalists and others involve expanding oil exploration and development on the Alaskan North Slope and, most particularly, in opening the Coastal Plain area of the Arctic National Wildlife Refuge (chapter 5, pp9–10).

The misgivings over the environmental safety promised by technological advances overshadowed the report's emphasis upon the national security issues involved, despite its explicit linkage between economy, standard of living and national security at its very outset. 'Energy policies that have emphasized reliance on market forces', according to the NEPDG, 'have led to major energy security gains over the past two decades ... Market solutions to limit the growth in our oil imports would reduce oil consumption for our economy and increase our economic flexibility in responding to any domestic or international disruption of oil or other energy supplies' (chapter 8, p1). However, being the consumer of over 25 per cent of worldwide oil production, American national interests clearly transcend its own borders. And since most of that oil will come from the Persian Gulf countries, 'this region will remain vital to U.S. interests' (chapter 8, p4). And those interests mean promoting foreign investment in the area through liberalized, 'transparent' markets. Furthermore:

> *Sanctions can advance important national and global security objectives and can be an important foreign policy tool, especially against nations that support terrorism or seek to acquire weapons of mass destruction. Nevertheless, sanctions should be periodically reviewed to ensure their continued effectiveness and to minimize their costs on US citizens and interests.*

Thus the NEPDG 'recommends that the President direct the Secretaries of State, Treasury, and Commerce to initiate a comprehensive review of sanctions. Energy security should be one of the factors considered in such a review' (chapter 8, p6). The comment may be directed at then existing sanctions against Iraq (such as the Food for Fuel programme initiated by the UN) and/or Iran. Saudi Arabia, with the largest known oil reserves, Yemen, the United Arab Emirates, Oman, Qatar and Kuwait are explicitly mentioned in the report as countries that have opened to international investment, but Iraq, the sixth largest supplier of US oil imports (after Canada, Saudi Arabia, Venezuela, Mexico, and Nigeria), goes unmentioned in the report, appearing only in one bar graph representing the countries of origin of imports (chapter 8, p4).

The suspicion of sanctions and advocacy of direct private investment abroad to advance American interests were characteristic of Vice-President Cheney's long-established positions (Mayer, 2004). And the emphasis upon the strategic importance of the Gulf was not new to US policy, of course, as the Carter Doctrine made clear. What distinguishes the NEP is its place within a more general military and economic strategy aimed at long-term access to foreign oil deposits. The strategy was foretold in a top-secret document from a high-level National Security Council (NSC) official in February 2001, seven months before the World Trade Center attacks. According to *New Yorker* writer Jane Mayer, the document, 'directed the N.S.C. staff to cooperate fully with the Energy Task Force as it considered the "melding" of two seemingly unrelated areas of policy: "the review of operational policies toward rogue states", such as Iraq and "actions regarding the capture of new and existing oil and gas fields"' (Mayer, 2004). The NSC memo is thus the link between the NEP and the National Security Strategy document, produced in September 2002.[10] The latter declared that one policy aim would be to 'strengthen our own energy security and the shared prosperity of the global economy by working with our allies, trading partners, and energy producers to expand the sources and types of global energy supplied, especially in the Western Hemisphere, Africa, Central

Asia, and the Caspian region'.[11] Once again, Iraq went unmentioned, though the document's endorsement of pre-emptive military action against 'rogue states' that posed a security threat to the United States was surely intended as a reference Iraq and Iran, the two-thirds of the notorious 'Axis of Evil' with direct importance to energy supplies.

The set of geopolitical and economic interests at play can be clearly enumerated. The projected demand for increased US oil consumption between 2001 and 2025 outstrips current domestic and foreign production. Furthermore, global energy demand over the same period would increase dramatically, particularly due to Chinese (and, to a lesser extent, Indian) economic growth. US policy must therefore be attuned not only to securing current levels of supply, but also toward increasing production. Furthermore, oil and natural gas prices must be kept within reasonable limits globally in order to guard against inflation, so an uninterrupted flow of oil must be secured. To even begin to meet the demands articulated within the NEP, foreign investment would be needed to upgrade production facilities in existing fields as well as for exploration and exploitation of new reserves. That is why the NEP targeted the Caspian Sea and African (principally Nigerian and Angolan) reserves, but the Middle East, containing two-thirds of the world's known reserves, was clearly central. And there, the potential threat posed by Saddam Hussein's Iraq to the main US ally in the region, Saudi Arabia, together with the danger of an anti-American Iranian regime that could disrupt passage of oil through the Straits of Harmuz loomed large. Added to these potential problems was the decline in Iraq's production capacity resulting from the effect of economic sanctions on investment in that country's oil infrastructure. In this multifaceted context, Michael Klare succinctly described the Bush administration's policies toward the Persian Gulf:

> As the administration saw it, a greater level of security in the Gulf required progress on three fronts: first, the stabilization of Saudi Arabia under the House of Saud; second, the removal of Saddam Hussein in Iraq and his replacement with a stable government capable of substantially boosting oil output; and, third, an escalation of pressure on the Iranian government leading, eventually, to the emergence of a leadership friendly to the United States. Together, these three goals – joined, after 9/11, by the war on terrorism – constituted the core elements of the Bush administration's Persian Gulf security policy. (Klare, 2004, p84)

While all of these policies have been pursued, none has resulted in complete success, at least thus far.

The implicit suggestion of the NEP that oil resources should take priority over concerns for weapons of mass destruction (WMDs) or terrorism was not negated but rather realized after 11 September. The invasion and occupation of Iraq, under the false pretenses of the war against terrorism and the threat of WMDs, was an action of imperial power within a larger plan to obtain unrestricted access to oil, the lifeblood of the American way of life. The involvement of Saudi citizens in the 11 September attacks and Saudi financial support for Islamic groups hostile to the United States were lost in the smoke as Washington turned its attention towards Afghanistan as a prelude to attacking Iraq, which had no ties to the attacks of 11 September but which was thought to have extensive untapped oil reserves.[12] It is hard to avoid the conclusion that there is a direct correlation between President Bush's call for Americans to shop in the wake of 11 September and the occupation of Iraq. After all, the president repeatedly said that the attacks on that day were attacks on the American way of life.

Jimmy Carter's concern for democracy was inner-directed. His presumption was that, in order to control its collective well-being, the country had to get control of its desire. His model for that, as for many of his World War II generation, was the collective sacrifice of desire in times of war. But that model had been outdated for some time, at least since the United States emerged from the 'good war' with a de facto imperial presence and the economic power that went with it. The fruits of that dominance were already on display when the Soviet leader Nikita Khrushchev visited the 'typical' American house built for an exhibition in Moscow in 1959 and engaged Vice President Nixon in the so-called kitchen debate. Nixon boasted of the new technologies in the house's kitchen and that the house was affordable for American workers and ex-servicemen. Khrushchev retorted that American houses were only built to last 20 years so builders could sell more of them, while Soviet houses were built to last. According to an account of the exchange, Nixon responded that the houses would last, but that 'after twenty years many Americans want a new home or a new kitchen, which would be obsolete then. The American system is designed to take advantage of new inventions and new techniques.'[13] Unimpressed, Khrushchev asked, 'Don't you have a machine that puts food into the mouth and pushes it down? Many things you've shown us are interesting but they are not needed in life. They have no useful purpose. They are merely gadgets'. Nixon pointed out Americans' freedom to choose which gadget they preferred.

It was Khrushchev and the Soviet system, of course, that wound up buried, if not by history then under all those gadgets. The American way of life President Bush saw under attack on 11 September takes its gadgets seriously. But the American way of life is the modern way of life distilled to its essence. The democracy of collective action Carter tried to evoke had long been replaced by the democracy of free choice on the model of the economic market. Bush's energy policy was all about exporting that model. Unlike Carter, he made no fruitless attempt to question it. The Carter Doctrine opened the door to the use of military power to secure US national interests in the Persian Gulf region; the Bush programme added economic power. 'Regime change' was meant to make Iraqis sufficiently American.

The failure of that programme does not obscure the fact that the energy crisis is endemic to modernity. Barack Obama's promise of hope and change does not alter that reality. The desire to promote so-called clean energy is perhaps genuine, but the method of doing so is every bit as committed to the market mechanism as was those of Obama's predecessors. No US president can avoid the promise of prosperity through economic growth and Obama is no different. While the new president has called for increased savings and investment to counteract the global financial crisis, the hope still remains that an increase in consumer spending will lead the way out of recession, and if US consumers are not presently up to the task, perhaps the Chinese can be persuaded to save less and consume more. Meanwhile, every time an iPod or a cell phone or any of the myriad of other little gadgets that have become necessities gets recharged, electricity is being used and that energy has to come from somewhere. David Hume saw imports from a burgeoning world market as spurs to domestic innovation, but those 18th-century imports were moving by quadruped and sail. Today's global market, supplying us with everything we did not realize we needed, moves by different means. And it moves at a feverish pace.

Notes

1   I follow Rosamond Kent Sprague's translation in Cooper, 1977, p743.
2   I follow G.M.A. Grube's translation, as revised by C.D.C. Reeve, in Cooper, 1977, p1011–1012 (emphasis in original).
3   The text of the speech is available at www.pbs.org/wgbh/amex/carter/filmmore/ps_crisis.html., last accessed 12 September 2010.
4   The text of this speech is available at www.jimmycarterlibrary.gov/documents/speeches/su80jec.phtml, last accessed 12 September 2010.
5   The irony gets harder to avoid when Carter says, in reference to the Soviet invasion, that, 'The Moslem world is especially and justifiably outraged by this aggression against an Islamic people'.
6   On the history of US policy vis-à-vis the Gulf, see Klare, 2004, Chapter 1.
7   The document is available at www.pppl.gov/common_pages/national_energy_policy.html, last accessed 12 September 2010.
8   It is perhaps worthy of note that, over the past 30 years, production of US coal has shifted significantly from underground mining in the Appalachian region to surface mining in the west, particularly in Vice President Cheney's home state of Wyoming. See the Energy Information Administration review of coal production, www.eia.doe.gov/cneaf/coal/page/coal_production_review.pdf, last accessed 12 September 2010. Table 2. US railroads have also been heavily promoting coal use, since they are its principal transporters (Associated Press, 2007).
9   The technologies that are available for 'washing' coal can only minimize sulphur dioxide, nitrogen oxide and particulate matter when burning coal. However, burning coal releases large quantities of carbon dioxide and is a major contributor to global warming. The technology to capture and store CO_2 emissions on a large scale does not as yet exist. See http://news.bbc.co.uk/1/hi/sci/tech/4468076.stm, last accessed 12 September 2010.
10 The document is available at http://georgewbush-whitehouse.archives.gov/nsc/nss/2002/, last accessed 12 September 2010.
11 http://georgewbush-whitehouse.archives.gov/nsc/nss/2002/, section VI, entitled, 'Ignite a New Era of Global Economic Growth through Free Markets and Free Trade'.

12 It was Paul Wolfowitz who, at a meeting of President Bush's security team on 15 September 2001, suggested that Iraq should be the first target, claiming that there was 'a 10 to 50 percent chance' that Saddam had something to do with 11 September (Woodward, 2002, pp83–84). It is doubtful that Wolfowitz was thinking solely about oil, but I speculate that he and Vice-President Cheney, who was also present, may well have had US long-term energy needs in mind.

13 See the account at www.turnerlearning.com/cnn/coldwar/sputnik/sput_re4.html, last accessed 12 September 2010.

References

Associated Press (2007) 'Railroads bet on coal despite pollution', available at www.abcmoney.co.uk/news/09200799969.htm (last accessed 12 September 2010)

Austin, M.M. and Vidal-Naquet, P. (1977) *Economic and Social History of Greece: An Introduction*, University of California Press, Berkeley and Los Angeles, CA

Coile, Z. (2004) 'New evidence of Enron schemes: Documents, tapes in Washington State case prompt lawmakers to demand regulators reopen probe into fallen energy company', *San Francisco Chronicle*, 15 June

Cooper, J.M. (ed) (1977) *Plato: Complete Works*, Hackett, Indianapolis and Cambridge

Egan, T. (2005) 'Tapes show Enron arranged plant shutdown', *The New York Times*, 4 February

Hume, D. (1978 [1739, 1740]) in L.A. Selby-Bigge (ed) *A Treatise of Human Nature*, (2nd edition), Clarendon Press, Oxford

Klare, M.T. (2004) *Blood and Oil*, Owl Books, Henry Holt, New York

Mayer, J. (2004) 'Contract Sport', *The New Yorker*, 16–23 February

Rawls, J. (1971) *A Theory of Justice*, Harvard University Press, Cambridge, MA

Woodward, Bob (2002) *Bush at War*, Simon & Schuster, New York

Xenos, N. (1989) *Scarcity and Modernity*, Routledge, New York and London

3

The Ghosts of Malthus: Narratives and Mobilizations of Scarcity in the US Political Context

Betsy Hartmann

Malthusianism has never really worked as a science. Nor does it amount to much as history. But it has always succeeded brilliantly as a prismatic compound of practices in which mathematics, economics, and Christian theology cannot be separated from metaphor, middle-class scare story, sacrifice ritual, and tragedy. It is partly through this inner breadth that Malthusianism has been able to organize so many productive scientific and bureaucratic enterprises and enter common sense through so many doors. Malthus's triumph, and the triumph of his successors, is that of conjoined poet, priest and rationalist. (Lohmann, 2005, p96)

At the turn of the 18th century British clergyman Thomas Malthus warned that human population growth, if left unchecked, would outstrip food production since population grew geometrically and agriculture only arithmetically. One of the architects of the 'dismal science' of modern economics, Malthus proposed that the main checks on population growth were those that increased death rates: hard labour, severe poverty, disease, war and famine, though later he acknowledged that 'preventative checks' such as late marriage could play a role in reducing births.[1] Through his principle of population, Malthus not only made scarcity a law of nature, but naturalized the social, economic and political inequalities of his time. The principle of population, he argued, proves that the cause of poverty 'has little or no *direct* relation to forms of government, or the unequal division of property; and that as the rich do not in reality possess the *power* of finding employment and maintenance for the poor, the poor cannot, in the nature of things possess the *right* to demand them' (cited in Hartmann, 1995, p35).

Two centuries have passed since Malthus wrote his essay on population. In that time food production has outpaced population growth (see Chapter 10, this volume, for a detailed analysis) and most countries have passed through a demographic transition to a smaller family size because of reductions in infant and child mortality that mean parents do not need to have many children to ensure that a few will survive, increasing education, urbanization, livelihood diversification and women's work outside the home. While world population is still growing and is expected to reach 9 billion by the year 2050, most demographers agree it will then stabilize and decline to somewhere around 8 billion in 2175. In fact, concern is now shifting from the negative consequences of rapid growth to the challenges of declining growth such as ageing populations and labour shortages.

Even though Malthus has been proved wrong, his ideas continue to flourish (see Chapters 8 and 10, this volume; they discuss the legacy of Malthus in the agriculture and food domains). Many modern neo-Malthusians, for example, believe that overpopulation not only causes hunger and poverty, but also environmental degradation and political conflict. Unlike Malthus, however, most neo-Malthusians put faith in family planning programmes as a way to drive birth rates down.

Why does Malthusianism have such remarkable staying power? Lohmann points to the intimate relationship between 'daylight' arithmetical Malthusianism so fundamental to modern notions of scarcity, and darker 'Us versus Them' terror narratives in which the overbreeding, dark-skinned poor threaten our survival. The two reinforce each other: the narratives papering over logical gaps in the theoretical argument while Malthusian arithmetic provides the necessary sense of tragic destiny to raise terror narratives to the level of Biblical parable. Malthus was a reverend after all (Lohmann, 2005).

There are also peculiarities about the US cultural and political context that help to explain the widespread acceptance of Malthusian ideas in popular, scholarly and policy venues. In this chapter I focus on the US for several reasons. First, since the end of World War II, US private and public agencies have played a major role in promoting population control in the global south as a cornerstone of international development and security policy (Hartmann, 1995). Secondly, neo-Malthusianism is such a powerful belief system in the US that most Americans assume the population bomb is still exploding out of control and are extremely fearful of looming scarcity. Mounting an effective challenge to neo-Malthusianism requires not only understanding its institutional structures but also the insidious ways it frames people's world views. In the chapter I look in turn at narratives and mobilizations of scarcity, focusing in particular on those to do with environment and security. I conclude with a few thoughts on how to challenge them.

This analysis draws on almost 30 years of experience working to transform population control ideologies and policies as both a scholar in development studies and an activist in the international women's health movement. It has been an interesting, if often frustrating, journey during which I have learned how hard it is to dislodge a dominant world view. Sometimes it feels as if one is beating one's head against a brick wall. Ultimately, the solution may be to jump over that wall – to find new ways of thinking, as this volume seeks to do, that are capable not only of better understanding the world but of capturing the popular imagination.

Narratives of scarcity

Malthusian narratives of scarcity are like church bells: sometimes they are rung one by one, sometimes they are rung all together and sometimes the bell-ringer makes a medley of old melodies and new. In the US the bell that has rung most consistently is that of environmental alarm. According to Wilmoth and Ball (1992), framing the population issue in environmental terms was probably the single most important factor in building a public consensus for population control in the US from the 1960s on. Most persuasive initially were narratives of ecological limits, legitimized and popularized by the computer models of the Club of Rome's 1972 study *Limits to Growth* (Dryzek, 1997). This was mainly a numbers game pitting projected aggregates of human numbers against aggregates of natural resources, but limits discourse also drew on the tropes and metaphors of conservation biology, particularly those of carrying capacity, in order to generate accompanying metaphors of people as exponentially growing pondweed, cancer cells, overgrazing cattle or bacteria in a petri dish.

There is a certain irony in the fact that the country with the most profligate waste and consumption levels became the most obsessed with planetary resource limits (and the least willing to do anything about them). Andrew Ross (1996) argues that in the US, fears about looming scarcities of natural resources paralleled the manufacturing of social scarcities by competitive capitalist regimes. In the public consciousness, imposed limits to growth in social welfare expenditures became intertwined with the notion of environmental limits (and not, unfortunately, with the pro-rich economic policies of the government and corporate elites).

In a somewhat different vein, Sandilands (1999) suggests that limits discourse resonates so well in the US because of Puritanical attitudes about the need to limit physical pleasure and sex. Sex is conspicuous by its absence in most Malthusian scarcity narratives, and when it is mentioned, the inference often is that women's sexuality is out of control and must be restrained.[2] There are interesting parallels here between blaming economic scarcity on the oversexed, overbreeding black 'welfare queen' or Latina immigrant, and blaming environmental scarcity on the hyperfertile developing world peasant woman.

Widespread cultural acceptance of the People versus Nature antagonism also helps explain the success of limits discourse. Because Americans live in such a rapacious resource-guzzling capitalist society, many assume that people are de facto bad for the environment. There is little understanding of the ways in which human agency can shape the environment in positive ways – in the US or anywhere.

The People versus Nature antagonism is reinforced by several factors. First is widespread parochialism and ignorance of the rest of the world.

Development education is almost unheard of in US public schools (or in the media); mainstream social studies texts, to the extent that they cover developing world issues, often utilize Malthusian stereotypes of the poor destroying forests and depleting soils (Hendrixson, 2001). Biology texts tend to be even worse in their alarmist portrayals of humans, especially dark-skinned ones, overshooting carrying capacity. In my children's high school, in a progressive school district, the standard biology text depicted overpopulation with a photo of overgrazing cattle next to one of a starving African child. 'Either we will voluntarily reduce our birth rate or various forces of environmental resistance will increase our death rate', the authors pronounce ominously. They also suggest that lenient immigration policies are preventing necessary population stabilization in the US (Audesirk and Audesirk, 1996, p865). Private population organizations, meanwhile, have developed problematic curricular materials for elementary school upwards that teach students to fear population-induced crowding and competition over scarce resources.[3]

In general, it is conservation biology, rather than social science, that frames population issues in the popular imagination. This can be attributed in part to the legacy of eugenics. Many early American conservationists were eugenicists who believed in maintaining the purity of both nature and the gene pool as well as in the manifest destiny of the white Anglo-Saxon race to steward (and colonize) the environment against the encroachment of immigrants (Stern, 2005). Eugenicists were also powerful players in both the pre- and post-World War II population control movement (Hodgson, 1991; Ramsden, 2001). Among them was conservation biologist Garrett Hardin, whose *Tragedy of the Commons* is still considered a classic text (Hardin, 1968; Chase, 1977).[4] Arguably, the influence of natural science and positivism on American social sciences may also play a role. In the case of demography, for example, Szreter writes that the dominant 'covering laws' school of thought 'recognizes no distinction in principle between the scientific study of social and natural phenomena' (Szreter, 1993, p690; also see Hartmann, 2003).

Another key factor is the wilderness ethic. William Cronon has described the unique place the idea of wilderness holds in the American psyche, both as a romantic, sublime, quasi-religious force and as a vehicle for frontier nostalgia. 'For many Americans', he writes, 'wilderness stands as the last remaining place where civilization, that all too human disease, has not fully infected the earth' (Cronon, 1995, p70). The wilderness ethic is problematic in many ways – for a start, it obscures the systematic forced migration and genocide of the Native Americans who once inhabited the 'wilderness'. It is hostile to sedentary agriculture and glorifies hunter-gatherers. Within the environmental movement, the privileging of wilderness has narrowed the scope of what is considered environmental activism, and reinforced white, wealthy male dominance of the movement (see Seager, 1993). At its most extreme, the wilderness ethic leads to a controversial Malthusian variant of deep ecology that is so hostile to people that some of its proponents have called for rapid reductions in human population, by as much as 90 per cent, and welcomed AIDS as a 'natural' check on population growth (Seager, 1993, pp232–235).

Another prominent set of Malthusian narratives – what I call 'degradation narratives' – draws on the People versus Nature antagonism, as well as old colonial stereotypes of destructive developing world peasants and herders. Contemporary degradation narratives go something like this: population pressure-induced poverty makes developing world peasants degrade their environments by over-farming or over-grazing marginal lands. The ensuing soil depletion and desertification then lead them to migrate elsewhere as 'environmental refugees', either to other ecologically vulnerable rural areas where the vicious cycle is once again set in motion or to cities where they strain scarce resources and become a primary source of political instability (Hartmann, 2003). The degradation narrative has proved particularly popular in western policy circles because it kills a number of birds with one stone: it blames poverty on population pressure, and not, for example, on lack of land reform or off-farm employment opportunities; it blames peasants for land degradation, obscuring the role of commercial agriculture and extractive industries; and it targets migration both as an environmental and security threat. It is a way of homogenizing all rural people in the global south into one big destructive force, reinforcing simplistic Us versus Them, West versus the Rest dichotomies.

During the latter decades of the Cold War, both the limits discourse and the degradation narrative increasingly intertwined with national security fears. In peace studies circles, fears of the nuclear apocalypse meshed well with a sense of impending environmental doom caused by overpopulation. For example, in 1988 Arthur Westing wrote that 'the huge mismatch between human population numbers and availability of natural resources' helped provide 'the support and impetus for the acceptability of war'. He called for drastic population control measures such as giving each adult a 'child-right chit' entitling the holder to have only one child; in overpopulated countries there would be only one chit for every two adults (Westing, 1988, p153). In a strange parallel with tradeable pollution permits, these chits would be transferable and negotiable commodities within nations.

At the same time the degradation narrative was taking root in sustainable development circles and influencing alternative visions of security (see Chapter 5, this volume, for a discussion on sustainable development and economics). The influential 1987 Brundtland report, for example, took a conventional neo-Malthusian view of population pressure causing poverty and resource depletion, asserting that:

> *Those who are poor and hungry will often destroy their immediate environment in order to survive. They will cut down forests; their livestock will overgraze grasslands; they will overuse marginal land; and in growing numbers they will crowd into congested cities.*
> (World Commission on Environment and Development, 1987, p28)

The report went on to identify these environmental stresses as important sources of conflict and advocates the use of sophisticated surveillance technologies to monitor indicators of environmental risk and conflict, such as 'soil erosion, growth in regional migration, and uses of commons that are approaching the thresholds of sustainability' (World Commission on Environment and Development, 1987, p302).

With the end of the Cold War, the field of environmental security came to occupy pride of place in the rethinking of security occurring in both the US academy and policy circles. While limits discourse resurfaced in mounting concerns about the possibility of resource wars over scarce water and oil (Klare, 2001), the degradation narrative underpinned influential neo-Malthusian models of environmental conflict, particularly those of Canadian political scientist Thomas Homer-Dixon. He maintained that scarcities of renewable resources such as cropland, fresh water and forests, induced in large part by population growth, contribute to migration and violent intrastate conflict in many parts of the developing world. In his own words:

> *Population growth and unequal access to good land force huge numbers of people onto marginal lands. There, they cause environmental damage and become chronically poor. Eventually, they may be the source of persistent upheaval, or they may migrate yet again, helping to stimulate ethnic conflicts or urban unrest elsewhere.* (Homer-Dixon, 1999, p155)

This conflict, in turn, can potentially disrupt international security as states fragment or become more authoritarian.

Homer-Dixon's work had a major influence on the Clinton administration (see Part II). Despite a number of critiques, it helped spawn a second generation of scarcity–security narratives.[5] Relocated to urban areas, for example, Homer-Dixon's destructive peasants become a 'youth bulge' of young men who are easily 'mobilized for violent political action, like terrorism' (Homer-Dixon, 2002). 'Youth bulge' theories and images figure prominently in the US 'war on terror'. They naturalize political conflict in the Middle East by attributing it to the population pressure of too many young Muslim men on scarce environmental and economic resources. Youth bulge theories also reinforce socio-biological views of young men as inherently more prone to aggression and violence (Hendrixson, 2004; Hartmann and Hendrixson, 2005).

Another iteration of youth bulge theory to attract the attention of the American press as well as of the CIA is a book published in 2004 by Valerie Hudson and Andrea den Boer called *Bare Branches: Security Implications of Asia's Surplus Male Population*. Using Homer-Dixon's methodological framework and accepting his assumptions about resource scarcity, the authors argue that surpluses of young males in countries like India and China, where sex selection in favour of male offspring is a widespread practice, and corresponding scarcities of young females are likely to cause increased crime, violence and militarization. According to Hudson, 'In 2020 it may seem to China that it would be worth it to have a very bloody battle in which a lot of their young men could die in some glorious cause' (cited in Glenn, 2004).

Although unbalanced sex ratios are certainly a serious social problem, portraying them as a menacing security threat is problematic, especially as scaremongering American journalists are currently trying to whip up renewed fear of the yellow peril.[6] The scarcity trope of 'bare branches' (unmarried males) is used throughout the book. It dehumanizes young men, reducing their behaviour to a function of too much testosterone, and reinforces gender stereotypes of young women as natural wives and reproducers, even as the authors present themselves as promoters of women's rights. A critical subtext of the book is fear of popular resistance to social and economic injustices. Migrants, who are pathologized throughout the book as 'transients', are made out to be particularly frightening. In addition to their high testosterone levels and low-life habits, 'transients' in China, for example, have had the audacity to engage in strikes and other protests over labour grievances. This kind of bare-branch 'disruptive behaviour' threatens the established social order.

Ironically, but not surprisingly, scarcity narratives also permeate discussions about declining birth rates in the west. The 'birth dearth' is a case in point (Wattenberg, 1989). The scarcity of white births is often juxtaposed against a surplus of immigrants and the supposed hyper-fertility of immigrant women.[7] In a cover story in *Foreign Policy* in 2004, Harvard political scientist Samuel Huntington, in a racist attack on Mexicans thinly cloaked in culture-speak, warned that high numbers of Hispanic immigrants (and their high birth rates) threaten America's Anglo-Protestant identity, values and way of life (Huntington, 2004).

In recent years anti-immigrant groups have strategically deployed scarcity narratives, blaming the population pressure of immigrants for depleting and degrading the American environment. Masquerading as environmentalists (with names like Carrying Capacity Network and Population-Environment Balance), they have tried to penetrate and take over liberal environmental groups, particularly the country's largest member-based environmental organization, the Sierra Club. Fortunately, researchers that monitor the Right are now exposing the links between these so-called environmentalists and white supremacist organizations such as the Council for Conservative Citizens. For example, anti-immigrant activist Virginia Abernethy, once a popular and 'respectable' spokeswoman on the population-environment circuit, is a member of the Council and has publicly stated that races should not mix (Southern Poverty Law Center, 2002).

Blaming immigrants for climate change is the latest iteration of this greening of hate. In August 2008, the nativist think-tank Center for Immigration Studies released a report placing the onus for rising US carbon emissions on immigrants and suggesting they remain in their home countries where they consume less energy. The message is that reducing immigration is a far more effective way of addressing global warming than investing in conservation and renewable energies (Kolankiewicz and Camarota, 2008)!

Fears of scarcity and immigration also feature in contemporary national security scenarios about global warming. In 2003, a Pentagon-commissioned report on the impact of abrupt climate change on US national security warned:

As abrupt climate change lowers the world's carrying capacity, aggressive wars are likely to be fought over food, water, and energy. Deaths from war as well as starvation and disease will decrease population size, which over time, will re-balance with carrying capacity. (Schwartz and Randall, 2003, p15)

It went on to warn of the threat of 'unwanted starving immigrants' pressing at our borders (p18).

Increasingly, Malthusian narratives about demographic pressures, resource scarcity and climate change coming together as the root cause of conflict in Darfur and elsewhere in the global south are making their way into mainstream US media and foreign policy circles. These are accompanied by apocalyptic projections of hundred of millions of 'climate refugees' roaming the globe and wreaking havoc (Hartmann, 2010). For example, a recent article in a respectable US environmental magazine paints a lurid picture of millions of destitute Bangladeshi environmental refugees as potential Muslim terrorists (Black, 2008).

That such scarcity scenarios exist is perhaps not surprising, but what is worrying is the credibility they enjoy – even in many liberal and progressive circles in the US. This is partly due to the confusion of neo-Malthusianism with women's rights and environmentalism. In the US, as well as in many other countries, neo-Malthusianism has long been associated with women's right to birth control.[8] In the public eye, population control is a win-win proposition: reducing birth rates not only cures, or buys time for curing, a whole slew of social, economic and environmental ills, it also helps emancipate women. The problem with this picture is that population control programmes designed to drive down birth rates as fast and efficiently as possible have often led to health and human rights abuses; they are very different indeed from birth control programmes whose goal is to meet women's needs for safe and voluntary contraception (Hartmann, 1995; Connelly, 2008).

In the 1980s and 1990s women's health activists brought these contradictions to the fore and achieved some reform of population policy. At the 1994 UN International Conference on Population and Development (ICPD) in Cairo, concerned about fundamentalist threats to family planning, they joined forces with population agencies to forge the strategic 'Cairo consensus' (Hodgson and Watkins, 1997). This consensus maintains that rapid population growth is still a major cause of poverty and environmental degradation, but that women's empowerment and reproductive health programmes are the solution to high birth rates, rather than the coercive population control programmes of the past. Though yet to be implemented effectively because of lack of funds and political will, the Cairo consensus has provided renewed legitimacy to neo-Malthusianism in liberal and progressive circles. Now there seems to be no downside to population control: you can be a Malthusian alarmist and a feminist at the same time.

However, one cannot view this phenomenon in isolation from the recent right-wing assault on reproductive rights. The political power of the anti-abortion movement in the US and former President Bush's retrograde domestic and international anti-family planning policies made the Cairo consensus look positive by comparison. This led to a kind of political self-silencing: for fear of playing into the hands of the Right, many reproductive rights advocates were wary of speaking out against population control programmes, even if they were based on faulty Malthusian logic and violate women's rights.[9] Furthermore, Bush's anti-environmental agenda made even neo-Malthusian environmentalism seem progressive by comparison.

This either/or political climate also impacts the ways in which fears of scarcity are strategically mobilized in the policy arena, which is the subject of Part II.

Mobilizations of scarcity

In early 2000, a colleague and I were invited to the offices of a prominent Washington population lobby group to speak to their staff about our concerns with their apocalyptic media messaging around the 'Day of Six Billion', the day in 1999 when world population ostensibly passed the 6 billion mark. Much to our surprise, after we presented our critique of Malthusian scare stories, the people in the room told us that they did not believe them either. The person in charge of their direct mail campaigns revealed that the main reason they use them is because fear sells, and it's OK to use fear since the money they get from the mailings is channelled into defending international family planning. In other words, liberal ends justify illiberal means.[10]

This incident illustrates how scarcity narratives are strategically deployed, in this case for raising funds from the public. In other cases, private foundations have used their funds to mobilize such narratives as a tool of policy change. A good example is the role played by the Pew Charitable Trusts in promoting fears of environmental scarcity and conflict as a way to build a constituency for the Cairo consensus.

In the early 1990s, the Pew Charitable Trusts, whose wealth derives from the Sun Oil Company, became the largest environmental donor in the US, as well as one of the most proactive (Dowie, 2001; Tokar, 1997). Expanding its mandate, Pew began to look more closely at foreign policy issues related to the environment and in 1993 created the Pew Global Stewardship Initiative (PGSI) to address population and consumption issues in preparation for the ICPD.

A central element of PGSI's plan was 'to assist foreign policy specialists in framing the related concerns of population, environment and sustainable development, and in identifying areas where demographic trends threaten regional or international stability' (PGSI, 1993a, p13). To develop the conceptual basis for this endeavour, PGSI would offer support for applied research on the linkages between population, environment and security. At the same time it also aimed to influence the media and popular opinion. For example, the opinion researchers it hired recommended adding 'an emotional component' and 'targeted visual devices' such as pictures of traffic jams and degraded landscapes to population messages in order to create the necessary alarm (PGSI, 1993b; pp73–74).

PGSI also hired Future Strategies, Inc., a consulting firm, to make recommendations on how to build a population and sustainable development campaign in Washington policy circles. Although it is unclear whether PGSI followed all the consultants' advice, the Future Strategies report provides a fascinating window on the marketing of demographic fears. As part of a 'grand strategy' to increase international family planning assistance, the report notes that Americans will have to be convinced that 'unchecked population growth and destruction of the environment are key national security concerns of the 21st century' (PGSI, 1994a, p31). So will specific constituencies, such as defence and intelligence policy-makers and intellectuals as well as Congressional actors, notably the Black Caucus who should be worried about the social chaos in Africa described by journalist Robert Kaplan in his (in)famous article 'The Coming Anarchy' (Kaplan, 1994).

The report considers a variety of arguments to sway the public and policy-makers, including fears of migration. The authors write: 'Unfortunately, the specter of "environmental refugees" driven by scarcity of resources and flooding American borders may be necessary to build the public support necessary for required increases in funding for population and sustainable development' (PGSI, 1994a, p33). Along with such arguments, it recommends using visual tools such as computerized mapping which overlays information about 'population growth, resource depletion, overt conflict and refugee movements' (p13), as well as adopting some of the campaign tools of the American Israel Political Action Committee (p33). As the former PGSI director, Susan Sechler, told me, 'People will get more aid if they are perceived to be dangerous than if they are pitied' (personal interview, 13 November 2000).

PGSI went on to fund two of Thomas Homer-Dixon's major research projects. The one with the most visibility was the Environment, Population and Security Project (EPS) which produced a number of country case studies and a briefing book designed to persuade policy-makers to take environmental conflict seriously. PGSI gave $300,000 to the project, including, at Homer-Dixon's urging, $30,000 for Robert Kaplan as a project consultant. (Hartmann, 2003).[11] It also constituted a high-level advisory committee on security which met with Homer-Dixon.[12]

PGSI's support and connections propelled Homer-Dixon's environmental conflict model, and his particular rendering of the degradation narrative, into a number of foreign policy arenas. From about 1994–1997, some mention of environmentally induced conflict seems *de rigeur* in official speeches and reports on the environment, whether emanating from the administration, State Department, intelligence community or Defense Department (Hartmann, 2003). In 1994 and 1995, even the administration's National Security Strategy, an important blueprint for foreign and defence policy, stated boldly in the preface that 'Large-scale environmental degradation, exacerbated by rapid population growth, threatens to undermine political stability in many countries and regions' (White House, 1995, p47).

It is not surprising that, under siege from the anti-abortion movement, population interests resorted to scarcity narratives to win support from legislators, policy-makers and the public for international family planning assistance. An example of this trend was the report from Population Action International, *The Security Demographic: Population and Civil Conflict after the Cold War* (Cincotta et al, 2003). Released with great fanfare at the prestigious Woodrow Wilson Center in Washington, DC, the report purported to prove that four demographic stress factors – (1) the youth bulge, (2) rapid urban growth, (3) competition for cropland and freshwater (with echoes of Homer-Dixon) and (4) AIDS-related deaths in the prime of life – contribute to a heightened risk of civil conflict in the developing world.

The report's end goal was to prove that reducing population growth will help reduce violent conflict. And the best way to reduce population growth is through women's empowerment and reproductive health – in other words the Cairo approach. The report thus once again married the Cairo reforms to national security threats. Its release rated a Reuters news story 'Study: Women's Health Linked to Unrest: High Birth Rates, AIDS Set Stage for Global Violence' (Reuters News Service, 2003) and news of it circulated, uncritically, on various progressive websites, including that of Common Dreams (Lobe, 2003).

While Barack Obama's victory is changing the political landscape in Washington, weakening the power of anti-abortion and anti-environmental forces at the federal level, it has also led to a new jockeying for position by the population lobby. Similar to the heyday of environmental security, the lobby's main strategy is to appeal to both environmentalists and national security interests by linking population growth to climate change and violent conflict (Hartmann and Barajas-Román, 2009). How influential their voice will be in the Obama administration is still open to question, but there are worrying signs that they are gaining ground. Hopefully, with the power of the Right somewhat diminished, reproductive rights activists will feel freer to speak out against a potential population control resurgence. It is also heartening that today in the US there is a strong and growing reproductive justice movement, led by women of colour, that combines support for reproductive rights with a critical analysis of population control policy and ideology (Silliman et al, 2004).

There is a saying that 'Guilt is the gift that keeps on giving'. Substitute scarcity for guilt and one gets an idea of why fears of it are so easily and frequently deployed. Scarcity just keeps giving, but it keeps taking too. No matter whether the intentions of its narrators are good or bad or somewhere in between, it can have dangerous effects.

On the ideological level, it obfuscates, totalizes and naturalizes, masking real-world, real-time, real-place political economy and political ecology. It produces and reinforces racial, ethnic and gender stereotypes. It turns entire populations into dangerous enemies.

It also has real policy effects. Dryzek (1997) notes that limits discourses (what he calls 'survivalism') lend themselves to authoritarian and elitist political prescriptions. Some of the key architects of the one-child policy in China, for example, were heavily influenced by the Club of Rome's *Limits to Growth*. As anthropologist Susan Greenhalgh writes:

> ... *practically all the key ideas on which China's one-child policy was based were borrowed from the West, and from Western science at that. The borrowers were a handful of natural scientists who defeated the social scientists in a major struggle for policy influence. The natural scientists' ideas got built into official policy, leaving China with a policy that may have restrained population growth, but did do at great human cost.* (Greenhalgh, 2003, p166)

More recently, the USAID-funded Futures Group in Washington aided and abetted the imposition of a discriminatory two-child norm by some state governments in India.[13] The Futures Group has a long history of persuading government officials in developing countries of the need for population control through the presentation of Malthusian scarcity scenarios (Hartmann, 1995).

Richard Matthew (2005) argues that the American environmental movement's promotion of doomsday neo-Malthusian thinking has had a negative impact on US national security policy. It has helped to persuade both the American public and policy-makers that the world is a dangerous and threatening place and, as a result, Americans 'no longer need much evidence to accept strong claims about grave threats, looming crises, bold preventive actions and firm responses'. Hence, the willingness to support the invasion of Iraq without real proof of the existence of weapons of mass destruction or of al Qaeda terrorist cells operating from the country. 'Unfortunately, the bold actions that follow may, from a security perspective, do more harm than good', Matthew comments, 'while lining the pockets of a few bureaucrats, contractors and consultants'. And the irony is that the interventions themselves may actually make the world more threatening, 'creating the conditions for a new round of alarming assertions' (Matthew, 2005, p243).

The mobilization of scarcity is serious business then, with potentially lethal consequences.

Challenging scarcity

How might we go about challenging these narratives and mobilizations of scarcity?

By way of conclusion, I would suggest that we need a multi-pronged, multi-faceted strategy. We need to disprove and debunk scarcity narratives through the provision of alternative information and evidence in a variety of venues, from academic publications to activist tools. For example, it can be very effective to show people actual scarcity images so they can literally *see* the deployment of racist stereotypes. The feminist group Committee on Women, Population and the Environment has developed a visual presentation of population imagery from the 1930s to the present to make audiences think critically about Malthusian assumptions and stereotypes (Population and Development Program, 2009).

Overturning deep-seated cultural assumptions in the US about People versus Nature and breaking the hold neo-Malthusianism has over liberal thought are more difficult challenges, especially when one does not want to play into the hands of the Right in terms of both its anti-choice and anti-environmental agendas.

Here alliances with other progressive political actors – e.g. reproductive rights advocates, environmental justice organizations, peace movements, immigrant rights groups – are essential. I also believe that one needs to reach people at a younger age. At Hampshire College, for example, we have developed an alternative population curriculum for high school students to counter both mainstream textbooks and the teaching resources put out by population lobbying groups and to introduce development education (Lugton and McKinney, 2004).

In terms of mobilizations of scarcity, scholars concerned with the construction and production of knowledge and the formation of policy can play an important role in researching and bringing to light the actors – private foundations, academics, policy-makers, public relations firms – that strategically employ fears of scarcity in pursuit of political goals. Without being a conspiracy theorist, one needs to expose the intentionality behind many mobilizations of scarcity and hold people accountable for their actions. One needs to name names when necessary.

And we need to join across academic disciplines and activist pursuits to put our heads together and come up with new ideas, new language, new images that reframe the population-environment relationship in rigorous but compelling ways that appeal to the policy-maker as well as the popular imagination. We need to show that the alternative to doomsday scarcity thinking is not triumphal free-market cornucopianism but rather an environmental equity ethic based on the precautionary principle, investments in green technologies and energy sources, social justice, peace and a political ecology that differentiates between people's negative and positive effects on the environment and clearly identifies who precisely is doing what. Without slipping into romanticism, it is important to point out the role many poor people play in protecting and enhancing the environment as a way of challenging negative Malthusian stereotypes (see Boyce and Shelley, 2003).

A crucial part of this task is identifying the key arenas in which to work. In many ways the time is ripe. In the academy, cross-disciplinary dialogue is helping to open up space for more critical views. Even in conservation biology, for example, long-standing Malthusian assumptions are coming under increasing scrutiny by younger scholars versed in both the natural and social sciences (McSweeney, 2005). Mounting concern about global warming also provides an opportunity to discuss environmental issues in new venues in new ways. The so-called 'War on Terror', by draining the national budget, starkly reveals the political creation of scarcity.

Scarcity is an idea whose time has come to go. Hastening that process is an important political project of our times.

Notes

1   See Avery, 1997, for an interesting historical account of Malthus' life and ideas.
2   In *The Population Bomb*, for example, Paul Ehrlich (1968) argued that women use their year-long sexuality in order to entice men into staying in family groups, and the resulting uncontrolled biological 'urges' lead to overbreeding (cited in Jaquette and Staudt, 1985).
3   For example, in a lesson plan for young children, 'Crowding Can Be Seedy', the Washington, DC-based Population Connection instructs teachers to give some students too many seeds to plant in a pot. When these seeds do not sprout and grow, students are asked: 'Think of your own home, and the people you share it with. What would it be like if there were two or three times as many of you living there? What things might there be too much or not enough of? (Possible answers: too much noise, trash, not enough beds, food, hot water, space, privacy, quiet, etc.) How do you think you and the people you live with would like that?' See Population Connection, 'Teaching Population – Hands-on Activities', CD, 2003.
4   Into the 1990s Hardin received funding from the Pioneer Fund, the major financier of eugenics research in North America (Hardin, 1993).
5   For a critique of Homer-Dixon, see chapters by Fairhead and Hartmann and the introduction in Peluso and Watts, 2001.
6   The cover story of the June 2005 *Atlantic Monthly* is 'How we would fight China: The Next Cold War', by Robert Kaplan. 'The Middle East is just a blip', he claims (Kaplan, 2005, p49).
7   See Krause (2005) for a fascinating case study of the politics and representations of sub-replacement-level fertility in Italy.
8   See Barrett (1995) for an interesting discussion of the mixed motives of neo-Malthusianism, especially with regard to concerns for both collective and individual welfare. See also Furedi (1997).
9   For a discussion of the complex politics around family planning, abortion and population control in the US, see Fried (2006).
10 For a more detailed account of liberal ends and illiberal means in the population policy arena, see Hartmann (2006).
11 The second was the Environmental Scarcities, State Capacity and Civil Violence project, with roughly half of the $400,000 financing coming from PGSI and the other half from the Rockefeller Foundation (Hartmann, 2003).
12 Among its members were Eileen Claussen, Senior Director for Global Environmental Affairs on the National Security Council; Kathleen McGinty, Director of the White House Office on Environmental Quality; and Enid Schoettle, National Intelligence Officer for Global and Multilateral Issues and a principal advisor to the CIA Director (PGSI, 1994b).
13 See Bhatia (2005) and SAMA (2005) for an overview of the effects of the two-child norm.

References

Audesirk, T. and Audesirk, G. (1996) *Biology: Life on Earth*, 4th edition, Prentice Hall, Upper Saddle River, NJ

Avery, J. (1997) *Progress, Poverty and Population: Re-reading Condorcet, Godwin and Malthus*, Frank Cass, London

Barrett, D.A. (1995) 'Reproducing persons as a global concern: The making of an institution', PhD thesis, Carolina Population Center, University of North Carolina at Chapel Hill

Bhatia, R. (2005) 'Ten years after Cairo: The resurgence of coercive population control in India', *DifferenTakes* No 31, Population and Development Program, Hampshire College, Amherst, MA

Black, G. (2008) 'The gathering storm: What happens when global warming turns millions of destitute Muslims into environmental refugees?', *Onearth*, Summer, pp22–37

Boyce, J. K. and Shelley, B.G. (eds) (2003) *Natural Assets: Democratizing Environmental Ownership*, Island Press, Washington, DC

Chase, A. (1977) *The Legacy of Malthus: The Social Costs of the New Scientific Racism*, Knopf, New York

Cincotta, R., Engelman, R. and Anastasion, D. (2003) *The Security Demographic: Population, and Civil Conflict After the Cold War*, Population Action International, Washington, DC

Connelly, M. (2008) *Fatal Misconception: The Struggle to Control World Population*, Cambridge, MA, Harvard University Press

Cronon, W. (1995) 'The trouble with wilderness; or, getting back to the wrong nature', in W. Cronon (ed) *Uncommon Ground*, Norton, New York

Dowie, M. (2001) *American Foundations: An Investigative History*, MIT Press Cambridge, MA

Dryzek, J.S. (1997) *The Politics of the Earth: Environmental Discourses*, Oxford University Press, New York

Ehrlich, P. R. (1968) *The Population Bomb*, Ballantine Books, New York

Fairhead, J. (2001) 'International dimensions of conflict over natural and environmental resources', in N.L. Peluso and M. Watts (eds) (2001) *Violent Environments*, Cornell University Press, Ithaca, NY

Fried, M. (2006) 'The politics of abortion: A note', *Indian Journal of Gender Studies*, vol 13, no 2, May–August, pp229–245

Furedi, F. (1997) *Population and Development: A Critical Introduction*, St. Martin's Press, New York

Glenn, D. (2004) 'A dangerous surplus of sons?', *The Chronicle of Higher Education*, April 30, available at http://chronicle.com/free/v50/i34/34a01401.htm (last accessed 2 May 2005)

Greenhalgh, S. (2003) 'Science, modernity, and the making of China's one-child policy', *Population and Development Review*, vol 29, no 2, pp163–196

Hardin. G. (1968) 'The tragedy of the commons', *Science*, vol 162, pp1243–1248

Hardin, G. (1993) *Living within Limits*, Oxford University Press, New York

Hartmann, B. (1995) *Reproductive Rights and Wrongs: The Global Politics of Population Control*, South End Press, Boston, MA

Hartmann, B. (2001) 'Will the circle be unbroken: A critique of the project on environment, population and security', in N.L. Peluso and M. Watts (eds) (2001) *Violent Environments*, Cornell University Press, Ithaca, NY

Hartmann, E. (2003) 'Strategic scarcity: The origins and impact of environmental conflict ideas', PhD Thesis, Development Studies Institute, London School of Economics and Political Science

Hartmann, B. (2006) 'Liberal ends, illiberal means: national security, "environmental conflict" and the making of the Cairo consensus', *Indian Journal of Gender Studies*, vol 13, no 2, May–August, pp195–227

Hartmann, B. (2010) 'Rethinking climate refugees and climate conflict: Rhetoric, reality and the politics of policy discourse', *Journal of International Development*, vol 22, pp233–246

Hartmann, B. and Barajas-Román (2009) 'The population bomb is back with a global warming twist', *Women in Action*, no 2, pp72–80

Hartmann, B. and Hendrixson, A. (2005) 'Pernicious peasants and angry young men: The strategic demography of threats', in B. Hartmann, B. Subramaniam and C. Zerner (eds), *Making Threats: Biofears and Environmental Anxieties*, Rowman and Littlefield, Lanham, MD, pp217–236

Hartmann, B., Subramaniam, B. and Zerner, C. (eds) (2005) *Making Threats: Biofears and Environmental Anxieties*, Rowman and Littlefield, Lanham, MD

Hendrixson, A. (2001) 'The industrious Europeans and the hungry third world masses: The story of population told by US high school textbooks', Working Paper No 2, Population Curriculum Project, Population and Development Program, Hampshire College, Amherst, MA

Hendrixson, A. (2004) 'Angry young men, veiled young women: Constructing a new population threat', The Corner House, Briefing 34, UK

Hodgson, D. (1991) 'The ideological origins of the Population Association of America', *Population and Development Review*, vol 17, no 1, pp1–34

Hodgson, D. and Watkins, S.C. (1997) 'Feminists and neo-Malthusians: Past and present alliances', *Population and Development Review*, vol 23, no 3, pp469–523

Homer-Dixon, T. (1999) *Environment, Scarcity and Violence*, Princeton University Press, Princeton, NJ

Homer-Dixon, T. (2002) 'Standing room only', *Toronto Globe and Mail*, 6 March, 'Why Population Growth Still Matters', available at www.homerdixon.com/pop/g&m_bottom.htm (last accessed 18 August 2003)

Hudson, V.M. and den Boer, A.M. (2004) *Bare Branches: Security Implications of Asia's Surplus Male Population*, MIT Press, Cambridge, MA

Huntington, S. (2004) 'The Hispanic challenge', *Foreign Policy*, March–April, pp30–45

Jaquette, J.S. and Staudt, K.A. (1985) 'Politics, population and gender: A feminist analysis of US population policy in the Third World', in K.B. Jones and A.G. Jonasdottir (eds) *The Political Interests of Gender*, Sage, London

Kaplan, R.D. (1994) 'The coming anarchy', *Atlantic Monthly*, February, pp44–76

Kaplan, R.D. (2005) 'How we would fight China', *Atlantic Monthly*, June, pp49–64

Klare, M.T. (2001) *Resource Wars: The New Landscape of Global Conflict*, Henry Holt, New York

Kolankiewicz, L. and Camarota, S.A. (2008) *Immigration to the United States and Worldwide Greenhouse Gas Emissions*, Center for Immigration Studies, Washington, DC, available at www.cis.org/GreenhouseGasEmissions (last accessed 2 January 2009)

Krause, E.L. (2005) *A Crisis of Births: Population Politics and Family-Making in Italy*, Thomson Wadsworth, Belmont, CA

Lobe, J. (2003) 'Rapid population growth fuels conflict, says new report', available at www.commondreams.org/headlines03/1217-01.htm (last accessed 13 February 2009)

Lohmann, L. (2005) 'Malthusianism and the terror of scarcity', in B. Hartmann, B. Subramaniam and C. Zerner (eds) *Making Threats, Biofears and Environmental Anxieties*, Rowman and Littlefield, Lanham, MD, pp81–98

Lugton, M. with McKinney, P. (2004) *Population in Perspective: A Curriculum Resource*, Hampshire College Population and Development Program, Amherst, MA, available at www.populationinperspective.org (last accessed 13 February 2009)

Matthew, R. (2005) 'Bioterrorism and national security: Peripheral threats, core vulnerabilities', in B. Hartmann, B. Subramaniam and C. Zerner (eds) *Making Threats, Biofears and Environmental Anxieties*, Rowman and Littlefield, Lanham, MD, pp237–246

McSweeney, K. (2005) 'Indigenous population growth in the lowland neotropics: Social science insights for biodiversity conservation', *Conservation Biology*, vol 19, no 5, pp1375–1384

Peluso, N.L. and Watts, M. (eds) (2001) *Violent Environments*, Cornell University Press, Ithaca, NY

PGSI (1993a) PGSI White Paper, July, PGSI, Washington, DC

PGSI (1993b) Report of Findings from Focus Groups on Population, Consumption and the Environment, conducted for PGSI by R/S/M, Melman, Lazarus Lake and Beldon & Russonello, July

PGSI (1994a) 'Building a coordinated campaign on population and sustainable development policy', report submitted to the PGSI by Future Strategies, Inc., Francis E. Smith and Pam Solo, March

PGSI (1994b) Report of Stewardship and Security Steering Committee Meeting, November 28, PGSI, Washington, DC

Population and Development Program (2009) 'Stop the blame: Population control imagery', available at http://popdev.hampshire.edu/stop-the-blame (last accessed 14 February 2009)

Ramsden, E. (2001) 'Between quality and quantity: The Population Council and the politics of "science-making" in eugenics and demography, 1952–1965', Rockefeller Archive Center Research Reports Online

Reuters News Service (2003) 'Study: women's health linked to unrest: High birth rates, AIDS set stage for global violence', 17 December

Ross, A. (1996) 'The lonely hour of scarcity', *Capitalism, Nature and Socialism*, vol 7, no 3, pp3–26

SAMA Resource Group for Women and Health (2005) *Beyond Numbers: Implications of the Two-Child Norm*, SAMA, New Delhi

Sandilands, C. (1999) 'Sex at the limits', in Eric Darier (ed) *Discourses of the Environment*, Blackwell Publishers, Oxford

Schwartz, P. and Randall, D. (2003) 'An abrupt climate change scenario and its implications for United States national security', commissioned by the Global Business Network for the Department of Defense, available at www.gbn.com/consulting/article_details.php?id=53 (last accessed 13 February 2009)

Seager, J. (1993) *Earth Follies: Coming to Feminist Terms with the Global Environmental Crisis*, Routledge, New York

Silliman, J., Fried, M., Ross, L. and Gutiérrez, E.R. (2004) *Undivided Rights: Women of Color Organize for Reproductive Justice*, Boston, South End Press

Southern Poverty Law Center (2002) 'The puppeteer', Intelligence Report 106, pp44–51

Stern, A.M. (2005) *Eugenic Nation: Faults and Frontiers of Better Breeding in Modern America*, University of California Press, Berkeley

Szreter, S. (1993) 'The idea of demographic transition and the study of fertility change: A critical intellectual history', *Population and Development Review*, vol 19, no 4, pp659–701

Tokar, B. (1997) *Earth for Sale: Reclaiming Ecology in the Age of Corporate Greenwash*, South End Press, Boston, MA

Wattenberg, B. (1989) *The Birth Dearth*, Pharos Books, New York

Westing, A. (ed) (1988) *Cultural Norms, War and the Environment*, Oxford University Press, Oxford

White House (1995) 'National Security Strategy of Engagement and Enlargement', July 1994 and February 1995, excerpted in Environmental Change and Security Project Report, no 1, pp47–50

Wilmoth, J.R. and Ball, P. (1992) 'The population debate in American popular magazines', *Population and Development Review,* vol 18, no 4, pp631–668

World Commission on Environment and Development (1987) *Our Common Future*, Oxford University Press, Oxford

Part II
Economics and Scarcity

Commentary

Lyla Mehta

According to popular opinion, scarcity is the creation of economists. In part, this has to do with Lionel Robbins' famous definition which is discussed by many of the contributors to this volume.[1] As discussed in this section his portrayal of economics solely as the science which studies the relationship between given ends and scarce means which have alternative uses was highly misleading for the 1930s when in the light of massive unemployment, so-called scarce resources could neither be used nor allocated across competing ends. The chapters in this section are written by both economists and non-economists and display divergent views about the nature of economics and the role of scarcity in economics.

Key to scarcity is the idea of value, which forms part of a long-standing debate that pre-dates economists and can be traced back to Plato and Aristotle's notion of value. The paradox of diamonds and water discussed by several authors in this volume is a useful starting point: early thinkers pointed out that diamonds were rare but pointless, whereas water was cheap but life-saving. Aristotle's idea of the 'good' led to him condemn all exchanges that were directly for profit and not undertaken for the satisfaction of needs. Political economists such as Marx reintroduced these ideas of use value, and some argue that Adam Smith's *The Wealth of Nations* was also concerned with the distinction between value in use and value in exchange (see Toye, 2005). In the 19th century the focus shifted to marginal utility and marginal costs which are discussed in the next chapter and laid the foundations for orthodox economics and its attention to supply and demand. Keynesian economics turned its attention to macro issues and went beyond the narrow definition of economics as a problem of allocation. Keynes also hoped for the end of the economic problems of supply and demand and for an age of abundance and leisure (ibid).

Changing notions of value are thus key to ideas of scarcity and the chapters in this section engage with both in different ways. In Chapter 4 Ben Fine discusses how, contrary to common belief among the proponents of mainstream economics and its critics alike, scarcity is (most of the time) peculiarly absent from economics. Like the Cheshire cat's grin, we know it is there but it disappears altogether when we seek to examine it a little more closely. This is because of the dogmatic attachment of economists to the technical apparatus of the optimizing individual and its aggregated counterpart in consideration of efficiency and general equilibrium theory, as if economic activity were the outcome of automatons. But in reality, this technical apparatus is often discarded due to market and non-market imperfections and economics is no longer simply the study of a needs and wants/scarcity dualism. These arguments are illuminated by examining Amartya Sen's work on entitlements, which marks a departure from earlier conceptions of scarcity. Still, he argues that entitlements analysis is neutral when it comes to underlying social relations, historical and cultural specificities around food and retains unresolved macro/micro tensions due to an adherence to a formalistic and individualistic frame.

Fred Luks' chapter (5) focuses on deconstructing economic interpretations of sustainable development. He argues that economics as a discipline could not exist in a world without scarcity. Seen from the perspective of economists, sustainable development is about scarcity and there are diverse ways to view sustainability. He demonstrates that both mainstream and alternative paradigms within economics tend to naturalize what is meant by scarcity and there is a continuum between the two positions. While ecological economics is highly critical of the mainstream view of unfettered and optimistic growth, it is also premised on notions of 'absolute' scarcity which fails to adequately problematize the socio-political aspects of both limits and scarcity. Refreshing alternatives are however emerging and can be found in 'discursive' and postmodern trends in economics, a re-reading of classical texts and also heterodox debates concerning happiness, waste and squander (an issue picked up in Chapter 7 by Michael Thompson who engages with rubbish theory).

The last two chapters in this section are written by non-economists and provide critical perspectives on how scarcity has been conceptualized by neoclassical economists. In Chapter 6 Sajay Samuel and Jean Robert argue that scarcity is a relational term. Still, in commodity-intensive societies the perception of endemic scarcity has intensified and become all-pervasive due to the limitless desire for accumulation which has been sparked and fed by the ideological commitments of mainstream economics. They contrast Aristotle's notion of the 'good' with Adam Smith's commitments to wealth-getting to bring this ideological ground into sharp relief. They argue that it is economic notions of supply and demand which have moved water from being the commons to something that is scarce and H_2O. They thus call for rethinking the basic assumptions of commodity-intensive society and re-evaluating self-sufficiency and the role of thresholds.

Michael Thompson uses cultural and rubbish theory in Chapter 7 to add new insights to understandings of value. He argues that the categories of transient objects (which decrease in value and have a finite lifespan) and durable objects (which increase in value and have an infinite lifespan) are not exhaustive. In addition, there is the neglected category of rubbish which explains why a rat-infested slum can end up a part of 'Our Glorious Heritage'. The idea of rubbish is neglected by economics and helps clarify and resolve serious problems with the concept of scarcity which Thompson demonstrates with interesting anecdotes, personal experiences and references to the perspectives taken by a diverse cast of characters: William Blake, Po Chu-I, John Maynard Keynes, Jackie Onassis and Miss Piggy.

These contributions highlight key challenges. There are diverse ways to view scarcity within economics and the authors clearly demonstrate that economics is not only about studying unlimited human wants and the scarce means to achieve them. Still, the neoclassical economic take on scarcity enjoys a privileged position in academic and policy thinking and has shaped dominant thinking concerning resources and their allocation. Several authors thus call for alternatives that challenge mathematically neat approaches that appear simple and logical. This means engaging more thoroughly with heterodox trends in economics (e.g. feminist economics), unpacking the level of aggregation and complementing conventional approaches with the constructivist ones as outlined by Luks in Chapter 5. While this might mean a more 'clumsy' set up (à la Thompson) that is less elegant than the dominant view of scarcity, the result will be more true to local realities and more useful in policy in the long run.

The global financial crisis of 2008–2009 has led to increased introspection, humility and reflexivity on the part of many economists who are looking to new approaches and disciplines to deal with instability, local level variation and heterodox ways to rethink human behaviour and conventional growth models (Elliot, 2010; Jackson, 2010). The crisis has also made it clear that many economists have been living in the illusion of a perfect and frictionless market system (Krugman, 2009). However, as argued by several contributors to this volume, the market is always embedded in culture, history and politics, and scarcity is not something that is just the creation of market forces. The idea of stable markets around which scarcity is the norm has largely emerged due to the power and reach of mainstream economics perspectives. This needs to give way to something messier that acknowledges the role of the symbolic, the reciprocal, the substantive, the political, the uneconomic and maybe even the irrational. This means revisiting the ideas of John Maynard Keynes, Karl Polyani, Ivan Illich and heterodox perspectives within economics while also drawing on complementary anthropological and socio-political perspectives to scarcity. It also urges us to be more upfront about social and power relations as well as historical and cultural specificities around resources which can ultimately help transcend the limited vision of *Homo economicus*.

Notes

1   'Economics is the science which studies human behaviour as a relationship between given ends and scarce means which have alternative uses.' (Robbins, 1932, p16)

References

Elliot, L. (2010) 'Rescuing economics from its own crisis', *The Guardian*, 5 April

Jackson, T. (2009) *Prosperity without Growth: Economics for a Finite Planet*, Earthscan, London

Krugman, P. (2009) 'How did economists get it so wrong?', *The New York Times*, 6 September

Robbins, L. (1932) *An Essay on the Nature and Significance of Economic Science*, Macmillan, London

Toye, J. (2005) 'What did economists do with scarcity?', presentation at the conference *Scarcity and the Politics of Allocation*, Institute of Development Studies, Brighton

4

Economics and Scarcity: With Amartya Sen as Point of Departure?[1]

Ben Fine

Foreword

Economics is the study of scarcity, how resources are allocated among competing uses. (Stiglitz, 2000, p23)

The older market failures were, for the most part, easily identified and limited in scope, requiring well-defined government interventions. Because virtually all markets are incomplete and information is always imperfect ... the market failures [of the new type] are pervasive in the economy. (Stiglitz, 1994, pp42–43)

Introduction

From the perspective of a more rounded social science, there are so many weaknesses in mainstream economics that it is difficult to know where to begin in laying them out, in offering alternatives and in explaining how the dismal science could have got itself into this state. Even so, despite having spent a working life in criticism of the orthodoxy, I can only be struck by the extent to which the notion of scarcity has attracted so little attention, in my contributions too, while being generally accepted as being indispensable to the mainstream.

This chapter seeks to resolve the paradox of centrality with neglect by re-examining some of my own earlier contributions on both the history of economic thought and the work of Amartya Sen for the light that can be shed on the economist's notion of scarcity and what turns out to be its total lack of relevance under close scrutiny even on its own terms. No wonder it has fallen out of the picture for proponent and critic alike.

But what does mainstream neoclassical economics itself understand by scarcity? It is based on the idea that resources are limited and wants and desires are not. This notion of scarcity within economics is dismissed by critics as too narrow in terms of the assigned meanings of resources and needs. I have considerable sympathy with this sort of criticism but closer attention is still required to the place of scarcity within economics itself. The rationale for this is brought out by consideration of the tensions across the two opening quotations from Stiglitz. Economics is the study of scarcity. But if market failures are the problem, scarcity is not (at least until made so by correction of those failures). This means that scarcity only prevails within economics in some ideal world of perfectly working markets, called Pareto-efficient, competitive, general equilibrium in technical terms, but going under the slogan of there being no such thing as a free lunch in popular neoliberal parlance.

Scarcity within economics then is something akin to the Cheshire cat's grin. We know it is there but it seems to disappear altogether when we seek to examine it a little more closely. In short, contrary to common belief among proponents of mainstream economics and its critics alike, scarcity is a peculiarly absent element from mainstream economics – most of the time. For it can only be there when examining the behaviour of isolated 'rational' individuals, *ceteris paribus* or in conceiving the workings of the economy as a whole in the ideal and unrealistic setting of general equilibrium theory that bears no relation to the realities of any economy in practice.

So why do economists, and critics, make such a hullabaloo over scarcity if it only pertains to a limited extent, in special cases, within their own analysis? The answer is not because of the analytical role of scarcity itself but the dogmatic attachment of economists to the technical apparatus that is used to define it in those special cases. That technical apparatus comprises methodological individualism, deductivism, the use of production and utility functions and so on, as if economic (and social) activity were the outcome of automatons. As will be shown in the first part of this chapter, the technical apparatus gained legitimacy by an extraordinary reduction of the problem of economics to the allocation of scarce resources to competing ends. Having in a sense exploited scarcity to this end, the notion has been discarded as the technical apparatus that it inspired becomes deployed across a range of applications in which economics is no longer simply the study of a needs and wants/scarcity dualism.

The second part of this chapter is an overview of some developments in the thinking of Amartya Sen. His most prominent work has its origins in social choice theory, itself an attempt to transform the complex problem of judging between different states of the world into the treatment of society as if it were a single choosing individual, an implicit reflection of scarcity in meeting needs. Not surprisingly in view of the earlier argument around the dispensable role of scarcity for ecnomics, in Sen's path from social choice to development as freedom, this notion of scarcity rapidly disappears (most notably in the entitlement approach to famine as opposed to food availability decline). But the technical apparatus to which it is attached lingers to a much larger and longer extent, and is to a degree still present at the close in terms of insufficient attention to the meaning and context, or active social construction of, entitlements, capabilities and freedom.

In other words, even in a scholar such as Sen, who is heavily critical of mainstream economics in many respects, the influence of its notion of scarcity is still present if only through the shadowy presence of the technical apparatus through which it is constructed. No doubt this in part reflects the need to get to grips with the material, even physical, realities of economic and social life, for which mainstream economics uses scarcity (or the technical apparatus underpinning it) as a quick fix. The concluding remarks point to alternative ways in which the material aspects of life, putatively addressed by the notion of scarcity, can be handled.

The peculiarity of scarcity within mainstream economics

The 'modern' notion of scarcity within contemporary mainstream economics has its origins in the marginalist revolution of the 1870s that was responsible for laying the foundations of orthodox economics as it is today. Crucial is the idea of economic rationality in the form of optimizing individuals. This is true of supply (the theory of the profit-maximizing firm) and of demand (the theory of the utility-maximizing consumer). There are corresponding implications for the notion of scarcity since such optimization only has any analytical purchase when the optimizing individual is confronted by the constraints of scarce resources. If such constraints are relaxed, there is a lessening of scarcity, so profits (and supply) and utility (and demand) can take on larger magnitudes.[2]

This notion of scarcity continues to prevail within contemporary economics, and it equally corresponds to popular notions. This does not mean that the notion has remained unchanged. This is so in two crucial, closely related but distinct, respects. First, at the time of the marginalist revolution, it was accepted that such economic rationality might be complemented by other motives or prompts to action. Further, the notion of (individual) utility had connotations much wider than the mere consumption (purchase or demand) of economic goods (for another discussion of the notion of water as an economic good see Chapter 12, this volume). Economic rationality, bounded by scarcity, applied only to a limited range of economic and social phenomena. The passage to contemporary notions of scarcity within economics has discarded these qualifications. For all economic (and social) behaviour is ultimately reduced to utility maximization or economic rationality. And utility itself is reduced to preferences over the options made available in light of resource constraints. Thus, the pursuit of utility maximization passes from a broad notion of welfare to become a simple and deterministic logic of choice between alternatives bound by scarcity interpreted as resource constraints.

Second, corresponding to the shifting meaning of scarcity since the marginalist revolution, is the idea that its definition in relation to *individuals* is simply projected into *social* scarcity. Just as individuals must choose between constrained options, so must society. This involves a systemic understanding of the economy in which individual and social scarcity exactly mirror one another. If it were otherwise, the notion of scarcity derived for the individual would be otiose from a social perspective as the constraints on individuals could be relaxed at the social level. Developments within economics since the marginalist revolution have been designed to ensure that the notion of scarcity attached to the individual does translate into a corresponding notion of scarcity at the level of the economy as a whole, as in the neoliberal mantra that there is no such thing as a free lunch.

This has all involved a number of elements in the evolution of mainstream economics. It requires, for example, that the individual who is more rounded than just a utility maximizer has to be discarded, otherwise aggregation over individuals would entail incursion of considerations other than those attached to the constraints on individuals – if I gain utility, for example, from activities (even thoughts and feelings, possibly of others) that do not require those 'scarce' resources. Such possibilities have tended by economists to be designated as irrational, a pejorative term for anything belonging to the non-economic or social, and so readily and illegitimately set aside as irrelevant, (although, as will be argued later, they have recently been brought back into account). Further, there is a shift from *partial* equilibrium (the scarcity attached to a single market) to *general* equilibrium (where all markets are analysed in interaction with one another). Then, one individual or sector of the economy can only gain at the expense of another. Yet, for a general equilibrium to exist and have scarcity (or welfare properties) comparable to those for the constrained individual, a legion of assumptions within the approach itself needs to be made about the nature of resource use and utility satisfaction. These include the absence of scale economies (productivity increases with higher output) and the absence of externalities in production and consumption, and the assumption that averaging across bundles of inputs to production and consumption is always superior to specialization. These are not merely highly restrictive assumptions, they defy comparison with general experience. Moreover, these technical assumptions apart, how the economy is conceived in translating individual to social scarcity is equally remarkably defiant of common sense. There is no money, and it is as if everybody barters with one another and there is no agent to set prices so that a fictional auctioneer is spirited into existence to declare them.

In effect, in establishing itself as a distinct discipline by virtue of its attention to economic rationality (optimization in the face of constraints), economics needed to strip down both its content and its applicability even from the already reduced content handed down by the marginalist revolution. The notion of scarcity within the newly emerging mainstream became totally subordinated to the technical content and methods of the discipline without regard to wider considerations let alone any sort of realism.

The peculiar scarcity of scarcity within mainstream economics

So, when in the early 1930s, Robbins (in)famously defined economics as the allocation of scarce resources between competing ends, he did so explicitly as an assessment of what economics should be, exaggerating the extent to which this was already the case. But he pinpointed what economics was becoming and what still remains the approach of the discipline to scarcity. To propel it along this path, he had to obliterate differences within the founders and followers of the marginalist revolution, as well as other traditions of economic analysis, in order to brush aside analytical absences and limitations. Only then could economics offer the pretence of being wedded to universal notions, reflecting the constraints on capacity to meet the (equally universal and insatiable) preferences of individuals.

The situation is, however, more complicated than this. First, Robbins' (1935) notion of economics was far from universally accepted and, in particular, attracted hostile reaction within the *Quarterly Journal of Economics*, from Talcott Parsons, trained as an economist and in the process of founding functionalist sociology. Second, Robbins (1971, p154) himself was later to come close to recanting in light of the policy consequences of 'the greatest mistake of my professional career' and his having 'become the slave of theoretical constructions which ... were inappropriate ... The theory was inadequate to the facts'. The latter were unavoidable in light of the massive unemployment of the 1930s for which 'scarce' resources were not being used, let alone allocated across competing ends. Rather, the microeconomics of (aggregated) individual optimization was transparently incapable of explaining the functioning of the economy as a whole for which an entirely separate theory was necessary. Following Keynes' interventions, analysis for the economy as a whole focused on macroeconomic aggregates, not microeconomic optimality (around scarcity). For Keynesianism, the problem is not scarcity (at the individual and social levels) but insufficient levels of effective aggregate demand to guarantee full use of existing available resources. Keynesianism and macroeconomics emerged, for which Robbins' definition is hardly apposite, and no alternative definition of scarcity follows for an economy at less than full employment.

Second, then, and more fundamentally, explicit reference to scarcity only makes sense in the context of the evolving microeconomics of mainstream economics – its explicit distinction from macroeconomics only emerging in the 1930s. Once macroeconomics is acknowledged as such, with one exception that proves the rule (that of Pareto-efficient general equilibrium), it necessarily undermines the microeconomic understanding of scarcity (in case of mis- or non-allocation or any form of dynamics that renders equilibrium otiose).

This is not an academic point, since Robbins' claim to define economics represented only the extreme position then being taken by economists in the wake of the marginalist revolution. The general position being adopted both within the economics profession and outside was that such a definition of economics (and, by implication, scarcity) was limited in its scope of application. For Keynes (1997),[3] for example, in a book described as the only one on economic methodology alone to appear before 1970 (Hutchison, 2000, pp4–5), the scope of economics concerns 'substantive *wealth*' and activities around its creation, appropriation and accumulation and corresponding institutions and customs.

To take Robbins then as representative of economics is highly misleading especially for the time when he was writing (Luks, also an economist, takes another position; see Chapter 5 in this volume). What is true, though, is that the microeconomics at the heart of his definition was undergoing prodigious development around that time in the two different but complementary ways already indicated: the partial equilibrium theory of individual optimization and the general equilibrium of interaction among such individuals. For, first of all, the marginalist revolution had established the niche from which that development could proceed, centring on the notion of rational economic agents in an environment of universal scarcity. In the wake of the marginalist revolution, with Marshall's partial equilibrium as stepping stone and Robbins' methodology as conduit, this niche was defined by the following elements:

- a separation of the social sciences into distinct disciplines with a corresponding division of subject matter and methods (albeit with overlaps);
- a division *within* economics between the deductive science attached to the axiomatics of individual economic rationality and the more rounded, inductive treatment of the individual, the macro-economy, the social and the historical (institutions, culture, etc.);
- a paradoxical presumption that the *universal* deductive approach to economics was at most of *limited* scope, with *market* behaviour alone as its core application.

On this basis, microeconomics was endowed with a space in which to evolve its own logic around the efficiency (or not) in equilibrium of the optimizing individual for whom scarcity in given endowments, alongside given preferences and technology, offer the key determining constraints. From the marginalist revolution onwards, the process involved the stripping out of both conceptual and technical obstacles to arrive at required solutions to the problem of market supply and demand from the perspective of a rational economic agent. The individual becomes an optimizing automaton without character or identity, denoted by a set of preferences or, more exactly, an ordering of a vector of goods, themselves without social or even physical properties to distinguish them. Thus, as observed, the notion of utility is metamorphosed through preferences to a logic of choice.

Such are the underpinnings of the demand theory attached to the consumer. Similarly, the process of production, or simply supply, becomes reduced to a technical relationship between inputs and outputs, setting aside considerations of production and work as socially and historically situated processes. Nor is there attention to how technology (and resources) are created, used and developed. Needless to say, the location of such an economy of choice is notable for the absence of the 'non-economic' to which it is attached and which makes it possible.

Alongside the supply and demand theory associated with the individual, such microeconomics also sought to aggregate the set of optimizing individuals as a whole. This is both to search out the possibility of a simultaneous equilibrium across all markets and to investigate the existence, uniqueness, stability and efficiency properties of such an equilibrium.

These two branches of microeconomics – optimizing and interacting individuals – both more or less fulfilled their potential simultaneously soon after World War II. As already hinted, the theory was driven by the technical assumptions necessary to derive the required results, with little or no deference to reality. These assumptions are prodigious even on their own terms, as with the absence of increasing returns and externalities for example. Significantly, in the meantime, other branches of economics could prosper. Most notable is Keynesian macroeconomics but also what would now be viewed as marginal heterodoxies – such as the old institutional economics, and the old or classical development economics. They could occupy the space created or vacated for them by the extreme limitations of the newly matured microeconomics, and by continuing traditions within economics itself.

Yet, once microeconomics had established itself in the way described, and on the terms of compromise within the discipline and with other disciplines, it began to carve out new areas of application, to challenge its traditionally limited scope. From a logical point of view, there remained the paradox of the universal applicability of utility maximization in principle and its limitation to market behaviour in particular. Consequently, once accepted, there is a case for extending the principle to non-market applications and deploying the theory as if a market were in place. Such is the impetus behind the first phase of what I have termed economics imperialism, the extension of economic principles to the other social sciences, most notable in any form of rational choice (Fine and Milonakis, 2009). Initially, its leading representative was Gary Becker, and its leading subject matter began with public choice and human capital. For Becker, all and not just market-based behaviour is rational or subject to the economic approach. Everything is reduced to a cost–benefit analysis of outcomes, with an equally universal scarcity constraining choices. Thus, Becker put Robbins' methodology for economics into practice, taking in the family, crime, addiction and anything else that took his and his followers' fancy. The universal application of the economic approach to all subjects leads to economics imperialism: the attempted colonization of the other social sciences by economics. It is an ironic venture, for the marginalist principles were only accepted in the first place in case of limited application and in light of their dependence upon the absence of broader economic and social content.

This all involves bringing back in what was originally left out in order to make the microeconomic core viable. But what is brought back in, and how, is very different from what was left out in the first place. For, how the 'non-economic' is treated is totally marked by the conceptual and technical apparatus that was established previously through the simple expedient of leaving it out. The 'non-economic', like the economic, is tied to production functions, utility maximization, equilibrium and efficiency, etc.

In short, while the traditional concept of scarcity within economics is highlighted by Robbins, its scope of application depends upon how widely rational choice methods are accepted within as-if-perfectly working markets. As late as 1990, in commenting on his economic approach to everything, George Akerlof (1990, p73) could say of Gary Becker (both Nobel Prize winners) that he knew how to spell banana (I prefer taramasalata) but that he did not know when to stop. Thus, Becker lies at one extreme of 'economics imperialism' for which the non-market is addressed as if it were akin to a *perfect* market (and everything is scarce from widgets to whatever is exchanged within the household). And, Becker is extreme by comparison with fellow economists, who call for a halt in application of the economic approach to non-economic subjects. These reservations are even stronger with respect to the methods and traditions of the other social sciences.

More recently, though, over the past couple of decades, there has been a corresponding shift in the way in which economics has sought to bring back in what it has left out in establishing its microeconomic core. It has appealed to a more refined and, in many respects, seductive form of reductionism of the economic and the social to individual behaviour, giving rise to a different and more virulent and appealing phase of economics imperialism. It has done so by focusing on economic theory on market – especially informational – *im*perfections. Buyers and sellers have different information and this can lead to markets failing to reflect scarcities in various ways. Without going into details, it is possible to explain why markets might not 'clear' (settle at a price for which supply is equal to demand), they might clear but be inefficient (exchanges do not take place that might be of benefit to both parties) and, at the extreme, potentially beneficial markets may fail to emerge altogether. This emphasis on market imperfections has given rise to a whole set of 'new' fields within economics – the new microfoundations of macroeconomics, the new trade theory, the new financial, the new development, the new institutional, the new labour economics – as well as new fields outside economics or influence upon the old – the new political economy, economic geography, economic sociology and so on. I have parodied such initiatives by the formula ss=e=mi^2. First, all economics is reduced to market imperfections, mi, and methodological individualism, also mi, (in the form of imperfectly informed rational economic agents). Then, all social science is reduced to such economics.

It follows that economics either relies upon its traditional concept of scarcity, as with Becker, or it complements it with some notion of market imperfection (whether macroeconomic, informational or institutional, etc.), only the correction of which would put us back on the track of competing ends. Either the market works perfectly in given and knowable conditions in which case scarcity prevails across competing ends but is of little interest, or the market does not work perfectly and, whatever the reason, it undermines the idea of scarcity as *the* constraint on competing ends. Economics, whether theory or policy, is only of substantive interest when it is not the allocation of scarce resources between competing ends, when Pareto efficiency does not and cannot prevail. This is illustrated by the quotations from Stiglitz, at the beginning of this chapter. The first routinely repeats that economics is as Robbins suggests. But Stiglitz's entire analytical corpus is based on an entirely different ethos. Whatever its own merits, this is the idea that correction of market failures is what economics is about. This means getting to the point where scarcity becomes the problem rather than it being the problem in the first place.

This whirlwind and partial tour across the history of today's mainstream economics sheds some light on the shadowy and contradictory role of scarcity within contemporary thought. For, first and foremost, that orthodoxy has become exclusively based on the technical apparatus of the optimizing individual and its aggregated counterpart in considerations of efficiency and equilibrium. This places considerable emphasis in principle upon the idea of general equilibrium as a balance between competing ends and scarce resources. But general equilibrium also serves as an abstract ideal, or standard, against which the real world might be judged by way of deviation. So, with few exceptions, general equilibrium has increasingly commanded how mainstream economists view the economy. Yet, with deviations from it, in light of market imperfections introduced as a way of bringing back in what has been left out (non-market factors), the corresponding notion of scarcity, narrow though it is in terms of analytical structure and conceptual content, no longer prevails until market or non-market imperfections are corrected. In a sense, the blindingly obvious inadequacy of Robbins in light of Keynesianism and the macroeconomic, has been generalized. Yet, mainstream economists still cling to the same technical apparatus that allowed scarcity to come to the fore. And, while the idea persists that scarcity lies at the heart of economics, this is soon forgotten and its nature and significance is rarely discussed. Otherwise, to reiterate, scarcity is not central, since market or other imperfections preclude it from being so.

From scarcity via social choice to freedom?

So, rather than being central to its methodology, scarcity has, from Robbins onwards, served as a legitimizing device for the general application of the technical apparatus and formal deductive methods of mainstream economics by appeal to the scarcity/needs and wants dualism in the totally rarefied context of isolated individual or general equilibrium. This elusive character of scarcity can be illustrated by reference to the trajectory of some of Amartya Sen's work. His contributions are often more than normally challenging to economics as a discipline, since Sen (1977) is no friend of rational choice and is especially rounded as an academic economist in relation to other disciplines. Not surprisingly, scarcity as such does not figure prominently within his work, in part because, although he continues to draw upon the technical apparatus of mainstream economics in some respects, he also seeks to break from it as well. Significantly, then, social choice theory has remained at the heart of his thinking, from the classic Sen (1970a) to his Nobel acceptance speech (Sen, 1999b).

Although social choice theory would appear to belong to a formal branch of political theory, it became prominent through an economist with the publication of Arrow (1951). At an abstract level, social choice is concerned with how to derive an outcome for society from the options available in light of the way in which individuals have preferences over those outcomes. Formally, however, in the hands of economists, social choice theory became a simple examination of the properties of voting systems. It is as if possible states of the world were candidates, each ranked by voters. What should be the result of the election in terms of social ranking of the candidates?

Thus, the whole motivation for social choice theory from the outset, even if stalled by Arrow's Impossibility Theorem,[4] was to derive a social ordering from individual orderings. Fundamentally, the problem of social choice is based upon how to reduce society to the status of an individual with derived preferences over alternatives, with these as-if-individual preferences reflecting trade-offs and, correspondingly, scarcity as traditionally conceived. The search for social choice reflects this goal, with different allocations of scarce resources, proxied by alternatives, across competing individual needs being ranked by the social as individual.

In retrospect, two central issues were raised initially and, on their own terms, have been resolved, with Sen a major contributor. First, supposing the value of alternative states of the world to different agents could be quantified, then *interpersonal* comparisons come to the fore – how much should one person's welfare count against another's? Second, a dual problem is the intensity of one individual's preferences – how much weight should be given to one individual's welfare in moving from one alternative to another of different utility? Clearly, such issues reflect a perspective building up traditionally from choice over scarcity. How do we rank the welfare of one person over another, and how do we rank the raised welfare of any person taken in isolation? Although, once again, scarcity does not appear explicitly, there is a general, if not universal, presumption that one person's welfare must be at the expense of another's, and choices must be made between them because of mutually exclusive increases of welfare in light of limited availability of resources.

Further, for social choice as practised by economists and in conformity to underlying technical apparatus, most if not all analysis has been purely formalistic. We have little or no idea who the individuals are, (poor, rich, men, women, etc.) nor what the alternatives are over which they have preferences (food, arms, etc.). In addition, society itself is absent – beyond somehow offering individuals unexamined choices, and otherwise itself being the outcome, in principle, of individual choices. The framework is one of deriving the social from the individual, with no feedback in the other direction. Sen (1995, p3) himself simply but devastatingly puts it, 'Another issue, related to individual behavior and rationality, concerns the role of social interactions in the development of values, and also the connection between value formation and the decision-making processes. Social choice theory has tended to avoid this issue'. In the context of scarcity, this leaves open how, why and whether needs/wants are generated let alone satisfied (or not) outside of individual choice over pre-existing alternatives.

One way of interpreting Sen's subsequent work is in rendering social choice less individualistic and formal. As Sen (1999b, p350) himself suggests:

> *Also, some investigations, while not directly a part of social theory, have been helped by the understanding generated by the study of group decisions (such as the causation and prevention of famines and hunger, or the forms and consequences of gender inequality, or the demands of individual freedom seen as a 'social commitment'). The reach and relevance of social choice theory can be very extensive indeed.*

How extensive in scope and depth is another matter, or a matter of time and development. In Sen's work, inequality (primarily of income) and poverty made up the next extensive step, beginning with *On Economic Inequality*. But the analysis, like that of the earlier social choice theory, has often remained formalistic – how to judge ethically between different distributions of income with the general presumption that more is better. In utility sum terms, the problems are how much to weight more income to a given individual and, given this, how much to weight one individual against another (or vice versa).

As I have shown elsewhere, (Fine, 1985), in generalizing the technical results of the highly cited Atkinson (1970), measuring inequality *between* individuals can be considered to be equivalent to measuring the relative worth of improvement for a *single* individual. In other words, valuing increase in my welfare more in and of itself offers the same ethical judgement as valuing my welfare more than yours.[5] This is hardly surprising but it highlights the formalism of the inequality literature and its corresponding limitations, and the presumption (if not necessity) that more for some is less for others (otherwise utility sum over all individuals can be made larger irrespective of weighting and comparison of individual incomes). For, while the two approaches to inequality (assigning weight to individuals as opposed to assigning weights across them) are mathematically equivalent, they are far from substantively equivalent. Comparison of given incomes between people is entirely different from comparison of different incomes for a single person. Further, the issues can only be engaged meaningfully at some level of detail concerning the nature of the people and the uses to which income is or can be put. For Sen, 'To try to make social welfare judgements *without* using any interpersonal comparison of utilities, and *without* using any nonutility information, is not a fruitful enterprise' (Sen, 1995, p8). In slightly more informal terms, for example, trading off between capacity for, and inequality in, enjoyment can hardly be pursued very far in the abstract. Do we reward those who are hard or easy to please and do we do so irrespective of why this is so and what are the rewards – the disabled as opposed to the depressive, and the private aeroplane as opposed to life's necessities?

In short, social choice theory and measurement of inequality have displayed a strong affinity both with the technical apparatus attached to mainstream economics and the presumption of enduring scarcity. Higher welfare or income for one is inevitably presumed to lead to lower income or welfare for others, so that intrapersonal and interpersonal comparisons have to be made to come to any view of what is better for society. Interestingly, one exception within social choice theory to this pervasive thrust is in Sen's 'Impossibility of a Paretian Liberal' (1970b). What he shows is that satisfying the Pareto criterion is questionable once one's own welfare depends upon pleasing others who may have illiberal preferences.[6] In other words, if we ask why people have the preferences that they do, we may not wish to satisfy them, and this makes scarcity in the face of competing ends as questionable as the ends themselves. This is, of course, nothing but common sense and hardly requires a course in ethics. If we do not like the preferences that others have (for excessive, even unhealthy consumption, for example), this means they may not be ends for us, and a source of scarcity from our perspective (although we might also be wary of being illiberal). However, once this can of worms is opened, it is lucky for economists that the normative is precluded from consideration. That is other than in presuming, crucially, that there are preferences that are insatiable and the world is better off the more they are satisfied, no matter what they are and how they have been derived.

As indicated, though, even on this narrow terrain, there is some need to make more progress in dealing with specificities of individuals and goods. Sen's turn from inequality and poverty to famine can be viewed in these terms. Food and the scarcity attached to starving are concrete applications. Sen is famed for having offered the entitlement approach (EA) to famine in which it is not caused by failure (or scarcity) of food supply as such but by the inability of those who are starved to access food. The contrast is with supply-side explanations, the food availability decline (FAD) approach, in which aggregate supply is presumed most likely to have occurred as a result of crop failure. Two features stand out from EA, marking continuities with previous work. First, the formal analytics of EA are derived from set-theoretic microeconomics, with generalization through access to non-market-related entitlements. What can I get from what I have, given the conditions for transforming one to the other? Consequently, EA is individualistic in methodology. Second, as is immediately apparent, the formal analytics of EA are not food-specific. They could apply equally to anything – whether basic needs or luxuries; are these to be interpreted as equally scarce?

This is not to suggest that EA, as deployed in practice, is purely micro-based, and never macro, and fails to be food-specific. As Sen (1999a, p170) argues, famine is dependent upon 'the exercise of power and authority ... the alienation of the rulers from those ruled ... the social and political distance between the governors and the governed'. Such considerations, however, tend to enter separately from the micro-analytics of entitlements. In part, macro references to food and famine arise directly out of empirical applications rather than from the theory. The macro-social also enters more obliquely through the incorporation of *social* relations, structures and processes. But these are superimposed, not built, upon the micro-foundations. An obvious example is the class of landless labourers. Unable to produce for their own consumption or to command sufficient (wage) revenue or payment in kind to gain sustenance, they are potentially subject to famine irrespective of overall aggregate supply of food. Yet, such arguments presuppose social relations on the land, between landlords and labourers, and in the distribution of food. None of these is reducible to the individualistic micro-analytics of EA.

These considerations aside, what is crucial for Sen's EA as opposed to FAD is that *scarcity* (of food supply) is not the underlying problem. Rather it is the shifting incidence of entitlements to a food supply that may even have increased. In a sense, this is a stunning illustration of the point posited earlier. Despite deploying much of the technical apparatus of microeconomics, suitably modified, Sen finds that scarcity is not necessarily the underlying cause of famine and, of course, it follows that scarcity can hardly be an underlying focal point for economics itself.[7]

My own assessment of EA, Fine (1997), was motivated less by consideration of famine as such than by earlier research on food that drew upon a broader study of the determinants of consumption (in the UK context with occasional attention to eating disorders if not famine).[8] The organizing theme was to hypothesize that commodities serving consumption are attached to distinct, integral 'systems of provision' – structurally integrated along the chain of activities from production to consumption itself, as in the clothing, energy and food systems (see for example Fine, 2002).[9] As a result, close attention was paid to the material (and social) relations surrounding the provisioning of different foods as we move along the food chain, thereby differentiating the sugar from the dairy system for example. This did, however, lead me to be acutely sensitive to the limited extent to which EA had in theoretical principle, if less guilty in empirical practice, addressed the specificity of food and of food systems as the latter vary by crop, time and place. And this lack of food-specificity in relation to provisioning has its counterpart in failing to address the meanings and cultures that are attached to foods as they are moved from field to plate.

In a nutshell, given its transparent conceptual and technical origins in the mainstream microeconomics of feasibility sets, EA is profoundly neutral with respect both to underlying social relations and historical specificity (except in defining endowments and their potential transformation into outcomes) and to the specificity of food itself in both material and cultural terms. Polemically, the scarcities associated with famine and entitlements look very different from a perspective that highlights the presence of global food systems that feed their cattle better than their humans, and the incidence of eating disorders, from obesity to anorexia, that are attaining epidemic proportions in the north (see Chapter 10, this volume, for contradictions in food policies and their impacts in the north).

These perspectives informed my assessment of EA. I suggested an unresolved tension in Sen's own work – between the micro-foundations of the entitlement analytics and the broader recognition of famine as irreducibly macro or systemic, not least because famine is more than the sum of its individual parts – not merely personal starvation for the many. Is famine the choice to starve by self or other on your behalf, a replicated but rational response to market imperfections? Sen commendably refrains from attaching the EA to the new micro-foundations despite his micro-analytics (and emphasis on the informational role to be played by a free press). Nor have I come across any sympathy for such an approach in his work, hardly surprising in view of his uncompromising stance on the limitations of the notion of 'rationality' as deployed by economists, (Sen, 1977).

Further, when he addresses the macro, it is from a perspective independent of the micro – as in the role of the free press and democracy in guarding against famine, although classes are at times perceived to have entitlements. Further, I argued that the same micro-macro tension is to be found in the EA debate. Those adopting a critical stance towards EA have not so much been engaging with it as an alternative to FAD as questioning whether their macro-interpretations of famine had been or could be accommodated within EA – issues of the nature of property, violence, culture and custom, all heavy with analytical content for the meaning of scarcity that departs from that attached to mainstream economics. All of this leaves the EA in an ambiguous relationship with scarcity – micro-choice from entitlements, on the one hand, but a critical stance to FAD, on the other.

This is an appropriate point to move on to well-being, capabilities, development and freedom, with Sen (1985) as a stepping stone. This constitutes more than a generalization and concretization of what has come before, as in the shift from inequality to famine. For, in the light of economics imperialism, there are other tensions than those attached to micro-macro. The marginalist revolution is recognized to have taken the social out of economics in two senses. It represented a shift to methodological individualism *and* the construction of the non-market as separate from the market. Information-theoretic economics claims to bring the social back in, on its own terms: through optimization subject to informational constraints. Similarly, the path followed by mainstream economics initially separates out material and cultural analyses and sets the latter aside. Yet, once again in its own inimitable style, the current phase of economics imperialism is reintroducing the cultural (trust, customs, norms, etc.) as an informational calculus.

Although Sen's work too has increasingly embraced the social and the cultural, once again, there is no evidence that he has been seduced by the unsubtle charms of economics imperialism. Indeed, if anything, there is a shift, at least discursively, away from the micro-analytic technicalities of EA. The practice was established in the context of famine and can, subsequently, float freely to serve intermediate or macro levels of analysis across capabilities more generally. In short, Sen sees a 'deep complementarity between individual freedom and social arrangements' (1999a, pxii). As in EA debate, commentators have questioned whether the macro, the social and the cultural have been or can be appropriately addressed on the basis of Sen's approach. Cameron and Gasper (2000), for example, edit a collection that explicitly assesses Sen's work in order to extend it.

Gasper, under the rubric of freedoms, achievements and meanings, says that 'whether to have more options is valuable depends on the meaning the options have for the actor and her audience', (p999). Giri (2000) is concerned with well-being as involving mental self-development and personal transformation towards sharing with others, Cameron (2000) with Sen's neglect of opulence or upper end of capabilities, and Carmen (2000) with 'capacitation'.

These all sit uncomfortably within an individualistic and formalistic methodology. The social and contextual are imperative. But, by extension of the earlier argument around the specificity of food (and other basic needs), it is essential to attach public as well as private contributions to capabilities to specific systems of provision (Fine, 2002). It is necessary to ask not only 'how are each of health, education, housing and welfare differentially created, distributed and used' but also how these are interactive with, and constitutive of, corresponding cultures, ideologies and political practices, each with their own construction of scarcity.

Whether for food or other capabilities, Sen's analysis does not appear to engage sufficiently with these issues to the extent that it remains formalistic/ individualistic. In arguing, controversially, that famine (dire under-provision for the many) is liable to be avoided by the presence of a free press and democracy, what exactly is the analytical content of such an observation? Is it specific to food, or does the same apply to housing and education (and excessive mortality of female children)? What are the mechanisms through which the free press and democracy work (or not)? Are they the same or different across different capabilities, entitlements and freedoms? My presumption is that they are different both for the nature, forms, levels and incidence of provision and their mode of functioning. By the same token, the nature and consequences of the mode of provision are diverse according to what is provided, by and for whom, and how. And the same applies to the nature and meaning of scarcity which, like the Cheshire cat's grin, has now simply disappeared as if it were never there. This is only more obvious for Sen than for mainstream economists because he appears to have no lingering attachment to the rational individual and general equilibrium as organizing concepts.

Concluding remarks

Many social scientists (see Chapter 6, this volume) and even economists (see Chapter 5, this volume) have reasonably been entirely dismissive of the notion of scarcity deployed by mainstream economics because of its limited conceptual and analytical content. But, as demonstrated here, that notion of scarcity is itself undermined once any attempt is made by economists themselves to move beyond, or away from, the rarefied assumptions required for their concept of scarcity to enjoy any legitimacy. It is, thus, hardly surprising that we hear very little about scarcity from economists except as the universal constraint that legitimizes the very technical apparatus that ultimately undermines it.

So, it is the technical apparatus that has priority, not the notion of scarcity, as has been illustrated by the cursory overview of Sen's work where scarcity is displaced by other concepts such as social choice, entitlements, capabilities and, ultimately, freedom. He has gone so much further than mainstream economists in undermining scarcity as an organizing principle but this is not to imply others have remained attached to it other than in principle. In practice, macroeconomics, market imperfections or whatever, all represent a departure from the notion of scarcity as determining factor. In short, scarcity is essentially an illegitimate legitimizing device for the methodology and technical apparatus of mainstream economics. Neither Cheshire cat nor its grin exists. Even Sen's work, though, has involved a dependence upon, as well as a departure from, the technical and conceptual apparatus of the mainstream.

This all raises two other issues. First, how might we reasonably persuade mainstream economists to think otherwise? I do not have the answer although I can observe that a critique of the notion of scarcity is not liable to be a powerful lever of influence since it is the technical apparatus that is sacrosanct, not scarcity as such. And economics has got itself into a position where that technical apparatus takes precedence over everything else – method, realism, critique and, it should be added, debate. For the technical apparatus of the mainstream has become sacrosanct within the discipline with neither tolerance nor capacity for dissent. Probably, the best strategy is to outflank economics as a discipline by offering an alternative political economy from within other disciplines.

Second, then, leaving economists to their own devices, how might scarcity itself be reasonably addressed by way of alternative? Of course, the putative material analysis offered by the mainstream by way of scarcity as constraint is sorely inadequate both in itself and as a starting point. But it is not a reason for abandoning material analysis in the understanding of scarcity altogether. There is a need for an alternative material analysis of who gets access to what, when and how. This is liable to be socially, historically and product-specific as the contributors in Part III of this volume argue (food is scarce in a very different way from oil and at different times and places). Not to accept this is almost certain to lead to universal notions of scarcity as characteristic of the human condition, as with Robbins and something, I suspect, uniquely characteristic of the ideology of a capitalist society.

This does not mean, however, that general analysis is entirely inappropriate. Indeed, a study of scarcity must surely take the political economy of capitalism as its starting point, and how this drives material provision in production, distribution and exchange. However, such an analysis in itself is not comprehensive because many forms of provision are not exclusively dependent upon production of commodities for profit, from non-capitalist production of all types through to welfare provision, the family, etc. These may, however, be subject to some form of commodification and/or attachment to the cash nexus. Capitalist commodity production acts as a standard against which these can be compared, often has a direct or indirect influence, and raises the issue of why there is a failure of capitalist penetration as a means of pinpointing alternative forms of provision.

Thus, taking capitalist commodity production as a starting point is not to reduce all notions of scarcity to its dull logic (or logics), even if not the one involving competing ends. For capital creates and coexists with non-capitalist forms in which material provision and corresponding notions of scarcity prevail. And, even where capitalist commodity production is involved, as previously indicated, there is wide variation in how provision takes place from commodity to commodity, and across time and place, with correspondingly differently constructed notions of scarcity. Environmental is different from human 'capital', and all the other plethora of 'capitals', as the term is attached to anything that vaguely connotes a resource. Such capitals are presumed to be scarce by extrapolation from Robbins, precluding the need either to develop a proper notion of capital or to specify the relations to which such capitals are differentially attached. Can sex tourism or violation be appropriately understood in terms of scarcity?[10] What is the scarcity attached to the anorexic? Like other authors in this volume, let me turn to the so-called water and diamond paradox. At a more mundane level, diamonds (dependent upon the longest-standing international cartel, de Beers) are different from water (newly privatized/commercialized). Consequently, how diamonds and water are made and perceived to be scarce differ, both across these commodities and, in turn, for each of them individually across socio-economic strata, especially for business as opposed to personal consumption.

Further, provision of a specifically attuned material analysis of scarcity will inevitably depend upon, and yield, close attention to the way in which the meaning of scarcity itself has been generated, deployed and transformed, a position taken by many authors in this volume. As I have argued in the context of consumer culture more generally, the notion of scarcity is liable to be product-specific, and in a symbiotic relationship to the way in which provision is made, from production through to consumption (and disposal). As such, notions of scarcity are liable to be attached to a system of beliefs, some general and some specific, but also subject to what I have ultimately dubbed the six Cs (although others could be added) (Fine, 2002; Fine, 2005). Thus, notions of scarcity will be contextual (time, place and product), construed (reflected upon and not simply received), chaotic (combining different beliefs from different sources, not necessarily coherently), constructed (in some correspondence to the material circumstances attached to provision), contradictory (tensions within material provision itself will be reflected in beliefs about it) and conflictual (or contested; one person's scarcity is another person's waste).

Notes

1 Personal commitments did not allow me to attend the 2005 workshop but I did draft a paper that was made available. This revised version benefits from having consulted the other chapters and various reports of proceedings, and from editorial suggestions. The discussion of Sen depends heavily upon purloining from Fine (2004). For a fuller account of the arguments over the history of economic thought, see Milonakis and Fine (2009) and Fine and Milonakis (2009).

2 Jevons, Walras and Menger are the three main founders of the marginalist revolution, but they differed from one another, see Chapter 6, this volume, for further discussion.

3 The author here is John Neville Keynes, father to John Maynard.

4 Essentially, an ingenious generalization of the voting paradox in which, across three voters and three candidates, each candidate has a majority over one of the others so none is victorious.

5 Atkinson (1970) uses a parameter ε to measure inequality aversion, essentially scaling incomes by the exponent, ε, before adding them together for utility sum across individuals. But to gain a measure of inequality, it is necessary to make interpersonal comparisons as well. Atkinson implicitly does this by treating all individuals equally, subject to transformed incomes, then adding these together for his measure. In contrast, I allow for weighted interpersonal aggregation, demonstrating that the less you rank more income for an individual, the more you favour the poor against the rich in interpersonal comparisons and vice versa (Fine, 1985).

6 See also Fine, 1975.

7 See Fine et al, 1996 and Fine, 1998.

8 See also Fine, 2005.

9 For a discussion of these issues, and the false opposition, for example, between commodity and gift, see Fine, 2002 and Lapavitsas, 2003.

10 See Radin (1996) for the idea that the treatment of sexual crime as an economic crime tends to make it (perceived to be) so.

References

Akerlof, G. (1990) 'George A. Akerlof', in R. Swedberg (ed) (1990) *Economics and Sociology, Redefining Their Boundaries: Conversations with Economists and Sociologists*, Princeton University Press, Princeton, NJ

Arrow, K. (1951) *Social Choice and Individual Values*, Wiley, New York

Atkinson, A. (1970) 'On the measurement of inequality', *Journal of Economic Theory*, vol 2, no 3, pp244–263

Cameron, J. (2000) 'Amartya Sen on economic inequality: The need for an explicit critique of opulence', *Journal of International Development*, vol 12, no 7, pp1031–1045

Cameron, J. and Gasper, D. (eds) (2000) 'Amartya Sen on inequality, human well-being, and development as freedom', *Journal of International Development*, vol 12, no 7

Carmen, R. (2000) 'Prima mangiare, poi filosofare', *Journal of International Development*, vol 12, no 7, pp1019–1030

Fine, B. (1975) 'Individual liberalism in a Paretian society', *Journal of Political Economy*, vol 83, no 6, pp82–96

Fine, B. (1985) 'A note on the measurement of inequality and interpersonal comparison', *Social Choice and Welfare*, vol 1, no 4, pp273–275

Fine, B. (1996) 'Reconciling interpersonal comparability and the intensity of preference for the utility sum rule', *Social Choice and Welfare*, vol 13, no 3, pp19–25

Fine, B. (1997) 'Entitlement failure?', *Development and Change*, vol 28, no 4, pp617–647

Fine, B. (1998) *The Political Economy of Diet, Health and Food Policy*, Routledge, London

Fine, B. (2002) *The World of Consumption: The Material and Cultural Revisited*, Routledge, London

Fine, B. (2004) 'Economics and ethics: Amartya Sen as point of departure', *The New School Economic Review*, vol 1, no 1, pp151–162, available at https://eprints.soas.ac.uk/6606/ (last accessed 7 September 2010)

Fine, B. (2005) 'Addressing the consumer', in F. Trentmann (ed) *The Making of the Consumer: Knowledge, Power and Identity in the Modern World*, Berg, Oxford

Fine, B. and Milonakis, D. (2009) *From Economics Imperialism to Freakonomics: The Shifting Boundaries Between Economics and Other Social Sciences*, Routledge, London

Fine, B., Heasman, M. and Wright, J. (1996) *Consumption in the Age of Affluence: The World of Food*, Routledge, London

Gasper, D. (2000) 'Development as freedom: Taking economics beyond commodities – the cautious boldness of Amartya Sen', *Journal of International Development*, vol 12, no 7, pp989–1001

Giri, A.K. (2000) 'Rethinking human well-being: A dialogue with Amartya Sen', *Journal of International Development*, vol 12, no 7, pp1003–1018

Hutchison, T. (2000) *On the Methodology of Economics and the Formalist Revolution*, Edward Elgar, Cheltenham

Keynes, J.N. (1997[1890]) *The Scope and Method of Political Economy*, 4th edition, Routledge/Thoemmes Press, London

Lapavitsas, C. (2003) *Social Foundations of Markets, Money and Credit*, Routledge, London

Marshall, A. (1959[1890]) *Principles of Economics: An Introductory Volume*, 8th edition, MacMillan, London

Milonakis, D. and Fine, B. (2009) *From Political Economy to Economics: Method, the Social and the Historical in the Evolution of Economic Theory*, Routledge, London

Radin, M. (1996) *Contested Commodities*, Harvard University Press, Cambridge

Robbins, L. (1935) *An Essay on the Nature and Significance of Economic Science*, Macmillan, London

Robbins, L. (1971) *Autobiography of an Economist*, Macmillan, London

Sen, A. (1970a) *Collective Choice and Social Welfare*, Holden-Day, San Francisco

Sen, A. (1970b) 'The impossibility of a Paretian liberal', *Journal of Political Economy*, Vol LXXVIII, no 1, pp152–157

Sen, A. (1973) *On Economic Inequality*, Oxford University Press, Oxford.

Sen, A. (1977) 'Rational fools: A critique of the behavioral foundations of economic theory', *Philosophy and Public Affairs*, vol 6, no 4, pp317–344

Sen, A. (1985) *Commodities and Capabilities*, North-Holland, Amsterdam

Sen, A. (1995) 'Rationality and social choice', *American Economic Review*, vol 85, no 1, pp1–24

Sen, A. (1999a) *Development as Freedom*, Oxford University Press, Oxford

Sen, A. (1999b) 'The possibility of social choice', *American Economic Review*, vol 89, no 3, pp349–378

Stiglitz, J. (1994) *Whither Socialism?*, MIT Press, Cambridge

Stiglitz, J. (2000) *Economics of the Public Sector*, 3rd edition, Norton & Company, New York

Swedberg, R. (ed) (1990) *Economics and Sociology, Redefining Their Boundaries: Conversations with Economists and Sociologists*, Princeton University Press, Princeton, NJ

Trentmann, F. (ed) (2005) *The Making of the Consumer: Knowledge, Power and Identity in the Modern World*, Berg, Oxford

5
Deconstructing Economic Interpretations of Sustainable Development: Limits, Scarcity and Abundance

Fred Luks

The meta-economics of sustainable development

Needs and limits are the cornerstones of sustainable development. Sustainable development is, according to the famous definition by the Brundtland Commission, 'development that meets the needs of the present without compromising the ability of future generations to meet their own needs' (WCED, 1987). Development is supposedly sustainable if it fulfils the requirements of intra- and intergenerational justice. This definition is probably one of the most quoted sentences on sustainable development. In order to understand the goal of sustainable development, particularly in relation to scarcity, it is important to also take into account the words that follow the definition. Sustainable development, we read, contains within it two key concepts: needs and limitations. In other words, sustainable development is about ends (in other words, meeting the needs of people living today and future generations) and limited means (namely, the environment, technology, institutions). In economic terms: sustainable development is about scarcity.

Sustainable development as a societal goal has been accepted by virtually every actor and institution. This was possible only because the term is open to very diverse interpretations. One important task for social science, then, is the analysis of the different interpretations that circulate in the discourse of sustainable development, the majority of which share an economic focus. Different interpretations of sustainable development are shaped by different understandings of terms like development, sustainability, growth, innovation –

and scarcity. Economics is involved even when it is not explicitly mentioned or considered because there is an 'economic construction of ecological reality' which is intimately linked to different notions of scarcity (Luks, 2000, p83ff; see also Luks, 2005a, 2005b and 2010; Höhler and Luks, 2004).

As discussed by several authors in this volume, the most famous definition of economics was provided by Lionel Robbins (1984 [1932], p16) in his *Essay on the Nature and Significance of Economics* in 1932: 'Economics is the science which studies human behaviour as a relationship between ends and scarce means which have alternative uses' (see also Chapter 4, this volume, for a further discussion of Robbins). Scarcity is to economics what the universe is to astrophysics, the human brain to brain science and society to sociology. The tension between means and ends, according to this world view, is a fundamental characteristic of the world. Scarcity is 'out there', simply because human beings always want more than there is, and economics is the scientific tool to deal with this fundamental problem of our existence. Very obviously, in a world without scarcity, there would be no such thing as economics.

Some would argue that this view of the relationship between economics and scarcity is too narrow. However, a look at mainstream economics textbooks such as Samuelson and Nordhaus (2005) shows that the picture that economics draws of itself is clearly dominated by scarcity as *the* 'economic problem' and efficiency as *the* economic way to deal with the world. Thus, Robbins' definition might not be shared by everybody, but nevertheless his *Essay* can (quite independently of what Robbins himself thought about it later on) still be read as a kind of constitutional text for the identity of economics as a science, since it has (successfully) defined scarcity as the ultimate subject matter of economics (Robbins, 1984). And resource efficiency (besides economic growth) is one of the overarching normative goals of economics as a science. As for the problem of unemployed resources, so important in macroeconomics, this unemployment can, from the viewpoint of economic science, be clearly interpreted as an inefficient waste that has to be eliminated in a world fundamentally shaped by scarcity.

Viewing the world as a place in which scarcity has become 'self-evident' in modernity (Xenos, 1989) is, in my opinion, also a product of economics. The economic discourse, with its focus on scarcity, has had an influence on how we think, speak and argue about nature, the environment, resources and sustainability. It has had a profound impact *beyond* economics. Even when 'non-economic' issues are debated, economics is with us and scarcity is all-pervasive. How nature is conceptualized in different economic perspectives is a case in point, which is something I turn to shortly. As an economist I have been long interested in how nature, limits to resources availability and sustainable development have been viewed by both the mainstream and by alternative paradigms within economics such as ecological economics. I demonstrate in this chapter that, while ecological economics provides some important critiques of the mainstream views of unfettered and optimistic growth, both mainstream economics and alternative approaches such as ecological economics tend to naturalize what they mean by scarcity. Due to its very important concern with sustainability and resource depletion, ecological economics is also premised on a notion of 'absolute scarcity' which does not adequately problematize the social and political context of limits and scarcity. Thus alternatives need to be found in the newly emerging 'discursive' and postmodern trend in economics, a re-reading of classical texts within economics and also in fanciful engagements with important heterodox debates concerned with happiness, waste and squander.

A matter of discourse

There are problems, but they are not merely 'out there'. To discuss something as a problem is already a social construction. This is why many approaches emphasize the role of language and construction, for example discursive, deconstructivist and rhetorical approaches – 'Rhetoric of inquiry is needed precisely because facts themselves are mute. Whatever the facts, *we* do the speaking – whether through them or for them' (Nelson et al, 1987, p8 [their emphasis]). Economics as a discipline had a very late 'linguistic turn' and the recognition that language matters has come later than in other disciplines. This was and still is a heterodox phenomenon many economists do not care about. But they should. Apart from some early scattered contributions like the one by Tribe (1978), the main line of economic thinking influenced by constructivism is the one initiated by McCloskey (1985; 1990; 1994) which can today be seen as part of emerging 'postmodern economics' (see Cullenberg et al, 2001; Ruccio and Amariglio, 2003). The rhetorical or discursive approaches in economics can be seen as part of a larger postmodern or (which is not the same) post-normal approach in the social sciences. I have argued elsewhere that the aforementioned approaches can be fruitfully applied to the investigation of scarcity and limits (Luks, 1998; Luks, 2005b; Höhler and Luks, 2004).

I distinguish between two forms of economic rhetoric, both relevant for this construction and for the role of scarcity: 'internal' rhetoric relates to the intra-scientific discourses; 'external' rhetoric refers to the use and abuse of economic concepts in societal discourses (Luks, 1998 and 1999). I use the term 'economic construction of ecological reality', first, for the 'internal rhetoric' of the representation of nature within economic theory. Second, there is an 'external' economic construction of ecological reality that relates to the fact that the discourse on sustainable development within society is shaped by economic terms, concepts and metaphors. The idea of scarcity is the centre of all economic thinking. Consequently, nature, in economic theory, is presented as a scarce resource that has to be used efficiently. To use the term coined by Schumpeter (1967 [1954]), the pre-analytical vision of economics is fundamentally shaped by viewing the world in terms of scarcity.

A constructivist perspective is of obvious importance for a discussion of finiteness, limits and scarcity. Nobody – not even hardcore mainstream economists – would deny that planet Earth is limited. The relevant question is how the nature, relevance and consequences of this fact are conceptualized and communicated. Thus it is important to provide a critique of concepts of limits, finiteness and scarcity. According to Michel Foucault (1992), a critique is not about saying that things are not right as they are, it is about pointing out on what kinds of assumptions, ideas and unchallenged modes of thought socially accepted practices rest. Critique, in this sense, means questioning concepts and categories that are generally taken for granted. I believe that this has to be applied to economics and the concept of 'scarcity' if social science wants to contribute meaningful ideas to 'sustainability'. As emphasized throughout the contributions to this volume, the fact that there is nothing 'natural' about scarcity and that there are different conceptions of scarcity is not only theoretically interesting but also relevant for political processes.

These processes are often shaped by the use of certain terms, arguments and metaphors which are frequently 'imported' from the scientific discourse. The following quotation from John Maynard Keynes' *General Theory* is the classic statement concerning the relationship between economics and politics:

> *The ideas of economists and political philosophers, both when they are right and when they are wrong, are more powerful than is commonly understood. Indeed the world is ruled by little else. Practical men, who believe themselves to be quite exempt from any intellectual influence, are usually the slaves of some defunct economist.* (Keynes, 1973 [1936], p383)

Looking at the discourse on sustainable development, one can see the validity of this perspective. Mainstream talk of sustainable development is linked with discussions of economic growth, environmental 'accounting' and the 'efficiency revolution'. These are but a few examples of the importance of economic thinking. Therefore, it is worthwhile to consider the world view that economics contributes to sustainable development and to ask what role the concept of scarcity plays in this context.

Following Hajer's (1995, p44) definition, a discourse can be described as 'a specific ensemble of ideas, concepts, and categorizations that are produced, reproduced, and transformed in a particular set of practices and through which meaning is given to physical and social realities'. Thus, our ways of understanding nature, the economy or political processes are always historically, culturally and socially specific and by no means 'natural'; something which is emphasized by many of the authors in this volume. Acknowledging this constructedness of facts leads to a focus on how problems and possible solutions are conceptualized.

This constructivist perspective, obviously, does not imply that there is no 'real' environmental change. I do not, of course, believe that climate change stops as soon as we stop talking about it. I agree with Rees and Wackernagel (1994, p387) that 'whatever one's ideological persuasion, there is a biophysical reality "out there" that is totally indifferent to human habit or preferences, important dimensions of which will always remain inaccessible to understanding'. Still, what has to be recognized is that we, as a society, funda-mentally depend on language and discourses:

> *A realist approach assumes incorrectly that the natural environ-ment that is discussed in environmental politics is equivalent to the environment 'out there'. This assumption fails to recognize that we always act upon our images of reality and are dependent on certain discourses to be able to express ourselves.* (Hajer, 1995, p16)

This is of highest relevance for the understanding of the contribution of economics to the issue of scarcity.

Ends, means, limits and the construction of scarcity

Long before neoclassical economics took over, economics was called the 'dismal science' by Carlyle. Even before economics as a systematic scien-tific discourse existed, Thomas Hobbes conceptualized scarcity as a central feature of society. Classical economists are usually seen as 'pessimists', especially because of their view concerning the relationship between popu-lation growth and the ability to produce food. However, while scarcity was surely at the centre of classical contributions to political economy, Smith, Malthus, Mill, Ricardo and others were very much concerned with long-term prospects for economic growth. With the famous and notable exception of John Stuart Mill, the classical economists were sure that the stationary state was the foreseeable and definite endpoint of capitalism and that this was a dull prospect.

With the rise of neoclassical economics in the 1870s, the analytical focus shifted from long-term macroeconomic considerations to microeconomic questions of allocation. Nature, so important to the writings of political economy up until then, virtually disappeared from economic literature. As late as 1865, Stanley Jevons wrote a very pessimistic book about the 'coal ques-tion'. When nature returned to economics with what we today call 'environ-mental economics', it was conveniently integrated into the mainstream vision of the analysis of allocation. Environmental problems came to be viewed as allocation problems, more specifically as market failure. Environmental prob-lems are there because markets 'fail': economic agents do not integrate the social costs into their calculations and therefore 'external effects' occur. It is important that this view, of course, implies that nature can be 'measured' in economic terms, in other words, in Euros or dollars.

One could say that mainstream economics starts with a pessimistic vision of scarcity but is, in the final analysis, optimistic because it claims that markets, technological innovation and substitution processes will help us out of the problems generated by scarcity. The fear of a 'stationary state', so present in classical political economy, is gone. Once we manage to inter-nalize external effects, the market processes will nicely signal the scarcity of different resources, substitution processes will occur, technology will help us to become sustainable. It is assumed that if there are problems, they will be solved through technological or other 'fixes'.

Ecological economics, an alternative paradigm that arose in the context of the sustainability discourse, criticizes this mainstream view as too optimistic. Mainstream economics is, in the words of Georgescu-Roegen (1986, p11), analysing 'superficial scarcity'. Many ecological economists share this view and agree with Ehrlich's (1989, p13) statement that we face 'meta-resource depletion' and therefore are confronted with 'absolute scarcity'. In a way, ecological economics criticizes mainstream economics by radicalizing its central assumption. Beyond the changing relationship between ends and means, and market processes and technological innovations notwithstanding, we face absolute scarcity that is identical with the biophysical limits to growth. It is no surprise that many ecological economists see themselves following a classical tradition. Like Malthus, ecological economics is pessimistic with respect to long-term growth; like John Stuart Mill, it is optimistic about the possibility for societal progress in a stationary or steady state.

As for the two aforementioned paradigms, what can a constructivist perspective teach us? Blühdorn (2000, p10) points out that:

> *a deeper understanding of the ecological problem cannot be achieved by double-checking, for example, whether or not oil spills really kill sea-birds, or whether civilisatory progress really diminishes biodiversity. The important question is rather for what reasons and to what extent such empirically measurable phenomena and developments can be conceptualised as problems and crises.*

Such crises, according to Blühdorn (2000, p14), 'are never empirically measurable phenomena occurring in the material world, but subjective conditions which are related to individual and social patterns of perception and consciousness'. With some adjustments, the same holds true for scarcity. Limits might be there, but the socially and politically relevant question is their conceptualization as scarcity. Luhmann (1994, p177), defines scarcity as the 'social perception of restrictions ... that can lead to social regulations' (my translation). In other words, scarcity presupposes the acknowledgement of finiteness as restrictions that include the necessity of choices (see also Chapter 6, this volume, for a discussion of finiteness). It is, Luhmann emphasizes, *not* self-evident that limits are perceived as scarcity (1994, p177ff). 'The fact', as Luhmann's example goes, 'that oil is only available in limited amounts, does not by itself make it scarce' (1994, p178) (my translation).

Is this an adequate understanding of the social construction and the function of scarcity? I think it is. As Blühdorn (2000, p49) puts it, 'Social constructions are the most real and most objective reality we have got, and nothing more real or more objective is accessible to us'. In other words, we don't really have a choice between dealing with the world out there and our social constructions. As for the frequent warnings not to fall into the 'constructivist trap' when applying 'postmodern' ideas to problems concerning the environment, it is helpful to distinguish between 'empirically measurable environmental *change* and the social perception of environmental *problems*' (Blühdorn, 2000, p41 [his emphases]; see also Mehta, 2005). Blühdorn (2000) states that this distinction is 'thoroughly comparable' with the distinction between sex and gender. The point is that there are biophysical and social facts that are not identical with the social perception, construction and communication of these facts. There are undeniable facts 'out there', but social dealing with these facts is a completely different issue. Applied to the issue at hand this means, yes, the world *is* limited, resources *are* used, we *can* measure environmental change – but when we talk about scarcity, we do not talk about these developments out there but refer to something that is fundamentally socially constructed. This holds true for *both* varieties of economic conceptions of scarcity.

It is an important contribution of ecological economics to move beyond the vision of mainstream economics by insisting on the relevance of limitedness. By providing an alternative economic construction of ecological reality, it has already had a productive function in the sustainability discourse. Ecological economics has put problems beyond relative scarcity and strategies beyond market orientation on the agenda. Far from being critical of the vision of general scarcity, it has nevertheless contributed to the deconstruction of the mainstream worldview of scarcity. *However*, this alternative approach itself calls for a deconstruction. In a way, the constructivist critique is harder to swallow for ecological economists than it is for mainstream economists. The reason is that many ecological economists are convinced that their approach to sustainability problems is more realistic than the dominating vision of the mainstream. From a constructivist position, this is not a valid claim. Finiteness, limits and 'absolute scarcity' are just as much social constructions as markets, prices and 'relative scarcity'. Neither the frequent recourse to entropy as the ultimate arbiter of scarcity (Daly, 1996, p29ff; Georgescu-Roegen, 1986) nor the insistence on the practical relevance of ecological limits (Ehrlich, 1989; Rees, 2006) is more than a social construction. Ecological economics can thus not claim that its analyses are in any way 'closer to the real world' – they aren't.

Markets, scarcity and growth. And scarcity. And growth. And scarcity. And ...

While mainstream and ecological economics have different versions of scarcity, both are based on the conviction that scarcity 'is there' and that it matters. While neither can claim to be more 'realistic' than the other, it is clear that both visions have different policy implications. This is particularly true for the different status that markets and growth have in mainstream and ecological-economic approaches. While mainstream economics prescribes internalization strategies that try to include environmental costs in the calculations of economic actors, ecological economics tries to contribute to macro policies that take seriously the limitedness of the world in which socio-economic development takes place. This includes erecting 'ecological guardrails' and *limiting* the scope of the market. Both the mainstream prescriptions of market correction (such as Pigouvian taxes) and market expansion (namely, the Coasian solutions of assigning property) attempt to enable markets to internalize external costs, or, in other words, to reflect scarcity more 'realistically'. Ecological economics, on the other hand, questions that the scarcities relevant for long-term sustainability can be reflected in markets. It insists that before the market does its work, the realm of the market has to be determined by political decisions.

From an ecological economic perspective, successful sustainability policies presuppose alternative problem constructions that provide meaningful information needed for policies that try to contribute to sustainable development in a finite world. While, at least theoretically, relative scarcities can be indicated by prices, in other words monetary indicators, the vision of 'absolute' scarcity implies the need for biophysical indicators based on concepts such as environmental space, societal metabolism or ecological footprint. However, based on the aforementioned constructivist arguments already provided, it seems naïve to suggest that physical indicators would bring us any closer to a clear and clean understanding of limits – these indicators are no less social constructions than other ways of expressing scarcity. *But*, and this has to be emphasized, physically based indicators are certainly more capable of 'constructing' and communicating biophysical limits than monetary indicators which, by definition, are measures of relative scarcity. Biophysically oriented calculations such as the ecological footprint provide a different picture of the interaction between economy and ecology and 'suggest the necessity of rethinking many of the assumptions about modernization and the economic measures of performance used to discuss public policy' (Dalby, 2002, p110). Ecological economics, then, also provides a critique of economic growth by analysing its relation to concepts such as development and progress and by problematizing its political function. Furthermore, by pointing out that on the grounds of simple economic logic, the possibility of uneconomic growth has to be considered. This is because further economic expansion may create more problems such as pressure on the environment that will undermine the quality of life (see, for example, Daly, 1996). This critique seems necessary in a socio-economic environment in which growth remains a central goal of economic policy and in which the idea of finiteness with respect to the environment is, to say the least, not very powerful.

It is safe to assume that the more 'absolute' the interpretation of scarcity, the more sceptical the attitude toward economic growth. Indeed, this distinction holds true from classical political economy and neoclassical economics (Jevons being an ambiguous case) to ecological economics. Barnett and Morse (1963) (who, interestingly enough, used the classical contributions by Malthus and Ricardo to distinguish different forms of scarcity) have set the tone that dominates mainstream contributions on scarcity to this date. This tone is optimistic, and the song repeatedly sung is about the compatibility of resource limits (the existence of which no neoclassical economist denies), continued economic growth and sustainable development. Again: the message is that market, innovation and substitution will prevent economic expansion from running against environmental limits. Ecological economics insists on the need for the rich countries to reduce their ecological impact on the global environment in order to leave space for development and growth for developing regions. 'It is ... time that the wealthy contemplate consuming less in order to *free up ecological space for the poor*' (Rees, 2006, p224 [emphasis added]).

Most ecological economists would not deny problems of 'underdevelopment' but would add that on a global scale, 'overdevelopment' – in other words a consumption level beyond carrying capacity – is just as serious. Ecological economics is, due to its emphasis on ecological limits, critical of economic expansion. While mainstream economics basically treats growth as something 'natural' and 'normal', ecological economists do not only question the possibility of further growth, but also point to the fact that, historically, growth is a quite exceptional phenomenon.

In his analysis of *Scarcity and Modernity*, Xenos (1989) shows how intimately ideas of growth, progress, scarcity and abundance are linked. Abundance can be seen as the other side of scarcity and is part of many ideas of progress. This includes sustainable development, for this concept promises a better world for everybody in which needs are met. The promise of abundance, however, is a false one (Xenos, 1989, p35ff). Many writers have described the link between higher output and expanding wants. Gerschlager (1996, p48), for example, observes a process of the permanent creation of needs. As long as the positive feedback loop between desire and production is not broken, every need satisfied leads to a new need. The productive removal of a need is at the same time the productive creation of scarcity. Xenos (1989, p70) emphasizes how much this is engrained in neoclassical theory:

> *Individuals decide that they have had enough of one thing only at the same moment as they decide that they want something else even more. Desire – restless, perpetually unfulfilled – underlies the marginalist notion of need.*

There is, in other words, a rat race between the fight against scarcity and the constant creation of new needs and desires. Against this backdrop, it comes as no surprise that there is a paradox concerning the relationship between income and happiness. In many industrialized countries, there is a decoupling between economic output and the quality of life. Happiness research has closely investigated this riddle (for an overview, see Easterlin, 2002; Frey and Stutzer, 2002). Two of the crucial and scarcity-related factors that have been identified are the so-called 'hedonic treadmills' and the relevance of positional goods. Hedonic treadmills (Brickman and Campbell, 1971, p299ff) occur when people sometimes very quickly adapt to new levels of consumption or wealth. Competition for positional goods such as a seat in the front row of the opera, exclusive real estate or an executive post is a zero sum game. Hence, 'individual demand for positional goods seeks the undeliverable' (Hirsch, 1976, p54). Attention and regard are positional goods of particular importance in post-industrial economies (see Franck, 1998; Offer, 2006, Chapters 4 and 10). It is obvious that both hedonic treadmills and positional goods are closely related to the modern version of scarcity. When adaptation creates ever more wishes, and when the supply of certain goods cannot by definition meet the demand, there can be no end to scarcity. The promise of modernity with its emphasis on development, growth, progress and abundance *cannot* be fulfilled.

Deconstructing naturalized economic scarcity

The task, then, is to deconstruct the dominant discourse and illuminate its contingency and to indicate alternatives that problematize the links between scarcity, growth and well-being. Interestingly, mainstream economics, so preoccupied with the relation between means and ends, refuses to consider ends. In the words of Robbins:

> *Economic analysis can simply point out the implications as regards the disposal of means of production of the various patterns of ends which may be chosen ... Economics is neutral as between ends. Economics cannot pronounce on the validity of ultimate judgments of value.* (Robbins, (1984 [1932], p147)

At the same time, mainstream economics simply assumes the infinity of human wants and analyses how scarce means can be used most efficiently. This is by no means a 'neutral' position but just as much a normative topic as the value discussions of ecological economics. The orientation toward market efficiency and the status of the goal of economic growth are normative postulates, not natural things. The same goes for optimality:

> *To privilege optimality is ... to make a straightforwardly normative value judgement that this is in some way the best or most appropriate criterion. This is, of course, a perfectly legitimate thing for economists to do, but in doing so no claims should be made to ethical neutrality. Nor should the economist expect society to regard his or her judgement as having any greater authority than that of anyone else.* (Jacobs, 1994, p76ff)

Normativity is relevant for many issues related to scarcity. It is worth re-emphasizing how intimate the link is between the assumption of general scarcity, the resulting prescription of increasing resource efficiency and the connection of this vision to the goal of economic growth. It has been noted that ecological economics, with its emphasis on limits and 'absolute scarcity', takes a much more critical stance towards economic growth. Many ecological economists emphasize that it is not enough to analyse how means can be used more efficiently. If one sees limits to the strategy of 'efficiency revolutions', the issue of *sufficiency* pops up quite naturally. Such a notion of 'enoughness' includes consideration of the distribution of income and wealth – not only on the national, but also on the global level. Growth has, in most industrialized countries, served to avoid distributional questions. In a finite world with an uneven distribution of resource use and increasing levels of consumption in many regions, this strategy is, according to ecological economic theory, no longer available. Thus, many ecological economists insist on the relevance of questions about the 'good life'. It is quite obvious that there is, then, a link between the study of sustainability and the field of happiness research. This relationship is becoming increasingly acknowledged (see, for example, Binswanger, 2006; Hinterberger, 2005; Luks, 2006) and should be included in the analysis of scarcity and its relevance for sustainable development. Bringing together both fields might be able to identify 'win-win-situations' in which a reduction of resource use can go hand in hand with an increasing quality of life.

To call for a (re)consideration of the 'good life', of luxury and, indeed, of non-efficiency may sound cynical in a world full of war, poverty and hunger. However, we might need these considerations and maybe even some anti-economic thinking to break the discursive chains of a universalized, naturalized and normalized notion of scarcity. Issues such as sufficiency, the good life and happiness shift the attention to subjective factors of wellbeing and economic behaviour. In this context, it has to be considered what the idea of scarcity means on the individual level. The relevance of this reaches far beyond ecological or sustainability issues:

> In the life-world of contemporary individuals the narrow questions to which the ecologist perspective has been reduced, that is absolute resource scarcity, nature-society metabolisms, biodiversity, ecological sustainability and so on are actually not that relevant ... identity issues, that is questions of self-construction and self-experience, take the central place formerly occupied by immediate material needs. Undoubtedly, questions of finiteness and limited resources do come into consideration. But in contemporary society, these issues enter the personal life-world primarily as issues of finite financial resources, and beyond this relative finiteness, absolute ecological limits play a rather subordinate role. (Blühdorn, 2000, p185 [his emphasis])

Blühdorn (2000, p50) argues that 'it is never the material side of a phenomenon of environmental change which triggers environmental concern, but always and exclusively the violation of established cultural norms of naturalness and acceptability'.

All this leads quite directly to a critique of naturalization. Blühdorn (2000, p177), in his *Post-ecologist Politics*, highlights 'the arbitrariness and contingency not just of traditional ecologism, but of all naturalisations in general, including the currently dominant naturalisation of the market principles and the new polarisation of society along the lines of material wealth'. This aim is of the utmost importance to an understanding of economic scarcity for the sustainability discourse and the search for alternatives. I think it is fair to say both conceptions of scarcity slip into different forms of naturalizations (and normalization). Whereas mainstream economics sometimes naturalizes the market, growth and the goal of efficiency, ecological economics clearly and quite obviously naturalizes – nature. In both mainstream and ecological economics, scarcity is naturalized. Constructivist thought challenges this and emphasizes the genuinely political character of such concepts. In sum: scarcity is not something natural, but something that is societal, cultural, political and economic (see also Luks, 2010).

A serious problem in this context is the 'dominance of modern economics as a language through which our thoughts and actions are identified and given meaning' (Zadek, 1993, p8). Thus, for a productive critique of scarcity, we have a desperate need for a consideration of ideas, metaphors, visions and theories that today may seem strange, funny, absurd or even cynical. We have a scarcity of ideas that reach beyond the current notion of scarcity that is in one way or the other linked to economic thinking. But I need to make my position clear. This does not mean that we have to do away with economics because there are many problems which need to be addressed through an economics lens. The point is that we also need something different, maybe something *very* different. When one views debates about ends and means, scarcity, nature, the environment, ecology, growth and happiness, contemporary discourses of sustainable development appear to be seriously stuck. As discussed, with both of the aforementioned paradigms of neoclassical and ecological economics, it is hard to get rid of the concept of scarcity. Both approaches have their merits in dealing with problems conceptualized as scarcity, but when it comes to the search for alternative visions of these problems, economics might not be the best candidate.

'The opposite of scarcity', writes Zadek (1993, p239), 'is not some quantitative, material abundance, but is a liberation from the constraints imposed on our understanding by social, political and other factors'. Zadek's *An Economics of Utopia* (1993) tries to contribute to this liberation and focuses on the concept of non-exploitation, which is presented as a criterion that is supposed to replace resource efficiency. Zadek's concept is based on a contextualization of scarcity and an analysis of the relationship between economic and utopian thinking that emphasizes the contingency of modern economic concepts. With its emphasis on the idea of non-exploitation, this concept is also related to the notion of reciprocity which is in turn linked to gift-giving. Both concepts – reciprocity and gifts – have a reputation for being able to deconstruct or at least question standard economic concepts such as scarcity or market (see, for example, O'Connor, 1999). But we need to take these potentially 'anti-economic' concepts such as gift-giving, generosity and even squander seriously (Luks, 2010). For explicitly anti-economic approaches such as Baudrillard's work on symbolic exchange and Bataille's 'general economy' teach us that inefficiency is not only a concept that works under specific contingent economic assumptions but that inefficiency, squander and waste are an intrinsic part of individual and social life. Bataille's heterology, in the words of Hegarty (2000, p27), 'stands for the way of looking at what is not normally considered, especially in the practices of either philosophy or science, these being matters pertaining to the sacred, horror, excretion, violent sexuality, states of excess'. Bataille is concerned with things beyond utility, and that is surely a field worth cultivating in order to deconstruct scarcity. (Thompson, Chapter 7 this volume, focuses on rubbish theory which also provides reflections on different ways to view utility.)

Apart from the empirical paradox of income growth without improvements in the quality of life, it is also useful to consider another theoretical paradox – the fact that there are 'goods' that increase in being spent. In other, and more radical terms, *some things become less 'scarce' when they are squandered*. If you spend (or share) happiness, love, joy and 'things like that', their 'quantity' is definitely increased, not diminished. This is not some romantic unscientific attempt to get out of the scarcity trap that economics has built, but a serious issue that has to be considered when one is interested in the sustainability of socio-economic development in a finite world. This means going beyond viewing only economic goods and services as scarce. One can surely also consider the scarcity of democracy, happiness, love – all 'things' that have a profound impact on well-being.

If we need to move beyond economic scarcity to tackle sustainability issues, it is certain that another 'resource' will be needed for that endeavour. This resource is fantasy. Scientific sources for inspiration can be found in philosophy, anthropology and sociology. The work of thinkers like George Bataille, Jean Baudrillard, Marcel Mauss, Marshall Sahlins, Georg Simmel and Pierre Bourdieu can certainly contribute to theoretical work that moves beyond scarcity and the narrow criterion of efficiency. It should not be overlooked, however, that there are also alternatives *within* economics. A rereading of economists like John Stuart Mill, Thorstein Veblen, Werner Sombart, John Maynard Keynes, Kenneth Boulding, Robert Heilbroner and others, including several postmodern economists, promises to be a fruitful undertaking in this vein. There are economic and anti-economic ideas that can contribute to creative thinking about what may not be 'the economic problem'. Things could be otherwise. That is what the contingency of scarcity is all about.

Acknowledgements

This chapter is based on my oral contribution to the workshop 'Scarcity and the politics of allocation', Institute of Development Studies, University of Sussex, Brighton, UK, 6–7 June 2005. I thank the participants for open (indeed rough) and inspiring discussions that have clearly led to an improvement of my argument. I am also indebted to Lexi von Hoffmann. Special thanks go to Lyla Mehta. Last but not least, I thank Doris Schnepf. This text draws on research in the context of the interdisciplinary research project NEDS which was funded by the programme 'Socio-Ecological Research' (SÖF) of the German Federal Ministry of Education and Research (BMBF) (#624-40007-07 NGS 11). Of course, I am solely responsible for content, opinion and oddities. This text is dedicated to Stefan H. Siemer.

References

Barnett, H.J. and Morse, C. (1963) *Scarcity and Growth: The Economics of Natural Resource Availability*, Johns Hopkins Press, Baltimore

Binswanger, M. (2006) 'Wachstum, nachhaltige Entwicklung und subjektives Wohlempfinden', *GAIA*, vol 15, no 1, pp69–71

Blühdorn, I. (2000) *Post-ecologist Politics: Social Theory and the Abdication of the Ecologist Paradigm*, Routledge, London/New York

Brickman, P. and Campbell, D.T. (1971) 'Hedonic relativism and planning the good society', in M.H. Appley (ed.) *Adaptation-level Theory*, Academic Press, New York, pp281–305

Cullenberg, S., Amariglio, J. and Ruccio, D.F. (eds) (2001) *Postmodernism, Economics and Knowledge*, Routledge, London/New York

Dalby, S. (2002) *Environmental Security*, University of Minnesota Press, Minneapolis

Daly, H.E. (1996) *Beyond Growth: The Economics of Sustainable Development*, Beacon Press, Boston

Easterlin, R.A. (ed.) (2002) *Happiness in Economics*, Edward Elgar, Cheltenham/Northampton

Ehrlich, P.R. (1989) 'The limits to substitution: Meta-resource depletion and a new economic-ecological paradigm', *Ecological Economics*, vol 1, pp9–16

Foucault, M. (1992) *Was ist Kritik?*, Merve Verlag, Berlin

Franck, G. (1998) *Ökonomie der Aufmerksamkeit: Ein Entwurf*, Carl Hanser Verlag, München/Wien

Frey, B.S. and Stutzer, A. (2002) *Happiness and Economics: How the Economy and Institutions Affect Well-Being*, Princeton University Press, Princeton/Oxford

Georgescu-Roegen, N. (1986) 'The entropy law and the economic process in retrospect', *Eastern Economic Journal*, vol XII, no 1, pp3–25

Gerschlager, C. (1996) *Konturen der Entgrenzung: Die Ökonomie des Neuen im Denken von Thomas Hobbes, Francis Bacon und Joseph Alois Schumpeter*, Metropolis, Marburg

Hajer, M.A. (1995) *The Politics of Environmental Discourse: Ecological Modernization and the Policy Process*, Oxford University Press, Oxford

Hegarty, P. (2000) *Georges Bataille: Core Cultural Theorist*, SAGE Publications, London/Thousand Oaks/New Delhi

Hinterberger, F. (2005) 'Eine neue Zukunft für ein glückliches Europa?', in H. Rauch and A. Strigl (eds) *Die Wende der Titanic: Wiener Deklaration für eine zukunftsfähige Weltordnung*, Oekom, München, pp293–298

Hirsch, F. (1976) *Social Limits to Growth*, Harvard University Press, Cambridge, MA

Höhler, S. and Luks, F. (2004) 'Die ökonomische Konstruktion ökologischer Wirklichkeit. Vorarbeiten, Thesen und Konkretisierungen zum Expertendiskurs der Nachhaltigen Entwicklung', NEDS Working Paper No 5, NEDS, Hamburg

Jacobs, M. (1994) 'The limits to neoclassicism: Towards an institutional environmental economics', in M. Redclift and T. Benton (eds) *Social Theory and the Global Environment*, Routledge, London/New York, pp67–91

Jevons, W.S. (1965 [1865]) *The Coal Question: An Inquiry Concerning the Progress of the Nation, and the Probable Exhaustion of our Coal-mines*, Augustus M. Kelley, New York

Keynes, J.M. (1973 [1936]) *The General Theory of Employment, Interest, and Money: The Collected Writings of John Maynard Keynes, Vol. VII*, Macmillan/St. Martin's Press London/Basingstoke

Luhmann, N. (1994) *Die Wirtschaft der Gesellschaft*, Suhrkamp, Frankfurt am Mein

Luks, F. (1998) 'The rhetorics of ecological economics', *Ecological Economics*, vol 26, no 2, pp139–149

Luks, F. (1999) 'Post-normal science and the rhetoric of inquiry: Deconstructing normal science?', *Futures*, vol 31, pp705–719

Luks, F. (2000) *Postmoderne Umweltpolitik? Sustainable Development, Steady-State und die Entmachtung der Ökonomik*, Metropolis, Marburg

Luks, F. (2005a) 'Innovationen, Wachstum und Nachhaltigkeit: Eine ökologisch-ökonomische Betrachtung', *Jahrbuch Ökologische Ökonomik*, 4: Innovation und Nachhaltigkeit, Metropolis, Marburg, pp41–62

Luks, F. (2005b) 'Ökologische Nachhaltigkeit als Knappheitsproblem: Ein kritischer Blick auf die ökonomische Konstruktion der ökologischen Wirklichkeit', *Natur und Kultur. Transdisziplinäre Zeitschrift für ökologische Nachhaltigkeit*, vol 6, no 1, pp23–42

Luks, F. (2006) 'Das Glück der Nachhaltigkeit und die Nachhaltigkeit des Glücks', *GAIA*, vol 15, no 4, pp250–251

Luks, F. (2010) *Endlich im Endlichen. Warum die Rettung der Welt Ironie und Groß-zügigkeit erfordert*, Metropolis, Marburg

McCloskey, D.N. (1985) *The Rhetoric of Economics*, University of Wisconsin Press, Madison, WI

McCloskey, D.N. (1990) *If You're So Smart: The Narrative of Economic Expertise*, University of Chicago Press, Chicago/London

McCloskey, D.N. (1994) *Knowledge and Persuasion in Economics*, Cambridge University Press, Cambridge

Mehta, L. (2005) *The Politics and Poetics of Water: The Naturalisation of Scarcity in Western India*, Orient Longman, New Delhi

Nelson, J.S., Megill, A. and McCloskey, D.N. (1987) 'Rhetoric of inquiry', in J.S. Nelson, A. Megil and D.N. McCloskey (eds) *The Rhetoric of the Human Sciences: Language and Argument in Scholarship and Public Affairs*, University of Wisconsin Press, Madison, pp3–18

O'Connor, M. (1999) 'Mana, magic and (post-)modernity: Dissenting futures in Aotearoa', *Futures*, vol 31, pp171–190

Offer, A. (2006) *The Challenge of Affluence: Self-Control and Well-Being in the United States and Britain since 1950*, Oxford University Press, Oxford/New York

Rees, W.E. (2006) 'Globalization, trade and migration: Undermining sustainability', *Ecological Economics*, vol 59, pp220–225

Rees, W.E. and Wackernagel, M. (1994) 'Ecological footprints and appropriated carrying capacity: Measuring the natural capital requirements of the human economy', in A. Jansson, M. Hammer, C. Folke and R. Costanza (eds) *Investing in Natural Capital: The Ecological Economics Approach to Sustainability*, Island Press, Washington, DC/Covelo, pp362–390

Robbins, L. (1984 [1932]) *An Essay on the Nature and Significance of Economic Science*, 3rd edition, Macmillan, London/Basingstoke

Ruccio, D.F. and Amariglio, J. (2003) *Postmodern Moments in Modern Economics*, Princeton University Press, Princeton/Oxford

Samuelson, P.A. and Nordhaus, W.D. (2005) *Economics*, 18th edition, McGraw Hill, Boston

Schumpeter, J.A. (1967 [1954]) *History of Economic Analysis*, edited from manuscript by Elisabeth Boody Schumpeter, 6th edition, George Allen & Unwin, London

Tribe, K. (1978) *Land, Labour and Economic Discourse*, Routledge & Kegan Paul, London

WCED (1987) *Our Common Future*, Oxford University Press, Oxford

Xenos, N. (1989) *Scarcity and Modernity*, Routledge, London/New York

Zadek, S. (1993) *An Economics of Utopia. Democratising Scarcity*, Avebury, Aldershot

6
Water Can and Ought to Run Freely: Reflections on the Notion of 'Scarcity' in Economics

Sajay Samuel and Jean Robert

Introduction

The spread of commodity-intensive society is a relatively recent and ongoing phenomenon, which provokes a historically new feeling of perpetual lack and ineradicable dearth. By definition, commodities come at a price, which necessitates dependence on money. This dependence is only deepened by the constantly stimulated desire for commodities. Not only is the capacity of self-reliance thereby frustrated and disabled, people are also incited and trained to devalue independence from commodities. Perhaps being disabled by the dependence on commodities would be acceptable were cash to grow freely on trees. But the collision between insatiable desires and a finite purse leaves the consumer in a state of perpetual dissatisfaction. Thus, commodity-intensive societies produce an incurable dis-ease: the frustration of never having enough, of feeling needy; that peculiarly modern condition of scarcity. For instance, the poor woman who cannot afford to buy bottles of the water that she once obtained freely from a tap or a well experiences scarcity as does the rich man who cannot quench his thirst with *Aquafina* after becoming aware of *Perrier*. Both are equally dependent on market values. Yet he, being enslaved to commodities, has forgotten what she still acutely remembers: the propriety of using water that can and ought to run freely.[1]

Scarcity means 'the insufficiency of supply; smallness of available quantity, number or amount, *in proportion to need or demand*' (Oxford English Dictionary, 1989, emphasis added). As such, scarcity is a relational term. While a certain quantity of a thing may be a necessary condition, excessive desire or demand is a sufficient condition for the experience of scarcity.

The overflowing shelves and garbage heaps of commodity-intensive society are proof of the abundance of things. And, as scientists inform us, the total quantity of the stuff named H_2O remains unchanged through the hydrological cycle, neither created nor destroyed. Yet, the perception of endemic scarcity intensifies. This, we argue, is due to the limitless desire for accumulation that subtends commodity-intensive societies, a kind of desire, in no small measure, sparked and fed by the ideological commitments of the mainstream of economic science.

In this chapter, we first contrast Aristotle with Adam Smith to bring this ideological ground into sharp relief. Smith centres the study of political economy on exchange value. In doing so, he overturns the traditional understanding of 'economics' in two ways: he excises use-value from its purview and also legitimizes vanity and greed. He understands and accepts that these vices drive the accumulation of wealth beyond use. Nevertheless, he masks their viciousness under the benign phrase 'bettering our condition'. In justifying limitless acquisitiveness or accumulation beyond use, mainstream economic thought produces scarcity. We show that neoclassical economics no less than the classical economics of Adam Smith actively hides its acquisitive foundations. The utility theory of neoclassical economics hides the assumption of 'more is better' under mathematical robes. In both cases, unfettered desire or demand is taken for granted and fuels the spread of ineradicable scarcity. Third, though the spread of economic thought leads to the ideology of more is better, we point out that the mathematical commitments of neoclassical economics requires it to be styled as a 'science of scarcity' in which scarcity is posited as quantitative constraints of time, means or money. Like Xenos, Chapter 2 this volume, we argue that by confusing finiteness (a question of quantities) with scarcity, mainstream economic science is blind to the fact that it helps produce the very problem it purports to solve. In making these arguments we draw on our past research and writing that uncover thought styles that bury or ignore vernacular forms of life (see for example, Robert 1994). Both of us are part of a group of itinerant thinkers, scholars, and activists deeply influenced by the thought and work of Ivan Illich and have focused on exposing the blind spots of modern economic science and political theory which serve as foot soldiers in the war against subsistence.

Like other authors in this volume, we also draw on the case of water (see Chapters 11 and 12 which also focus on water scarcity). It is economic notions of demand, supply, production, consumption, allocation, distribution and prices that suffuse the discourse on 'water scarcity'. The hegemony of economic terms reinforces the notion that water is a resource, as is also argued by Jairath in Chapter 12 of this volume. Instead, as we argue in the conclusion to this chapter, the urgent task in adequately grasping the question of scarcity in the context of water is to see first that water is a commons.

From the good to values

For over 2000 years, 'economics' was a branch of politics or moral philosophy. From Xenophon's *Oikonomikos* in the fourth century BC, to Adam Smith's teacher, Francis Hutchinson's *Short introduction to Moral Philosophy* in 1742, *oeconomics* referred to the ethical art of running a household: of how to deal with food stores, the training towards virtue of women, children and servants (Finley, 1985, pp17–21).[2] What are now accepted as the subjects of economic science – trade and exchange, money, distribution and so on – traditionally belonged to the study of politics, understood as reflections on the highest good for man. To buttress this point, it is perhaps sufficient to note that all of Aristotle's writings on 'economics' appear either in *Ethics* or *Politics*. The first lines of these works reveal the traditionally understood end of ethics and politics and, more emphatically, the proper end of 'economic' matters.[3] In the Aristotelian tradition that infused western thinking on 'economics' until the early modern period, trade, barter and exchange are species of human activities practised within polities. Since both human actions and political arrangements strain naturally towards the good, 'economic' affairs are necessarily subject to considerations of the good.

Aristotle's discussion of the arts of acquisition provides a clear explanation for why exchange relations ought to be subjected to ethics and politics. In *Politics*, he distinguishes two kinds of acquisitive arts. The first is the art of acquisition oriented by natural needs and therefore a proper part of household management; oikonomia (see also Chapter 2, this volume).[4] The second, called 'the art of wealth-getting', *khrèmatistikè*, is exemplified by 'retail trade'. Retail trade or buying goods for the purpose of reselling them at a profit produces wealth solely through exchange.

Aristotle argued that activities ordered by profit-seeking are unfitting and unnatural because animated by the purpose of accumulating money for itself. Accordingly, wealth-getting is perverse in two ways. First, the heterogeneity of human actions and of things is effaced when subjected to the reign of exchange. When purchased for the purpose of resale, a shoe is not qualitatively different from a table; both are transmogrified into commodities. Commodities subsume and bury that heterogeneity of things which is partly conferred by the distinct uses to which they are put. Similarly, as paid services, cooking is equated to gardening, both rendered homogenous as undifferentiated forms of 'labour', which effaces the meaningfulness of human actions.[5]

Second, and equally important for Aristotle, was the fact that the accumulation of money for itself is unchained from natural ends – those of needs or use. When purchased for resale, no quantity of shoes is enough. Shoes then become a cipher for money whose accumulation has no inherent end or principle of self-limitation. Unhinged from natural needs or use, accumulation leads to the fate of Midas – who starved to death while sitting on a hoard of coins. Therefore, for Aristotle, to live by exchange exhibits a derangement of reason: the retailer unreasonably forgets the distinction between merely living and living well.[6] Politics and ethics were oriented by the good and implied reflections on the good life. The art of wealth-getting which aims at profit-making, because inherently limitless, is destructive of ethics and politics. It is precisely for this reason that Aristotle censures getting wealth through exchange.

In his *Inquiry into The Nature and Causes of the Wealth of Nations*, Adam Smith turned the Aristotelian tradition on its head. Instead of grounding his inquiry on the questions of the good and the just, he legitimized the art of wealth-getting. It is this overturning that constitutes his lasting bequest to modern economics. To properly grasp his innovation, therefore, one should begin by considering his stated purpose for undertaking the inquiry.

Smith defines 'political economy' as a science exclusively directed by two ends: to enable individuals and the state to acquire wealth.[7] He thus legitimizes the acquisition of wealth and thereby frees acquisitiveness from ethico-political restraints. Despite the arrangement of words in Smith's 'political economy', the principle of commercialism is not subservient in rank to that of politics. Instead, justice is reduced in status to a handmaiden of wealth-getting. The witness of Andrew Millar, an auditor of Smith's lectures on jurisprudence, is instructive in this regard:

> *In the last part of his lectures he [Smith] examined those political regulations which are founded not upon the principle of justice, but that of expediency, and which are calculated to increase the riches, the power and the prosperity of a state ... What he delivered on these subjects contained the substance of the work he afterwards published under the title of An Inquiry into the Nature and Causes of the Wealth of Nations.* (cited in Cannan, 1904)

By placing economic science in the service of accumulating wealth, Smith stakes out its purpose. It is to achieve this end that he also restricts its subject matter to the determinants of market prices; to the sphere of exchange-value. He accepted Locke's arguments: that labour is the foundation of property rights; that applying labour transforms the commons into private property; that money ignites the spirit of acquisitiveness; and that accumulation beyond use is just.[8] Smith curtails his inquiry to exchange-value in full awareness of the contrasting 'value-in-use' and is perhaps the first who, in recognizing that traditional distinction, nevertheless rules out use-value as a legitimate subject of an inquiry on wealth.[9]

In this context, consider the distinction Smith draws between diamonds and water (see Chapters 2 and 4, this volume, for further discussions of the water and diamonds paradox). He recognizes that water is useful but of little value in exchange, whereas diamonds are almost useless but nevertheless expensive (Smith, 1875, Book 1, Chapter 2). Well before him, it was known that the most useful stuff for life is free and that superfluities could be expensive. For instance, even as late as the 17th century, Pufendorf could still write:

> ... *those things are of the least account of Value without which*
> *Human Life is least able to subsist; and therefore not without*
> *the most singular Providence of Almighty God, Nature has been*
> *very bountiful in providing a plentiful store of those things. But*
> *the wanton Luxury of Mankind has set extravagant Rates upon*
> *many things which Humane life might very well be without, for*
> *instance upon Pearls and Jewels.* (Samuel Pufendorf, in Kauder,
> 1953, p650)

In contrast, Smith does not follow this Aristotelian tradition in evaluating the propriety of value-in-exchange by value-in-use. He therefore eschews any ethical or moral judgement on the sphere of exchange-values, and instead focuses the study of political economy on the sphere of the useless. He could thereby 'ignore' use-value by naturalizing perversity, that is, by ennobling the quest for wealth. He disavowed the Aristotelian ethico-political restrictions on exchange by explicitly enjoining men and states to acquire riches. For Aristotle, the retailer exhibits a derangement of reason. For Smith, every man is reasonable insofar as he lives as a retailer.[10] For Aristotle, the retailer's deranged acquisitiveness was unnatural because it suppressed or perverted his natural sociability. For Smith, man's sociability was the outcome of his selfishness or self-interest, expressed in the natural propensity to truck, barter and exchange.[11]

And yet, though Smith recognized that the causes of wealth were rooted in unseemly passions or vices, he was chary to call them as such. Indeed, his earlier reflections on the moral sentiments can be read as an attempt to rhetorically remove the sting of viciousness from vice. He recognized the 'avarice and ambition' that attended the endless 'pursuit of wealth, power and pre-eminence' as he did the 'emulation which runs through all the different ranks of men'. He emphasized it was vanity, rooted in 'the belief of our being the object of attention' and 'not the ease or the pleasure' that drove men to 'pursue riches and avoid poverty' (Smith, 1858, Part 8, Section 2, Chapter 3).

But, as he argued, 'virtue consists not in any one affection but in the proper degree of all the affections' and it is 'sympathy' or the 'correspondent affection of the spectator' that 'is the natural and original measure of the proper degree [of virtue]' (Smith, 1858, Part 8, Section 2, Chapter 3). Yet in Smith, 'sympathy' is a neutral scientific term that cannot discriminate between good and bad.[12] Men sympathize with those who 'make a parade of their riches'. And women show off to provoke the sympathy of others. Mutual sympathy is the glue bonding (wo)men to that ceaseless 'toil and bustle' necessary to acquire more than they need. Therefore, 'sympathy' is neither the compassion felt for the poor and downtrodden nor the fellow feeling towards the sick and distressed. Instead, in Smith, 'sympathy' is the reward for vanity in commercial society.

And if 'sympathy' was not neutral enough, Smith also introduces the more benign phrase 'bettering our condition' to better justify and legitimize the vainglorious pursuit of wealth.[13] The continued importance of this phrase is underscored by the fact that it is as recognizable and acceptable today as when he first advanced it. For who now would deny the benign effort to 'better one's condition'? He argued that the desire to better our condition 'comes with us from the womb and never leaves us till we go to the grave' and that it excites a 'uniform, constant and uninterrupted effort' towards wealth-getting that fuels both public and private opulence.[14] Smith thereby legitimizes acquisitiveness by rephrasing it as a natural desire to better our condition.

Thus Smith lays the ideological scaffolding for modern economics. By making plausible exchange for the purpose of accumulation as the inevitable outcome of the natural propensity to truck and barter, Smith clears the grounds for justifying commodity-intensive market society. By transforming the vice of vanity and envy into the natural desire to better our condition he makes these causes of wealth palatable. He thus displaces the traditional reflections on 'economics', which began from considerations of the good. No pre-modern could think to hold in esteem that which was not estimable. Neither Aristotle nor the scholastics could conceive the accumulation of wealth for itself as good. Instead, Smith extricated 'economics' from its traditional moorings in ethics and politics to better accept the purpose of political economy as the accumulation of wealth. Yet, this also legitimizes the sufficient condition for scarcity, the limitless desire for acquisitions that exceeds both need and use.[15]

Utility is not useful

Despite the many differences between classical and neoclassical economics, they share a common ideological ground. In this mainstream of economic science, use-value is ignored and unfettered acquisitiveness ennobled. Whereas Smith used the phrase 'bettering our condition' to mask and make palatable the ignoble causes of wealth, neoclassical economics achieves the same result through its notion of utility. Utility is assumed to increase with the more one possesses, so that three chairs and three tables offer greater utility than two of each (Chapter 4, in this volume, also provides an analysis of the marginal revolution). The assumption that 'more is better' therefore throws mathematical clothes over the skeleton of unfettered desire. (Thompson, in Chapter 7 discusses Miss Piggy's obsession with 'more is more' and the non-satiety principle in modern economics.)

Popularly enshrined as marking the 'marginal revolution' in economic thought, neoclassical economics is now considered the new and improved version of economic science. Broadly, the marginal revolution consisted of the discovery that the intensity of the desire for a thing determined, in the last analysis, its value-in-exchange. The novelty of the utility theory of value supposedly lies in replacing the objective quantity of labour time with the purely subjective feeling of desire as the ground of exchange value. Yet, classical economists had already accepted the need or desire for a thing as a necessary though not sufficient condition of its exchange-value.[16] Moreover, as Marx noted, 'usefulness does not dangle midair ... it is conditioned by the physical properties of the commodity ...' (1954).

What is decisively new in neoclassical economics is that 'utility' becomes a placeholder for a mathematical construct.[17] Already, in Bentham, utility had become the subject matter of an abstract principle subtending a 'felicific calculus'. His 'principle of utility' allowed the calibration of individual pleasures and pains and the purported calculation of the greatest happiness for the greatest number. Yet, it is no mere Benthamite abstraction that is affirmed by the marginal revolution in economics. Instead, when for example, Jevons asserts 'value depends entirely on utility', he reinterprets everyday experience and language to suit a mathematical function. It is well known that the invention of 'diminishing marginal utility' constitutes the real and lasting novelty of neoclassical economics, obtained by fitting economic thought to the structure of differential calculus. If a differentiable function is named 'utility' and its first derivative 'marginal utility,' then the quasi-concavity of that function is sufficient to establish 'diminishing marginal utility'. Jevons is a good witness to the convolutions required in retrofitting ordinary experience to suit mathematical functions. He refers to water as an example to lend everyday credibility to his formulations, but then strains ordinary credulity by suggesting that men drink water to the point of being sickened by it.[18]

Despite its overt mathematization, neoclassical economics shares the ideological conceit of unlimited acquisitiveness bequeathed to it by classical economics. Perhaps Marshall states the proposition most succinctly, 'There is an endless variety of wants, but there is a limit to each separate want' (Marshall, 1898, p155). Whereas the second part of his proposition reflects the innovation of diminishing marginal utility, the first recognizes vanity as the wellspring of commodity-intensive society. The assumption of limitless wants is axiomatic in neoclassical economics, and usually ascribed to 'tastes and preferences' beyond the scope of economic analysis. Thus, it assumes acquisitiveness is an ineradicable aspect of human nature instead of a socially conditioned behaviour. The techniques of utility maximization and the geometry of indifference maps obscure the fact that neoclassical economics takes as its foundational assumption the very behaviour or attitude that produces the experience of scarcity. Regardless of quantities or availability, unbounded desire will necessarily create scarcity, and this dynamic is buried at the heart of mainstream economic thought.

Smith placed use-value in the blind spot of economics though he recognized usefulness as the first meaning of 'value'. Neoclassical economists identified 'value' with what was obtained in exchange and could no longer comprehend usefulness. Blind to what Smith had blinkered beyond economics, neoclassical economists could not imagine alternatives to market society.[19] However, by legitimizing unfettered acquisitiveness prompted by vanity, through such rhetorical flourishes as 'bettering our condition' or mathematical obscurities as 'utility' and 'indifference maps', the mainstream of economic science propagates the sufficient condition of scarcity.

Scarcity is not finiteness

Yet, the notion of scarcity as a universal and ineradicable condition was only given scientific credence by 20th-century economists. 'Scarcity', like 'utility', is a word deployed to make mathematical economics ordinarily comprehensible. Leon Walras was perhaps the most active in transferring the mathematics of energy physics to economics. Unsurprisingly, it is also he who most clearly formulated 'scarcity' as the indispensable source of economic value.[20] Yet, the idea that scarcity defines 'the raison d'être of economic science' was not widely accepted until the 1930s, which is when mathematical formulations become central to it.[21] As an endemic human condition justifying economics, scarcity usually shows up only in the popularization of economics in trade and text books. Indeed, it would not be a great exaggeration to suggest that it was Lionel Robbins who gave wide currency to the notion of 'economics as a science of scarcity' even though, as Fine demonstrates, he may have subsequently detracted from this view.[22]

The mathematics of constrained optimization is the kernel of 20th-century economic theorizing.[23] Consumers are said to maximize their utility subject to the constraint of income, producers are said to maximize their output given the quantity of capital and labour available, as Robinson Crusoe allocates his labour among tasks given the constraint of time. Without constraints, whether of time, money or means, there is no economic problem. It is in the context of the mathematical technique of constrained maximization then, that 'scarcity' in economics must be understood. Specifically, 'scarcity' is to constraints as 'marginal utility' is to a differentiable and quasi-concave function. Modern economists rarely consider 'scarcity' a technical term and unlike 'balance of payments', or 'n-person games', scarcity does not usually appear in technical treatises on economics.[24] Scarcity, however, is rhetorically convenient for popularizing economic science. It fuels that perception that economics deals with problems necessitated by the limited quantity of means, or money, or time (see Fine, this volume, for a discussion on the elusive nature of scarcity in economics).

In contrast, when classical economists spoke of 'scarcity', they typically meant 'rare', 'little' or 'infrequent'. They did not imagine any scarcity in the case of producible goods. Ricardo's reasoning seems persuasive: in distinguishing between two kinds of price, he notes that the 'scarcity price' is independent of the quantity of labour. Instead, such prices are applicable only to rare objects that are necessarily limited in number. The prices of such rarities are therefore determined by the competing desires of those who wanted to possess them. To the classical economist however, this 'scarcity price' was an exceptional phenomenon in the sphere of exchange and could not be used to explain the value of what was abundant. After all, the glut in manufactured goods was self-evident to them.[25]

Scarcity is an inherently relational concept. It refers to the dearth, the insufficiency of something; that is, the quantity of something in relation to the need, want or desire for it. Scarcity should be distinguished from finiteness, which is not a relational concept. Finiteness is an objective property of things independent of the needs or purposes of women and men. Obviously, finite quantities do not imply fixed quantities – the quantity of rainwater in the Sahel may vary from year to year but in each year there is a finite amount. In contrast, whether a finite quantity of water is insufficient depends on the purposes of its use. The amount that is excessive for a home with a dry toilet will be insufficient for one with five flush toilets and a lawn. Thus, insufficiency or scarcity necessarily entails judgements on the appropriateness of needs and wants. Evaluations of scarcity or abundance, of too little or too much, are non-quantifiable judgements utterly distinct from numerical measurements.[26]

This contrast between finiteness and scarcity is not sufficiently drawn either in economics or more generally.[27] In Chapter 2, Xenos also argues that finitude is not scarcity. Scarcity is a relational measure of experience, inextricably binding the quantity of things to the purposes of men. For this reason, scarcity is always a socially constructed experience and never a natural phenomenon. Scarcity is a measure of the *insufficiency* of finite quantities and cannot itself be measured by number. In contrast, the finiteness of a thing can be measured in numbers. That water is finite is a truism that does not imply that water is scarce. Despite the conceptual distinction between finiteness and scarcity, the latter has a strange connotative power. Typically, the phrase 'X is scarce' draws attention to the quantity of X, while passing over the purposes for which it is insufficient. The phrase 'water is scarce' tends to mistakenly emphasize only the necessary but not sufficient condition that makes water scarce; it tends to reduce the experience of scarcity to the quantity of water.

Neoclassical economists are heirs to the classical economists insofar as they accept acquisitiveness as a natural condition. To popularize constrained maximization as the 'science of scarcity' they however foster a systematic confusion between finiteness and scarcity. The 'scarcity' that they invoke is endemic and ineradicable. It is not caused by the unavailability of things. After all, the landfills that have grown to the size of small hills are enough proof that modern societies waste more than previous generations have ever consumed or used. Instead, scarcity now appears ineradicable because needs have metastasized into endless wants. Yet the tendency of 'scarcity' to be identified with limited quantities suggests otherwise. Perhaps the connotative power of 'scarcity' is a leftover from bygone days when needs were culturally bound and stable. Perhaps it is now actively maintained to prevent judgement on the appropriateness of wants and desires. In either case, the use of 'scarcity' today tends to reinforce the illusion that it is caused by the unavailability of things instead of the excessiveness of wants. And it is the mainstream of economic science since Adam Smith that has cemented this illusion. On the one hand it legitimizes and propagates the sufficient condition of the experience of scarcity – insatiable desires; and on the other, proposes to solve the very problems created by such limitless acquisitiveness.

Water is a commons

This dual dynamic of attempting to solve a problem with the very style of thought that fuels it, is painfully obvious in the case of the so-called 'water scarcity'. In the context of this discourse, water is considered a resource. Caught in the conceptual web of demand and supply, policy-makers can only think of ways to increase the quantity or decrease the consumption of water resources (see Chapters 11 and 12, this volume, for a discussion of conventional responses to water management and scarcity). And, unsurprisingly, they focus on the price mechanism as a panacea. They want to price water so that the gifts of nature can be converted into private property. They want to price water to spur increases in supply by, for example, turning seawater into fresh water. They want to price water to restrict the effective demand for it. They propagate the reign of prices to transmute the needs of all into the wants of the few who can pay.[28] In their rush to find efficient solutions to the problem of water scarcity, they have conveniently forgotten that the ideology subtending commodity-intensive society necessarily produces and propagates scarcity. For where cash is king, self-sufficiency and the commons are cast into exile. Under the rule of prices, the abundant can also be unaffordable. Moreover, prices may reduce the effective demand for *Perrier* and flush toilets but can also spark the envious desire for them.[29] Unlike their predecessors, modern economists who propagate the price mechanism forget what Adam Smith knew: it is vanity that fuels the engine of commercial society.

Therefore, the question of scarcity today cannot be divorced from the question of human needs and wants. Addressing the question of needs and wants is pre-eminently a process of judging when something is too much or too little; of judging if and when needless wants have replaced useful needs. Is industrial farming counter-productive? Do dams damage? Are flush toilets and green lawns necessary? Are desalination technologies appropriate? These are questions of ethics and politics. They cannot be comprehended in the terms of an economic science, which was consciously established beyond ethics and politics. Blind to use-values while celebrating acquisitiveness, mainstream economics is of little help in thinking about the proposition that 'water is scarce'. A discourse based on thinking about water as a resource, caught within the conceptual pincers of demand and supply, rife with 'allocation', 'distribution', 'production' and 'consumption' only obfuscates the modern experience of scarcity. What it contributes to with one hand, it pretends to solve with the other.

That the unfettered spread of commodity-intensive society has led to the despoliation of the air, soil and water is obvious enough. That commodity-intensive society has produced a cornucopia of things the majority cannot afford is equally obvious. However, that commodity-intensive society induces scarcity by fuelling acquisitiveness is not sufficiently obvious. From its inception, mainstream economics has been chained to the ball of market exchange. Its proponents can only tout more markets as solutions to the very problems created by market society, that is, to create more scarcity in the pretence of eradicating it.

One way out of the mental prison wherein water appears as a resource is to recall that water is a commons. The contrast between water as a commons and as a resource was well exposed at the turn of the 19th century. *Aqua currit et debet currere*; 'water runs and ought to run' ruled the judge in the Merritt *v* Parker case (1795, New Jersey). He thus recalled that well-worn maxim of common law which prohibited interference to water-course flows. For as Blackstone noted, 'water is a moving, wandering thing, and must of necessity continue to be common by the law of nature so I can only have a temporary, transient, usufructuary property therein' (cited in Shiva, 2002, p20). Historically, diverting or significantly obstructing the natural course of water was judged illegal unless agreed to by all parties affected. Yet, barely 10 years later, the judges in the case of Palmer *v* Mulligan (1805, New York) ruled legitimate the damming of water for the purpose of a mill. The difference between the two rulings defined the 19th-century transformation in the legal conception of property. Law would no longer protect the liberty to the quiet enjoyment of property that was once honoured by the common law maxim *sic utere tuo, ut alienum non laedas*, 'so use yours that others be not harmed'. Instead, the liberty to quiet and harmless enjoyment was legally destroyed when the rights of ownership were recast to permit the commercial development of property, even if to the detriment of another's use.

It was to legalize economic growth and commodity-intensive society that judges began to use a brand new economic and utilitarian criterion to assess legal damages: the economic efficiency gained from restricting liberty. Accordingly, the commons could be exploited for private purposes as long as the cash value to the one owner outweighed the loss of another's liberty. Law was thus wielded as an instrument of commercialism to separate what was kept together by common law for centuries: the coincidence of injurious misuse and legally determined damages. It did so by comparing what could only be contrasted: legal rights and civil liberties. Instrumental law not only defanged neighbourly conflict by reducing politics to the economic calculus of cost and benefit but also legally transformed water into a privately exploitable resource.[30]

To see water as a commons, again, requires attending to both our forebears and contemporaries who, like those in the Thar desert of Rajasthan today, live well without suffering from the scarcity of water (Shiva, 2002). It requires being free of the debilitating effects of economic styles of thinking. It calls for a revaluation of self-sufficiency and of living within natural thresholds, which for the Nobel Laureate, Herbert Simon, occurs only in fast-disappearing black zones of 'autarky' of the modern world (1991, pp25–44). Perhaps the effort to recover water as a commons will lead to clarifying the distinction between the commons and the market, between the subsistence and commodity dependence and between needs and wants. Such an effort may even lead to the realization that there is no scarcity of water and that the stuff we think of as scarce is better named H_2O (Illich, 1985).

Notes

1   The literature on the contrast between commodity-intensive society and its antithesis is extensive. For an orientation to this contrast that admits no synthesis, consult Illich, 1980. He rehabilitates the word 'vernacular' to indicate social arrangements, past and present, wherein the 'the home-grown, home-bred and home-spun' dominate the dependence on purchased goods and services. William Leiss coined the phrase 'high-intensity market setting' to refer to 'a market economy in which there is a very large number of commodities available to a large number of people, and in which many commodities are the result of highly complex industrial production processes involving sophisticated scientific and technological knowledge' (Leiss, 1988, p7). The works of Karl Polanyi (Polanyi, 1944; Polanyi et al, 1957; Dalton, 1968) clarify the historicity of commodity-intensive societies, made visible when nature and human action become widely priced as land and labour respectively. Marshall Sahlins (1972) and Finley (1985) confirm that pre-modern societies, whether Aboriginal Australia or Western Antiquity, got on quite well without it. Jacques Le Goff (1988) emphasizes the aim of the medieval 'economy' as that of subsistence, of providing for necessities. The continuing modern war on subsistence and the resistance to it is well documented. Consult for example, Thompson, 2000; Wolf, 1969; Shanin, 1977; and Marcos, 2001). Scott (1999) argues that visionary plans to modernize society invariably fail and usually leave their beneficiaries worse off for the attention. Study the key terms collected in Sachs (1992) as commands that rally the troops to the war against subsistence.

2   When Adam Smith wrote *The Theory of Moral Sentiments* (1858) some 17 years before publishing *An Inquiry into the Nature and Causes of the Wealth of Nations* (1875), he still adhered to this traditional meaning of *oeconomics*.

3   The first sentence of the *Nicomachean Ethics* reads 'Every art and every inquiry, and similarly every action and choice, is thought to aim at some good; and for this reason the good has rightly been declared to be that at which all things aim' (Bk.1, 1094a1). Similarly, the first sentence of *Politics* reads 'Every state is a community of some kind, and every community is established with a view to some good; ... [and] the state ... aims ... at the highest good' (Bk.1, 1252a1).

4   'Of the art of acquisition then there is one kind which by nature is a part of the management of a household, in so far as the art of household management must either find ready to hand, or itself provide, such things necessary to life, and useful for the community of the family or the state, as can be stored. They are the elements of true riches; for the amount of property which is needed for a good life is not unlimited ...' (Aristotle, *Politics*, Bk.1, Ch.8, 1256b).

5   The *Nicomachean Ethics* contains Aristotle's discussion on the (in)appropriateness of the commensurability entailed by exchange. See Scott Meikle (1995) for an outstanding treatment of the (un)resolved problem of commensurability that haunts modern economics. Hannah Arendt (1958) finely crafts the distinctions between 'work', 'labour' and 'action'.

6   'The origin of this disposition (accumulation of coin for itself) in men is that they are intent upon living only, and not upon living well; and as their desires are unlimited, they also desire that the means of gratifying them should be without limit ... [Thus] some men turn every quality or art into a means of getting wealth; this they conceive to be the end, and to the promotion of the end they think all things must contribute' (Aristotle, *Politics*, Bk.1, Ch.9, 1258a). 'There are two sorts of wealth-getting, as I have said; one is a part of household management, the other is retail

trade: the former necessary and honourable, while that which consists in exchange is justly censured; for it is unnatural, and a mode by which men gain from one another' (Aristotle, *Politics*, Bk.1, Ch.10, 1258a & b).

7 'Political economy ... proposes two distinct objects: first, to ... enable [people] to provide a (plentiful) revenue or subsistence for themselves, and secondly, to supply the state or commonwealth with a revenue sufficient for the public services'. Though 'political economy [is] considered as a branch of the science of a statesman or legislator ...', its stated purpose is 'to enrich both the people and the sovereign' (Smith, 1875, Bk.4, Introduction). The phrase 'political economy' was used by James Steuart (1712–1780) in *An Inquiry into the Principles of Political Economy* (1767) but there refers to the paternalistic task of a prince. The phrase in its Smithian sense will run through Ricardo, Mill, and Jevons until Marshall's *Principles of Economics* first published in 1890. There Marshall contracts 'political economy' to 'economics' and he defines it on the ground laid by Smith. Thus, 'Political Economy or Economics is a study of mankind in the ordinary business of life; it examines that part of individual and social action which is most closely connected with the attainment and with the use of the material requisites of wellbeing'.

8 The importance of Locke to Smith is evident in his paean to property. 'The property which every man has in his own labour, as it is the original foundation of all other property, so it is the most sacred and inviolable', (Smith, 1875, Book 1, Chapter 10, Part 2). For reasons of space, we do not offer detailed quotations from Locke to support our argument of Smith's dependence on him. However, see John Locke (1988).

9 '... money has become in all civilized nations the universal instrument of commerce, by the intervention of which goods of all kinds are bought and sold, or exchanged for one another. What are the rules which men naturally observe in exchanging them either for money or one another, I shall now proceed to examine'. 'These rules determine what may be called the relative or exchangeable value of goods.' '... The word value, it is to be observed, has two different meanings, and sometimes expresses the utility of some particular object, and sometimes the power of purchasing other goods which the possession of that object conveys. The one may be called "value in use"; the other, "value in exchange"' (Smith, 1875, Book 1, Chapter 4).

10 A man 'supplies the far greater part of them (his wants) by exchanging that surplus part of the produce of his own labour, which is over and above his own consumption, for such parts of the produce of other men's labour as he has occasion for. Every man thus lives by exchanging, or becomes in some measure a merchant, and the society itself grows to be what is properly a commercial society' (Smith, 1875, Book 1, Chapter 4).

11 Thus, 'we are not ready to suspect any person of being defective in selfishness' (Smith, 1858, Part 8, Section 2, Chapter 3). 'This division of labour, from which so many advantages are derived, is not originally the effect of any human wisdom, which foresees and intends that general opulence to which it gives occasion. It is the necessary, though very slow and gradual consequence of a certain propensity in human nature which has in view no such extensive utility; the propensity to truck, barter, and exchange one thing for another' (Smith, 1875, Book 1, Chapter 2).

12 We are aware of the 'Adam Smith Problem', usefully summarized by Leonidas Montes (2003, pp63–90). 'The *Problem* as such, states that there is an irreconcilable difference or inconsistency between *The Theory of Moral Sentiments*, with its sympathy-based concept of human nature, and *The Wealth of Nations*, founded on

an egoistic theory of self-interest' (p66). We contend that since Smith's 'sympathy' is sparked by vanity and nourished by envy, 'Das Adam Smith Problem' is not Adam Smith's problem.

13 'It is because mankind are disposed to sympathize more entirely with our joy than with our sorrow, that we make parade of our riches, and conceal our poverty ... Nay, it is chiefly from this regard to the sentiments of mankind, that we pursue riches and avoid poverty. For to what purpose is all the toil and bustle of this world? What is the end of avarice and ambition, of the pursuit of wealth, of power, and preheminence? Is it to supply the necessities of nature? The wages of the meanest labourer can supply them ... If we examined his oeconomy with rigour, we should find that he spends a great part of them upon conveniencies, which may be regarded as superfluities, and that, upon extraordinary occasions, he can give something even to vanity and distinction ... From whence, then, arises that emulation which runs through all the different ranks of men, and what are the advantages which we propose by that *great purpose of human life which we call bettering our condition*? To be observed, to be attended to, to be taken notice of with sympathy, complacency, and approbation, are all the advantages which we can propose to derive from it. It is the vanity, not the ease, or the pleasure, which interests us. But vanity is always founded upon the belief of our being the object of attention and approbation' (Smith, 1858, Part 1, Section 1, Chapter 3 [emphasis added]).

14 See his discussion on 'bettering our condition' in Smith, 1875, Book 2, Chapter 3. Here, in *The Wealth of Nations* he assumes what he argued for in *Moral Sentiments*: that avarice, ambition and vanity can be reduced to 'bettering our condition'.

15 How mimetic desire becomes acceptable because it is functional for commercial society can be read in the writings of Hobbes, Locke, Hume, Mandeville and Rousseau up to the classical economists. Desire is endlessly stoked and never satisfied when 'I want what you have'. From Mandeville to Keynes the perception that vice produces wealth depends on seeing that desire unhinged from use – acquisitiveness – can never be satisfied. Social scientists lack such perception. For scarcity as rooted in mimetic desire, consult Mandeville, 1924; Keynes, 1972; Girard, 1976; Dumouchel and Dupuy, 1979; Xenos, 1989; Achterhuis, 1993.

16 David Ricardo clearly states the role of utility in classical economics. 'Utility then is not the measure of exchangeable value, although it is absolutely essential to it. If a commodity were in no way useful – in other words, if it could in no way contribute to our gratification – it would be destitute of exchangeable value, however scarce it might be, or whatever quantity of labour might be necessary to procure it' in Ricardo, 1821, Chapter 1, Section1.

17 See Philip Mirowski, 1989, and its useful summary in Mirowski 1988, where he writes, 'It is the second thesis of this chapter that the hard core of neoclassical economic theory is the adoption of mid-nineteenth century physics as a rigid paradigm ... [which] ... explains the preference for techniques of constrained maximization over any other analytical technique', (p24). More generally, he offers compelling evidence for the argument that 'utility' in neoclassical economics was identified with 'potential energy' in 19th-century physics. He emphasizes the futility of this attempted identification by noting that it is meaningless to speak of the sum of income and utility being conserved through market exchanges, as does the sum of kinetic and potential energy when a ball falls to the ground.

18 'Water, for instance, may be roughly described as the most useful of all substances. A quart of water per day has the high utility of saving a person from dying in a most distressing manner. Several gallons a day may possess much utility for such

purposes as cooking and washing; but after an adequate supply is secured for these uses, any additional quantity is a matter of comparative indifference. All that we can say, then, is, that water, up to a certain quantity, is indispensable; that further quantities will have various degrees of utility; but that beyond a certain quantity the utility sinks gradually to zero; it may even become negative, that is to say, further supplies of the same substance may become inconvenient and hurtful' (Jevons, 1988, Chapter 3).

19 By the end of the 19th century, value-in-use lost all meaning as noted by Alfred Marshall. 'The word "value", says Adam Smith, has two different meanings, and sometimes expresses the utility of some particular object and sometimes the power of purchasing other goods which the possession of that object conveys. But experience has shown that it is not well to use the word in the former sense. The value, that is the exchange value, of one thing in terms of another at any place and time, is the amount of that second thing which can be got there and then in exchange for the first. Thus the term value is relative, and expresses the relation between two things at a particular place and time' (Marshall, 1898, Book II, Chapter II).

20 The term or concept does not appear of any importance in Jevons or Marshall. Menger has the concept without the word. It was Leon Walras, perhaps the most mathematical of 19th-century economists, who is the outstanding exception. 'Whether labour is all or part of social wealth is beside the point. In either case, why is labour worth anything? Why is it exchangeable? That is the question before us. Adam Smith neither asked nor answered it. Surely, if labour has value and is exchangeable, it is because it is both useful and limited in quantity, that is to say because it is scarce. *Value therefore comes from scarcity.* If there are things other than labour that are scarce, they will also have value and be exchangeable. So the theory which traces the origin of value to labour is a theory that is completely devoid of meaning rather than too narrow, entirely gratuitous rather than merely deficient' (in Jolink, 1996 [emphasis added]).

21 See Pearce, 1986, p379. The thorough-going mathematization of economic science is a 20th-century phenomenon and tracks the spread of marginalism in economics. 'In the 1930's new uses for the marginal concept were introduced in the journals and the specialized literature' (Howey, 1989, pxxxii).

22 The much-quoted, and by our investigations the most quoted statement, by Robbins to support the notion that economics is a science of scarcity appears in a trade book for non-technical readers. 'We have been turned out of Paradise. We have neither eternal life nor unlimited means of gratification. Everywhere we turn, if we choose one thing we must relinquish others which, in different circumstances, we would not wish to have relinquished. Scarcity of means to satisfy given ends is an almost ubiquitous condition of human behaviour. Here, then, is the unity of the subject of Economic Science, the forms assumed by human behaviour in disposing of scarce means' (Robbins, 1932, p15). We have vainly searched for an entry on 'scarcity' in Seligman (1930), Sills (1968), Higgs (1926) and Smelser and Baltes, 2004. It makes a late appearance in reference books as the organizing principle of economic science after being so popularized in textbooks, including that reliable standard by Paul Samuelson, *Economics*, first published in 1948.

23 'Optimizing, a catch-all term for maximizing, minimizing … lies at the heart of economic analysis … Indeed, optimizing subject to constraints has been considered by many as defining the essential nature of economics' (Lancaster, 1968, pp9–10). To make constrained optimization meaningful in everyday language, he invokes the quotation from Robbins.

24 When a technical meaning is imposed, 'scarcity' becomes ordinarily meaningless as evident in the entry on 'scarcity' in Eatwell et al, 1988. 'But the meaning of scarcity within marginalist theory of distribution is very peculiar: it concerns only the *relative* quantities of the factors employed in production. We may say that a factor is *scarce* when increasing quantities of it applied to a given quantity of the other gives rise to decreasing returns.'

25 'There are some commodities, the value of which is determined by their *scarcity* alone. No labour can increase the quantity of such goods, and therefore their value cannot be lowered by an increased supply. Some rare statues and pictures, scarce books and coins, wines of a peculiar quality, which can be made only from grapes grown on a particular soil, of which there is a very limited quantity, are all of this description. Their value is wholly independent of the quantity of labour originally necessary to produce them, and varies with the varying wealth and inclinations of those who are desirous to possess them' (Ricardo, 1821, p2 [emphasis added]).

26 Study Plato's *The Statesman* (Plato, 1997) for a decisive account of two kinds of measurement – the one 'arithmetic' (corresponding to finiteness) and the other 'geometric' (corresponding to scarcity). The philosophical implications and practical consequences of the distinction between these kinds of measurement have been well drawn out by Rosen, 1985.

27 Many chapters in this volume emphasize the relational nature of 'scarcity'. See the excellent Chapter 12 in this volume by Jasveen Jairath who recognizes the importance of having a different word for quantitative measures of a thing. Obviously, we propose 'finiteness', as Fred Luks (Chapter 5) does explicitly and Nicholas Xenos (Chapter 2) implicitly, both in this volume.

28 Chapters in this volume provide ample evidence of the extent to which the idea of a market in water to reduce effective demand and increase supply dominates contemporary thinking on the topic. For an illustrative example in the burgeoning literature on water scarcity, see Saleth and Dinar, 2001, pp119–132. That scarcity and abundance are endemically viewed through the economic prism of demand and supply is perhaps most convincingly laid out in Gleick, 2004. The report is based on the unquestioned acceptance that water is an economic resource. Consequently, all its solutions to the problem of water can be seen as attempts that either increase water supply or manage the demand for it.

29 Even the most 'obvious' economic law of an inverse relation between price and quantity demanded becomes dubious by slightly shaking one of the foundational assumptions of mathematical economics. See Stiglitz, 1987, pp1–48. He shows that changing the assumption of costless information upsets much of the neoclassical applecart. It is a matter of elementary logic that assumptions known to be false cannot lead to correct conclusions, except by accident.

30 Consult Jean Robert (1994) for extensive historical and theoretical analyses of water built on the distinction between water understood as commons and misunderstood as economic resource. See Illich (1985) to enter into the historical rupture in perception attending the transmogrification of water into a techno-scientific economic resource. The cases and argument presented above are culled from Horowitz (1977), especially Chapter 2. He emphasizes that in the US, 'the evolving law of water rights had a greater impact than any other branch of law on the effort to adapt private law doctrines to the movement for economic growth' (p34).

References

Achterhuis, H. (1993) 'Scarcity and sustainability', in *Global Ecology: A New Arena for Political Conflict*, Zed Books, Boston, MA

Arendt, H. (1958) *The Human Condition*, University of Chicago Press, Chicago, IL

Aristotle (1984) *Politics*, in J. Barnes (ed) *The Complete Works of Aristotle*, Princeton University Press, Princeton

Aristotle (1984) *Nicomachean Ethics*, in Jonathan Barnes (ed) *The Complete Works of Aristotle*, Princeton University Press, Princeton

Bentham, J. (1823) *Introduction to the Principles of Moral and Legislation*, London

Cannan, E. (1904) 'Introduction', in A. Smith (1875[1776]) *An Inquiry into the Nature and Causes of the Wealth of Nations*, Methuen, London

Dalton, G. (ed) (1968) *Primitive, Archaic and Modern Economies*, Anchor Books, New York

Dumouchel, P, and Dupuy, J.-P. (1979) *L'Enfer Des Choses*, Seuil, Paris

Eatwell, J., Milgate, M. and Newman, P. (eds) (1988) *New Palgrave Dictionary of Economics*, Macmillan, New York

Finley, M.I. (1985) *The Ancient Economy*, University of California Press, Berkeley, CA

Girard, R. (1976) *Deceit, Desire and the Novel*, Johns Hopkins Press, Baltimore, MD

Gleick, P. (ed) (2004) *The World's Water: The Biennial Report on Freshwater Resources*, Island Press, Washington, DC

Higgs, H. (ed) (1926) *The Dictionary of Political Economy*, Macmillan, NY

Horowitz, M. (1977) *The Transformation of American Law, 1780–1860*, Harvard University Press, Cambridge, MA

Howey, R. (1989) *The Rise of the Marginal Utility School*, Columbia University Press, New York

Illich, I. (1980) 'The war on subsistence' (Chapter 3), and 'Vernacular values' (Chapter 2) both in *Shadow Work*, Marion Boyars, London, pp27–52, 53–74

Illich, I. (1985) *H₂O and the Waters of Forgetfulness*, Haydey Books, Berkeley, CA

Jevons, S. (1988) *The Theory of Political Economy*, 3rd edition, Macmillan, London

Jolink, A. (1996) *The Evolutionist Economics of Leon Walras*, Routledge, NY

Kauder, E. (1953) 'Genesis of the marginal utility theory from Aristotle to the end of the 18th century', *The Economic Journal*, vol 63, pp638–650

Keynes, J.M. (1972 [1930]) 'Economic considerations for our grandchildren', in *Essays in Persuasion*, Collected Works, vol IX, Macmillan, New York

Lancaster, K. (1968) *Mathematical Economics*, Dover, New York

Le Goff, J. (1988) *Medieval Civilization, 400–1500*, Blackwell, London

Leiss, W. (1988) *The Limits to Satisfaction*, McGill University Press, Kingston

Locke, J. (1988) 'On property' (Chapter 5), in P. Laslett (ed) *Two Treatises of Government*, Cambridge University Press, Cambridge, revised edition

Mandeville, B. (1924) *The Fable of the Bees, or Private Vices, Publick Benefits*, Oxford University Press, Oxford

Marcos, Subcomandante Insurgente (2001) *Our Word is our Weapon*, Seven Stories Press, New York

Marshall, A. (1898) *Principles of Economics*, 4th edition, London

Marx, K. (1954 [1887]) *Capital*, vol 1, Progress Publishers, Moscow

Meikle, S. (1995) *Aristotle's Economic Thought*, Clarendon Press, Oxford

Mirowski, P. (1988) 'Physics and the "marginalist revolution"', in *Against Mechanism: Protecting Economics from Science*, Rowman & Littlefield, New York

Mirowski, P. (1989) *More Heat than Light: Economics as Social Physics; Physics as Nature's Economy*, Cambridge University Press, Cambridge

Montes, L. (2003) 'Das Adam Smith problem: Its origins, the states of the current debate, and one implication for our understanding of sympathy', *Journal of the History of Economic Thought*, vol 25, pp63–90

Oxford English Dictionary (1989) Oxford University Press, Oxford

Pearce, D. (ed) (1986) *The MIT Dictionary of Economics*, MIT Press, Cambridge, MA

Plato (1997) *The Statesman* in J.M. Cooper (ed) *Plato: The Complete Works*, Hackett Publishing, Indianapolis, IN

Polanyi, K. (1944) *The Great Transformation*, Reinhart, New York

Polanyi, K., Arensberg, C. and Pearson, H. (eds) (1957) *Trade and Markets in Early Empires*, The Free Press, New York

Ricardo, D. (1821) *On the Principles of Political Economy and Taxation*, Cosimo Inc., New York, 3rd edition

Robert, J. (1994) *Water is a Commons*, Habitat International Coalition, Mexico City

Robbins, L. (1932) *The Nature and Significance of Economic Science*, Macmillan, London

Rosen, S. (1985) *The Limits of Analysis*, Yale University Press, CT

Sachs, W. (ed) (1992) *The Development Dictionary*, Zed Books, Boston, MA

Sahlins, M. (1972) *Stone Age Economics*, Adline, New York

Saleth, M. and Dinar, A. (2001) 'Preconditions for market solutions to urban water scarcity: Empirical research from Hyderabad City, India', *Water Resources Journal*, vol 37, pp119–132

Samuelson, P. (1948) *Economics*, McGraw Hill, New York

Scott, J. (1999) *Seeing Like a State*, Yale University, Princeton, NJ

Seligman, E.R.A. (ed) (1930) *Encyclopaedia of Social Sciences*, Macmillan, New York

Shanin, T. (1977) *The Awkward Class*, Cambridge, London

Shiva, V. (2002) *Water Wars: Privatization, Pollution and Profit*, South End Press, MA

Sills, D. (ed) (1968) *The International Encyclopaedia of Social Sciences*, The Free Press, New York

Simon, H. (1991) 'Organizations and markets', *Journal of Economic Perspective*, vol 5, pp25–44

Smelser, N. and Baltes, P. (eds) (2004) *International Encyclopedia of the Social and Behavioral Sciences,* Elsevier, New York

Smith, A. (1858[1759]) *The Theory of Moral Sentiments*, A. Millar, London

Smith, A. (1875[1776]) *An Inquiry into the Nature and Causes of the Wealth of Nations*, Methuen, London

Steuart, J. (1767) in A. Millar and T. Cadell (eds) *An Inquiry into the Principles of Political Economy*, Strand, London

Stiglitz, J. (1987) 'The causes and consequences of the dependence of quality on price', *Journal of Economic Literature*, vol 1, no 1, pp1–48

Thompson, E.P. (2000) 'The moral economy of the crowd', in D. Thompson (ed) *The Essential E.P. Thompson*, The New Press, New York

Wolf, E. (1969) *The Peasant Wars of the 20th Century*, Harper & Row, New York

Xenos, N. (1989) *Scarcity and Modernity*, Routledge, London

7

A Bit of the Other: Why Scarcity Isn't All It's Cracked up to Be

Michael Thompson

Opened in 1903, the Karl Ernst Osthaus Museum (in Hagen, Germany) was the first museum of modern art in the world. It is also the only museum to be run explicitly on rubbish theory principles, which helps explain why, to mark its centenary, it republished my book *Rubbish Theory* (Thompson, 1979) in a new German translation by the museum's director, Michael Fehr. *Rubbish Theory* sets out to answer the question that economics, you might think, would have answered but hasn't: how does something second-hand become an antique; how does a rat-infested slum become part of Our Glorious Heritage? My argument will be that, by rectifying this omission on the part of economics we can clarify and resolve some serious problems with the concept of scarcity.

The basic idea is that there are two mutually exclusive cultural categories that are 'socially imposed' on the world of objects: a *transient* category (the members of which have decreasing value and finite expected lifespans) and a *durable* category (the members of which have increasing value and infinite expected lifespans). If these two categories exhausted the material world then the transfer of an object from one to the other would not be possible (because of the mutual contradiction of the categories' defining criteria). But, of course, they are not exhaustive; they only encompass those objects that are valued, leaving a vast and disregarded realm – rubbish – that, it turns out, provides the one-way route from transience to durability (see Figure 7.1). Hence Michael Fehr's nice insight that there are just two destinations: the rubbish tip and the museum. Once produced, a transient object will decline in value and in expected lifespan, eventually reaching zero on both. In an ideal (for some, at any rate) world it would then, having reached the end of its usefulness, disappear in a cloud of dust. But often this does not happen; it lingers on in a valueless and timeless limbo (rubbish) until, perhaps, it is 'discovered' by some creative and upwardly mobile individual and transferred across into the durable category.[1]

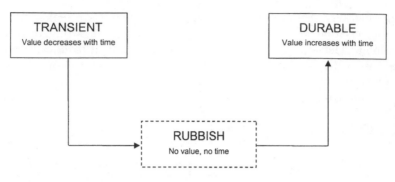

Source: Thompson (1979, p10)

Figure 7.1 *Cultural categories of objects and the possible transfers between them*

There is, of course, a great deal more to rubbish theory than this, but already we can see some of the serious inadequacies of neoclassical economics:

- Thanks to its insistence on the notion of scarcity (it defines economics as 'the allocation of scarce resources to alternative ends')[2] neoclassical economics restricts itself to the realm of value – the transient and durable categories – and turns its back on everything else (see Chapters 4, 5 and 6, this volume, for diverse perspectives on scarcity and economics). This, of course, is why it cannot account for something second-hand becoming an antique, or for all those Georgian terraced houses in inner London that, far from having been swept away (as was the planners' intention back in the 1960s) are now designated as conservation areas and statutorily listed as being of 'outstanding architectural or historical interest' (and worth many millions of pounds each!)
- Neoclassicists, of course, will claim that they have not ignored the realm of the valueless, and that it is taken care of by their notion of *waste*. But waste is not the same as rubbish, because it is still under the thrall of scarcity: if it hadn't been scarce to start with it wouldn't have been wasted! For instance, once fresh water has been defined as scarce, every drop of it that reaches the sea, and has therefore not been diverted to some productive end, is a drop wasted. In the same way, a recent World Bank review of urban infra-structure programmes in developing countries noted that many municipal water authorities were 'grossly inefficient and wasteful of scarce supplies' (Black, 1998, p52). And much the same scarcity-framing is evident in the notion of *bads* – goods, as it were, that happen to have negative value. Neither waste nor bads equate to rubbish: to valuelessness and timelessness[3]
- Nor can neoclassical economics, with its utilitarian logic, cope adequately with the durable category. Turnover-maximization (as in the old Tesco

supermarkets' dictum 'Pile it high and sell it cheap') can make little sense of objects that get more and more valuable by just sitting there doing nothing.[4] Hence the strange labels economists attach to durable objects: 'non-use value', 'existence value', 'positional goods' and so on

- Some economists, of course, may seek to expand their 'territory' by imposing scarcity where none existed before. Thus we find passengers on London's Underground being reclassified as 'customers' (as if they could take their custom to some other, rival Underground) and, turning to the developing world, water being redefined as an 'economic good': the leitmotif of the development community over the past decade or so (e.g. Garn, 1998; Briscoe, 1997). Indeed, one expert has even gone so far as to insist that the water that is brought to us by reservoirs and pipes is a 'product' not a service! Furthermore, it must be kept scarce, if need be by increasing demand relative to supply.

> *A programme's designers and managers must understand that they are selling a product, not providing a service. Where sufficient demand exists, the facilities and services offered must be tailored to that demand; where demand is not strong, it must be stimulated.* (Cairncross, 1992, pv)

This discourse of scarcity, if it becomes hegemonic, will drown out the contending 'water as a human right' discourse (and the general well-being and public health discourse) as, for instance, happened for a while in Britain where families that were not able to pay their water bills were disconnected (see Mehta, 2003, for a discussion of these discourses in the water domain). If the disconnectees were living in high-rise public housing (and many were) the health risks were not just to themselves, since they resorted to hurling their excrement from their balconies in polythene bags that then burst open when they hit the ground.

So neoclassical economics, thanks to its overeager attachment to scarcity, is making a pig's ear of it all; what is needed is some sort of systems theory approach that can take in both the valued and the valueless *and* the dynamic relationship between them.[5] And, in order to get some idea of what that systems approach might be, we need to return to Karl Ernst Osthaus's remarkable museum.

Utility versus utopia

At the time I was writing *Rubbish Theory* I was much involved with some early conceptual artists – The Art and Language Group – and so I was delighted to be offered the chance of another dabble:[6] this time as a curator of, and contributing artist to, the major exhibition – Museutopia – that was mounted in celebration of the Karl Ernst Osthaus Museum's centenary.[7] 'What would life be like', ran Michael Fehr's invitation to his international stable of artists, 'in a situation where all our material needs have been met?'.

My 'exhibit' was an outline for a play – a one-act farce – that, it was hoped, would be performed in the Hagen museum by the Bonn Shakespeare Players, a student theatre group. Unfortunately, getting from my idea to an actual performance would have required something akin to the intense and gruelling process by which a Mike Leigh play or film sees the light of day, and this was simply not feasible for the Bonn Shakespeare Players (for one thing, they had their exams to pass!). So my artwork ended up becoming part of the documentation for the exhibition (Fehr and Rieger, 2003), a curious resource that I will now draw on to try to answer the question we are faced with: how do we make the neoclassical pig's ear into a systems theory silk purse?

The farce, I should explain, has a *dramatis personae* of five, none of whom ever met any of the others in 'real life':

William Blake (visionary and utopianist);
Po Chu-I (retired mandarin and poet);
John Maynard Keynes (economist and would-be dentist);
Jackie Onassis (insecurity advisor and slimming expert);
Miss Piggy (consumer and architectural critic).

The plot in outline

'Keynes', his biographer Robert Skidelsky (2000, p478) concludes, 'was not a socialist. But like Blake he strove to realize a utopia beyond the economics of industrialism ...' If we take 'beyond the economics of industrialism' as synonymous with the state of affairs where all our material needs have been met (as in Michael Fehr's invitation) then Keynes's and Blake's and our Museutopia are essentially one and the same (and different from the socialist utopias that champions of liberal democracy now see as things of the past).[8]

Keynes, true to his early mentor, the Cambridge philosopher G.E. Moore,[9] always looked forward to the time when economists would be 'like dentists':[10] a time when, as he put it:

> ... we shall once more value ends above means and prefer the good to the useful. We shall honour those who can teach us how to pluck the hour and the day virtuously and well, the delightful people who are capable of taking direct enjoyment in things, the lilies of the field who toil not, neither do they spin. (Keynes, as quoted by Skidelsky, 2000, p478)

Keynes, though perfectly serious, is being deliberately outrageous ('impish' is the word used by those who knew him well); he *has* to be outrageous because what he is saying contradicts the *non-satiety requirement* that underpins pretty well all of economic theorizing and analysis – the insistence that, as the very careful wording has it, a person will always prefer a larger bundle of goods to a smaller one.[11]

More than a thousand years before Keynes and his beloved Bloomsbury Group, and on the other side of the globe, the retired mandarin Po Chu-I said much the same, the title of his famous work – *A Mad Poem Addressed to My Nephews and Nieces*[12] – indicating that he too was well aware of the outrageousness of this utopia: a utopia in which, in gentle but firm defiance of the non-satiety requirement, a smaller bundle of goods is consistently preferred to a larger one:

What I shall need are very few things.
A single rug to warm me through the winter;
One meal to last me the whole day.
It does not matter that my house is rather small;
One cannot sleep in more than one room!
It does not matter that I have not many horses;
One cannot ride on two horses at once!

And more recently, and almost half a world away again, the best-selling book, *Your Money or Your Life* (Dominguez and Robbin, 1992) has become a bible to all those North Americans who have decided to *downshift* and, in the process, to radically redefine The American Dream. Here, the defiance of the non-satiety requirement is rather more strident than it is in Keynes or in Po Chu-I: 'Even if you win the rat-race, you're still a rat'. And it is here, in this pithy one-liner, that we can detect the essence of my argument, which is that the denial of the non-satiety requirement entails its confirmation: that to downshift you have first to have something to downshift *from*. In other words, being one way is possible only when there is another, contradictory, way to define oneself against.

Nor, of course, do we have to look far to find this other. The philosophy of plenitude (the term 'plenitude' comes from another rejector of the non-satiety requirement, Lewis Mumford (1964, p400) would never have cut much ice with Jackie Onassis, who famously declared 'You can never be too rich or too thin'. And Miss Piggy, when she learnt about the aesthetic principle that underlay Mies van der Rohe's architecture – 'Less is more' – was having none of that nonsense. 'More is more', she insisted in her unstoppable way, and that was that![13]

The non-extinguishability of the other – in this case, the Jackie Onassises and Miss Piggys who make our utopia unattainable in its totality – far from being a setback, gets us off a rather awkward hook: *the end of technology.*

- If we all agreed that all our material needs had finally been met then our technology would stop. But technology can't stop (or, at least, if it did stop it would not be able to stay where it was!). As Langdon Winner observed (1977), 'We don't just use technology; we *live* it', which means that Keynes' utopian moment – when ends are once more valued above means and the good above the useful – may well be a long time in coming. The trouble is that we and our technology are simply not separable in this way. Like a bike and its rider, the whole thing is only viable if it is bowling along. People who can balance themselves on a stationary bicycle are found only in circuses!

- Worse still, if our technology stopped so would our utopian thinking. This is because the whole point of utopias is to mobilize and motivate actions of one sort rather than another: to sink costs into our preferred path of technological development – small is beautiful, say (if our utopia is one in which all differences are equalized, like Pol Pot's) or bigger is better (if our utopia is one in which there is a place for everyone and everyone in his or her place, like Plato's Republic) – and thereby prevent those costs being sunk into other paths that are preferred by those other actors to whom our utopia is distinctly dystopian. (Buckminster Fuller's vision of an intercontinental electricity grid, which would enable North America to transfer its summertime excess of generated power to South America and vice versa, would be seriously at odds with the 'small is beautiful' utopia that is espoused by, for instance, several 'deep ecologists')
- This crucial and unbreakable connection between the ideational realm and the material base also explains the otherwise bizarre attention given by utopianists (think of Speer's detailed drawings for the new capital of Europe at Linz – Hitler's birthplace) to the physical forms that their New Jerusalems will take: Thomas More's capital city and its 53 satellite towns, the farmers, the clothing of the men and the women, the absence of iron (and hence the need for external contact and trade) and so on.

After all, if ideas were only ideas (as they would be if we were no longer concerned about our material needs) there would be no point in having them! So we should be grateful to the Jackie Onassises and Miss Piggys of this world precisely because, in preventing the attainment of our utopia, they actually make it possible. Striving, not arriving, is the utopian essence![14]

'Nothing very farcical in all that', you might say, but the entertainment is mostly in the details: the high seriousness of the Bloomsbury Group (with their religion of 'timeless ecstasy') when it is brought face-to-face with Po Chu-I's 'hermit peace'[15] or with Miss Piggy's philosophy of 'more is more' and so on. So, in order to preserve the farcibility of it all, I have put these details into the rather copious endnotes. That way, the reader can have a chuckle or two at the expense of these diverse utopianists without interrupting the flow of my argument (and the justification for my title): that there is an *essential contention*[16] between all those visions of the future, and that neoclassical economics, thanks to its blanket and unreflexive imposition of the notion of scarcity, has totally failed to recognize that. Instead, it has latched onto just one of those visions – Miss Piggy's – and sought to wipe out the others. Not a sensible thing to do if your very life depends on their being there.

Mapping the essentially contested terrain

If people quite often transgress the non-satiety requirement – and only Miss Piggy, among our five characters, does not transgress it[17] – then perhaps there are more ways of economizing than neoclassical economics allows. So we can begin where economics should have begun: by asking how many ways of economizing are logically possible. There turn out to be five, each of which recommends itself to the upholders of one of the five forms of social solidarity that have long been familiar to social scientists, and that have now been systematized by cultural theory.[18] All this can be set out by summarizing the chapter 'Making ends meet' in the book *Cultural Theory* (Thompson et al, 1990).

'Making ends meet' is ordinary language for economizing, and the ends in question are needs and resources. But needs and resources are not just given; to some considerable extent, we make the ends themselves before we make them meet. Cultural theory is built upon this 'social malleability'; it gives formal expression to the everyday observations that some people are more needy than others, and that some are more resourceful than others. Its basic hypothesis is that whether a person[19] is able to manage his needs and his control over resources depends on the way in which he is caught up in the process of social life. Po Chu-I, for instance, was not able to prefer a smaller bundle of goods to a larger one until he had withdrawn from the sort of social involvements that went with his privileged yet demanding life as a mandarin – in his case, a regional governor. There are, therefore, four logical possibilities:

1   You can manage neither your needs nor your resources
2   You can manage your needs but not your resources
3   You can manage your resources but not your needs
4   You can manage your needs and your resources.

As you go down this list of possibilities, needs and resources get more malleable. At Possibility 1 they are not malleable at all; they are 'frozen up'. At Possibilities 2 and 3 there is one degree of freedom; one scope – to manage needs in the first case, to manage resources in the second – has 'thawed out'. And at Possibility 4 there are two degrees of freedom; nothing is frozen up (Figure 7.2).

Reasoning in terms of degrees of freedom, though quite common in the natural sciences, is something of a rarity in social science, so I will have to go carefully.

- At Possibility 1 you cannot really develop a strategy. All you can do is try to cope, as best you can, with a situation over which you have no control
- At Possibility 2 you can only increase your ability to choose by managing your needs down so that they lie more comfortably within your fixed resources
- At Possibility 3 you can increase your ability to choose by managing your resources up, thereby lessening the risk of them being overwhelmed by your fixed needs
- Possibility 4, because it involves two degrees of freedom, is more complicated and gives rise to two strategies:
    - Possibility 4a: depending on how you mix your two managements, you can gain a third degree of freedom. You can, if you are managing them

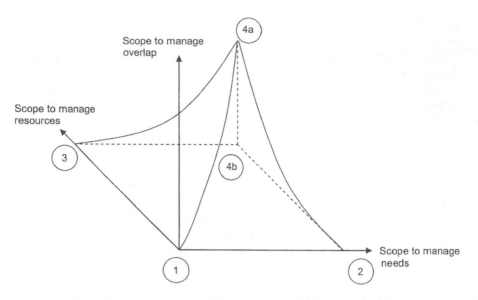

Figure 7.2 *The three degrees of freedom and the five need-and-resource managing strategies*

both up or both down (and, of course, you can periodically switch back and forth between up and down), also manage the size of the overlap between them. As Mr Micawber famously remarked: 'Annual income twenty pounds, annual expenditure nineteen pounds nineteen and six, result happiness. Annual expenditure twenty pounds ought and six, result misery' (Charles Dickens, *David Copperfield*, Chapter 12). So this strategy fits with what is sometimes claimed to be the benefit of a classical education: that it enables you to enjoy life without all the things it prevents you from getting!

– The other strategic option – 4b – is to ignore overlap management and, through energetic involvement in ego-focused networks, to manage both needs and resources up as high as possible. This, of course, is Miss Piggy's strategy, and it is the one of the five that is countenanced by neo-classical economics, and enshrined in its non-satiety requirement. Only in this situation does the exuberant businessman's quip – about being unable to reconcile his net income (command over resources) with his gross habits (ever-proliferating needs) – make any sense.

So this curious space (Figure 7.2) with its five corners – or *singularities* as mathematicians call them – each defining a quite distinct way of economizing, is the basic framework for cultural theory.[20] And, once we have that framework, we can see just how poverty-stricken neoclassical theory is: it has tucked itself into just one of the five corners, denied the other four, and then convinced itself that this little provincial niche is the universe!

So what's wrong, and what's right, with scarcity?

We should be careful not to demonize scarcity. Scarcity, after all, is a wonderful thing; if things – some things – were not scarce we would not be able to get markets to work, nor would hierarchical actors be able to step in and set prices in those situations where markets (perhaps because of spiralling transaction costs) have failed. But markets and hierarchies – the standard duo in institutional economics, and in much political science theorizing – are only two out of the five forms of social solidarity: the five ways of economizing (markets correspond to Possibility 4b; hierarchies to Possibility 3). And it is important that the other three are not squeezed out of the picture, which of course is precisely what happens when the notion of scarcity becomes 'hegemonic'. So it is not scarcity *per se* that we need to worry about; it is when scarcity-based arguments and policy decisions go uncontested – when the voices of the likes of Po Chu-I, Keynes and Blake are silenced – that the little red warning lights should start blinking.[21]

Finally, coming back to the rubbish theory with which I started, there is the question of how its system of transitions – Transient-to-Rubbish and Rubbish-to-Durable – relates to the five ways of economizing with which I have ended up. Until quite recently, I could not really answer this question. Though there was obviously some affinity between rubbish theory's socially imposed categorizations and the 'systemic constructivism' (as Charles Tilly (2007) calls the approach taken by cultural theory) that is involved in the separating out of the five strategies for making ends meet, I could not see how to bring them together. Eventually it dawned on me that the latter are actually inherent in the rubbish theory system (Thompson, 2003). It is not an easy argument, but the gist is that the state of affairs in which the two sets of transfers – Transient-to-Rubbish and Rubbish-to-Durable – happen at exactly the rates needed to maintain the status quo – keeping the whole ever-evolving process by which objects are produced, consumed and conserved going in such a way that power (loads of money, for instance) and status (feeling at ease with Durables, for instance) are continually realigned – is something of a special case.

Each of these two rates can go too slowly or too quickly, in the sense that they can easily diverge from the specific rates that would ensure that the class-based social order (in which power and status are always aligned) exactly reasserts itself through all the changes in the material 'markers' by which that social order is achieved. If things go too slowly then power and status will no longer be fully aligned, and we will find ourselves being transformed into a caste-based society (as in the classical Indian system in which the meat-eating Rajah sits firmly at the head of the power structure but defers to the vegetarian Brahmin within the hierarchy of status). Conversely, if things go too quickly, the Durable category will collapse under its own weight, the status currency will be debauched, and the totality will move away at right-angles to the class-caste axis.

As status differences disappear, transactions become increasingly symmetrical, and we move onto the 'level playing field' so beloved, for instance, by those who have embraced Margaret Thatcher's 'enterprise culture'.

So, with the 'hydraulic' system moving this way and that across this two-dimensional space, depending on which hands manage to turn which 'taps' which way, we end up with four extremities, each of which is attractive to one of the four 'engaged' solidarities (fatalists just have to accept the way things happen to be) and unattractive to the other three. Neoclassical economics (along with its emphasis on scarcity) makes good sense of the level playing field extremity, but you will need Georgescu-Roegen's (1974) thermodynamic economics or Schumacher's (1973) Buddhist economics (or perhaps ecological economics) to cope with how things are at the egalitarian extremity, and a hefty dose of the new institutional economics (Williamson, 1975) to get a handle on the hierarchical extremity. And so it goes, though the fatalistic affinity (dependency theory, perhaps) and the hermit affinity (the absence of economies of scale, perhaps, since that rather does away with competition) are currently more speculative. All of which suggests that the elegance that goes with the notion of scarcity needs to give way to a clumsier set up: one in which each dogma has its day, and neoclassical economics – Alan Greenspan's 'self-interest ideology' along with the Washington consensus – has had its!

Notes

1 Though not without resistance. There are many powerful actors – social scientists often call them 'gatekeepers' – who are intent on preserving what is sometimes referred to as 'the canon'. See Thompson (2003).

2 Economics was formalized, and given this explicit scarcity focus, in the 1920s and 1930s, most notably at the London School of Economics. Before that, it was much more grounded in production processes (Adam Smith's pin factory, for instance) and in the dynamics of industrial organization (Engel's work in the Manchester area, for instance). And Alfred Marshall, though one of Britain's leading mathematicians, refused to mathematize his economics, on the grounds that that would divert him from his ultimate goal: to understand 'the forces that cause movement'. The redefinition, in its original form, went as follows: 'Economics is the science which studies human behaviour as a relationship between ends and scarce means which have alternative uses' (Robbins, 1932, Chapter 1, Section 3).

3 For more on how waste and 'bads' have been uncritically employed in economics, see Gilmartin (2003) and Thompson (1998) respectively.

4 Turnover maximization, of course, is just one of the ways in which economic actors may try to conform to the neoclassical norm of utility (or profit) maximization.

5 This, as was pointed out by an eminent mathematician (Stewart, 1979), is what rubbish theory is trying to do, and I have recently returned to that task by showing how cultural theory (which I set out in the second half of this chapter) can be derived from rubbish theory (Thompson, 2003).

6 An instance of this first dabble was an article (Thompson, 1971) in the journal *Art Language*. There were only two issues of this pretentious and hilarious publication (it was modelled on the journal *Mind* and aimed to overthrow the tyranny of the art object by producing art that was impossessable – a sculpture, for instance, in the

form of a vast and gently widening square-sectioned column of air, rising vertically from an arbitrarily selected 1-kilometre grid square in an ordnance survey map of Oxfordshire and extending all the way to the upper atmosphere).

I was intrigued, 30 or so years later, to see a copy of one of these issues of *Art Language* displayed as *an art object* in London's Whitechapel Gallery (in a retrospective exhibition of early conceptual art). Proof that even the most impossessable of art can be made possessable, if that is what the art market demands.

7   The exhibition, as befits conceptual art, was only a part of it. It was preceded by an international seminar on 'Utopia Thinking' and this, in turn, led to the museum being asked to develop a major international conference on a related theme for the Nord-Rhein Westfalia Institute for Advanced Studies (see respectively, Fehr and Rieger, 2005; Rüsen et al, 2004).

8   An American academic who attended one of our Museutopia meetings told us he had had to lie to his colleagues about the purpose of his trip to Europe. Utopias, he told us, were considered so *passé* that his career would have been in danger if he had told the truth!

9   G.E. Moore, it is probably fair to say, has not worn well, perhaps because, as has often been argued, the Edwardian world in which he flourished (his *Principia Ethica* – the formal enunciation of the doctrine around which the Bloomsbury Group formed itself – was published in 1902) was so completely swept away by World War I. At the time, however, Moore's teachings were, as one of Keynes' biographers observes, 'exceptionally appealing to the spirited young' (Lekachman, 1966, p17). Keynes himself has bequeathed us a marvellous summary of this doctrine:

> *Nothing mattered except states of mind, our own and other people's of course, but chiefly our own. These states of mind were not associated with action or achievement or with consequence. They consisted in timeless, passionate states of contemplation and communion, largely unattached to 'before' and 'after'. Their value depended, in accordance with the principle of organic unity, on the state of affairs as a whole which could not be usefully analysed into parts. For example, the value of the state of mind of being in love did not depend merely on the nature of one's own emotions, but also on the worth of their objects and on the reciprocity and nature of the object's emotions, but it did not depend, if I remember rightly, or did not depend much, on what happened, or how one felt about it, a year later, though I myself was always an advocate of a principle of organic unity through time, which still seems to me only sensible. The appropriate subjects of passionate contemplation and communion were a beloved person, beauty and truth, and one's prime objects in life were love, the creation and enjoyment of aesthetic experience and the pursuit of knowledge. Of these love came a long way first.* (Keynes, 1949)

The doctrine, Lekachman continues, was 'highly aristocratic and highly personal' and it 'assumed a society sufficiently stable and satisfactory in its social, financial and practical arrangements to enable the practitioners of Moore's ethics to devote all their time to the acquisition of desirable states of mind' (Lekachman, 1966, p17). In other words, as in the Museutopia project, it assumed a world where all our material needs have been met. Since this, clearly is not how the world was back in 1902, the doctrine, it has always been assumed, was accessible only to a privileged few: those, like the writer E.M. Foster and the other, rather more firmly attached, members of the Bloomsbury Group, who had substantial private incomes.

10 Even, or perhaps especially, in the depressed years of the 1920s Keynes looked forward to that not-far-off day when the problems of scarcity that so exercised economists (and so elevated their skills, not least in their own eyes) would disappear: the time when, as in our Museutopia, all our material needs have been met:

> *Do not let us overestimate the importance of the economic problem, or sacrifice to its supposed necessities other matters of greater and more permanent significance. It should be a matter for specialists, like dentistry.* (Keynes, 1931)

'Possibly', as Lekachman (1966, p42) has wryly observed, 'displeasing both professions at a stroke', Keynes spelt out his idea of the economist's role in this utopian scheme of things, 'If economists could manage to get themselves thought of as humble, competent people, on a level with dentists, that would be splendid.'

11 Economists are careful not to deny the truism that you can have too much of a good thing. People, they argue, can become pig-sick of smoked salmon, say, and they are careful to stress that the insatiability applies to things in the plural, not to this or that particular thing. Hence the 'bundle of goods' form of words (see Awh, 1976). We should also note that if people were not insatiable they would not have to prioritize their ever-proliferating needs so as to bring them within their more limited resources, and if they didn't do that the whole edifice of neoclassical economics would collapse. So it is the theory that *requires* the non-satiety.

12 Translated (c1918) Arthur Waley, *Chinese Poems* (Allen & Unwin, London, 1918). Po Chu-I flourished around the first half of the 9th century. For a more extensive treatment of him, particularly of how his way of economizing relates to the other four ways that are socially possible (only one of which is consistent with the non-satiety requirement) see Chapter 2 of Thompson et al (1990).

Po Chu-I's needs, far from spiralling ever onwards and upwards, are non-proliferating and, moreover, so undemanding that they fit comfortably within his quite modest resources. No need, therefore, for all the prioritizing that is so central to economic theorizing. Indeed, were Po Chu-I to start prioritizing his needs he would scupper his distinctive management style, which depends on him maintaining the comfortable gap between his needs and his resources by all the time redefining the former in relation to the latter.

But *is* Po Chu-I a full-blooded utopian? I think not, because his concern is simply to explain and justify his hermit peace; not to struggle, Blake-like, his sword never sleeping in his hand, until everyone (whether they like it or not) is in the same condition. Nor is he utopian in the way Keynes was: confident that, the moment our society moves beyond the 'economics of industrialism', we will all make the switch of our own volition, and there will simply be no need for all the Blakean paraphernalia: arrows of desire, bows of burning gold, chariots of fire and so on.

So Blake, Keynes and Po Chu-I, though they all contradict the non-satiety requirement, have very different commitments. Blake, you could say, is the 'muscular utopian': determined to bring everyone to his Jerusalem, whatever the cost in mental fight. Keynes is a 'languid utopian': assured that, when the conditions are at last right, we will all make the transition of our own enlightened choice. And Po Chu-I is neither muscular nor languid: concerned only with achieving that utopian condition for himself and, in a very quiet way, letting other people know that such a transition is possible. It is my argument that only the Po Chu-Is of this world will avoid disappointment; the others have set their hearts on a universal state of affairs that is achievable only in part.

13 Here I am indebted to the distinguished Miss Piggy scholar, Mark Sagoff, who also alerted me to the non-satiety requirement, and to its crucial importance for modern economic theory (see Sagoff, 1993).

Just as there are important differences between Blake, Keynes and Po Chu-I, even though they all contradict the non-satiety requirement, so Jackie Onassis and Miss Piggy, though they are both in line with that requirement, are not quite the same. Jackie Onassis is insecure, in that she has an elevated social status to maintain, while Miss Piggy, being unconcerned (unaware, even) of the potential 'falls from grace' (nicely depicted in Tom Wolfe's (1987) *The Bonfire of the Vanities*) that so exercise Jackie Onassis, is wondrously self-assured. Miss Piggy's money is not old, nor is she at all interested in making it old, which, of course, explains why, unlike Jackie Onassis, she loses no sleep over her ample girth. Economists would be more pleased with Miss Piggy, and would have to wheel in Thorsten Veblen and his *Theory of the Leisure Class* (1899) or Fred Hirsch (1977) and his notion of 'positional goods', in order to cope fully with Jackie O.

14 Blake was careful not to show us Jerusalem complete as a rebuilt city. Rather (and here we see the common strand in his and Keynes' utopianisms) it is a state of mind, to be built by all of us at all times – ongoing work, contingent, provisional, and always under threat. The threats, however, were there all right, and Blake was not reticent about showing us those; most famously, perhaps, in his depiction of three miserable little figures – they turn out to be Bacon, Newton and Locke – framed by a trilithon from the reconstructed Stonehenge. His three archetypal scientists, we learn, are mutations/combinations of Albion's 12 sons, and Blake is here associating the corrupting influence of Reason and Science with the Druids' perversion of patriarchal religion towards oppressive laws and human sacrifice. Greek and Roman art were likewise demonized, and Blake asserted, in direct contradiction of the orthodoxy of his day, that 'Rome & Greece swept Art into their maw and destroyed it'. 'Mathematic Form', which Blake saw as being embodied in 'The Classics', had to be replaced by 'Living Form' – Gothic (and half a century or so later, with what Summerson (1945, p292) has called 'The Revolution Against Taste', and the consequent ascendancy of Pugin's 'pointy architecture', it was). Gothic, of course, was eventually dislodged by modernism, by which time the Bloomsbury Group (Keynes included) were merrily making themselves at home in the classical Georgian architecture that had so incensed Blake. All of which just goes to show how sensible Blake was not to provide us with any pictures of his Jerusalem!

15 In Endnote 12 I distinguished Po Chu-I's 'hermit peace' from both Blake's 'Jerusalem' and Keynes' 'timeless ecstasy'. Where Blake and Keynes saw everyone eventually arriving at their utopias, Po Chu-I was content just to arrive there himself, and to then quietly let people know that such a destination existed and was reachable. Even so, the threats were still there for Po Chu-I, just as they were for Blake (and also for Keynes, though he managed to keep them at bay with a combination of intellectual brilliance and startling rudeness). (Also, there were many who, whenever he mounted his utopian hobby-horse, simply refused to believe he was being serious. Had they realized he was they might have been moved to do something about it.) The main threat for Po Chu-I was from the almost hegemonic hierarchical social order of China at that time: an order that he was challenging (very quietly,

admittedly) by taking it on himself to define his needs and his resources where they, in a hierarchical order, are determined for him by his rank and station. In the book *Cultural Theory* (Thompson et al, 1990, p41) we made this threat real by magically transporting Po Chu-I into present-day Britain:

> *But then comes a knock on Po Chu-I's door. It is a small deputation of public officials come to tell him that he has been living below the poverty line; he does not have enough bedclothes; he is not eating enough; his mobility is inadequate; his small house is in contravention of current housing standards. He is to be moved into an old people's home where he will be properly clothed, fed and housed. As he makes this involuntary transition to the old people's home, his needs are expanded for him until they reach their 'correct' level.*

Poor old Po! Completely off his chump, obviously: thinking he, of all people, could know what his needs were!

16 An *essentially contested concept*, following Gallie (1955) is one that can never be pinned down in a single way but can be clarified only through regular argument, that is, through discourse.

17 Jackie Onassis almost satisfies the requirement, but her concern for status lets her down (see note 13).

18 See Thompson et al, 2006.

19 Strictly speaking, a *dividual*, since most of us live different parts of our lives in different solidarities – workplace and home, for instance.

20 There is a great deal at stake here, in that cultural theory, in taking us from the neo-classicist's 'one component' system to a fivefold interplay, takes us from simplicity (in the technical sense of the word) to complexity. This is something that institutional economics (e.g. Williamson, 1975) does not do, even though, to its credit, it recognizes the existence of two of the five singularities – markets and hierarchies. Such a twofold system, however, is still simple, because, like neoclassical economics, it is still deterministic: if you're tipped out of markets you'll end up in hierarchy and vice versa. But go beyond two and the dynamics become unpredictable.

Indeed, if we take our freezing and thawing-out metaphor literally, we can see that the 'heat' in this system is defying the second law of thermodynamics. It is flowing from the 'cold' bodies to the 'hot' bodies, in that those dividuals who are able to create freedoms for themselves are doing so largely at the expense of those who are not able to do this. There is, in other words, a breaking of symmetry, in which tiny random imbalances, far from cancelling one another out, are magnified into mutually sustaining differences of kind. It is this sort of disequilibrating mechanism – the more, the more; the less, the less ('To those that have shall be given; from those that have not shall be taken away, even that which they have') – that is at the centre of theories of self-organization generally. For the breaking of symmetry see Thom (1972). For self-organization see Prigogine and Stengers (1984). For non-ergodicity (the failure of small historical events to cancel one another out) see Arthur (1989a and 1989b).

21 The short answer to the question 'why should we heed these warning lights?' is that, if we do, we can avoid an awful lot of what Aaron Wildavsky (1981) called *curvilinearity*. Curvilinearity is when, as you are doing something that is giving you more and more of what you want – trust, say, or profit or even 'hermit peace' –

you cross some invisible threshold and start getting less and less of what you want and eventually, if you persist, the exact opposite of what you want. George Soros' argument – that if you were somehow able to get rid of anti-capitalism you would destroy capitalism (Soros, 1997) – rests on this notion of curvilinearity, and we sometimes see it lampooned in that common bureaucratic response 'Hierarchy isn't working; we need more hierarchy!'

Curvilinearity cuts in, so the cultural theory argument runs, when some of the solidarities' 'voices' become so loud that some of the others are drowned out. And that, of course, is what has happened in all those situations in which the scarcity notion goes unchallenged. For a number of worked policy examples – both elegant failures (where voices are being drowned out) and clumsy successes (where each of the voices is heard, and responded to, by the others) – see Verweij and Thompson (2006).

References

Arthur, W.B. (1989a) 'Self-reinforcing mechanisms in economics', in P.W. Anderson and K.J. Arrow (eds) *The Economy as an Evolving Complex System*, Santa Fe Institute Studies in Complexity, Addison-Wesley, Reading, MA

Arthur, W.B. (1989b) 'Competing technologies, increasing returns and lock-in by historical events', *Economic Journal*, vol 99, pp116–131

Awh, R. (1976) *Microeconomics: Theory and Applications*, John Wiley, New York

Black, M. (1998) *Learning What Works: A 20 Year Retrospective View on International Water and Sanitation Cooperation*, UNDP-World Bank Water and Sanitation Program

Briscoe, J. (1997) 'Managing water as an economic good: Rules for reformers', in M. Kay, T. Franks and L. Smith (eds) *Water: Economics, Management and Demand*, Chapman and Hall, London

Cairncross, S. (1992) 'Sanitation and water supply: Practical lessons from the decade', UNDP-World Bank Water and Sanitation Discussion Paper No 9, UNDP-World Bank, Washington DC

Dominguez, J. and Robin, V. (1992) *Your Money or Your Life*, Penguin, New York

Fehr, M. and Rieger, T. (eds) (2003) *Museutopia: Schritte in andere Welten*, Neuer, Hagen Folkwang-Verlag im Karl Ernst Osthaus-Museum

Fehr, M. and Rieger, T. (eds) (2005) *Thinking Utopia*, Berghahn, Oxford

Gallie, W.B. (1955) 'Essentially contested concepts', *Proceedings of the Aristotelian Society*, vol 56, pp167–198

Garn, M. (1998) *Managing Water as an Economic Good: The Transition From Supply-Oriented to Demand Responsive Services*, The World Bank, Washington, DC

Georgescu-Roegen (1974) *The Entropy Law and Economic Progress*, Cambridge, Harvard University Press, MA

Gilmartin, G. (2003) 'Water and waste: Nature, productivity and colonialism in the Indus Basin', *Economic and Political Weekly*, vol 38, no 48, pp5057–5065

Hirsch, F. (1977) *Social Limits to Growth*, Routledge & Kegan Paul, London

Keynes, J.M. (1931) *Essays in Persuasion*, Macmillan, London

Keynes, J.M. (1949) 'My early beliefs', *Two Memoirs*, Kelly, Village Station, New York

Lekachman, R. (1966) *The Age of Keynes*, Penguin, Harmondsworth

Mehta, L. (2003) 'Struggles around "publicness" and the right to access: Perspectives from the water domain', in I. Kaul (ed) *Global Public Goods: Making Globalisation Work for All*, Oxford University Press, New York

Mumford, L. (1964) *The Pentagon of Power*, Secker and Warburg, London

Prigogine, I. and Stengers, I. (1984) *Order Out of Chaos: Man's New Dialogue with Nature*, Bantam Books, New York

Robbins, L. (1932) *Essay on the Nature and Significance of Economic Science*, Macmillan, London

Rüsen, J., Fehr, M. and Ramsbrock, A. (eds) (2004) *Die Unruhe der Kultur: Potentiale des Utopischen*, Vebrück Wissenschaft, Göttingen

Sagoff, M. (1993) 'Ethical dimensions of consumption and stewardship', unpublished research proposal submitted to the Pew Charitable Trusts by the Institute for Philosophy and Public Policy, University of Maryland, MD

Schumacher, E.F. (1973) *Small Is Beautiful*, Blond and Briggs, London

Skidelsky, R. (2000) *John Maynard Keynes Vol. 3: Fighting For Britain 1937–1946*, Macmillan, London

Soros, G. (1997) 'The capitalist threat', *The Atlantic Monthly*, vol 279, no 2, pp45–58

Stewart, I. (1979) 'Review of "Rubbish Theory"', *New Scientist*, 23 August, p605

Summerson, J. (1945[1962]) *Georgian London*, Pelican, Harmondsworth

Thom, R. (1972) *Stabilité Structurelle et Morphogénèse*, Benjamin, Paris

Thompson, M. (1971) 'Category and action', *Art Language*, vol 1, no 2

Thompson, M. (1979) *Rubbish Theory: The Creation and Destruction of Value*, Oxford University Press, Oxford (republished (2003) in a new German translation by Michael Fehr, as *Mülltheorie: Über die Schaffung und Vernichtung von Werten*, Klartext-Verlag, Essen)

Thompson, M. (1998) 'Waste and fairness', *Social Research*, vol 65, no 1, pp55–73

Thompson, M. (2003) 'Time's square: Deriving cultural theory from rubbish theory', *Innovation*, vol 16, no 4, pp319–330

Thompson, M., Ellis, R.E. and Wildavsky, A. (1990) *Cultural Theory*, Westview, Boulder, Colorado

Thompson, M., Ellis, R. and Verweij, M. (2006) 'Why and how culture matters', in R.E. Goodin and C. Tilly (eds) *The Oxford Handbook of Contextual Political Analysis*, Oxford University Press, Oxford

Tilly, C. (2007) 'Three visions of history and theory', *History and Theory*, vol 46, no 2, pp299–307

Veblen, T. (1899) *Theory of the Leisure Class*, republished 1953, New American Library, New York

Verweij, M. and Thompson, M. (eds) (2006) *Clumsy Solutions for a Complex World*, Palgrave Macmillan, Basingstoke

Wildavsky, A. (1981) 'Rationality in writing: Linear and curvilinear', *Journal of Public Policy*, vol 1, pp125–140

Williamson, O. (1975) *Markets and Hierarchies*, Free Press, New York

Winner, L. (1977) *Autonomous Technology*, MIT Press, Cambridge, MA

Wolfe, T. (1987) *The Bonfire of the Vanities*, Jonathan Cape, New York

Part III
Resource Scarcity, Institutional Arrangements and Policy Responses: Food, Agriculture, Water and Energy

Commentary

Lyla Mehta

The preceding sections examined why scarcity matters and its role in economics. This section now turns to specific resources and resource scarcity with a focus on food, agriculture, water and energy. The chapters on food and agriculture concentrate on the problems of hunger and agricultural production in both the north and south

In Chapter 8 Nicholas Hildyard focuses on how scarcity often emerges as a political strategy. While numerous empirical studies locate the cause of deprivation in power imbalances and struggles over access to and control over resources, neo-Malthusianism has shifted focus to population growth as a cause of absolute scarcity in the future. Neo-Malthusianism is used to colonize the future to serve particular interests, be it to privatize the commons or water or promote biotechnology. The scare of unbridled population growth in the future is used to legitimize the present takeover of a range of resources. Projections and scares of future resource crises and a Malthusian world (witness, for example, current debates on climate change, mass migration and resource scarcity) are privileged over practice/lived reality. This is clearly demonstrated in Chapter 9 by Ian Scoones on soil fertility which looks at two ways of seeing scarcity. The global vision focuses on different levels of nutrient imbalance based on aggregate input-output models (which is reproduced in the Commission for Africa report). In contrast, local farmers view scarcity in a very different way, often identifying lack of fertility as an opportunity. In Chapter 10 Erik Millstone argues that even though productivity in agriculture has increased more rapidly than the population, the problem of chronic hunger persists. In different parts of the world, obesity and starvation are often two sides of the same coin in that they both result from political forces that distort prices, putting food out of the reach of some and making only unhealthy food available to others. In industrialized countries, rising productivity and government intervention in markets have led to the generation of surpluses, the production of foods that people won't eat, and the creation of human-induced scarcities.

The final three chapters turn to water and energy resources and on distinctions between different aspects of scarcity. Water management debates usually focus on first-order issues of physical scarcity. These debates, however, ignore both the multiple aspects of scarcity and the appropriation of water by powerful actors. The resulting interventions, such as 'integrated water resource management', can intensify control over the resource and existing inequities. In Chapter 11 Bruce Lankford argues that scarcity is often viewed in volumetric logics in terms of redressing demand and supply balances. This concern is often nurtured by the material realities of water politics, policies and budgets and only partially recognizes how water is shared and can contribute to exacerbating scarcity, especially in the dry season. By drawing on a case study in Tanzania he proposes viewing water scarcity through a facilitative 'share' response which is more suitable for water allocation in highly dynamic environments.

Scarcity is also aggressively promoted by the water establishment in India as demonstrated by Jasveen Jairath in Chapter 12. Policy-makers in India shy away from the social dimensions of water management. By focusing on absolute notions of water scarcity, legitimacy is created for large-scale projects that focus on augmenting water supply through top-down engineering models. But the governance context of such policy implementation docs not necessarily reallocate augmented water supplies according to democratic norms. Most marginalized people do not gain access to new water sources due to discriminatory access and control by the powerful. Thus, rather than focusing on creating 'more water' and water scarcity, it is important to focus on the social and political factors that cause inaccessibility and perpetrate exclusions. In Chapter 13 Dipak Gyawali and Ajaya Dixit also focus on the dominant development ethos as propagated by donors and planners which creates new demands and scarcities where none existed before. In Nepal, powerful players such as the World Bank and politicians have used the discourse of TINA (there is no alternative) to promote flawed and expensive white elephants such as the hydropower project, Arun III, and expensive highways at the cost of cheaper and more decentralized options. Thus, there is the need for civil society and other social auditors to forge alternative paths that allow for more plural debate, where simplistic dichotomies are rejected and there is scope for innovation and alternatives.

These chapters highlight the need to link the discursive framings of what we mean by scarcity with value and how we determine what is scarce.[1] Governmentality (in other words, the technologies and rationalities of the state) is key to understanding how issues of scarcity can legitimize policy and we need to be aware of wider political and economic forces that tend to aggravate and perpetuate scarcity. Clearly, simplistic portrayals of resource 'crises' must be challenged and local realities need to be a part of policy responses to resource management and allocation processes. This means engaging proactively with global processes such as the Millennium Development Goals (MDGs) in ways that will ensure that local complexities as well as diverse and dynamic aspects of resources can inform high-level policy debates. These need to be combined with improving democratic processes in decision-making around resource management where experts acknowledge local people's own understandings of resources and ways to govern them. This must however not gloss over local power and relations around scarce resources (for example, mythical and symbolic implications of water in different societies can also be a form of social control). Finally, to avoid looking at future resource scarcities in mono-causal and deterministic ways, we need to develop a pedagogy and reflexivity that will question the role of institutions that colonize the future in specific ways without drawing from lessons of the past.

Notes

1   Some of the ideas expressed here draw on the insightful comments of the discussants Tim Forsyth, Alan Nicol and Jan Selby, to whom I am most grateful.

8

'Scarcity' as Political Strategy: Reflections on Three Hanging Children

Nicholas Hildyard

A preoccupation with the future not only prevents us from seeing the present as it is but often prompts us to rearrange the past. (Hoffer, 1954)

Those who know Thomas Hardy's novel *Jude the Obscure*, or who have seen the film of the book, may recall the gut-wrenching scene where Jude's eldest child throttles his younger sister and brother and then hangs himself. And all because of 'scarcity'.

Set in the mid-19th century, the story revolves around Jude Fawley, a stonemason, who has been thwarted at every turn in his life: his efforts to 'better himself' by seeking a place at Oxford university – a place he is intelligent enough to obtain – have run foul of Oxford's 'four centuries of gloom, bigotry, and decay'; his union with his cousin, Sue Bridehead, has made him an outcast, thrown out of job and home because they are not married; and his ambitions have been repeatedly dashed by poverty and class. With the family about to be evicted from their lodgings, and learning that another child is on the way, his eldest boy, left alone with the other children while Jude and Sue seek new accommodation, takes matters into his own hands. The adults return, successful in their quest, to find all three of their children hanging from the coat pegs on the back of the bedroom door. A note lies on the floor: 'Done because we are too menny'.

The reader, of course, knows better. Bigotry, the rigidities of the class system and the poverty in which Jude has become trapped are the cause of his predicament, not too large a family. And because we know this, the child's actions are all the more shocking. How could young Jude – such a serious, reflective boy – have got it all so wrong? How had he come to believe that the problem lay with him and his siblings,[1] not prejudice and inequality? For all the child's intelligence, his analysis is ultimately that of a child experienced in the ways of the world but ill-equipped to make sense of them. He has put two and two together – and made four: but the premises he was working from were wrong and his answer reflected the wrong question. We rage because, far from being the level-headed pragmatist he thinks he is, whose calculating will save Jude and Sue, his wrong-headedness sends the couple spiralling into further grief and disaster. We forgive him only because he is naïf – a child.

Presciently, Hardy portrayed Jude's son as the harbinger of a coming way of thinking.[2] And Hardy was right. Wherever environmental crises or developing world poverty are at issue, young Jude stalks the commentaries of political pundits, World Bank officials and barflies alike – at least in the north. At times, his appearance is almost gratuitous:[3] at others, cynical;[4] but, for the most part, subliminal.[5] The grammar and spelling have become more polished, but the message remains the same: 'because we are too menny'.

Some questions …

I mention young Jude because his tragic history encapsulates two of the most striking features of the notion of 'scarcity' within modern economic theory: its failure to explain what it purports to explain and its enduring appeal despite this evident failure.

Both require investigation. Why do we recognize young Jude's disastrous misreading of his family's circumstances – but grant the same misreading such legitimacy when it is applied by economists, demographers, planners, corporate financiers and politicians to the wider world? What are the politics that permit the transformation of 'because-we-are-too-menny' from a tragic, childish error into a statement of the unpalatable but obvious, an analysis that reflects distance and maturity, even into a badge of political courage?[6]

Or, to probe deeper, is young Jude's 'means-ends' thinking *really* the driver behind human behaviour? Is scarcity the inescapable fact of life as Lord Robbins, the early 20th-century British economist, insists? (See Chapter 4, this volume, for nuanced discussions of Lord Robbins' notion of scarcity.)[7] Are we condemned by our 'nature' to be forever making ruthless choices as we tirelessly seek to allocate the limited means available to us between ever-expanding and competing ends? Or is scarcity (as opposed to dearth) the *product* of state planning and market forces, at least in the most recent past?

Or, again, does *Homo economicus*, that obsessive rent-maximizing archetype whose brain is apparently wired to disregard society and act only in response to the ruthlessly Procrustian calculus of cost-benefit analysis, really exist outside of those bureaucracies whose rules are designed to enforce such behaviour? Are the sacrificial 'trade-offs' spawned by cost–benefit analysis – suicide and murder versus trusting one's parents to find new cheaper lodgings; a forest lost here versus improved macroeconomic growth there; children's lives versus a new power station – an inevitable part of the human condition?

Or simply the inevitable product of an economic system expanding under the rule of scarcity (see Fairlie et al, 1993)? What about those numerous other societies (typified by commons-based regimes),[8] that have been organized around avoiding such choices?[9]

And how has the modern economist's notion of scarcity survived as a respectable theory when it fits the realities of everyday behaviour as uneasily as Cinderella's slipper fitted the Ugly Sisters' feet?

... and some observations

As someone who constantly runs up against Malthusian 'explanations' of poverty, hunger, environmental degradation and resource shortages in my solidarity work with communities whose livelihoods are affected by large-scale infrastructure projects, such as dams and oil and gas developments, these questions cry out for inquiry. In this chapter, I focus on how Malthusian explanations are far from politically neutral – and are best viewed and approached as political strategies, not least to foreclose debate and 'colonise the future'.

Some observations may be appropriate.

The first is that there is plentiful empirical evidence from many fine-grained ethnographies of decision-making within both industrial and pre-industrial societies that forcefully debunks the notion that economic behaviour can somehow be separated from other social behaviour (see Polanyi, 2002; LeClair and Schneider, 1968). *Homo economicus* is simply a figment of the economist's imagination (see Part II, this volume, for a range of perspectives on economists, scarcity and *Homo economicus*). In the real world, including the world of large financial institutions,[10] the vast majority of people do not spend their time single-mindedly weighing off scarce resources against supposedly unlimited needs, wants and desires. They make decisions, certainly, but those decisions reflect a plurality of values and concerns whose weight changes with context. In effect, real-world economic behaviour is *never* independent from social behaviour: it is society, culture and power relations – rather than the nostrums of economic theory – which ultimately shape the operations of markets.

Second, needs are not unlimited. Nor do most people conceive of them as such – despite the efforts of the advertising industry and the protestations of economists. As Gustavo Esteva has noted of the new communities that have sprung up on the margins of Mexico City in the wake of successive economic crises:

> People do not assume unlimited ends, since their ends are no more than the other side of their means, their direct expression. If their means are limited, as they are, their ends cannot be unlimited. Within the new commons, needs are defined with verbs that describe activities embodying wants, skills and interactions with others and with the environment. Needs are not separated into different 'spheres' of reality: lacks or

expectations on one side, and satisfiers on the other, reunited through the market or the plan. (Esteva, 1992, p21)

Third, no amount of empirical evidence or counter theory is likely *in and of itself* to undermine the enduring hegemony of the means-ends model of 'economic rationality'. One reason for this is that 'scarcity' as used in modern economic and political thought is best approached as *political strategy* (an endlessly malleable means of legitimizing a particular set of social and political relations, institutions and policies and of blocking inquiry) rather than as theory (a testable hypothesis that stands or falls on its ability not only to explain but also to predict). Empirical evidence, coupled with political organizing around other explanations, may temporarily deny political space to those who would use the strategy in one arena but it does not (and will not) prevent its proponents from using it in other arenas where its power has not been weakened. On the contrary, so long as it remains useful – primarily as a means of diverting attention from causes of poverty that might implicate the powerful – it will be recast, adapted and reused whenever and wherever possible, regardless of the empirical evidence that is built up to counter it.

It is this last point that I would like to explore in a little more depth by drawing on examples from agriculture. I hope that it may assist in our discussions on ways in which the 'scarcity discourse' within dominant strands of modern economics might be countered.

Power not numbers

Within agriculture the scarcity discourse has been largely framed by Malthusian images of demand ('too menny people') outstripping supply, a point elegantly made by both Betsy Hartmann and Erik Millstone in their chapters for this volume (3 and 10). Such Malthusian thinking has not gone unchallenged. On the contrary, detailed sociological and political attention to what is actually happening on the ground has invariably located the causes of hunger not in an *absolute* scarcity but in *socially-generated* scarcity arising from imbalances of power that deny people access to food and water (see Chapters 10, 12 and others in this volume).

More than enough food is currently produced to provide everyone in the world with a nutritious and adequate diet (FAO, 2000), yet one-seventh of the world's people (some 800 million people) go hungry. India, Pakistan and Bangladesh are home to half that number – despite grain silos bursting with a surplus of 59 million tonnes of food (Esteva, 1992, p21; Vidal, 2002; Sainath, 2001; Coronel and Dixit, 2006, p17).[11, 12] If people starve or go malnourished, it is because there is not the food to feed them but because they lack the money to buy it or land on which to grow it (see also Chapter 10, this volume).

As the UN Food and Agriculture Organization (FAO) states: 'After 50 years of modernization, world agricultural production today is more than sufficient to feed 6 billion human beings adequately. Cereal production alone, at about 2 billion tonnes or 330kg of grain per caput/year and representing

3,600 calories per caput/day, could to a large extent cover the energy needs of the whole population if it were well distributed' (FAO, 2000).[13]

The scarcity mill in agriculture

Taking a step back, it is possible to identify a range of power imbalances that lie at the root of the manufactured scarcity that is the hallmark of food poverty, whether yesterday or today. A very incomplete list of such imbalances might include: the enclosure of commons (Fairlie et al, 1993); lack of access to land (Colchester and Lohmann, 1993); unequal gender relations (Agarwal 1995, 1998); ethnic and racial discrimination (Lohmann, 1999);[14] sexism;[15] intra-household inequalities;[16] denial of human rights;[17] the political exploitation of famine (see, for example, Keen, 1984); agricultural modernization;[18] market liberalization;[19] and ecological degradation.[20]

Access to land, for example, is vital to the livelihoods of the world's poorest people. Lack of access to land not only denies people the ability to grow or to gather their own food: it is also excludes them from a source of power. Who controls the land – and how they do so – affects how land is used and to whom the benefits for its use accrue.

Despite land reform programmes being undertaken in many countries, however, highly concentrated patterns of land ownership continue to be a source of impoverishment and hunger worldwide. In Bolivia, just 50,000 families, a mere 0.6 per cent of the country's 8.9 million people,[21] own 90 per cent of the country's productive land, while four-fifths of the rural population remain in poverty.[22] In Brazil, which has the second most concentrated land ownership system in the world,[23] 2.8 per cent of landowners own over 56 per cent of arable land: 45 per cent of the total area is occupied by only 1 per cent of agricultural holdings.[24] The 18 largest landowners own an area equivalent to that of The Netherlands, Portugal and Switzerland combined. In Guatemala, just 2 per cent of the population own 72 per cent of agricultural land, which is used predominantly for sugar, coffee, bananas and rubber plantations, in addition to cattle ranching (Krzaric, 2005).

The corollary of such concentration of land ownership in the hands of the few is land scarcity for the many. Two-thirds of the rural Brazilians rely on smallholder production – but have access to only 2.5 per cent of the total land available for agriculture (Centre Europe – Tiers Monde, 1999, p32, see note 24). In the Philippines, about 68 per cent of rural households with at least one member working in agriculture (three-fifths of the Philippine population) are landless (Rosario-Malonzo, 2005). As in Brazil,[25] official land reform programmes have made little impact (Rosario-Malonzo, 2005, p35; Stocking, 2002). Meanwhile, in the wake of the 'credit crunch' and resulting international financial crisis, many investors are ploughing their money into buying land in southern countries, a 'sector' that is viewed as a potential safe haven in turbulent financial times (Hildyard, 2008).

Even where small producers do have access to land, the unequal terms on which they enter the market, both as producers and consumers, leave them vulnerable to debt and impoverishment. While northern countries continue to protect their farmers – to the tune of $1 billion a day – southern governments have been forced to lower import barriers and remove agricultural subsidies (see Chapter 10, this volume, for a critique of northern agricultural and food policies). Rural incomes have plummeted, as farmers have been left unable to compete with the flood of subsidized imports from rich countries. In 2001 alone, cotton farmers in America received subsidies valued at $4bn – more than the US provides in aid to the whole of Africa (Stocking, 2002).[26] By stimulating overproduction, the subsidies drove down worldwide cotton prices, costing cotton exporting countries in sub-Saharan Africa an estimated $301 million in lost export earnings (Stocking, 2002, p38). Speculation, particularly by hedge funds, has also exacerbated the vulnerability of both poorer consumers and producers, as prices fluctuate wildly (Hildyard, 2008).

For poorer farmers, the structural inequalities embedded in local, regional and world markets make the difference between surviving and starving. Those with wealth and influence win out over those without. Only those who, in the economists' jargon, have the income to translate their biological needs into 'effective demand' get to eat. In today's global supermarket, people earning $25 a year – if they are lucky – must compete for the same food with people who earn $25 an hour, or even $25 a minute.

It is this market logic – and the power structures that drive it – that lies behind the paradox of people starving despite abundant local harvests; that explains why shiploads of grain were exported daily from the famine-stricken Horn of Africa during the 1980s to feed already well-fed Europeans; and that ensures that, even in the rich north, cats and dogs belonging to European pet owners can be better fed than children of low-paid or unemployed European workers.

Colonizing the future

Rooting deprivation firmly and squarely in power relations provides proof – if proof was needed – that no matter how much food is produced or water harnessed, how few babies are born or how dramatically human numbers fall, it is the nature of inequity remorselessly to generate 'scarcity'. Without changes in the social and economic relationships that currently determine the production, distribution and consumption of food and water, there will always be those who are judged 'surplus to requirements' and who are thus excluded from the wherewithal to live. The human population could be halved, quartered, decimated even, yet hunger would still remain. So long as one person has the power to deny food to another, even two people may be judged 'too menny'.

Unsurprisingly, detailed sociological studies that locate the cause of deprivation in struggles over access to – and control over – resources and power have made both the past and the present increasingly hostile territory for Malthusian explanations of scarcity: neither the historical record nor contemporary realities support the view that numbers, rather than power relations, are responsible for scarcity. As a result, fewer and fewer people now suggest that today's or yesterday's famines and water crises lie in absolute scarcities caused by population growth.[27]

But the future is another country – an as yet unoccupied political space where the 'noise' of political economy can be blanked out and Malthusian mathematics are granted an explanatory power that they no longer enjoy when applied to the past and the present. Plugging into the Malthusian notion of 'population' as an inexorable force that spurs humans to breed unchecked, neo-Malthusians have shifted their focus from human numbers as the cause of *current* scarcity[28] to population growth as the cause of absolute scarcity in the *future*.

In agriculture, for example, the prospect of (primarily dark-skinned) babies yet to be born causing global famine is being used by a range of interests – from biotech to water supply companies – to colonize the future for their particular interests. In Malthus' day, the resource that private interests most sought to lay hold of was community land – the forests, fields and pastures that villagers held and managed in common – and the labour that survived on it. Two centuries later, the push is towards the privatization of other publicly shared resources: seeds, water and air – resources that until recently have been taken for granted as common goods, albeit goods that (in the case of seeds and water) have generally been subject to complex communal rules governing their access and use. And, just as Malthus justified the privatization of communal land through dystopian predictions of population-induced scarcity, so the arguments for privatizing seeds, water and are being promoted through a similar scarcity discourse.

The selling of biotechnology is illustrative. The messaging is resolutely future-oriented, with the predicted avalanche of extra mouths to feed being used first to establish a foothold for biotechnology as a 'partial solution' to world hunger[29] – and then to expand that foothold by smothering discussion of alternatives, notably the redistribution of wealth and power. Although the structural causes of hunger are acknowledged, they are dealt with solely in the context of the 'present': the future is used to thrust them unceremoniously into the background, casting them as petty distractions that are of purely academic interest when compared with the overwhelming task of boosting future food production. In the process, questions over the very real role that genetic engineering itself will play in exacerbating the structural causes of hunger – not least through the privatization of seeds – are effectively parried (The Corner House, 1998).

The persuasive power of the future to depoliticize the debate on food poverty and channel decision-making towards a genetically engineered future is evident in the response of the UK's influential Nuffield Council on Bioethics to the introduction of genetically engineered crops. Redistribution is briefly considered as an option for addressing hunger but summarily dismissed as infeasible:

> *Political difficulties of redistribution within, let alone among, countries are huge. Logistical problems and costs of food distribution also militate against sole reliance on redistributing*

> *income (i.e. demand for food) to meet present, let alone future,*
> *needs arising from increasing populations in less developed*
> *countries ... What is required is a major increase in support*
> *for GM [genetically-modified] crop research and outreach*
> *directed at employment-intensive production of food staples*
> *within developing countries.* (Nuffield Council on Bioethics,
> paras 4.8, 4.10)

Elsewhere, future threats to environment and society are similarly being used to capture the present – and thereby colonize the future itself. In climate, the talk is of teeming numbers of Chinese and Indians causing whole cities to be lost to flooding through their greenhouse gas emissions – unless companies are granted property rights in the atmosphere through carbon-trading schemes; in water, of the 'gloomy arithmetic' (World Commission on Water, 2000, p15) of future thirsty slum dwellers condemning us to water wars – unless, following Malthus,[30] market discipline is brought to water use primarily through water pricing.[31]

It goes without saying that the 'war-room' mentality generated by such predictions of scarcity-driven apocalypse serves admirably to divert attention away from the awkward social and environmental history of the discredited policies and projects – from dams to nuclear power stations and genetic engineering – that the public is now invited to embrace in the interests of meeting globally aggregated predictions of demand.

Learning from the future?

Indeed, such is the power of 'scarcity' to colonize the future that even those who, quite properly, locate today's scarcities in political conflict, frequently crumble when confronted with projections of future population growth, setting aside the insights of political economy in favour of Malthusian metaphors that emphasize numbers over power relations as the explanation for future shortages.

In doing so, they grant Malthusianism an explanatory power that they would actively deny to it when applied to the present and the past. Instead of the past being a guide to future action, the future (implausibly) becomes a guide to the present.[32] George Santayana's dictum that 'those who cannot remember the past are condemned to repeat it' (Santayana, 1905) is jettisoned in favour of the ungrounded, and thus politically even more malleable, exercise of 'learning from the future'. In the process, 'scarcity' is rehabilitated: removed from the messy political realities of the present, it regains its authority as an abstract model, redeploying its mesmerizing powers over those who would privilege theory over lived experience.

Yet future crises are likely to be rooted in the same dynamics in which they are rooted today: political conflict, exploitative distributive institutions, sexism, racism, human rights abuses and environmentally destructive practices. If society wants to prepare for future resource crises (and there surely *will* be future scarcity of one kind or another) it would therefore be more prudent to look to the present rather than to some theoretical Malthusian model of the future. The future will grow out of the present, not out of society suddenly turning Malthusian. The better way of dealing with 'future crisis' is not imagining a future Malthusian world which bears no relationship to what exists now or ever has existed, and then imagining how to stave off that hypothetical Malthusian world, but rather dealing with current scarcities *now* on the realistic assumption that what causes scarcity today is going to go on causing scarcity in the future.

Denying Malthusianism a refuge in the future is thus of critical importance if the past is not destined to be repeated and the present forgotten. But it is also important if 'scarcity' (as it is currently used in economic discourse) is to be marginalized as a political strategy for diverting attention from the root causes of hunger, environmental degradation, conflict and the like. For granting Malthusianism a space in the future is one of the principal everyday actions through which the scarcity-terrorized thinking of young Jude – and the power relations and activities that it helps to support – are reproduced, rejuvenated and allowed (even when debunked by practical experience) to return to haunt the present.

As Betsy Hartmann notes (Chapter 3, this volume), undermining the power of Malthusian scarcity ideologies and policies is one of the most important political projects of our time. I join with her in hoping that this volume will further the political organizing that will undoubtedly be essential if young Jude is not to stalk the future along with Malthus' ghost and the shambling remains of Lord Robbins.

Notes

1 'I think that whenever children be born that are not wanted they should be killed directly, before their souls come to 'em, and not allowed to grow big and walk about!' (Hardy, 1896)
2 'Such boys springing up amongst us – boys of a sort unknown in the last generation – the outcome of new views of life.' (Hardy, 1896)
3 See, for example, Bales, 1999. Bales cites increased human numbers as one of the main causes of the continuation of slavery into the modern era: 'Two factors are critical in the shift from the old slavery to the explosive spread of the new. The first is the dramatic increase in world population ... Especially in those areas where slavery had persisted or was part of the historical culture, the population explosion radically increased the supply of potential slaves and drove down their price' (p12). Yet the detailed examples of modern slavery presented in the book, and the analysis of their dynamics, do not substantiate this claim and barely even raise the theme of population again. On the contrary, the causal factors that the author documents suggest that the roots of slavery lie elsewhere: in political and economic systems that allow one person to exert control over another (p12); the sex trade (p34ff); the insecurity that has followed the implementation of modern development programmes; globalization (p12); criminal gangs; insecure land tenure or the lack of land tenure; the erosion of traditional 'social order' (p29 and p65); corruption; and 'chaotic' Third World governments (p244). The population argument is so overwhelmingly refuted by the evidence presented in the book, that its mention would appear almost entirely gratuitous.

4   Paul Harrison, a well-known commentator on 'population' issues, argues that reducing human numbers must take priority over addressing the structural roots of the environmental crisis because it is easier than curbing consumption or adopting environmentally sound technologies. See, for example, Harrison, 1992.

5   Typically, reports on the economy and politics of southern countries – invariably the 'problem' of population is deemed a southern problem – will begin with citing population figures, even though these may have no relevance to what follows. However, the figures once cited, frame the subsequent discussion, skewing both the identification of problems and of solutions. This subliminal framing is superbly analyzed by Timothy Mitchell in his article, 'The use of an image: America's Egypt and the development industry' (Mitchell, 1996). Mitchell shows how Egypt is typically depicted by USAID (United States Agency for International Development) and other development agencies as the narrow valley of the River Nile, hemmed in by desert and crowded with rapidly multiplying millions, a picture which enables Egypt's poverty to be ascribed to demography and geography. Such an image obscures the political and social inequalities that underlie Egypt's ability to feed itself – and the part played by USAID-funded agricultural projects in exacerbating such inequalities.

6   See for example, Coward, 2002. Coward sees a conspiracy of silence on the issue of population which she blames on 'fear of offending non-western societies'. Tellingly, she overlooks both the resurgence of population discourse in discussions of immigration and in the War on Terror and the dominance of population thinking in many international development institutions. One might also ask: when have western societies ever shown show fear of offending the finer feelings of non-western societies? For discussion of new population discourses, see Hendrixson, 2004; Krause, 2006.

7   Robbins defined economics as 'the science which studies human behaviour as a relationship between ends and scarce means which have alternative uses' (Robbins, 1932).

8   Commons-based societies are characterized by social, economic and political arrangements that place the shared right to survival above 'exclusive individual rights to possess, exchange and accumulate' (Lohmann, 2006). Typically, land, water, labour and other critical elements of livelihoods are managed communally and are inalienable. For discussion, see Fairlie et al, 1993.

9   This is not to argue that such societies have thereby avoided scarcity. Periodic shortages of food and other necessities may be common. But such dearth is not permanent – and, critically, it is experienced differently than in those societies where there are fewer cultural constraints on the ability of one group or individual to exercise power over key livelihood necessities.

10 See, for example, Granovetter, 1985; Abolafia, 1997. Abolafia's ethnography of Wall Street traders documents how the stock, bond and futures markets are socially constructed institutions in which the behaviour of traders is 'suspended in a web of customs, norms, and structures of control'. What propels Wall Street 'is not a fundamental human drive or instinct, but strategies enacted in the context of social relationships, cultural idioms, and institutions – a cycle that moves between phases of unbridled self-interest and collective self-restraint'.

11 India, currently a 'boom' economy, has more hungry people than any country on Earth.

12 Nor is hunger-amid-plenty a phenomenon that is restricted to poorer developing world countries. In 1998, it was estimated that 23 million Americans are food

insecure, of whom 11 million, including 4 million children, experienced chronic hunger – this in a country that produced 40 per cent more food than it needs. See Eisinger, 1998; Pretty and Hine, 2002.

13 Similarly, if over 1 billion people do not have access to safe drinking water, it is not because the water is lacking: there is more than enough water available, even in water-stressed areas, to provide sufficient water for basic household needs (40 litres per capita per day) to all those classified as 'unserved' today – and the extra 2 billion expected by 2025. To understand why people go short of water – or any other resource – it is necessary to go beyond the statistics that weigh numbers against supply and look at the complex workings of power at the local, regional, national and international levels. The reality is – and always has been – that water (like food) flows to those with most bargaining power: industry and bigger farmers first, richer consumers second and the poor last. In the process, the water supplies that the poor rely on are polluted by industrial effluent, exported in foodstuffs or poured down the drain through wasteful consumption. See UNDP, 2006; Chapter 12, this volume.

14 For a case study of racism in the oppression of swidden agriculturalist hill peoples in Thailand, see Lohmann, 1999.

15 See Agarwal, 1995 and 1998. In many cases, women have been denied rights to land under land reform programmes because the land is allocated solely to males, who are assumed to be the 'heads' of households. For experience in Karnataka, India, see Brown et al, 2002.

16 See O'Brien and Gruenbaum, 1991; Berstein et al, 1990. Intra-household tensions can disadvantage women whose access to food within households, even within relatively equitable commons regimes, has historically been skewed by gender biases. Food owned by the household, for example, is not always shared equally: gender subordination results in women often being the last to eat and explains why, in a number of recent incidences of famine, food shortages have resulted in women being 'neglected, abandoned, divorced and sold into prostitution in the interests of male survival'.

17 See, for example, Via Campesina, 2006. The report notes, 'Violations of economic, social and cultural human rights go together with violations of civil and political rights. Peasant leaders, agrarian reform activists, rural women leaders etc. face severe oppression and often persecution, particularly if economic assets are involved. Freedom of expression, the right to organize themselves, to demonstrate politically, to act as social movements are rights that have frequently been attacked. If social movements, such as peasants' organisations, begin to assert their rights, they face persecution or even assassination'.

18 For example, the promotion of off-farm inputs – chemical fertilizers, pesticides and improved seeds – has forced farmers to buy what was previously free, in addition to locking them into a cycle of diminishing returns on fertilizers and increasing pesticide use. As a result, thousands of small farmers – including those who had gained land under previous land reform programmes – have fallen into debt and frequently seen their land holdings bought up by richer neighbours. See, for example, Bello and Rosenfeld, 1990.

19 For examples of the impacts of trade liberalization in the south and the north's continuing protectionism, see: Institute for Agriculture and Trade Policy Trade Observatory; UNCTAD (United Nations Conference on Trade and Development); Madeley, 2000. For case studies of impacts on rice farmers in Bangladesh, see Rashed et al, 2005.

20 By inexorably undermining the capacity of land to produce food, the ecological damage caused by intensive farming is creating the conditions for absolute scarcity, where even equitable economic and social arrangements may prove insufficient to prevent widespread human impoverishment. Artificial fertilizers and chemical sprays, for example, have disastrously undermined the natural fertility of soils. As farmers have ceased to apply manure and other organic material to the land, so the soil's structure in many areas has begun to break down, increasing its vulnerability to erosion. Such degradation is now in itself a major cause of socially generated scarcity.

21 Bolivia Population Statistics, available at www.indexmundi.com/g/g.aspx?c=bl&v=21 (last accessed 30 July 2010)

22 'Bolivia: land battles', *The Economist*, 23 September 2006, p58

23 'Red April in Brazil', IDS News, undated

24 Centre Europe – Tiers Monde, 'Land concentration in Brazil: a politics of poverty', Human Rights Sub-Commission 1999, Statement on Item 2: question of the violation of human rights and fundamental freedoms in any part of the world. Written statement, UN symbol: E/CN.4/Sub.2/1999/NGO/24, available at www.cetim.ch/en/interventions_details.php?iid=129 (last accessed 30 July 2010)

25 See Movimento dos Trabalhadores Rurais Sem Terra, www.mstbrazil.org (last accessed 30 July 2010); Bastos, 2006; Kingstone, 2005. For discussion on failures of the 2001 'market-led' reforms of the previous Cardosa government, see Domingos, 2003.

26 In aggregate, the rich countries of the Organisation for Economic Cooperation and Development subsidize their farmers to the tune of $400 billion a year. See Bidwai, 2006, p45.

27 Even former bastions of Malthusianism, such as the FAO and the International Food Policy Research Institute (IFPRI), a public-private research agency backed by 64 governments, now acknowledge that politics rather than too many people lies at the heart of continuing famine and malnutrition. As Eugenio Díaz and Sherman Robinson of IFPRI note, 'A world with an adequate supply of food is clearly more desirable than a Malthusian world in which food is scarce, food prices are high and rising, and people are in conflict over scarcity. However, providing an adequate aggregate food supply will not eliminate malnutrition and hunger, now or in the future. To do that requires much more. To achieve food security for the entire world population, countries must work to reduce poverty and achieve a more equitable distribution of income – tasks that technology alone can only support, not achieve' (Díaz and Robinson, 2003).

28 There is increasing recognition, at least in public, that distributional issues are the key factor in determining scarcities. However, this does not prevent neo-Malthusians from seizing on the statistics of hunger to make a case for absolute limits having been met wherever they can. For example, it is often argued that countries which are not self-sufficient in water or food have already exceeded local 'carrying capacity', even though the food imports often reflect changing dietary patterns or the inability of local farmers to compete with heavily subsidized exports from richer countries.

29 See, for example, the testimony of David Sandalow, Assistant Secretary of State for Oceans and International Environmental and Scientific Affairs, to the Subcommittee on International Economic Policy, Export and Trade Promotion of the Senate Committee on Foreign Relations, Washington, DC, 12 July 2000: 'How do we feed a growing population – which some estimate will reach 9 billion in the next

30 years – when most arable land on the planet is already under cultivation? How do we find new ways to deliver desperately needed medicines to desperately poor people? Modern biotechnology is part of the answer. Modern biotechnology is not a panacea, but it can help make a difference in the fight against hunger and poverty. Using this new technology, we can feed hungry children, raise incomes, fight disease and protect the environment.'

30 Malthus never intended his *Essay on Population* to be an exploration of the mysteries of human fertility: rather, it was a polemic in defence of private property. Market forces and market reasoning, he argued, bring discipline into the chaos that is Nature. Property brings prudence and prudence separates the deserving from the undeserving. Absent private property and, thanks to 'population', the world is catapulted headlong into scarcity: the four horsemen of the Apocalypse ride unopposed. 'Population' was the tool that Malthus used to elevate these politics into a theory and to use that theory as a political battering ram: by harnessing his politics to mathematics, he furnished the privatization movement with a spuriously neutral, pragmatic set of arguments for promoting a new political correctness – one that denied the shared rights of everyone, however poor, to subsistence, sanctioning instead the rights of the 'deserving' over the 'undeserving', with the market as arbiter of entitlements. This was the essence of the Malthusian argument – and the political goal to which 'population' was first strategically deployed.

31 'Commission members agreed that the single most immediate and important measure that we can recommend is the systematic adoption of full-cost pricing for water services ... Without full-cost pricing the present vicious cycle of waste, inefficiency, and lack of service for the poor will continue. There will be little investment from the private sector, services will be of poor quality and rationed, and there will be little left for investing in water quality and other environmental improvement', World Commission on Water for Water for the 21st Century, 2000, p46.

32 For example, the futurologist Herman Khan (1922–1983), reputedly the model for Stanley Kubrick's Dr Strangelove, stated, 'Anyone can learn from the past. These days it is more essential to learn from the future' (Khan, cited in VaTech Hydro 2001, p33).

References

Abolafia, M.Y. (1997) *Making Markets: Opportunities and Restraints on Wall Street*, Harvard University Press, Cambridge, USA

Agarwal, B. (1995) *A Field of One's Own: Gender and Land Rights in South Asia*, Cambridge University Press, Cambridge, UK

Agarwal, B. (1998) *Gender and Command over Property: An Economic Analysis of South Asia*, Kali for Women, New Delhi

Bales, K. (1999) *Disposable People: New Slavery in the Global Economy*, University of California Press, Berkeley

Bastos, A. (2006) 'Brazilian bishops and pastors call Lula's land reform a work of fiction', March, available at www.brazzilmag.com/component/content/article/34/5963-brazilian-bishops-and-pastors-call-lulas-land-reform-a-work-of-fiction.html (last accessed 30 July 2010)

Bello, W. and Rosenfeld, S. (1990) *Dragons in Distress: Asia's Miracle Economies in Crisis*, Institute of Food and Development Policy, Food First, San Francisco, CA

Berstein, H., Crow, B., Mackintosh, M. and Martin, C. (1990) *The Food Question: Profits versus People?*, Earthscan, London

Bidwai, P. (2006) 'From what now to what next: Reflections on three decades of international politics and development', *Development Dialogue*, no 47, June

Brown, J., Ananthpur, K. and Giovarelli, R. (2002) 'Women's access and rights to land in Karnataka', RDI Reports on Foreign Aid and Development, no 114, RDI, May, available at www.rdiland.org/images/publications/RDI_114.pdf (last accessed 30 July 2010)

Colchester, M. and Lohmann, L. (eds) (1993) *The Struggle for Land and the Fate of the Forests*, World Rainforest Movement, Zed Books, London

Coronel, S. and Dixit, K. (2006) 'Setting the context: The development debate thirty years after What Now', *Development Dialogue*, no 47, June

Coward, R. (2002) 'The Numbers are the beasts', *The Ecologist*, October

Díaz, E. and Robinson, S. (2003) 'Biotechnology, trade and hunger', Biotechnology and Genetic Resource Policies Brief, 2, IFPRI, January, available at www.ifpri.org/publication/biotechnology-trade-and-hunger-0 (last accessed 30 July 2010)

Domingos, M. (2003) 'Backgrounder Part I: Land reform in Brazil', February, available at www.landaction.org/display.php?article=63 (last accessed 30 July 2010)

Eisinger, P. (1998) *Toward an End to Hunger in America*, Brookings Institute Press, Washington DC

Esteva, G. (1992) 'Development' in W. Sachs (ed) *The Development Dictionary: A Guide to Knowledge as Power*, Zed Books, London

FAO (2000) 'The socio-economic impact of agricultural modernisation' in FAO, *The State of Food and Agriculture 2000*, FAO, Rome, available at www.fao.org/docrep/x4400e/x4400e10.htm (last accessed 30 July 2010)

Fairlie, S., Hildyard, N., Lohmann, L. and Sexton, S. (1993) *Whose Common Future? Reclaiming the Commons*, Earthscan, London

Granovetter, M. (1985) 'Economic action and social structure: The problem of embeddedness', *American Journal of Sociology*, vol 91, no 3, November, pp481–510

Hardy, T. (1896) *Jude the Obscure*, Osgood, McIlvaine, London

Harrison, P. (1992) 'Population', *The Guardian*, 29 May

Hendrixson, A. (2004) 'Angry young men, veiled young women: Constructing a new population threat', Corner House Briefing, 34, December, available at www.thecornerhouse.org.uk/resource/angry-young-men-veiled-young-women (last accessed 30 July 2010)

Hildyard, N. (2008) 'A (crumbling) wall of money: Financial bricolage, derivatives and power', Corner House Briefing, 39, October

Hoffer, E. (1954) *The Passionate State of Mind*, Harper and Row, New York

Keen, D. (1984) *The Benefits of Famine: Political Economy of Famine and Relief in Southwestern Sudan 1983–1989*, Princeton University Press, Princeton, NJ

Kingstone, S. (2005) 'Modest gain in Brazil land reform', BBC News, 20 January, available at http://news.bbc.co.uk/1/hi/world/americas/4190335.stm (last accessed 30 July 2010)

Krause, E.L. (2006) 'Dangerous demographies: The scientific manufacture of fear', *Corner House Briefing*, 36, July, available at www.thecornerhouse.org.uk/resource/dangerous-demographies (last accessed 30 July 2010)

Krzaric, R. (2005) 'The limits of pro-poor agricultural trade in Guatemala: Land, labour and political power', Occasional Paper, UNDP, available at http://hdr.undp.org/docs/publications/background_papers/2005/HDR2005_Krznaric_Roman_17.pdf (last accessed 30 July 2010)

LeClair, E.E. and Schneider, H.K. (1968) *Economic Anthropology*, Holt, Rinehart and Winston, New York

Lohmann, L. (1999) 'Forest cleansing: Racial oppression in scientific nature conservation', Corner House Briefing, vol 13, January, available at www.thecornerhouse.org. uk/resource/forest-cleansing (last accessed 30 July 2010)

Lohmann, L. (2006) 'Activism, expertise, commons' in 'What next? Setting the context', *Development Dialogue*, no 47, June, Special Issue

Madeley, J. (2000) *Hungry for Trade: How the Poor Pay for Free Trade*, Zed Books, London

Mitchell, T. (1996) 'The use of an image: America's Egypt and the development industry', *The Ecologist*, vol 26, no 1, pp21–22

Nuffield Council on Bioethics (1999) 'Genetically modified crops: The ethical and social issues', available at www.nuffieldbioethics.org/go/ourwork/gmcrops/publication_301.html (last accessed 30 July 2010)

O'Brien, J. and Gruenbaum, E. (1991) 'A social history of food, famine and gender in twentieth-century Sudan' in R.E. Downs, D.O. Kerner and S.P. Reyna, *The Political Economy of African Famine*, Gordon and Breach, Reading

Polanyi, K. (2002) *The Great Transformation: The Political and Economic Origins of Our Times*, Beacon Press, Boston

Pretty, J. and Hine, R. (2002) 'Reducing food poverty with sustainable agriculture: A summary of new evidence', interdisciplinary Centre for Environment and Society, University of Essex, Colchester, available at www.essex.ac.uk/ces/occasionalpapers/ SAFErepSUBHEADS.shtm (last accessed 30 July 2010)

Rashed, T., Ahmed, M.I. and Sarwar, M.M.G. (2005) 'Undercutting small farmers: Rice trade in Bangladesh and WTO negotiations', Unnayan Onneshwar, available at http://unnayan.org/Other/Unnayan%20Onneshan_TNLP_Agriculture.pdf (last accessed 30 July 2010)

Robbins, L. (1932) *An Essay on the Nature and Significance of Economic Science*, Macmillan, London

Rosario-Malonzo, J. (2005) 'Market oriented land reform and the World Bank', *APRN Journal*, vol 13, December, available at www.aprnet.org/journals-a-policy-papers/53-volume-13-december-2005/285-market-oriented-land-reform-and-the-world-bank (last accessed 30 July 2010)

Sainath, P. (2001) 'None so blind as those who will not see', available at www.unesco. org/courier/2001_06/uk/medias.htm (last accessed 30 July 2010)

Santayana, G. (1905) *The Life of Reason*, Volume 1, Constable, London

Stocking, B. (2002) '"To them that hath": How world trade policies undermine poor producers' in L. Howland, J. Holden and D. Stedman Jones (eds) *Foodstuff: Living in an Age of Feast and Famine*, Demos, London

The Corner House (1998) 'Food? Health? Hope? Genetic engineering and world hunger', Corner House Briefing, 10, October, available at www.thecornerhouse.org. uk/resource/food-health-hope (last accessed 30 July 2010)

UNDP (2006) 'Human development report 2006 – Beyond scarcity: Power, poverty and the global water crisis', available at http://hdr.undp.org/hdr2006/ (last accessed 30 July 2010)

VaTech Hydro (2001) 'Annual report 2001', VaTech Hydro, Vienna

Via Campesina (2006) 'Violations of peasants' human rights: A report on cases and patterns of violence 2006', available at http://viacampesina.org/main_en/images/ stories//annual-report-HR-2006.pdf (last accessed 30 July 2010)

Vidal, J. (2002) 'Time to come clean on the dirty secret of starvation', *The Guardian*, 10 June, available at www.guardian.co.uk/comment/story/0,3604,730487,00.html (last accessed 30 July 2010)

World Commission on Water for Water for the 21st Century (2000) 'A water secure world: Vision for water, life and the environment', World Water Council, Marseille, available at www.worldwatercouncil.org/fileadmin/wwc/Library/Publications_and_reports/Visions/CommissionReport.pdf (last accessed 30 July 2010)

9

Seeing Scarcity: Understanding Soil Fertility in Africa

Ian Scoones

Introduction

Notions of scarcity have dominated policy debates about soil fertility in sub-Saharan Africa over many decades. Too few nutrients (usually nitrogen or phosphorous) means more fertilizer (usually inorganic, chemical fertilizers) is the oft heard cry to action. The high-profile report of the Millennium Project on how to meet the first Millennium Development Goal of reducing hunger argues, for example, that improving soil health through addressing soil nutrient imbalances is the first entry point for improving agricultural productivity and central to halving hunger by 2015, particularly in Africa (UN Millennium project, 2005, p13).[1]

Yet such global, broad-brush, generalized approaches to defining scarcity (or similar terminologies such as gaps, deficits or imbalances) and so defining solutions (and programmatic interventions, projects and flows of aid funds) are only one way of seeing scarcity. This chapter offers two contrasting perspectives on scarcity and, with these, two different ways of understanding the problem of soil fertility in Africa. The result is two divergent responses, with implications for development agencies, national governments and farmers.[2] Seeing scarcity in different ways means asking: what exactly is scarce? When? Where? For whom? With what consequences? Reflecting on different ways of seeing scarcity requires a focus on the politics of knowledge: how notions of scarcity are constructed, and in turn how understandings of soil fertility – and its management – are framed.

These themes have been the focus of my work on resource use and management in Africa over the past 20 years. How resources are seen and by whom has a huge impact on how policies unfold; too often the framings deployed by policy-makers are detrimental to the livelihoods of rural people. My work, in collaboration with researchers from different parts of Africa, has attempted to look at these questions from different perspectives, seeing resources – such as soils, water, forests, rangelands, livestock, wildlife and so on – and particularly the constructions of their use and availability, from the standpoint of rural people themselves. Counterposed against dominant visions imposed by policy elites, donors and others, such alternative ways of seeing can be given power and presence in the ongoing struggles around knowledge and politics at the heart of development practice.

The chapter has two main parts reflecting first on a global, generalized framing and second on more local understandings, drawing in particular on work in southern Ethiopia. These are examined in relation to policy and field implementation debates in Africa over the last decade. The conclusion returns to the implications of taking account of the politics of seeing scarcity in different ways.

Global visions

Much international development discourse must frame discussions in generalized, broad-brush terms. To garner support, enlist networks of actors, make a splash and so raise limited funds, corners must be cut, simplifications must be made and an overarching appealing narrative presented. Just as in so many other areas, this has been the case in the soil fertility debate. The UN Millennium Project task force (see above) coordinators – Pedro Sanchez and M.S. Swaminathan – have had long experience of operating at this global level. Swaminathan, of course, had been centrally engaged in launching the 'green revolution' in India, whereby new seeds, together with fertilizers and water, were critical to the agricultural productivity boosts seen in Asia from the 1970s and the banishing of food scarcities. Sanchez, formerly the head of a Kenya-based international agricultural research centre, (ICRAF – International Centre for Research on Agroforestry), and now a director of the Millennium Villages Project based at the Earth Institute at Columbia University, has successfully argued for an integrated approach to soil fertility management as key to agricultural productivity enhancement across Africa. ICRAF was also central to a now-shelved Africa-wide Soil Fertility Initiative, pushed by the World Bank, the International Fertilizer Development Centre (IFDC) and the fertilizer industry, among others. Sanchez was also lead editor of the highly influential Soil Society of America 1997 special edition entitled 'Replenishing Soil Fertility in Africa' (Sanchez et al, 1997). This made a strong case for seeing scarcity of soil nutrients in terms of imbalances, based on input and output assessments of nitrogen and phosphorous carried out at a continental level:

> *The magnitude of nutrient depletion in Africa's land is enormous. Calculations ... indicate an average of 660kg of nitrogen per hectare per year, 75kg of phosphorous per hectare per year and 450kg of potassium per hectare per year during the last 30 years has been lost from about 200 million ha of cultivated land in 37 African countries.* (Sanchez et al, 1997, p4)

The data that this argument derives from have become iconic 'facts' in the debate about African soil fertility. Derived from nutrient balance models, initially at a national scale (aggregated up to a continental level), these figures combine rough judgements and guesswork with, at least at the beginning, some very limited empirical studies. The 1990 document produced for the UN Food and Agriculture Organization (Stoorvogel and Smaling, 1990) offered a stark warning: soil nutrients in Africa are scarce and getting scarcer. This analysis offered the opportunity for generating considerable interest in soil fertility in Africa during the second half of the 1990s.[3] The dramatic (and large) figures were transformed into vivid maps of the continent, plastered in red, warning both explicitly and subliminally of imminent danger and impending catastrophe (see Figure 9.1). As a rallying call for an issue which had seen little international attention for decades, many

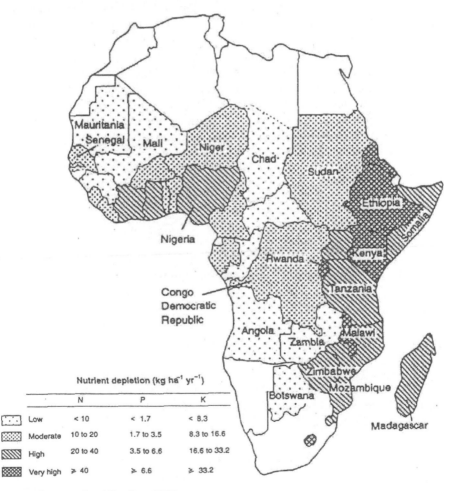

Source: Stoorvogel and Smaling, 1990

Figure 9.1 *Nutrient depletion in Africa*

reflected that the generalizations, simplifications and aggregations involved in linearly scaling-up mini-plot studies were warranted, even if accuracy was lost in the process (see Smaling et al, 1999). Others, however, questioned the approach, arguing that sometimes inappropriate conclusions were drawn from aggregated nutrient budget studies (see Scoones and Toulmin, 1998).

There are a number of characteristics of these global visions which are worth unpacking because they give clues to how scarcity is seen, based on a particular politics of knowledge operating at the international (or at least Africa-wide) level. Three characteristics are highlighted below.

Inputs and outputs: Accounting and economics metaphors

The metaphors of accountancy and economics have a strong lure in development debates. As many commentators noted, if dollar values can be attached to the deficit, then bells ring in decision-makers' ears. The input-output nutrient budgets were perfect for this. Analysts could prove that very large numbers of dollars were being lost each year through 'soil mining', sometimes adding up to significant proportions of the GDP (Gross Domestic Product) of small, poor countries. This was dramatic stuff, something that the dry talk of complex nutrient soil nutrient dynamics (of adhesion and immobilization, of biological-mineral interactions, of breakdown and fixation rates and so on) was fundamentally unable to capture. As one well-respected international scientist observed:

> *Nutrient budgets were successful because they were simple; the message was simple ... you can't take money out of the bank without putting something in. The principle of mining is understood by everybody. Mining leads to lower yields, that's clear. But in the details it's not so simple.* (quoted in Keeley and Scoones, 2003, p49)

Through the language of 'balancing the books', of inputs and outputs, depleting capital stocks, creating deficits and generating scarcity, discursive connections between the worlds of science, planning and policy-making are made, via the well-understood precepts of accounting economics. Sanchez et al (1997, p11) argued: 'There is an exact congruence between the concepts of capital stocks and service flows in economics and that of pools and fluxes in soil science'. This allowed key actors – such as Sanchez and colleagues – to push the soil management, and particularly 'nutrient replenishment' agenda, into the limelight and bravely request large amounts of money for the Africa-wide Soil Fertility Initiative (SFI).

Crisis and simplicity: Black-boxing uncertainty

A key characteristic of the global vision, as already noted, is its stark simplicity and its portrayal of impending crisis. This narrative style is of course well used to generate policy interest and enlist coalitions of actors and organizations around an issue. For a period, this was done to good effect in the case of

African soil fertility. The SFI coalition was constructed around a set of stylized 'facts' about nutrient scarcities and depletion rates, built into an argument of replenishment through a large-scale, continent-wide, integrated approach (World Bank, 1996). As one advocate passionately argued, there was an urgent need for 'closure' around the soil fertility issue – there was now a need for action: 'We need the bigger picture, then we go down to the villages and the farms', he said (quoted in Keeley and Scoones, 2003, p50). For him, dealing with uncertainty, ambiguity and contests over interpretations was a diversion when getting the debate on to the table and getting it funded. There was plenty of time, he argued, for fine-tuning responses when the argument had been won and the initiative funded.

But black-boxing uncertainties in order to build an actor network (see Latour, 1987) advocating a particular position, is not straightforward, as the story of the SFI illustrates (see Keeley and Scoones, 2003, Chapter 3). Not everyone was prepared to play ball. For a start scientific debates raged (sometimes with fairly overt attempts at suppression) over the desirability and feasibility of one-off rock phosphorous additions as a solution to phosphorous scarcities. Others doubted the replicability of ICRAF's favoured 'wonder plants', Tithonia and Sesbania, with 'improved fallows' as a solution to nutrient-poor soils. Still others questioned whether the logistics of the proposed large-scale programmes were really thought through. One sceptic observed: 'I don't believe in one-off recapitalisation. It's logistically impractical for one thing ... but modest things get no money'.

For a period, though, a coalition formed, avoiding, ignoring or suppressing such debates that did not fit with a particular way of seeing scarcity. This often involved a neat coincidence of interests. ICRAF needed a higher profile and funds as a new CGIAR centre (Consultative Group for International Agricultural Research), the World Bank and the FAO had to be seen to be doing something about Africa and had a long track record of supporting fertilizer projects. In this way, the IFDC's own raison d'être was reinforced, the fertilizer industry lobby (through the Paris-based Fertiliser Industry Association) was unsurprisingly keen, and African governments too were also enthusiastic, seeing the opportunity of some other way of getting subsidized fertilizer imports after many years of being told that all subsidies had to be removed. (See Chapters 8 and 10, this volume, for discussions of the politics of scarcity and food.)

Bureaucratic imperatives: Creating gaps to fill

A number of important bureaucratic imperatives at the heart of this coalition helped frame the African soil fertility problem in this way. Scarcities, deficits, gaps, are all tangible conditions that the donor community – and the associated research organizations dependent on their largesse – can easily latch on to. Gap analysis has defined so many development debates – from energy to wood fuel to water to food, and so too soil fertility. But a rising graph with a deficit beneath it, or a dramatic map with scarcities marked in red is something that donors can respond to. The bureaucratic imperatives of donor organizations – hitting targets, disbursing funds, being seen to be linked to the 'big issues' – thus define scarcities in particular ways.

The bureaucratic practices and cultures of aid organizations, whether in the UN system, the multilateral banks or the bilaterals, all (in importantly different ways) have systems in place which define an internal politics of knowledge that finds its way into funding priorities, programmes and policies: complexity, difference, ambiguity, debate are out; simplicity, uniformity and certainty are in. Seeing scarcity therefore in more nuanced ways is almost impossible at an institutional level, where a lethal combination of a disbursement goal budget culture and a target-driven audit culture set the terms. As a result, funds are cut if the crisis is questioned, the gap is seen to be less large (or different in form), or the solutions more complex than originally envisaged.

The SFI, for a time, managed to ride the wave, garnering both scientific and bureaucratic/funding support. But it did not last. The standardized global narrative began to dissipate; the case for the SFI could not be sustained. As the science was unpacked and the complexities and uncertainties exposed, key actors failed to join up and the once tight actor network began to unravel. Local contexts and particularities became impossible to ignore, as diverse and dynamic local contexts and practices failed to match the simplified global narrative (Keeley and Scoones, 2003, Chapter 3). In other words, different ways of seeing scarcity came to disturb the global vision.

Local dynamics and diversity

Understandings of local complexity, dynamics and diversity in soil management stand in sharp contrast to the global visions just described (see Chapters 11 and 12, this volume, for similar analyses in the realm of water). These complicate, disturb and challenge the simple global vision, and, in key respects, were part of the SFI's downfall.

A long tradition of study has emphasized local knowledge and practice in soil management, deeply embedded in social, cultural and institutional settings (see Schoffeleers, 1979; Mukamuri, 1995; Jacobson-Widding and van Beek, 1990; Fairhead and Leach, 1996, Ostberg, 1995 among many others; see Fairhead and Scoones, 2005 for a short review). Such work sees scarcity (or rather scarcities) in different ways: plural, differentiated, complex, dynamic – not singular, uniform, simplified and static. Importantly such work does not suggest there is not a 'soil fertility problem' in Africa, as some seem to think;[4] it is just that the problem is defined in different ways, with sometimes dramatically different implications for interventions and policies. Three themes are introduced in the following sections.

Different scales, different dynamics

Since the now classic 1990 paper on soil nutrient budgets that sparked the explosion of global visions and ambitions described above (Stoorvogel and Smaling, 1990), there have been numerous other studies that have taken the

original to task. These have made concerted attempts to disaggregate understandings of soil fertility dynamics, often through discussions and participatory involvement of farmers themselves. These local-level (disaggregating to
field and farm scales) nutrient budget analyses often tell a very different story
(see for example Eyasu and Scoones, 1999; Harris, 1998; DeFoer and Scoones,
2001; de Jager et al, 1998). Instead of the simplistic aggregate picture, a
pattern of accumulation and loss, patchy patterns of scarcity and plenty and
a complex spatial and temporal dynamics is made clear. Even using the highly
simplistic tool of nutrient balance assessments, a much greater complexity is
evident. This is further added to by an appreciation of within-field micro-
variability (of leaching, siltation, deposition, etc.) across small slopes, rills and
gullies (see Brouwer and Powell, 1998; Brouwer and Bouma, 1997).

At different scales, then, different dynamics of nutrient scarcity and surplus
are evident, with different implications for management. For the international
research organizations, donors and others, the scale of concern is continental
or global – this is where their targets are set and how funds can be disbursed
in large tranches. For farmers, by contrast, it is farm-level micro-variation that
is important. For example, it may be that soil loss (erosion and nutrient depletion) is actually encouraged in some places in order for organic matter and
nutrients to accumulate elsewhere where they are more manageable.[5] Scarcity
is thus a spatially and temporally specific concept which is not fixed, but can
be managed through skill and investment.

Managing scarcities: Farming skills

The accounting metaphors used by the nutrient budget approaches detract
from a field-level way of seeing scarcity. This instead emphasizes skill, practice, invention, experimentation and performance in soil management. Rather
than seeing soil management as simply an issue of making up the deficit, filling
the gap or addressing a scarcity with an input, farmers often express a different
view. Managing scarcities (which unquestionably exist) is about deploying
multiple skills, not just physical inputs. Nitrogen, phosphorus and potassium
are of course important, but not the only ingredients. As Paul Richards (1989)
put it, farming is a performance, usually with multiple stages and variable
scripts. Skill- and practice-based knowledge is essential (see Stone, 2004),
allowing farmers to combine seeds, soils, nutrients, water and sunlight in ways
that are always improvised and responsive. Simple blueprint-style, one-size-
fits-all solutions are well known not to work in agricultural development (see
Chambers et al, 1989) and interventions must be responsive to context and
suited to adaptation and elaboration.

Participatory approaches to integrated soil fertility management (DeFoer
and Scoones, 2001; DeFoer and Budelman, 2000) have demonstrated the
promise of complex responses to nutrient scarcities through the use of both
organic and inorganic applications. Farmers are not very interested in the
debate between organic (muck and manure) versus inorganic (chemical fertilizers); they are interested instead in attuned responses to local needs which

inevitably require an integrated approach. Thus across a farm different diagnoses of scarcity are evident, resulting in different responses.

For example in Wolayta, southern Ethiopia, farms are differentiated into broadly four different sections in farmers' own characterizations (see Figure 9.2, from Konde et al, 2001, p65). Each has different types of scarcity; each requires different forms of soil fertility management. The *enset* (false banana) patch close to the home requires large amounts of organic matter to build up a rich mulch suitable to protect *enset* (a key dry season and famine food) from dry periods and ensure strong growth of a large plantation which, after some time, is increasingly self-sustaining as residues are recycled in the *enset* garden. This garden also becomes a site for growing other vegetables and fruit trees once a 'strong' soil is developed. Further away from the home an intensively managed maize garden (*darkoa*) is also created. The *darkoa*

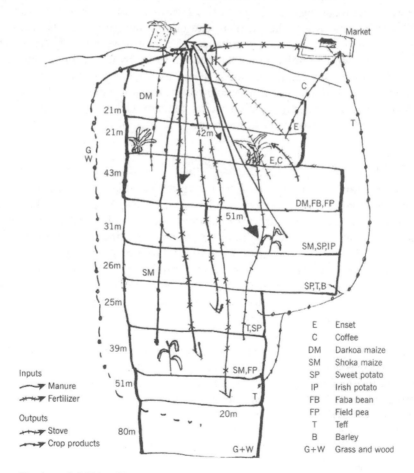

Source: Konde et al, 2001, p65

Figure 9.2 *Resource flow diagram, Wolayta, Ethiopia*

again is reliant on intensive application of organic material (crop residues and manure). This is built in a number of stages, starting with the planting of taro on mounds, where soil is improved through systematic digging, hoeing, turning and incorporation of organic materials. When the soil is improved sufficiently maize is planted, before a new cycle of renewal is entered into.

Further away from the house in the main field (*shoka*) the soils (and associated scarcities) are treated quite differently. Here inorganic fertilizers are applied if they can be afforded, often in very small amounts and with spot applications. In these unimproved soils, the lack of key nutrients (mostly nitrogen) is well recognized. Soil erosion is managed carefully with bunds and ditches, the use of termite mounds and with accumulations and depletions within field areas well-known by farmers. In particularly depleted areas, where nutrients are especially limiting, then single teaspoons of inorganic compound fertilizer may be added to growing plants. Overall at a per hectare level, the fertilizer applications are minimal, but by ensuring high levels of nutrient use efficiency (in other words, very effective uptake) scarcities can be offset at the micro-plant level with levels of input far lower than suggested by higher-scale assessments of deficit and scarcity. The furthest plot from the house is a grass and tree section (*mita gidiya*) where cultivation does not take place. However, this is a source of biomass for other parts of the farm and, with livestock often tethered there, a place where manure accumulates.

Thus different areas within the farm have drastically different management regimes, associated with different types of scarcity. Seeing scarcity in this differentiated way, as farmers do, means that a blanket statement that 'the farms of Wolayta are scarce in nutrients and so require major fertilizer inputs' is actually rather meaningless. For example, the *enset* and *darkoa* maize garden may make up less than 10 per cent of the total field area, but it is this area that yields the most food. Nutrient scarcities in these areas are addressed as an utmost priority, with a combination of valuable organic matter skilfully and carefully applied to improve the soil in a step-wise systematic way over time. 'Creating gardens' (see Konde et al, 2001) is not just about balancing nutrients. Soil management is much more than this; balancing soil moisture, organic matter, nutrient levels, pH and soil biota in complex combinations through skilful, practised interventions. By contrast, the *shoka* outfields are treated more opportunistically. If fertilizers are available (and affordable) they will be applied but, if not, labour is insufficient to transform them and they are left, with ongoing depletion (through removal of grains and residues) and relatively low yields accepted.

Meanings of scarcity: Social and cultural dimensions

Transforming soils from 'weak' to 'strong', from 'skinny' to 'fat', from 'sleeping' to 'awake' is not only a technical, ecological process. Such transformations are intimately bound up in social, institutional, cultural and political dynamics in any African farming society (see Dea and Scoones, 2003, for southern Ethiopia; Fairhead and Scoones, 2005, for an overview). Farmers have an intimate relationship with soils and their fertility, with often numerous terms used to describe their status and transformation. For example, in Wolayta, southern Ethiopia, over 10 different soil types are identified, while only one broad type is conventionally defined for the area. Farmers can engage in almost endless conversation about strategies for changing a soil from *arada* (infertile) to *lada* (fertile). As Ato Toma from Lasho Peasant Association in Wolayta explained:

> When I inherited this land, the soil fertility was poor. The *darkoa* garden was very small. The soils in almost all other parts were dying, and very skinny (gilka). Luckily I started working them before they died (haigoa) and were completely ruined. Now I have expanded my darkoa and also fattened (anquara) the soils in my land through my own efforts. Currently the soils in my land are more fertile than most of the farmers around here. This was made possible through continuous investment and work (ossua) and the effective keeping (nagua) of the land. Soils need continuous tending and care, just like one does with children and cattle. (interview August 1995, quoted in Dea and Scoones, 2003, p469)

Investment, work, care and attention are thus all part of Ato Toma's understanding of soil fertility management. 'Keeping the land' is a further dimension which is also often mentioned. Here Ato Toma is referring to the link between the physical management of soils and the broader spiritual world within which soils are situated. Scarcity is thus not just a matter of physical (and so economic) dearth, but something associated with how soils are being cared for in a broader sense. Scarcity can, in this view, be imposed through inappropriate behaviour and cultural malpractice. In Wolayta, soils are traditionally thought to be governed by the 'spirit of the soil' (*bita talahia*). Soil health, just as human health, is sustained through appropriate sacrifices and propitiation ceremonies. Failure to comply results in *gomia* (the evil eye), with dire consequences for soil fertility and productivity. Christian religious discourses also define appropriate behaviour towards soils, and sinners (*nagara*) are blighted with poor soils and low production (Dea and Scoones, 2003, p470–471).

Soil transformations are thus entwined with cultural and social understandings of the physical world. Soil fertility management is therefore intimately bound up with the life cycles, histories and so biographies of people, fields and their soils. Konde et al (2001, p56–59) document the changing fortunes of three different farmers from Wolayta, southern Ethiopia. Political changes (including land appropriation and changes in tenure regime), life-cycle shifts (marriage, the birth of children, external employment), disease incidence (resulting in deaths in the family or loss of livestock through trypanosomiasis) and changing institutional arrangements (such as the decline in group-based work parties and the rise of church-focused labour pooling) all combine to affect the ability of different farmers to invest in their soil resources. Conjunctures of events combine to result in sometimes major, seemingly irreversible, shifts. The result is a shifting pattern of soil investment in different sites over time, with the boundary between the *darkoa* home garden area and the *shoka* outfields moving as assets and abilities change – notably labour and oxen (and so manure and ploughing options).

Conclusions

There is a startling disconnect between the global visions of donors, international research organizations and national ministries vying for funds and policy spaces and the local dynamics, complexities and practical realities on the ground. For those pushing a global vision – with its associated funding flows, bureaucratic imperatives and scientific black-boxing – a particular way of seeing scarcity is (almost inevitably) constructed. This simplifies, homogenizes and aggregates, resulting all too often in blueprint, generalized solutions. By contrast, while not denying the very real problems of scarce nutrients, farmers at a more local level emphasize complex dynamics and diverse responses in a broader socially and culturally embedded vision of soils and their fertility.

Seeing scarcities through different lenses has thus highlighted how it is the politics of knowledge, values and interpretation that matters. This is not a technical issue: depending on the scale – both spatial and temporal – we can measure whether a particular place for a particular time period has a deficiency of nutrients for a particular use or not. But which measurement is relevant? For whom? As Mortimore and Harris (2005, p43) show, the 'dominant narrative [of general soil degradation and erosion] is deficient as a guide to policy'. With cases from across West Africa they show how farmers' investments at the local level buck the trend and contradict the gloomy predictions of agricultural productivity and performance of the dominant view.

Scarcities, of course, do exist, wherever we look. That, however, is not the issue. Whose versions and visions of scarcity, and whose responses count, are the much more important questions. How we see scarcity is thus a political choice, and one that needs far greater attention in thinking about development and policy responses. A key challenge for all involved in soil fertility issues (or any other natural resource management debate for that matter) is to ensure that the dominant, well-connected and so well-funded versions are unpacked, interrogated and scrutinized with far greater rigour than is sometimes permitted or expected, and alternative ways of seeing scarcity are given space at the policy table.

Notes

1   Major initiatives on soil fertility in the last decade have echoed this. For example, the Alliance for a Green Revolution in Africa (AGRA) – has launched a major new 'Soil Health' programme aimed at 4.1 million farmers across Africa, with the Bill and Melinda Gates Foundation committing $198 million to the effort. The Abuja declaration, following on from the African Fertilizer Summit of 2006, set the scene for major investments in boosting fertilizer supplies. CAADP – the Comprehensive

African Agricultural Development Programme – has been active in supporting this effort, particularly through its work on improving input markets and fertilizer supply. Other initiatives abound, including the Millennium Villages programme, Sasakawa-Global 2000, the activities of the Association for Better Land Husbandry, among many others. All see soil fertility as central, although the suggested solutions and policy requirements are very different.

2   This chapter is based on work carried out between 1995 and 2002 in Ethiopia, Mali and Zimbabwe together with over 30 collaborators from Africa and Europe. This chapter was written in 2005 for the workshop on which this book is based. The project was funded by the European Commission (TS3-CT94-039) and coordinated by the International Institute for Environment and Development. The results are published in Scoones, 2001. Follow-up work funded by the Economic and Social Research Council on policy processes was published in Keeley and Scoones, 2003.

3   A veritable industry in nutrient budget studies was generated, with some useful reflection on the problems of these by some of the originators (see Smaling et al, 1999). However, even in 2004 more general assessments (see Sheldrik and Lingard, 2004) were being published, justifying an ongoing focus on input markets as 'the problem' (see Crawford et al, 2003).

4   See numerous case examples from all over Africa of farmer practice in Scoones, 2001 (focusing on soil fertility) and Reij et al, 1996 (focusing on soil erosion and water conservation).

5   Manipulation of termite activity to enhance soil and water characteristics is an oft-commented on facet of soil management in Africa (see, for example, Fairhead and Leach, 2000 for an assessment for West Africa).

References

Brouwer, J. and Bouma, J. (1997) 'Soil and crop growth variability in the Sahel. Highlights of Research, 1990–94', ICRISAT, Pantcheru and Wageningen Agricultural University, Wageningen

Brouwer, J. and Powell, J. (1988) 'Increasing nutrient use efficiency in West African agriculture: The impact of micro-topography on nutrient leaching from cattle and sheep manure', *Agriculture, Ecosystems and Environment*, vol 71, pp229–239

Chambers, R., Pacey, A. and Thrupp, L.-A. (eds) (1989) *Farmer First. Farmer Innovation and Agricultural Research*, Intermediate Technology Publications, London

Crawford, E., Kelly, V.A., Jayne, T.S. and Howard, J. (2003) 'Input use and market development in sub-Saharan Africa: An overview', *Food Policy*, vol 28, no 4, pp277–292

Dea, D. and Scoones, I. (2003) 'Networks of knowledge. How farmers and scientists understand soils and their fertility. A case study from Ethiopia', *Oxford Development Studies*, vol 31, no 4, pp461–478

DeFoer, T. and Budelman, A. (eds) (2000) *Managing Soil Fertility: A Resource Guide for Participatory Learning and Action Research*, KIT Publications, Amsterdam

DeFoer, T. and Scoones, I. (2001) 'Participatory approaches to integrated soil fertility management', in I. Scoones (ed) *Dynamics and Diversity: Soil Fertility and Farming Livelihoods in Africa*, Earthscan, London

de Jager, A., Kariuki, I., Matiri, F., Odendo, M. and Wanyama, J. (1998) 'Monitoring nutrient flows and economic performance in African farming systems, NUTMON IV. Linking nutrient balance and economic performance in three districts in Kenya', *Agriculture, Ecosystems and Environment*, vol 71, pp81–92

Eyasu, E. and Scoones, I. (1999) 'Perspectives on soil fertility change: A case study from southern Ethiopia', *Land Degradation and Development*, vol 10, pp195–206

Fairhead, J. and Leach, M. (1996) *Misreading the African Landscape: Society and Ecology in a Forest-Savanna Mosaic*, Cambridge University Press, Cambridge

Fairhead, J. and Leach, M. (2000) 'Termites, society and ecology: Perspectives from West Africa', in D. Posey (ed) *Culture, Ecology and Post-modernity*, Cambridge, Cambridge University Press

Fairhead, J. and Scoones, I. (2005) 'Local knowledge and the social shaping of soil investments: Critical perspectives on the assessment of soil degradation in Africa', *Land Use Policy*, vol 22, pp33–41

Harris, F. (1998) 'Farm-level assessment of the nutrient balance in northern Nigeria', *Agriculture, Ecosystems and Environment*, vol 71, pp201–214

Jacobson-Widding, A. and van Beek, W. (1990) 'Chaos, order and communion in the creation and sustenance of life', in A. Jacobson-Widding and W. van Beek (eds) *The Creative Communion: African Folk Models of Fertility and the Regeneration of Life*, Uppsala, Acta Universitatis Upsaliensis, Uppsala Studies in Cultural Anthropology, pp15–34

Keeley, J. and Scoones, I. (2003) *Understanding Environmental Policy Processes: Cases from Africa*, Earthscan, London

Keeley, J. and Scoones, I. (2004) 'Understanding policy processes in Ethiopia: A response', *Journal of Modern African Studies*, vol 42, no 1, pp149–153

Konde, A., Dea, D., Jonfa, E., Folla, F., Scoones, I., Kena, K. and Berhanu, T. (2001) 'Creating gardens: The dynamics of soil fertility management in Wolayta, southern Ethiopia', in I. Scoones (ed) *Dynamics and Diversity. Soil Fertility and Farming Livelihoods in Africa*, Earthscan, London

Latour, B. (1987) *Science in Action*, Cambridge, MA, Harvard University Press

Mortimore, M. and Harris, F. (2005) 'Do small farmers' achievements contradict nutrient depletion scenarios for Africa?', *Land Use Policy*, vol 22, pp43–56

Mukamuri, B. (1995) 'Local environmental conservation strategies: Karanga religion, politics and environmental control', *Environment and History*, vol 1, pp297–311

Nyssen, J., Mitiku, H., Moeyersons, J., Poesen, J. and Deckers, J. (2004) 'Environmental policy in Ethiopia: A rejoinder to Keeley and Scoones', *The Journal of Modern African Studies*, vol 42, pp137–147

Ostberg, W. (1995) 'The land is coming up: The burunge of Central Tanzania and their environments', *Stockholm Studies in Social Anthropology*, p34

Reij, C., Scoones, I. and Toulmin, C. (eds) (1996) *Sustaining the Soil: Indigenous Soil and Water Conservation in Africa*, Earthscan, London

Richards, P. (1989) 'Farming as performance', in R. Chambers, A. Pacey, and L.-A. Thrupp (eds) *Farmer First. Farmer Innovation and Agricultural Research*, Intermediate Technology Publications, London

Sanchez, P.A., Shepherd, K.D., Soule, M.J., Place, F.M., Buresh, R.J. and Izak, A.-M. N. (1997) 'Soil fertility replenishment in Africa: An investment in natural resource capital', in R. Buresh, P. Sanchez and F. Calhoun (eds) *Replenishing Soil Fertility in Africa*, SSSA, Wisconsin

Scoones, I. (ed) (2001) *Dynamics and Diversity: Soil Fertility and Farming Livelihoods in Africa*, Earthscan, London

Scoones, I. and Toulmin, C. (1998) 'Soil nutrient balances: What use for policy?' *Agriculture, Ecosystems and Environment*, vol 71, pp255–267

Schoeffeleers, J. (ed) (1979) *Guardians of the Land*, Gwelo, Mambo Press

Sheldrik, W. and Lingard, J. (2004) 'The use of nutrient audits to determine nutrient balances in Africa', *Food Policy*, vol 29, no 1, pp61–98

Smaling, E., Oenema, O. and Fresco, L. (eds) (1999) *Nutrient Disequilibria in Agroecosystems. Concepts and Case Studies*, CABI Publishing, Wallingford

Stone, G. (2004) 'Biotechnology and the political ecology of information in India', *Human Organization*, vol 63, pp127–140

Stoorvogel, J. and Smaling, E. (1990) 'Assessment of soil nutrient depletion in sub-Saharan Africa', Winand Staring Centre, Wageningen

UN Millennium Project (2005) 'Halving hunger: It can be done. Summary version', The Earth Institute at Columbia University, New York

World Bank (1996) 'Restoration of soil fertility in sub-Saharan Africa', concept paper and action plan, World Bank, Washington, DC

10
Chronic Hunger: A Problem of Scarcity or Inequity?

Erik Millstone

The central argument of this chapter is that in our world chronic hunger is not a natural or inevitable phenomenon but an artefact of social, economic and political processes. In aggregate, there is more than enough food in this world for everyone but the institutions of ownership and relationships of commerce entail that it is distributed inequitably. In aggregate, affluent countries and communities that already have sufficient access to food are gaining access to even more, while those with insufficient access to food are finding their access diminishing. Those perverse patterns are the product of policy regimes that need to be reformed.

Since 1974 I have been studying the causes and consequences of technological change in food and agriculture, focusing almost entirely on industrialized countries. It was obvious that hunger in developing countries was a more important issue than, for example, the use of food additives, pesticides and veterinary medicines in the food systems of the industrialized world. But since scholars such as Dumont in 1974, George in 1976 and Lappe and Collins in 1977, had torpedoed below the waterline suggestions that chronic hunger is a problem of aggregate scarcity, it seemed appropriate to focus some attention on other problematic aspects of the food and agricultural systems that had escaped scrutiny. Thirty-five years later it is evident that Malthusian mythological dragons that repeatedly assert that chronic hunger and under-nutrition are caused by scarcity rather than by poverty still need to be combated (as has been argued by Hartmann (Chapter 3), Hildyard (Chapter 8) and others in this volume).

In late 2007 and during 2008 food prices rose abruptly across many international and local markets, and many commentators interpreted those changes as evidence of increasing underlying scarcity. A more accurate account would have acknowledged the instability of the food system and the rising probability of food price volatility, and acknowledged that chronic hunger is produced by the prevailing policy regime.

Those who assume or argue that scarcity is an ineradicable feature of the human condition typically argue or assume that millions of people are hungry and/or starving because there is insufficient food in the world to feed everyone; or to put the same point slightly differently, that there are too many people to feed given the total available food supply (see also Chapter 8, this volume). Those assumptions have historically been associated with Thomas Malthus and his *Essay on the Principles of Population as it affects the future improvement of society*, which was first published in 1798 (Malthus, 1798).

Malthus argued that, other things being equal, human populations would grow rapidly, while food production can at best grow only slowly. Malthus argued that food scarcity would be the main constraint on population growth and size, apart from sexual restraint and late marriage. He assumed that, self-restraint apart, human beings would reproduce as rapidly as possible until there were too many mouths to feed, given the available food supply. Consequently, he argued that the only natural check on population growth was starvation. He interpreted the hunger that he witnessed in Britain as proof that population in the late 18th century had already exceeded the limit that British agriculture could possibly sustain. Part of the persuasiveness of Malthus' claim derived from the fact that it could be encapsulated in mathematical language, namely in the claim that population size could grow 'geometrically' while the supply of food could at best grow 'arithmetically'.

Contesting theoretical approaches

Malthusian attempts to use 'scarcity' as an explanatory narrative of chronic hunger have been found persuasive by many protagonists but not by all, and contests have ensued over competing analyses and bodies of evidence (see also Chapters 3 and 8, this volume, for detailed discussions of neo-Malthusianism and Malthusianism and current political issues). Anti-Malthusianism has not, however, constituted a unified position but has been composed of a heterogeneous collection of contrasting arguments. There has never been just one dominant anti-Malthusian narrative but several competitors. During the 19th century a range of contrary accounts tried to provide explanations for (and/or the avoidance of) hunger and starvation, emphasizing for example the impact of technological change (Babbage, 1832; Comte, 1853), the impact of entrepreneurial creativity (Mill, 1852), institutional changes (Durkheim, 1893) and socio-economic inequalities (Marx, 1887).

Interpretations of, and responses to, Malthusianism have evolved, varying across both place and time. Hodgson for example has argued that in the USA prior to the 1890s Malthusian ideas seemed implausible, given that American society saw itself as having plentiful natural resources such as cultivable land but confronted by a scarcity of labour and needing to occupy and tame 'the wild west' (Hodgson, 1991, pp3–4). Hodgson also argued that in the USA in the late 19th century and early 20th century Malthusianism became increasingly plausible to some US commentators, once European migrants started to fill the cities and especially their slums, rather than shifting to the western and southern frontiers. As Hodgson explained, 'A new Malthusianism arose, then, among many late nineteenth-century students of population that differed from the classic sort. The vision of a 'filled' America facing resource limitations did not produce simple calls to slow population growth. The addition of racist and Darwinian ideas heightened compositional concerns' (Hodgson, 1991, p5). (For recent socio-political debates in the US context see Chapter 3, this volume.)

In Europe in the 19th century, including the UK, Darwin drew explicitly on Malthus, and so too did social Darwinists such as Herbert Spencer, whose discourse of 'the survival of the fittest' tended to characterize those whose survival was in peril as 'unfit' (Spencer, 1851). On the other hand, as McDonagh has argued, the Chartists were among the most vigorous critics of Malthus' ideas (McDonagh, 2003). Charles Dickens' *A Christmas Carol* has been interpreted for example by James Henderson as an anti-Malthusian tale (Henderson, 2000). Later in the UK, Galton and the eugenicists drew on the work of both Darwin and Malthus (Galton, 1864, 1865). In Germany, Nietzsche drew heavily on Malthus, while rejecting key elements of Darwinism (Nietzsche, 1914). Hitler and Nazi ideologists drew on both Malthus and social Darwinism.

In the late 20th century some 'third world structuralists', especially in Africa, argued in a robustly anti-Malthusian fashion that population growth can make a positive contribution to economic growth and development. Population growth, they contend, can have beneficial effects by stimulating demand and encouraging technological innovation to accommodate the new growth.[1] Boserup has also actively articulated an anti-Malthusian position arguing that population growth can be a source of demand that drives the intensification of cultivation, particularly among subsistence and peasant producers (Boserup, 1965, 1981). In the second half of the 20th century in the USA, Malthusian ideas were advocated and popularized, for example, in works such as *The Population Bomb* by Paul Erlich (Erlich, 1964). They were, however, vigorously contested for example by George (1976) and Lappe and Collins (1977).

Empirical anti-Malthusian evidence

Not merely have Malthusian ideas been theoretically contested, they have also been challenged by reference to empirical data, and frequently found wanting. The most persuasive critiques of Malthusian accounts of hunger have drawn attention to, and repeatedly emphasized that, historical data and experiences do not bear out Malthusian predictions and that they contradict Malthusian analyses. When Malthus was writing his *Essay on the Principles of Population* in the 1790s the world's population was less than 1 billion people. Since then the total size of the human population has grown approximately 8–10 fold. Still, as demonstrated below, there is currently sufficient food produced annually on the planet to feed everyone, and in aggregate and on average sufficient food has been available every year since 1800 to feed the population then alive.

In retrospect it is evident that Malthus was mistaken about the dynamics of both human population changes and developments in agricultural productivity. Over the past 200 years, the global population has grown, but in aggregate and over the long term food has become more rather than less plentiful and agricultural production has grown at a faster rate than population. The impact of technological and commercial changes in agriculture has been far greater than Malthus and the Malthusians expected.

Figures used to represent estimates of the current size of the human population and aggregate levels of food production are notoriously imprecise. In practice, it is unrealistic to expect such aggregated figures to be accurate to ± 20 per cent. Estimates of those uncertainties are typically conspicuous by their absence; error bars, confidence limits or standard deviations are rarely provided by institutions such as the UN FAO and the Worldwatch Institute that aspire to being treated as authoritative. Fortunately, for the purposes of this discussion, such imprecision is tangential, since a discussion of orders of magnitude can be sufficient.

In 2005, the FAO estimated that, when aggregated, the world's total production of cereals was ~2,230,000 million tonnes. The FAO also estimated the world's population in 2005 at ~6,464,750,000 or ~6.5 billion.[2] Consequently, to a reasonable first approximation, in 2005, in aggregate the *per capita* food availability was ~340kg/cap/year, or ~1kg per person per day. If those cereal supplies had been uniformly distributed across all of humanity they would have been sufficient to support healthy lives for all who were not otherwise unwell. One kilogramme of cereals is sufficient to provide more than 2300 calories per day, per person. Of course, there are post-harvest losses of cereals, but people also eat fruits, vegetables, nuts, fish, meat and dairy products. Notwithstanding the pessimism of Malthusians, the data are sufficiently reliable to show that, in aggregate there is a surplus of food rather than a shortage – in relation to total global population.

Moreover, since the late 18th century, there has never been evidence of aggregate global scarcities of food. There have been too many periods during which there have been localized scarcities, and too many of those periods have lasted too long. Since the mid-18th century, however, aggregate food production has grown at a more rapid rate than the size of the human population. Over the last 250 years, on average, the productivity of farming globally has grown more rapidly than population, and more rapidly than productivity in almost every other sector, with the possible exception of micro-electronics in the last 20 years (Johnson and Quance, 1972).

I entirely agree with the Worldwatch Institute and with Amartya Sen that:

> *poverty – rather than food shortages – is frequently the underlying cause of hunger ... nearly 80 percent of all malnourished children in the developing world in the early 1990s live in countries that boasted food surpluses. The more important feature common to these countries is pervasive poverty, which limits people's access to food in the market or to land, credit,*

and other inputs needed to produce food. Poverty also means poor access to non-food services, including health care, education, and a clean living environment, which increases the likelihood of hunger. (Sen, 1981; Gardner and Halweil, 2000)

Almost all problems of chronic hunger arise not because there is too little food, but because food is distributed very inequitably; not in proportion to need but in proportion to effective demand. One implication of that analysis is that hunger and malnutrition cannot be understood by an approach that deals only in terms of aggregates and averages, without reference to inequitable patterns of access and distribution.

Another important aspect of Sen's work has been to show that even in the case of acute famines, as opposed to chronic under-nutrition, people often starve not because of any localized net scarcity of food in aggregate but rather because their 'entitlements' to food collapse for some other reason, such as loss of earnings (Sen, 1981). Sen also showed that often, during localized famines, foodstuffs are exported from regions suffering famines because the levels of effective demand have fallen even as the levels of need have risen. To use a slightly different vocabulary, analyses of both chronic hunger and acute famines can benefit from a focus on the politics of allocation rather than on hypotheses of aggregate scarcities; distributional issues are crucial in a world in which some 20 per cent of the world's population consume approximately 80 per cent of the resources (see Chapter 4, this volume, for a discussion of scarcity with Amartya Sen as a point of departure).

The food surpluses, and the patterns of distribution and consumption, that have emerged and can be documented are neither natural nor inevitable; they are rather the results of human actions and policies. In particular, the policies of the governments of the industrialized countries have had a considerable impact on levels of production and patterns of trade and distribution, especially since the 1930s, and so the evolution and impacts of those policies deserve consideration. For example, the European Common Agricultural Policy (CAP), particularly from the 1960s to the 1980s, provided farmers with subsidies that encouraged overproduction of cereals, meat, milk and dairy products, which in turn generated huge surpluses that were then often dumped on to world markets depressing prices for farmers outside Europe. A similar but even more extravagant regime was operating in the US. Moreover the European and US authorities also subsidized the sale of surplus fats, sugars and starches to their domestic food processing industries, which in turn contributed very substantially to the rising incidence of diet-related chronic pathologies such as heart disease, diabetes and obesity. Overconsumption in the industrialized countries and chronic under-nutrition in poor countries have been opposite sides of the same coin.

Agricultural policy contradictions

Public policy-makers in the industrialized countries have had to struggle with agricultural policy; the challenges of deciding whether or not to intervene, and if so how, have been complex. Policy-makers have often not been able to avoid intervening in agricultural markets, yet they have had to grapple with two powerful contradictory tendencies. Unregulated agricultural markets can be extremely unstable; and food shortages are politically costly and exceedingly unpopular, while conspicuous surpluses of food products can destabilize farm incomes. Consequently, in the industrialized countries since the 1930s, public policy-makers have been actively trying to ensure that aggregate domestic scarcities do not occur, while also trying to ensure that the resultant surpluses do not undermine the viability of the domestic agricultural economy. The needs of hungry people in developing countries have, at best, been secondary.

The volatility of unregulated agricultural markets

The market for staple foods (especially in affluent countries) is, in several important respects, an untypical market. Historically, unregulated food markets have been more volatile and unstable than the markets for almost all other types of commodities; this is because food supplies can fluctuate markedly while demand (at least for staple foods) is remarkably stable. The *supply* of foods can easily vary sharply from season to season, especially in response to the weather and disease patterns. The *demand* for basic foodstuffs is, however, notoriously price-inelastic. If the price of potatoes halves in affluent societies very few people would double the quantity of potatoes they eat. If the price of basic foodstuffs doubles, many people will choose to pay those higher prices and forego expenditure on other commodities or services, especially luxuries, to ensure that they and their families have enough to eat. Those patterns cannot be easily reconciled with orthodox neoclassical economic assumptions that human wants are unlimited and that requisite resources are invariably scarce. While many people may prefer luxury foods to staples, very few people keep eating until they become nauseous, although many eat sufficiently for their weight to increase; indeed a large percentage of the citizens in industrialized countries at any one time claims to be trying to stick to weight-reducing diets or diets intended to control their weight. In 2007 the market for commercial diet products in the UK was valued at about £11 billion (or €16 billion).[3] In February 2003, Datamonitor issued a report estimating that the European diet market, including foods, drinks and supplements, was valued at €93 billion and that in 2002 some 230 million people across Europe attempted to follow weight-loss diets, but only 3.8 million kept any weight off for over a year (NutraIngredients.com, 2003).

The markets for fashionable clothes, books and recorded music are, for example, markedly different from the market for staple foodstuffs. If the price of books or CDs is halved, people might well buy twice as many books or CDs than before, while if prices were to double, sales would decline sharply. Many markets can reach saturation, but markets for staple foodstuffs are more readily saturated than most; a modest oversupply can result in a collapse in farm-gate, wholesale and retail prices, especially for perishable commodities, while suggestions of an imminent scarcity of foodstuffs have often provoked panic buying.

In poor countries, and in poor communities in affluent countries, the pattern would be different. A sharp decline in the price of staple foodstuffs might well result in sharply increased consumption, while a sharp increase in prices might well result in severe malnutrition and fatalities, but the domestic agricultural policies of the governments of industrialized countries have been focused on domestic rather than overseas welfare.

In the late 19th and early 20th centuries, unregulated agricultural markets in the industrialized world were prone to what economists refer to as the 'bunching' of investment. That phenomenon can be illustrated with what in US agricultural history is known as the 'corn-hog cycle' (Haas and Ezekiel, 1926; Craig and Holt, 2005). If each individual farmer tries to decide which commodities to concentrate on and invest in for next season, e.g. by planting seeds or breeding and buying stock, they will typically select that (or those) commodities which then command the highest price(s). When the price of hogs rose, many US farmers moved out of corn and into hogs, only to find that by the time their animals were ready for market the price of hogs had fallen and the price of corn had risen. When the subsequent set of investment decisions was taken, they were consequently bunched in the opposite direction, with similar alternating consequences, driving the cycle round again.

Given the price inelasticity of demand for staple foodstuffs, and the instabilities in supplies resulting from seasonal variations and the bunching of investment, the net result in unregulated markets was sharp fluctuations in both prices and supplies, to the distress of both urban consumers and rural producers. The magnitude and consequences of the fluctuations in food supplies and prices were, moreover, reinforced and exacerbated by the impact of the high rates of technological change that have characterized the agricultural and food sectors.

With the possible exception of the micro-electronics industry referred to above, over the past 250 years it has been the agricultural sector that has seen the fastest and most sustained rate of growth in productivity and aggregate production compared to all other major productive sectors. Since the early 18th century, technical improvements in, for example, tools, seeds, stock-breeding, methods of cultivation and husbandry, harvesting and processing, preservation, storage and distribution have been pervasive and sustained. On average, and over the long term, the relative prices of agricultural commodities have consequently fallen more rapidly than those of the goods and services for which agricultural commodities can be exchanged; the terms of trade have deteriorated from the farmers' point of view. The combination of the long-term deflationary effects of technological change on agricultural prices, together with the instability of prices and supplies, meant that unregulated agricultural markets in the late 19th and early 20th centuries became exceedingly volatile. Not only were farmers and farm workers discontent, so too were urban consumers.

The dominant policy assumptions of governments, ministers and officials in the industrialized countries were frequently that intervention would be inappropriate and counter-productive. However, powerful economic and social pressures from both impoverished farmers and landowners on the one hand and urban discontent at unreliable supplies and prices on the other were sufficient in the mid-20th century to persuade governments to intervene and take responsibility for stabilizing agricultural markets (van Zwanenberg and Millstone, 2005). The main events that transformed agricultural policies from *laissez faire* regimes to interventionist ones were wars, especially the two World Wars, as well as the inter-war depression. In the US, active official public intervention in agricultural markets began with Roosevelt's New Deal (Lang and Heasman, 2004). After 1945, the agricultural policies of the governments of all industrialized countries were predicated on the assumption that governments had an indispensable role to play in stabilizing agricultural markets, food prices and food supplies.

For much of the period since 1945, European and North American farmers have received subsidies, and those subsidies have stimulated investments in agricultural productivity, which have resulted in the generation of large agricultural surpluses. The farms of the industrialized countries are producing too much food in at least two senses: first, there is more food than the farmers are able to sell, and second, there is more food than it is good for the populations of the OECD (Organisation for Economic Co-operation and Development) countries to eat. Many of the diet-related health problems such as obesity, diabetes and heart disease are a consequence of eating too much food, rather than too little (WHO, 2002, 2003).

Key features of the historical process can be inferred from the following graph, showing annual average wheat prices in the USA from 1866 to 1998, adjusted for inflation.

The long-term downward trend in wheat prices, and other food prices too, can be attributed to the effects of technological changes discussed above, but the graph in Figure 10.1 also illustrates another important point. The contrast between the period prior to 1945 and the period following the end of World War II is also highly significant. During the period prior to 1945 the graph reveals far greater price volatility than is evident in the post-war period. After 1945 a range of price stabilization measures had the effect of considerably damping price volatility. Those measures typically involved mechanisms for setting what were in effect floors and ceilings to market prices, restricting and damping their volatility.

A set of initiatives in the early 21st century among the OECD countries aimed at market liberalization ran the risk of reintroducing the kind of volatility that was evident from 1866 to 1954. Similarly, shifts in public policy interventions earlier this decade in, for example, the US and EU to encourage the cultivation of crops for biofuels, contributed to amplifying recent food price volatilities.

The chronic surpluses that have arisen as a consequence of technological and commercial changes and public policy measures have posed considerable problems for governments and for the farming and food industries. Governments have responded in a variety of different ways. First, they have used public resources to subsidize exports of products that were themselves produced with

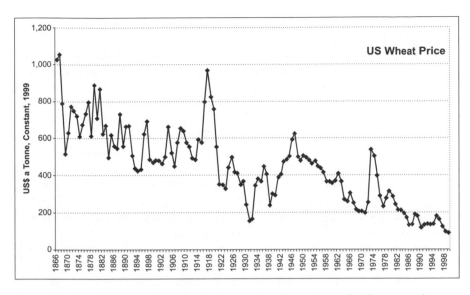

Source: Data from US Department of Agriculture www.usda.gov/nass/pubs/ (last accessed March 2009)

Figure 10.1 *US wheat prices, annual averages, 1866–1998*

the help of subsidies. The consequences of subsidized exports from the industrialized countries for farmers in underdeveloped countries (UDCs) have been severe and have contributed to their impoverishment, and consequently to rural deprivation and hunger. While retail food prices in developing countries may have fallen, that often did not lead to improved nutrition for the poor but rather to declining rates of pay for manual labourers.

Second, OECD governments have often encouraged the recycling of surplus staples up the food chain and into processed food products, since there was little scope for profitably marketing surplus foodstuffs to people too poor to pay for them. In Europe, prior to 1992, huge agricultural surpluses were accumulated (European Commission, 2004). The farming and food industries were then encouraged to take cheap and plentiful proteins, vitamins and carbohydrates and to convert them into scarce and expensive products. In particular, large quantities of grains and pulses (especially maize and soy beans) have been fed to cattle, pigs and poultry to produce meat, milk, dairy products and eggs. To the extent that those products were, in turn, in surplus, the food processing industry has been encouraged to transform those ingredients into 'value added' processed products such as pizzas, burgers, chips/fries, crisps/chips and more recently 'ready meals' (Maunder, 1970; Hightower, 1975; Desrosier and Desrosier, 1971; Elinder, 2005).

The surpluses in the EU were diminished by the McSharry reforms of 1992, which started replacing guaranteed commodity prices with a new regime of direct compensatory payments to farmers if prices fell below a certain level, and offered compensation to farmers who pursued environmentally friendly practices (Diaz-Bonilla et al, 2006). Since the mid-1990s European agricultural surpluses have diminished, but it remains the case that substantial subsidies from the EU's Common Agricultural Policy still help food processing companies by reducing their costs and enabling them to sell greater quantities of obesogenic foods (Whitehead and Nordgren, 1996; Consumer in Europe Group, 1994). For example in 2003–2004 Tate & Lyle Europe received a total of £127,324,713 from the CAP and Nestlé UK Ltd received £12,478,212.[4] In a letter to *The Guardian* in December 2005 the Deputy Director general of the UK Food and Drink Federation insisted that UK foods manufacturers '... are not given subsidies, but are entitled to compensation for the artificially high prices they pay for certain raw materials ...' (Paterson, 2005). To some that seemed like a distinction without a difference, and failed to explain why consumers were not 'entitled' to such 'compensation'.

Some commentators have argued that if affluent consumers in the industrialized countries were to eat significantly less meat, or none at all, then the amounts of vegetable protein that would become available could then be accessed by poor and hungry people in developing countries (Lappe, 1965). That argument ignores the problem of poverty; if less meat was consumed by affluent people, but the poor became no less poor, it would still not be profitable to sell grains and pulses to poor people, and so after a brief transition period in which the prices of grains and beans declined, less grain and pulses would be produced.

Agricultural economists have long appreciated that one of the central challenges of food policy in the industrialized countries has been coping with food surpluses that cannot be profitably sold (Johnson and Quance, 1972; Tarrant, 1980). Over 30 years ago Thomas T. Poleman pithily explained that:

> ... if US farm policy over the past half century can be thought of as having a theme, it has been to prevent [farmers'] productivity from driving down prices ... the tinkering with the market mechanism has been on a scale befitting the world's wealthiest nation. From Soil Bank to Public Law 480 to drowning baby pigs, little that might elevate prices has not been tried. (Poleman, 1975)

Poleman's analysis was no less true then for other industrialized countries, and it remains pertinent in the first decade of the 21st century.

The policy of paying farmers to take land out of production began in the US during the New Deal: Public Law 480, enacted in 1954, represented the main post-war institutional mechanism for exporting surplus agricultural commodities. In the development of the post-1945 European Common Agricultural Policy, production subsidies were combined with export subsidies and the so-called 'set aside' regime, in which farmers were paid not to plant crops or to raise livestock. Joseph Heller's portrayal in *Catch 22* of one key aspect of the New Deal provides a brilliant condensation of the eccentricities of this aspect of agricultural policies in the industrialized economies:

> *Major Major's father ... was a long-limbed farmer, a God-fearing, freedom loving, law-abiding rugged individualist who held that federal aid to anyone but farmers was creeping socialism ... His speciality was alfalfa, and he made a good thing out of not growing any. The government paid him well for every bushel of alfalfa he did not grow. The more alfalfa he did not grow, the more money the government gave him, and he spent every penny he did not earn on new land to increase the amount of alfalfa he did not produce. Major Major's father worked without rest at not growing alfalfa. On long winter evenings he remained indoors and did not mend harness, and he sprang out of bed at the crack of noon every day just to make certain that the chores would not be done. He invested in land wisely and soon was not growing more alfalfa than any other man in the county. Neighbours sought him out for advice on all subjects, for he had made much money and was therefore wise.* (Heller, 1975, pp94–95)

The absurdity of the arrangement was internal to the policy rather than an artefact of Heller's literary talent.

From the point of view of the food processing industry, surplus production and low food prices are not an unmixed blessing. Food companies are quite happy to obtain their ingredients at progressively lower prices, but if they have to sell their products correspondingly more cheaply, their incomes and profits are likely to decline, just as farm incomes used to fall before governments initiated their subsidy programmes. If, however, food companies can buy cheaply but sell high-priced so-called 'value-added' products then their incomes may rise rather than fall. The processing industry therefore takes advantage of low-priced agricultural ingredients and transforms them into relatively more expensive and profitable processed foods. The transformation of raw potatoes into crisps and chips provides a clear example of how low-cost surplus food staples (for which price and income elasticities are low) can be transformed into relatively scarce products that can command far higher prices and for which price and income elasticities are far more commercially favourable. That analysis suggests that apparent excesses of foods and apparent scarcities of foods are opposite sides of the same coin (Lang and Heasman, 2004). Over-consumption of calories in the north and underconsumption of calories in the south are co-produced by global socio-economic and technological processes.

Agricultural policies in developing countries

Government agricultural policies in developing countries have been significantly different from those in the north. Under colonial conditions, attempts were made to commercialize agriculture, to provide products for export, often to the colonizers' home market and, more generally for the extraction of surpluses. In post-colonial times, there have been some occasional and intermittent attempts by individual governments to subsidize domestic farmers, but those attempts have often been frustrated by an overall lack of resources, by competing claims on government expenditures and complicated by neo-patrimonial criteria for selecting recipients. As Chinsinga has indicated, for example, Malawi's experience reveals a lengthy contest between the Malawian government and its domestic constituencies on the one hand and OECD governments, the World Bank and donor agencies on the other, over the issue of subsidies for poor farmers to help them obtain fertilizers (Chinsinga, 2007). In 2006, the government of Malawi turned its back on the Washington Consensus and decided to invest in subsidizing supplies of maize seeds and fertilizers to poor farmers. The resulting harvest in 2007 reached a record level, but the desirability and sustainability of such measures remains highly contested (DFID, 2007; Chinsinga, 2007). Governments in the global south have often been advised and instructed by governments of industrialized countries, and institutions such as the World Bank especially under its 'structural adjustment' programmes, to reduce or eliminate domestic agricultural subsidies. The implicit narrative seems to be: do as we say, not as we do. In the context of a speech to the Second Kenyan National Agricultural Sector Conference, in November 2008, Akin Adesina, representing the Alliance for a Green Revolution in Africa (AGRA), said:

> Farmers' get subsidies everywhere, except Africa ... [in the USA and EU they are] doing the right thing, so can we also do the right thing? ... What we need today is not a Washington Consensus, we need an African Consensus. (Adesina, 2008)

Given the extent and complexity of agricultural policy debates within Africa, it might be unrealistic to expect a consensus within Africa or even within a single African country, but the perspectives of poor African farmers and farm workers could more effectively be taken into account by policy-makers.

One of the key issues during the contested Doha Development Round of the World Trade Organization has been the reluctance of the US and the EU to agree to cuts in subsidies to their farmers and to their agricultural exports. Some of the governments of developing countries have tried to encourage the development of a domestic processing industry capable of transforming domestically produced crops into higher-value processed products, such as instant coffee, to try to gain more from the agricultural value chain and to counteract the effects of declining terms of trade for unprocessed agricultural commodities, but those manufactured goods have often not had unrestricted access to the markets of the industrialized countries. The 'playing field' is anything but level. If the 'playing field' of public support for farmers were to be less uneven, and favoured poor farmers over wealthy farmers, there would be fewer chronically hungry communities.

As other authors in this volume have argued, even though there is a very substantial body of evidence indicating that Malthusian assumptions are mistaken, Malthusian ideas have not lost their attractiveness or superficial plausibility. In the social sciences, refuted paradigms often do not fade away but can persist despite the availability of evidence that undermines their basic assumptions. This predicament implies, however, that those who currently articulate Malthusian accounts of chronic hunger most energetically are often among the least well-informed.

Summary and conclusion

In summary, therefore, in practice and in aggregate there is not, and for at least 200 years there has not been, any overall global aggregate scarcity of food. Millions of people have gone, and still go, hungry: not because food is unavailable but because they are too poor to gain access to the food that is plentiful. Moreover, huge agricultural surpluses have been generated by public policy measures in the industrialized countries, although other policy measures and commercial initiatives have meant that a superficial impression of scarcity has been created by taking plentiful staple foods and industrially transforming them into scarce, relatively expensive and profitable products. Chronic hunger in poor countries is therefore a consequence of poverty and an artefact of commercial and industrial transactions and policy decisions, not a fact of nature – even less an inevitable one. The global food system exhibits the bizarre pathology of simultaneously producing underconsumption and hunger in poor countries and chronic overconsumption in the industrialized countries. Neither of those nutritional pathologies is natural or inevitable, rather they are both interconnected socio-economic artefacts. In general, and for the most part, the appearance of scarcity of foodstuffs has been the artefact of public and corporate policies and strategies. Claims of scarcity of food need to be taken not with a 'pinch of salt' but rather with a large skip-full.

Notes

1   See for example www.svf.uib.no/sfu/nsw/staff/florence.shtml (last accessed March 2010).
2   See http://faostat.fao.org/Default.aspx (last accessed April 2009).
3   See www.nutraingredients.com/news/printNewsBis.asp?id=74769 (last accessed July 2007).
4   Data available from farmsubsidy.org at http://farmsubsidy.org/ (last accessed July 2007).

References

Adesina, A. (2008) 'Improving access to agricultural inputs and output markets for enhanced productivity', speech to the Second Kenyan National Agricultural Sector Conference, in November 2008, available at www.ascu.go.ke/DOCS/conference%20programme%20291008.pdf (last accessed April 2009)
Babbage, C. (1832) *On the Economy of Machinery and Manufacture*, Charles Knight, London
Boserup, E. (1965) *The Conditions of Agricultural Growth*, Aldine, Chicago

Boserup, E. (1981) *Population and Technological Change*, University of Chicago Press, Chicago

Butler, C. (2006) 'Population growth, migration and four Millennium Development Goals', available at www.appg-popdevrh.org.uk/Publications/Population%20Hearings/Evidence/BODHI%20evidence.doc, (last accessed April 2009)

Chinsinga, B. (2007) 'The Social Protection Policy in Malawi: Processes, Politics and Challenges', Future Agricultures Consortium, available at www.future-agricultures. org/pdf%20files/SP_policy_malawi.pdf (last accessed February 2008)

Comte, A. (1853) *Cours: The Positive Philosophy of Auguste Comte* (translated and edited by H. Martineau), Chapman, London

Consumer in Europe Group (1994) *The Common Agricultural Policy: How to Spend £28 Billion a Year Without Making Anyone Happy*, Consumer in London Group, London

Craig, L.A. and Holt, M.T. (2005) 'A history of the corn-hog cycle in the USA', September, available at www.american.edu/cas/econ/WAEHS/Papers/Craig%20 10-2005.pdf (last accessed July 2006)

Desrosier, N.W. and Desrosier J.N. (1971) *Economics of New Food Product Development*, AVI, Westport, Connecticut

DFID (2007) 'A record maize harvest in Malawi', May 2007, Department for International Development, available at www.dfid.gov.uk/casestudies/files/africa%5 Cmalawi-harvest.asp (last accessed March 2009)

Diaz-Bonilla, E., Frandsen, S.E. and Robinson, S. (eds) (2006) *WTO Negotiations and Agricultural Trade Liberalization: The Effect of Developed Countries' Policies on Developing Countries*, CABI, Wallingford

Dumont, R. (1974) *Agronone de la faim*, Laffont, Paris

Durkheim, E. (1893) *De La Division du travail social*, Les Presses Universitaires de France, Paris, translated by S. Simpson (1947) *The Division of Labour in Society*, The Free Press, Glencoe, Illinois

Elinder, L.S. (2005) 'Obesity, hunger and agriculture: The damaging role of subsidies', *British Medical Journal*, vol 331, pp1333–1336

Erlich, P. (1964) *The Population Bomb*, Ballantine, New York

European Commission (2004) *The Common Agricultural Policy Explained*, Brussels, available at http://ec.europa.eu/agriculture/publi/capexplained/cap_en.pdf, see esp. p10, (last accessed July 2007)

Galton, F. (1864) 'Hereditary character and talent', Part I, *MacMillan's Magazine*, vol 11, November, pp157–166

Galton, F. (1865) 'Hereditary character and talent', Part II, *MacMillan's Magazine*, vol 11, April, pp318–327

Gardner, G. and Halweil, B. (2000) *Overfed and Underfed: The Global Epidemic of Malnutrition*, WorldWatch Paper 150, March, p17

George, S. (1976) *How the Other Half Dies: The Real Reasons for World Hunger*, Penguin Books, Harmondsworth

Haas, G.C. and Ezekiel, M. (1926) 'Factors affecting the price of hogs', *US Department of Agriculture Bulletin*, vol 1440, pp67–68

Heller, J. (1975) *Catch 22*, Corgi Books, New York

Henderson, J.P. (2000) '"Political economy is a mere skeleton unless ..." What can social economists learn from Charles Dickens?', *Review of Social Economy*, vol LVIII, no 2, pp141–151

Hightower, J. (1975) *Eat Your Heart Out*, Random House, New York

Hodgson, D. (1991) 'The ideological origins of the Population Association of America', *Population and Development Review*, vol 17, no 1

Johnson, G.L. and Quance, C.L. (eds) (1972) *The Overproduction Trap in US Agriculture: A Study of Resource Allocation from World War I to the Late 1960s*, Johns Hopkins University Press, Baltimore

Lang, T. and Heasman, M. (2004) *Food Wars: The Global Battle for Mouths, Minds and Markets*, Earthscan, London

Lappe, F.M. (1965) *Diet for a Small Planet: How to Enjoy a Rich Protein Harvest by Getting Off the Top of the Food Chain*, Ballantine Books, New York

Lappe, F.M. and Collins, J. (1977) *Food First: Beyond the Myth of Scarcity*, Houghton Mifflin, New York

Malthus, T.R. (1798) *Essay on the Principles of Population as it Affects the Future Improvement of Society*, first published anonymously by J. Johnson, London; available at www.econlib.org/library/Malthus/malPop.html (last accessed 15 April 2009)

Marx, K. (1887) *Capital: A Critique of Political Economy*, 3 vols, Lawrence and Wishart, London

Maunder, P. (1970) 'The UK food processing and distributive trade: An appraisal of public policies', *Journal of Agricultural Economics*, vol 21

McDonagh, J. (2003) *Child Murder & British Culture 1720–1900*, Cambridge University Press, Cambridge

Mill, J.S. (1852) *Principles of Political Economy*, 3rd edition, Parker, London

Nietzsche, F.W. (1914) *Beyond Good and Evil: Prelude to a Philosophy of the Future*, translated by Helen Zimmern, Foulis, London

NutraIngredients.com (2003) 'Keeping dieters dieting – the key to market growth', 19 February, available at www.nutraingredients.com/news/printNewsBis.asp?id=37340 (last accessed July 2007)

Paterson, M. (2005) 'Letter to the editor', *The Guardian*, 16 December, p35

Poleman, T.T. (1975) 'World food: A perspective', *Science*, May, pp510–518

Sen, A. (1981) *Poverty and Famines: An Essay on Entitlement and Deprivation*, Oxford University Press, Oxford

Spencer, H. (1851) *Social Statics*, John Chapman, London

Tarrant, J.R. (1980) 'Government intervention in agriculture', in *Food Policies*, John Wiley & Sons, Chichester and New York

van Zwanenberg, P. and Millstone, E. (2005) 'The evolution of the UK's agriculture and food policy regimes', in *BSE: Risk, Science and Governance*, Oxford University Press, Oxford

Whitehead, M. and Nordgren, P. (eds) (1996) 'Health Impact Assessment of the EU Common Agricultural Policy', Swedish National Institute of Public Health

WHO (2002) 'The European Health Report 2002', WHO Regional Publications, European Series No 97, Copenhagen

WHO (2003) 'Diet, Nutrition and the Prevention of Chronic Diseases', WHO Technical Report Series 916, Geneva

11

A Share Response to Water Scarcity: Moving beyond the Volumetric

Bruce Lankford

Introduction

This chapter examines water scarcity through a facilitative 'share' response, arguing that scarcity is too often seen as volumetric imbalance to be dealt with by saving, storing and delivering more water. However, these may be responses that only partially recognize how water is shared and that therefore continue to exacerbate scarcity and inequity. In emphasizing a 'para-volumetric' response to scarcity, the chapter contains a framework of supply, demand and share responses and argues that, alongside demand and supply solutions, the allocation of water between users[1] increases in significance. An additional dimension of scarcity beyond the volumetric shortage occurs in dynamically supplied environments where water is variably apportioned between users semi-automatically or semi-consciously as a result of existing institutions and infrastructure. The chapter concludes that, while scarcity might indeed be a universal backdrop, it is society's experimentations with water interventions under conditions of rapid hydrological change that are the acid tests of how scarcity is understood.

For the purposes of political expediency, water scarcity, seen as limited or decreasing water supply in the face of existing or increasing demands,[2] proves to be useful in two ways. First, it is easier to blame a natural shortage of water than to accept the full liabilities related to the sharing of limited amounts. Second, 'lack of water' allows for policies that are not so much related to how water can be managed and shared but more to concerns about how to fix or solve the lack of supply (see also Chapter 12, this volume). A concern with volumetric shortages rather than with the details of water management, particularly the distribution of water between users, is nurtured by the material realities of water politics and policies; budgets to be spent, a desire to 'keep things simple'[3] and a political milieu of lobbying, ballot intentions, donor-client agendas and public accountability. By drawing on a case study in Tanzania, particularly ideas developed in Lankford and Beale (2007), this chapter attempts to show differences between the volumetric logics of redressing demand-and-supply balances and approaches that facilitate the sharing of water under conditions of a highly varying supply.

Whether users face relative temporary or semi-permanent water scarcity in comparison to periods of water abundance is not disputed here because water supply in nature is inherently variable. Furthermore, the objective is not to comment on the efficacy of demand and supply solutions as others have done admirably (Mehta, 2006; Molle and Berkhoff, 2007). I move beyond the *volumetric* supply, demand and allocative origins and solutions of scarcity. Thus while Mehta (2001 and 2005) has focused on anthropogenic influences on water scarcity (such as over-exploitation of groundwater and devegetation) as well as the constructed nature of scarcity and its naturalization, these are volumetric commentaries on supply and demand. By contrast, I highlight the exacerbation of natural and social scarcity by anthropogenic structures inappropriately designed to share out water.

As well as shortages of water and degrees of access to water supplies, inequitable allocation of water is identified in the water scarcity literature as a 'crisis' (Clarke, 1991; Gleick, 1993; Brown, 2001). For example, the causes of the crisis of the Aral Sea (Micklin, 2007) are attributed to upstream irrigation. While allocation is acknowledged to play a role in scarcity in such writings, this tends to be couched in a volumetric analysis of which sectors are provided with water using long-term sum-balances. I seek to go beyond 'sum-balance' allocation perspectives to the contemporaneous sharing of water in certain environments.

Share management is defined here as a set of interventions designed to propagate proportions of available supply through a hierarchy of competing users, taking into account variability of supply, the number of users and their demands. This proportional distribution of water occurs over different scales, levels and time windows. As a theoretical framework, it supersedes (and incorporates) water allocation because of the need to accept the paradigmatic challenges of water distribution in highly dynamic environments – the latter defined by semi-arid conditions or rapid climate change particularly in closed river basins – where variable intensities of scarcity and insufficiency occur rapidly and unpredictably both in time and space. The particularities of such environments may not be served by current models of either integrated water resources management or adaptive water resources management where both models undertake a normative regulatory approach to water allocation. In other words, allocating water from one user to another via regulation of the former's demand may not be enough – in highly transient situations water sharing is mediated by a number of other means.

Water scarcity

A brief overview of commentaries on the construction of scarcity is provided before moving on to an examination of the tendency towards volumetric thinking. From a seemingly neutral definition of a mathematical conception of balance between supply and demand, scarcity is undergoing an increasingly sophisticated level of analysis.

In disciplinary terms one might distinguish between scientists who study water balances as hydrologists might, technical instrumentalists who reflect on the role of the built environment (e.g. lack of storage) in determining scarcity, social scientists concerned with relationships between society, power over and access to and distribution of water and economists who endeavour to understand water scarcity as an expression of financial scarcity, inappropriate pricing and market behaviour.

In addition, scholars have considered other forms of deficit (e.g. financial or political will) that drive water shortages. Turton and Ohlsson (1999) termed a focus on water shortages a first-order analysis of scarcity and other types of capabilities as second-order analyses. Mehta (2006) explored four types of resources, primary to quaternary, physical, economic, adaptive and political. Mehta's capability and well-being approach to scarcity is an example of a multi-strand examination of scarcity, and argues for a detailed look at underlying capabilities, moving beyond first-order resource solutions that often propose 'more water' via supply technologies to help solve water imbalances. Ohlsson (1998) argued for a social water stress index to reflect adaptive capacity. Furthermore, our understanding is not simply a product of the range of incorporated perspectives as suggested by Turton, Mehta and others but is also a result of the depth and breadth within those disciplines and perspectives.

Scarcity is commonly analysed from a supply side or a demand side (or conservation), or in terms of how water is shared between sectors, termed here 'share management'.[4] Although I draw on the literature on allocation within an integrated water resources management (IWRM) framework and particularly on Homer-Dixon's third category (which he termed 'structural') (Homer-Dixon, 1999) and the use of 'water allocation' by the Comprehensive Assessment of Water Management in Agriculture (Molle, 2003; Molle et al, 2007), I make a special case for the term 'share management' alongside demand and supply management.

The bias towards supply management (e.g. building dams) or demand management (e.g. fixing leaks) is revealing not only of trends among donor thinking but also of how 'scarcity response' narratives are constructed. Of late, the International Water Management Institute (IWMI) and the World Bank have argued that per capita storage is low in sub-Saharan Africa and that additional storage is required; a reflection of the economic scarcity of investment (World Bank, 2007; Rosegrant et al, 2002). The ambivalent treatment of share management in these literatures suggests that a more profound look at the technical management of scarcity adds to demand and supply thinking, enhances the outcomes of additional storage and enriches our engagement with the political construction of scarcity. It should be said that this chapter does not take issue with the *how* and *whether* water is 'saved' in one sector – a debate where precise communication is required (Perry, 2007).

Tending towards volumetric responses to water scarcity

A volumetric response to water scarcity is a natural logic. The evolution of this logic to scarcity can be seen in the last 40–50 years, with the supplanting of supply management ('if water is scarce, increase supply') by demand management ('if water is scarce, reduce demand'). Evolution has continued with both supply and demand management promulgated, combined with the emergence of allocation within an IWRM framework (GWP, 2000), a central tenet of which is regulation via pricing water volumetrically or licensing water provision. These tend to be expressed volumetrically as either annual volumes (cubic metres) or discharges (litres or cubic metres per second) rather than in proportions or percentages of available flow.

As indicated above and in the chapter to follow by Jairath, the quality of scarcity thinking is most revealed when indicators of scarcity or recommendations are promulgated. The water stress index, one of the most widely adopted (Falkenmark, 1989), proposes a threshold of 1700m^3 of renewable water resources per capita annually, below which countries are said to be water-stressed (see also Rijsberman, 2006). This index functions when boundaries are carefully defined (e.g. basin, country level) but cannot express the extent to which water is shared between a unit's population or users (see also Chapter 12, this volume, for a discussion of supply and demand management issues). The same omission applies to the Water Poverty Index (WPI) (Sullivan, 2002), constructed from five main indicators (water availability, access to water, capacity for sustaining access, the use of water and the environmental factors that impact on water). Although WPI moves away from being a volumetric measure it does not describe how water is shared between users in a given area.

An introduction to supply and demand management

A careful framing of responses to scarcity is predicated on a specification of the concepts of demand and supply management guided by Tables 11.1 and 11.2, and Figure 11.1. In this analysis, water supply is taken as the amount of water extraneous to a user, while water demand is the amount of water utilized and managed 'within' a user from the point of abstraction. We can describe the 'amount' of water supplied, used or saved in three ways; *volumetrically* which includes three subtypes of depth (in millimetres), total volume (cubic metres) and discharge (litres/second); as an *intensity* calculated as a specific or tertiary ratio, a common one being the hydromodule in litres per second per hectare; and as a *proportion* (percentage) of total supply or total demand. Without formulating water use as 'intensity', or recasting demand as a proportion of supply or total demand, water wastage and overuse is difficult to judge accurately.

Table 11.1 *Framework of supply management as a scarcity response*

Scarcity response	Subtype	Definition
Amount descriptors	Volumetric (depth, volume or discharge)	Water supply, usage or saving within a sector expressed as a depth equivalent (mm), volume (cubic metres), or discharge (litres/second)
	Intensity or specific	Water supply, usage or saving expressed as a ratio to a field or person (litres/second/hectare)
	Proportion	Water supply, usage or saving within a sector expressed as a percentage of total water supply
Supply management	Access	Establishing infrastructure that *extends access* to existing freshwater, for example a deeper borehole
	Buffer (or capital)	Establishing or managing infrastructure to store or create freshwater, for example a reservoir
Includes five types of shifts	'Mining' – long time shifts	Acquiring and accessing geological water that moves slowly within the hydrological cycle
	Storage – short time shift	Acquiring water that represents a shift of water within the hydrological cycle over a short time-span
	Place shift	Managing water that entails a move of the resource; e.g. inter-catchment transfer
	Quality shift	Cleaning up or improving otherwise unusable water; e.g. desalinization
	Phase shift	Rain cloud-seeding and condensation technologies to provide drinking water from vapour

'Supply management' suggests the augmentation of water to sectors or a sector, while 'demand management' describes the reduction in demand for water via the improved management of water within a sector to fit the available supply (Radif, 1999). Supply management can be understood as increasing the amount of water either by extending access to existing flows, or by increasing the reserve volume (or buffer) by capturing flows that otherwise would have been lost to beneficial use. Examples include reservoirs and groundwater recharge systems. Conceptually, supply management shifts existing water either spatially, temporally or through changing quality and phase. Thus, storage of wet season flow to the dry season is an intra-annual shift in the hydrograph. Accessing groundwater comprises a shift on longer, even geological, timescales. Desalinization gives more water via improving water quality, while pollution, representing a decline in water quality, reduces water availability. Condensation technologies for drinking water are a phase shift from vapour to liquid, and may become increasingly important supply side solutions (Lindblom and Nordella, 2007). See also Molle (2003) for four types of water sources; rainwater, streamwater, controlled, and potential controlled.

Table 11.2 *Framework of demand management as a scarcity response*

Amount descriptors	Volumetric (depth, volume or discharge)	Water supply, usage or saving within a sector expressed as a depth equivalent (mm), volume (cubic metres), or discharge (litres/second)
	Intensity or specific	Water supply, usage or saving expressed as a ratio to a field or person (litres/second/hectare)
	Proportion	Water supply, usage or saving within a sector expressed as a percentage of total water supply
Demand management – requires reductions in one or more of these 'fractions'	Withdrawal (gross or cap)	The total amount of water required by a sector at the point of diverted supply including the 'inefficient' or non-beneficial (tare) part
	Consumptive use (beneficial and non-beneficial)	Water is depleted from the hydrological cycle during usage – irrigation is an example. This describes the amount of water removed by a user after recoverable return flows have been computed. From the source's point of view, this can be seen as a net depletion. Beneficial water is when it is consumed or used to produce societal benefits (e.g. crops or environmental goods)
	Non-consumptive	Water is minimally depleted but its quality might be changed during usage (industrial use is an example)
	Recoverable fraction	Water is returned to the hydrological cycle
	Non-recoverable fraction	Non-consumed water cannot be used for beneficial use within the hydrological cycle
	Supply-driven	Demand fluctuates as a result of short- or long-term changes in the availability of supply
	User-driven	Demand adjusts as a result of purposive measures taken by a user to reduce water consumption

Multiple concepts of demand management also require careful unpacking. Much work has been done by the IWMI (Molden et al, 2003). Table 11.2 identifies 10 dimensions to demand management. There are three components to water use and savings; net, tare and gross. Net is the component of gross water use that generates benefits to the user, and arises from consumptive or nonconsumptive use (consumption is equivalent to depletion). Tare is the 'inefficiency' component arising from delivering water to provide the net requirement and gross is the combination of net and tare and leads to a gross requirement at the point of abstraction. Water demand in a user can be expressed from the point of view of the resource whereby returned water (and therefore net demand from the point of view of the hydrological cycle) can be computed.

Two drivers reduce demand; the first is that demand reductions are driven by the availability of water, meaning that a reduced supply, either from natural variation or growing competition, forces a reduced demand. The second, less likely

Table 11.3 *Framework of share management*

Amount descriptors	Volumetric (depth, volume or discharge)	Water supply, usage or saving within a sector expressed as a depth equivalent (mm), volume (cubic metres), or discharge (litres/second)
	Intensity or specific	Water supply, usage or saving expressed as a ratio to a field or person (litres/second/hectare)
	Proportion	Water supply, usage or saving within a sector expressed as a percentage of total water supply
Share management (determining both current and future division of water)	Appropriation	Share of current and future water over the longer term • external regulatory and dialogue environment • demand management within one user • growth over time of favoured user
	Allocation	Allocation of water between sectors or users by using allocation and regulation tools via IWRM framework
	Translation	Inter-seasonal change in share of controlled water between sectors or users as a result of new or altered institutions or infrastructure
	Modification	Intra-seasonal contemporaneous change in share of water between users or sectors as a result of an ongoing changing supply mediated by existing institutions and infrastructure
	Scheduling	Time period management of water distribution between users and sectors within proportions determined by allocation of water to users and sectors
Three types of water movement between users	Surface	Movement of water via channels, pipes and rivers
	Subsurface	Movement via soil water and geological water
	Vapour	Movement of water via atmosphere

option, is that savings (or reductions in non-beneficial use) are made within the sector without reference to the external supply of water. In keeping with IWMI's framework, demand management should refer to, among other dimensions, consumptive, non-consumptive, beneficial and non-beneficial components.

Mental agility is required because demand management within one user frees up water for another user, and could be seen as a supply solution. Another confusion arises from a literal perspective; visible alterations to the 'supply' such as exchanging an open channel for a pipe to save water are 'demand' solutions (Merrett, 2004 contains an example of this confusion).

A facilitative response – water share management

For this analysis of scarcity, a third option exists, outlined in Table 11.3 and depicted in Figures 11.1, 11.2, 11.3 and 11.4. 'Share' determines how a stable or varying supply is apportioned between users resulting in currently supplied proportions of water and in future changes in proportions in either short or long timescales. Timescale and spatial scale are critical to our understanding of how share management functions and where a normal understanding of 'allocation' sits (Figure 11.1). Following Table 11.3, changes in apportionment of water between users occur via five mechanisms:

1   The first, *appropriation*, is the implicit and unforeseen shift in shares enabled by the growth of one user that then *ceteris paribus* reduces water for other users. This is most visible over timescales of 5–10 years and is seen more clearly in Figure 11.2 as a rising share of water accruing to user D1
2   The second is the *allocation*[5] of water between users by using decision-making tools and devices (markets, licences) within a regulatory IWRM framework. This is how most commentators perceive water sharing alongside demand and supply management. Associated with allocation is the parallel application of demand management to a 'donating' sector (this is depicted towards the right-hand side of Figure 11.2)
3   *Translation* covers the (often implicit and unintended) change in shares of water between users as a result of new or altered supply side infrastructure integrated over a longer time (seasonal) period of the hydrograph. For example, surplus water stored in a dam during the wet season takes environmental water and holds it back for another user, perhaps irrigation. Translation implies a temporal inter-seasonal shift in water usage with a concomitant shift in apportionment between sectors (see Figure 11.3)
4   *Modification* describes contemporaneous changes in the share of water between users as a result of a changing extraneous supply being altered by existing infrastructural architecture. This is significant in environments with highly varying flows. In brief, the flow characteristics of abstractions determine the amount of water taken by users at any given time as a discharge – yet when expressed as a percentage of the total supply, shares between users alter. For example, two neighbouring irrigation intakes might both take 200 litres per second, amounting to 5 per cent of a river discharge of 8000 litres per second. When the river flow declines to 400 litres per second, they would then take an equal share of 50 per cent each of a river flow. As the dry season progresses, and the river flow falls to 200 litres per second, this gives unequal shares of 100 per cent to the first intake and 0 per cent to the second intake. See Lankford and Mwaruvanda (2007) for more on the implications of intake design for water distribution and basin governance
5   *Scheduling* is concerned with the short time period movement of water between users but within shares determined by the allocation of water to users. Scheduling does not result in any net long-term changes, but can critically resolve inter- and intra-sectoral water shortages where timing of delivery is important. For example, water flows can be scheduled between an irrigation system and a downstream wetland to sustain their respective ecologies. Scheduling is important where decisions about water sharing between users are best taken at a devolved level.

Five types of water sharing and their association with demand and supply management

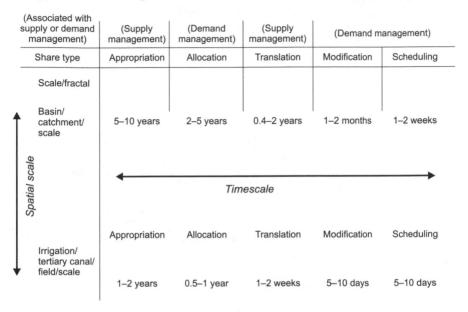

(Associated with supply or demand management)	(Supply management)	(Demand management)	(Supply management)	(Demand management)	
Share type	Appropriation	Allocation	Translation	Modification	Scheduling
Scale/fractal					
Basin/ catchment/ scale	5–10 years	2–5 years	0.4–2 years	1–2 months	1–2 weeks
	Appropriation	Allocation	Translation	Modification	Scheduling
Irrigation/ tertiary canal/ field/scale	1–2 years	0.5–1 year	1–2 weeks	5–10 days	5–10 days

Spatial scale

Timescale

Figure 11.1 *Scale and time acting on water sharing options*

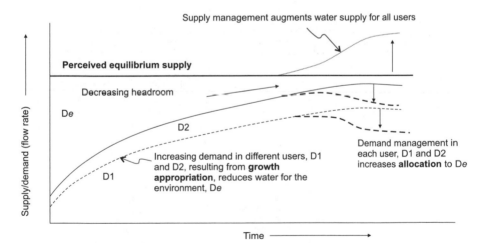

Supply management augments water supply for all users

Perceived equilibrium supply

Decreasing headroom

De

D2

Increasing demand in different users, D1 and D2, resulting from **growth appropriation**, reduces water for the environment, De

D1

Demand management in each user, D1 and D2 increases **allocation** to De

Supply/demand (flow rate)

Time

Figure 11.2 *Supply and demand curves deemed to be in broad equilibria*

The five options describe *how* water is moved between users and sectors, distinguishing 'sharing processes' from 'sharing claimants'. As presented in Figure 11.1, the five definitions are to some extent 'fractal'. In other words, they apply to different levels of spatial scale and at different timescales, for example to the allotment of water between irrigation, industry and the environment on

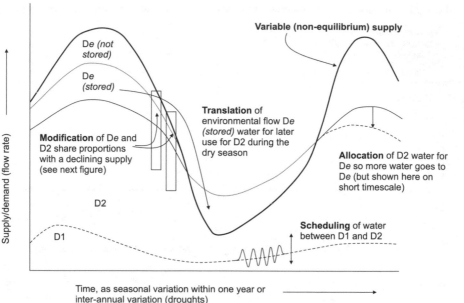

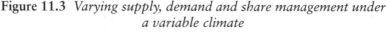

Figure 11.3 *Varying supply, demand and share management under a variable climate*

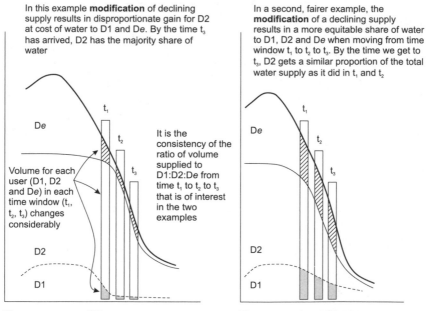

Figure 11.4 *Detail demonstrating modification of shares in a declining supply*

the same river or to a series of irrigation intakes on a river or to canals within an irrigation system.

Categorized with share management are the three ways in which water moves between users; surface, subsurface and vapour. This hints at the likelihood of saved water being made available to another sector, or whether it may be captured by the same sector, depending on the spatial and hydrological route the water takes (see Molle et al, 2004). The route that water takes affects notions of certainty and timing, in that water moving via groundwater flow is slow and difficult to gauge while water moving between users as atmospheric vapour is even less 'knowable'.

Note that a change in water apportionment via allocation and scheduling arises from active management and governance, while a change in water apportionment arising from translation and modification occurs primarily from a variable supply interacting with existing infrastructural architecture and is therefore more passive (although these are subject to change as well).

The five types of share management apply to different river basin conditions with profound implications for how water is governed. Setting aside the first, appropriation, I contend that in an equilibrium climate (e.g. oceanic, temperate) where the supply of water varies relatively little, shares between users are determined by purposive demand or supply management in one or more sectors linked with allocation share management. Thus water saving in irrigation, cascaded up to a cap on abstraction, adds water to other sectors.

However, with a greater amplitude of hydrological variability associated with pulse-driven semi-arid environments or climate change, translation and modification share management becomes more important (Figures 11.3 and 11.4). When supply increases or decreases over orders of magnitude within relatively short periods of time (rivers might vary from 0.1 cumecs during a dry season to 100 cumecs during a wet season), this imposes shifts in demand but disproportionally upon different sectors, depending on how users differentially access an increasing or decreasing rate of supply.[6] This can be seen as a modification of the supply variability upon demand variability, and therefore of the share proportions of users. At times of very low water supply in such arid environments, scheduling becomes more important too.

A conceptual framework of scarcity logic

Moving beyond a volumetric mission for balancing supply and demand opens up space for considering how inter-user shares can be managed, particularly in dividing water to users contemporaneously in the face of a variable supply. Figure 11.5 schematically expresses a single-axis concept of contrasting responses to scarcity. The left hand side tends towards tackling scarcity volumetrically, while the right side proposes a share response that recognizes – in the face of a dynamic supply – the allocative dimensions of scarcity, the facilitative nature of providing shares, and the need to cascade shares down levels of use. The middle territory suggests a mixed approach.

Response	Volumetric/quantity logic			Composite 'facilitative' logic
Order of response	Primary; 'solving the water balance'		⟷	Layered, composite; 'propagating equitable shares'
Climate & agro-ecology	Humid, temperate, oceanic, stable		⟷	Seasonal, semi-arid, dynamic
Hydrological predictability & stability	Equilibrium, predictable		⟷	Non-equilibrium, unpredictable
Approach	Supply mgt	Demand mgt	Share mgt (allocation)	Share mgt (modification, translation, scheduling)
Managerial intention	Alter volume balance within a supply phase			Alter share balance when moving between phases
Water unit of measurement	Volume or discharge or depth			% Proportion or intensity/specific
Means of water measurement	Metering			Non-metering solutions
Water rights	Volumetrically specified			Temporally and/or proportionally specified

Figure 11.5 *A conceptual framework of scarcity response*

It is worth noting that water metrics are integral to the approach chosen. Thus supply and demand management, associated with 'quantity-balance' logics, primarily considers volume (cubic metres) or discharge (litres per second). The facilitative and composite approaches are inherently concerned with managing existing shares as proportions and/or specific flows expressed as an intensity (e.g. litres per second per hectare).

The framework comments on water responses to scarcity utilizing an equilibrium and non-equilibrium lens (Lankford and Beale, 2007) – drawn in turn from ecological theories of natural resource and ecological governance recognizing parallel challenges of meeting demand and supply at the local and landscape scales (Behnke and Scoones, 1993; Sullivan, 2003). Thus, when water scarcity is primarily held to be a problem of volumetric scarcity arising out of an imbalance of supply and demand linked under conditions of *perceived* average 'equilibria', analysts favour a response logic tending towards supply side or demand side solutions (see also Chapter 12, this volume). Apart from the risks of whether such technologies materially boost supply or reduce net demand, the key risk is that the interpretation of the environment is incorrect – hence the term 'perceived'.

A 'quantity-balance' logic, while important, is not necessarily complete or accurate enough in semi-arid environments – seen as non-equilibrium environments marked by considerable fluxes of scarcity. For two reasons, pulse-driven environments require additional thinking. First, supply and demand are not in step with each other either inter- or intra-seasonally, and second they are not moving towards a broad equilibrium over time (see Figure 11.3). The additional thinking is that we are not able or obliged to balance supply and demand in the same way, but to give emphasis to propagating shares between users in ways that are locally transparent and beneficial and facilitating user communities to transit from wet to dry periods.

This framework throws light on supply side solutions for non-equilibrium semi-arid environments. Given a new reservoir, the manner in which that additional water volume is shared within the locality becomes significant, recognizing the paramount importance of timeliness of water arrival for ecological functioning in semi-arid climates. How this takes place, with implications for guarding against unplanned appropriation, for purposive water allocation (setting the broad limits on water apportionment for domestic, productive or environmental purposes during dry and wet seasons), for translation (proportions changed through the presence of the dam), for modification (the interference of other infrastructure on the intended outcome of reservoir releases) and for scheduling (switching the dam's water between users) has to be critically addressed.

How society *shares* a variable supply between different users rather than attempts to 'climate-proof' such an environment by boosting supply is a fundamental question. This is particularly so as we recognize differences between types of users and stakeholders characterized by their proximity to a secure supply (e.g. powerful top-enders versus impoverished tail-enders) and dependence on small, timely amounts of clean water (contrasting irrigators with domestic users). Moreover, it is the relative lack of political voice of the less advantaged that diminishes society's obligations to consistently prioritize a more equitable sharing of limited, varying supplies. It is posited that this water scarcity framework, while nevertheless subject to claims for water by socially differentiated groups, puts into the hands of water managers a more explicit tool for interpreting intended and unintended impacts of water interventions.

Case study example of the framework

The differences between volumetric and facilitative approaches to scarcity are now briefly explored, exemplified by work conducted by the author in Tanzania during the period 1999–2005.[7] The case study is the basin of the Usangu wetland forming the headwaters of the Great Ruaha River, which is a major tributary of the Rufiji River. The area covers 20,800km², of which 23 per cent is alluvial plains at an elevation of 1000 to 1100m above sea level, and the remaining 77 per cent forms the high catchment, ranging in altitude from 1100 to just under 3000m above sea level. The high catchment receives 900–1500mm of rainfall annually while the plains receive 650–800mm. Rainfall is highly seasonal, occurring mainly between December and April. A long dry season occurs between May and November.

The Usangu basin contains a number of water resource subsystems. The relatively wet high catchment on the southern and western boundary of the area forms the source for a number of perennial and seasonal rivers which flow into the Usangu Plains. The plains consist of alluvial fans forming an almost continuous band around the margins of the central plains, and seasonally flooded open grassland and perennial swamp towards the centre.

Irrigated agriculture is situated on the middle to lower parts of alluvial fans on the southern margin of the Usangu wetland, consisting of large state-owned rice farms and separate informal smallholder areas. Irrigation using diverted river water is the greatest source of demand for water within Usangu. Paddy rice is irrigated in the wet season, while maize and vegetables are irrigated in the dry season. Below the irrigation systems are grasslands and wetlands – the latter expanding and contracting depending on inflows. Water exits the north end of the Usangu wetland over a natural rock sill which acts as a spillway. The outflow supplies the Great Ruaha River which flows northeastwards through the Ruaha National Park forming an important source of water for wildlife. Downstream of the Park, the river flows into the Mtera and Kidatu hydropower reservoirs that provide approximately 50 per cent of Tanzania's electricity supply.

A World Bank project 'River Basin Management and Smallholder Irrigation Improvement Project' (RBMSIIP), funded in Tanzania to support river basin management (World Bank, 1996), sought to allocate water in the Usangu basin via the implementation of a formal regulatory approach. The main aim was to reduce irrigation abstraction so that more water remained in the Great Ruaha River supporting the Usangu wetland, the Ruaha National Park and hydropower. This utilized new water rights sold in litres per second, combined with changes to intake design where an 'improvement' from traditional designs was deemed necessary (Lankford, 2004). One rationale for introducing water rights was to attach fees as an incentive for water conservation.

Research in the area by van Koppen et al (2004) demonstrated that the new volumetric water rights were poorly matched to the problems encountered. The water rights did not recognize existing customary water rights; they failed to accommodate swings in water supply due to rainfall and seasonality; could not be tied to actual water taken because no flow measuring structures were in place; and in many cases were not related to the discharge capacities of new intakes or to the demand of irrigation systems.[8] Furthermore, the rights were not, when cumulatively added to other water rights, related to the overall supply in the river systems (which varied by several orders of magnitude from wet to dry seasons) and were difficult to update in a constantly changing situation.

The design of irrigation rights and intakes by RBMSIIP influenced water allocation materially and in unintended ways. Downstream users were subjected to extreme low flows in the dry season as a result of upstream full crest ('blocking') weirs taking all the water. These conventionally designed types of irrigation intake aggravated a delicate situation where dry season flows of only 100–200l per second had to be shared between intakes and instream users along a catchment. The intakes did not increase irrigation efficiency in the ways intended because it was mainly affected by in-field water management and reuse of drain water by peripheral irrigators (Machibya,

2003). Thus a volumetric solution of water rights and intake 'improvements' based on equilibrium thinking exacerbated downstream water scarcity once the wet season was over and flows declined during the dry season.

A facilitative alternative (see Table 11.4) is provided in the legal infrastructure framework of Lankford and Mwaruvanda (2007) for managing formal and informal rights and river basin infrastructure. It rationalizes the interface between formal volumetric water rights (where the capped abstraction determines allocation between users in the wet season) and customary agreements (that relate to shares of instream water during the dry season). The framework demonstrates how, if strengthened and supported, local customary negotiations, combined with formal water management interventions, apportion water during both wet and dry seasons. The framework argues that the current design of irrigation intakes, in terms of maximum capacity, adjustability and any proportional capability, needs to be rethought so that the intakes fit and help support their associated, seasonally-relevant, sharing arrangements.

On the left hand side of Table 11.4, with a volumetric bias, water rights require water measurement to charge users for the amount of water used (an economic incentive for demand management). Therefore, the logic runs, water

Table 11.4 *Comparing approaches for managing dynamic supply in sub-catchments*

Water governance dimension	RBMSIIP approach	Alternative 'facilitative' approach
Seasonal change reflected in intake design	Weir and orifice intake has to be manually adjusted in dry season to reduce inflows	Proportional flume design embeds sharing of water during dry season
Intake component most closely associated with this change in design	Gate is usually opened to the maximum setting enabled by design. The focus here is litres/second	Design to allow passive proportional abstraction of available river flow with maximum intake capacity being the volumetric cap. The main focus is percentage of division
Type of rights most closely associated with wet and dry season	Formal water permit (volumetric) with no recognition of informal shares or rights	Formal water permit (volumetric) is the maximum cap during wet season while customary agreements are proportional during dry season (or time schedule basis)
Water measurement	If to support volumetric rights, then a measuring structure is necessary (yet open channel variable flow measurement is problematic)	No measurement necessary, volumetric cap designed into the intake, and proportional rights aided by proportional design
Role of intake improvement from traditional to 'improved'	To improve irrigation efficiency via regulation designed using normative irrigation engineering procedures	To help share water between users intra- and inter-sectorally within and below the catchment. Focus is on the catchment sharing of water

discharges should be volumetrically measured.[8] Yet, water can be 'measured' in three other ways: by proportional division, by time measures (with off/on gate settings) and by modular gate technology, all of which establish transparent means of satisfying managerial gaps in the apportionment of water.

In summary, contemporary water rights issuance in Tanzania was a volumetric response to scarcity. RBMSIIP hoped that these volumetric rights would ensure demand management and therefore bring about reduced upstream demand thereby effecting inter-sectoral allocation from upstream irrigation to downstream hydropower. The framework proposed by Lankford and Mwaruvanda (2007) suggests a need to distinguish between the wet and dry season sharing of water, between paper 'rights' and concrete structures, and between proportional as well as volumetric division of water. As well as local power interests, one obstacle to the implementation of the approach in Table 11.4 is current momentum towards normative irrigation intake design. Even if implemented, the success of the framework would rely on an ongoing effort to socially explore water apportionment between water rich top-enders and water poor tail-enders combined with experimentation of gate dimensions, adjustments and flows.

Conclusions

In presenting a wider framework of supply, demand and share management responses to scarcity, I propose a number of conclusions. First, with regards to scarcity responses, clarity is required, not simply in definitional terms but in terms of intentions and material outcomes; what aims to boost supply can then increase demand and what can seem to be demand management may not affect total abstraction. More particularly, in highly dynamic environments, imperfectly considered interventions regarding demand or supply management might exacerbate unfair water apportionment and not alleviate scarcity for some. Within highly politicized debates about water scarcity, particularly to address scarcity under climate change, the need to define meanings, causalities, quantities, intentions and outcomes is paramount.

Second, I argue that a supply-and-demand 'volumetric' logic runs the risk of being a partial response to water scarcity, occluding dimensions of water management that address the sharing and scheduling of limited and varying water supplies. A composite framework that examines the supply, demand and share of water is proposed, emphasizing in particular modification and translation dimensions of sharing water during transitions from high to low water sufficiency and back again. Pursued to outputs, this approach might nevertheless require additional storage or water-saving technologies – but they would be encapsulated within a prioritized set of ideas regarding water apportionment contrasted against dominant volumetric scarcity narratives.

Drawing from political ecology approaches, we might observe that crises and technical responses are framed by those who have an ability to shape policy narratives (e.g. Sullivan, 2000). Thus, orthodoxies of supply and demand management that appear to have a *straightforward* and *sensible* technical basis should nevertheless be thoroughly contested. One example of this is that irrigation efficiency can be addressed by shifts to micro-irrigation or canal lining. While this is technically generalizable, it omits a definition of boundaries that define whether savings actually result in a reduction of net irrigation abstraction and the extent to which such interventions address how small amounts of water are apportioned to needy users during periods of drought or aridity at the landscape scale.

Third, the chapter elevates irrigation abstraction technology (mostly neutral in the demand and supply management debate, or potentially mistaken as a technology to improve irrigation efficiency) to being critical for considering how share management functions contemporaneously in the face of a varying supply. Seeing intakes and other abstraction points as technologies for flow switching or dividing a river flow might be a useful way of reimagining these as representing share infrastructure, just as storage is supply infrastructure.

Fourth, the appropriate selection of supply, demand and share management responses represents a matter of water governance – and does so in two ways. First, share and demand management requires an effort of governance over and above providing the capital and infrastructural elements of storage. Second, governance theory must be in a position to comment on the interlinkages between, and respective relevance of, supply, demand and share management, thus shaping a policy response to a particular context.

Fifth, the framework has critical implications for equilibrium and non-equilibrium theories of water apportionment between users. Under equilibrium conditions where water is perceived to be predictable and knowable in terms of supply and amount, the regulatory 'allocation' of averaged volumes via IWRM may be the most appropriate response to water sharing. However, in semi-arid conditions where water supply is unpredictable and highly variable over short timescales, 'translation', 'scheduling' and 'modification' become more significant as mediating mechanisms for water sharing between users. In addition, under such conditions, regulators might entertain water rights expressed as proportions (percentage) of the available supply.

To conclude: we may too often underestimate the interplay between demand, supply and share management in different types of landscapes and environments. Put simply, if water systems and management are held to be manifold, composite and complex, then approaches change from being direct and volumetric to being composite and 'para-volumetric'. Share management, together with demand and supply management, describes a tripartite view of scarcity management, underpinning an objective of facilitating a water-using society to transit to different states of water sufficiency during wet and dry periods by organizing resources at a locally and temporally relevant scale. It is about adaptive guises – society tends to default to volumetric adaptations to shortages rather than adaptations to shortages that accommodate the nature of water management (high variability, continuous flows, poor transparency, timeliness). This returns to an underlying adaptive or 'knowledge scarcity' which suggests that we do not critically unpack scarcity, particularly when scarcity responses are reinforced politically and materially by programmes that spend on storage infrastructure without making good the potential benefits of that extra storage through enhanced water apportionment, especially transiting from wet to dry periods.

Notes

1   The term 'user' covers all types of water sectors, stakeholders, individuals and groups.
2   As several authors in this volume note, water scarcity is something that is usually socially constructed. The term 'water sufficiency' could be explored as an alternative to encompass a decrease in the volume of water available per capita or to an area over time. However, it is beyond the scope of this chapter to deal with the social meanings of water scarcity or sufficiency.
3   The author has commonly heard this refrain at water workshops and meetings attended by policy-makers and scientists, particularly when dealing with IWRM.
4   'Share' is preferred to the word 'allocation', which has already acquired other meanings in IWRM, and for its tonal and grammatical verbal similarities to the words 'demand' and 'supply'.
5   'Allocation' covers reallocation; both are purposive, utilizing the same devices.
6   The Tanzanian case study saw irrigation intakes sequentially abstract water upstream to downstream. Upstream intakes received disproportionally more water during low flow periods.
7   This work provided the inspiration for non-equilibrium and facilitative approaches to water apportionment. A number of publications can be referred to as background reading (Lankford, 2004; Lankford et al, 2004; Lankford et al, 2007; McCartney et al, 2007; SMUWC, 2001).
8   I refer to emails with the World Bank in November 2003 on their long-term aims of RBMSIIP to support water measurement so fees could be set volumetrically.

References

Behnke, J.R.H. and Scoones, I. (1993) 'Rethinking range ecology: Implications for rangeland management in Africa', in I. Scoones, C. Kervin and R.H. Behnke Jr (eds) *Range Ecology at Disequilibrium: New Models of Natural Variability and Pastoral Adaptation in African Savannas*, ODI, IIED and Commonwealth Secretariat, London, pp1–30

Brown, L. (2001) 'How water scarcity will shape the new century', *Water Science and Technology*, vol 43, pp17–22

Clarke, R. (1991) *Water: The International Crisis*, Earthscan in association with the Swedish Red Cross, London

Falkenmark, M. (1989) 'The massive water scarcity now threatening Africa: Why isn't it being addressed?', *Ambio*, vol 18, pp112–118

Gleick, P.H. (ed) (1993) *Water in Crisis: A Guide to the World's Fresh Water Resources*, Oxford University Press, New York

GWP (2000) *Integrated Water Resources Management*, TAC 4, Global Water Partnership, Stockholm

Homer-Dixon, T.F. (1999) *Environment, Scarcity, and Violence*, Princeton University Press, NJ

Lankford, B.A. (2004) 'Irrigation improvement projects in Tanzania: Scale impacts and policy implications', *Water Policy*, vol 6, no 2, pp89–102

Lankford, B.A. and Beale, T. (2007) 'Equilibrium and non-equilibrium theories of sustainable water resources management: Dynamic river basin and irrigation behaviour in Tanzania', *Global Environmental Change*, vol 17, pp168–180

Lankford, B.A., Merrey, D., Cour, J. and Hepworth, N. (2007) 'From integrated to expedient: An adaptive framework for river basin management in developing countries', Research Report 110, International Water Management Institute, Columbo, Sri Lanka

Lankford, B.A. and Mwaruvanda, W. (2007) 'A legal-infrastructural framework for catchment apportionment', in B. van Koppen, J. Butterworth and I. Juma (eds) *Community-based Water Law and Water Resource Management Reform in Developing Countries*, CABI Publishing, Wallingford, pp228–247

Lankford, B.A., van Koppen, B., Franks, T. and Mahoo, H. (2004) 'Entrenched views or insufficient science? Contested causes and solutions of water allocation; insights from the Great Ruaha River Basin, Tanzania', *Agricultural Water Management,* vol 69, no 2, pp135–153

Lindblom, J. and Nordella, B. (2007) 'Underground condensation of humid air for drinking water production and subsurface irrigation', *Desalination*, vol 203 (1–3), pp417–434

Machibya, M. (2003) 'Challenging established concepts of irrigation efficiency in a water scarce river basin: A case study of the Usangu Basin, Tanzania', PhD thesis, University of East Anglia, Norwich

McCartney, M.P., Lankford, B.A. and Mahoo, H.F. (2007) 'Agricultural water management in a water stressed catchment: Lessons from the RIPARWIN project', Research Report 116, International Water Management Institute, Columbo, Sri Lanka

Mehta, L. (2001) 'The manufacture of popular perceptions of scarcity: Dams and water-related narratives in Gujarat, India', *World Development*, vol 29, no 12, pp2025–2041

Mehta, L. (2005) *The Politics and Poetics of Water: Naturalising Scarcity in Western India*, Orient Longman, New Delhi

Mehta, L. (2006) 'Water and human development: Capabilities, entitlements and power', background paper for the 2006 Human Development Report, 'Beyond scarcity: Power, poverty and the global water crisis', Institute for Development Studies, UK

Merrett, S. (2004) 'The demand for water: Four interpretations', *Water International*, vol 29, no 1, pp27–29

Micklin, P. (2007) 'The Aral Sea disaster', *Annual Review of Earth and Planetary Sciences*, vol 35, pp47–72

Molden, D., Murray-Rust, H., Sakthivadivel, R. and Makin, I. (2003) 'A water productivity framework for understanding and action', in J.W. Kijne, R. Barker and D. Molden (eds) *Water Productivity in Agriculture: Limits and Opportunities for Improvement*, Comprehensive Assessment of Water Management in Agriculture, Series, No 1 International Water Management Institute, Colombo, Sri Lanka

Molle, F. (2003) 'Development trajectories of river basins: A conceptual framework', Research Report 72, International Water Management Institute, Colombo, Sri Lanka

Molle, F., Mamanpoush, A. and Miranzadeh, M. (2004) 'Robbing Yadullah's water to irrigate Saeid's garden: Hydrology and water rights in a village of central Iran', Research Report 80, International Water Management Institute, Colombo, Sri Lanka

Molle, F. and Berkoff, J. (2007) 'Irrigation water pricing: The gap between theory and practice', Comprehensive Assessment of Water Management in Agriculture Series, No 4, CABI Publishing, Wallingford

Molle, F., Wester, P. and Hirsch, P. (2007) 'River basin development and management', in *Water for Food, Water for Life: A Comprehensive Assessment of Water Management in Agriculture*, Earthscan, London and International Water Management Institute, Colombo, Sri Lanka

Ohlsson, L. (1998) 'Water and social resource scarcity', FAO Issue Paper, FAO, Rome, Italy

Perry, C. (2007) 'Efficient irrigation: Inefficient communication; flawed recommendations', *Irrigation and Drainage*, vol 56, pp367–378

Radif, A.A. (1999) 'Integrated water resources management (IWRM): An approach to face the challenges of the next century and to avert future crises', *Desalination*, vol 124, pp145–153

Rijsberman, F.R. (2006) 'Water scarcity: Fact or fiction?', *Agricultural Water Management*, vol 80 (1–3 Special Issue), pp5–22

Rosegrant, M.W., Cai, X. and Cline, S.A. (2002) *World Water and Food to 2025: Dealing with Scarcity*, IFPRI/IWMI, International Food Policy Research Institute, Washington DC and International Water Management Institute, Colombo, Sri Lanka

SMUWC (2001) 'Sustainable management of Usangu Wetlands and its catchment', Final project reports, Directorate of Water Resources, Ministry of Water, Government of Tanzania, Dar es Salaam

Sullivan, C. (2002) 'Calculating a water poverty index', *World Development*, vol 30, no 7, pp1195–1211

Sullivan, S. (2000) 'Getting the science right, or introducing science in the first place? Local "facts", global discourse – "desertification" in north-west Namibia', in P. Stott and Sian Sullivan (eds) *Political Ecology; Science, Myth and Power*, Arnold, London, pp15–44

Sullivan, S. (2003) 'On non-equilibrium in arid and semi-arid grazing systems', *Journal of Biogeography*, vol 29, pp1595–1618

Turton, A.R. and Ohlsson, L. (1999) 'Water scarcity and social stability: Towards a deeper understanding of key concepts needed to manage water scarcity in developing countries', Occasional Papers No 17, SOAS/KCL Water Issues Group, University of London

van Koppen, B., Sokile, C., Hatibu, N., Lankford, B.A., Mahoo, H. and Yanda, P. (2004) 'Formal water rights in Tanzania: Deepening the dichotomy?', Working Paper 71, International Water Management Institute, Colombo, Sri Lanka

World Bank (1996) 'River Basin Management and Smallholder Irrigation Improvement Project (RBMSIIP): Staff Appraisal Report', World Bank, Washington, D.C.

World Bank (2007) 'Investment in agricultural water for poverty reduction and economic growth in sub-Saharan Africa: A collaborative programme of AfDB, FAO, IFAD, IWMI and World Bank', Synthesis Report, available at http://siteresources.worldbank.org/RPDLPROGRAM/Resources/459596-1170984095733/synthesisreport.pdf (accessed 30 July 2010)

12
Advocacy of Water Scarcity: Leakages in the Argument

Jasveen Jairath

Context

The current discourse on water from the global to the local level bears the unambiguous stamp of 'absolute water scarcity' and associated concerns of 'water security'. This uncritical message of water scarcity permeates both highly formal and scholarly research as well as prominently projected voices at public water fora (see for instance Elkington, 2008; Schneider, 2009).

These opinions have acquired the power of a dogma, which (like all fundamentalisms) professes to be self-evident and self-rationalizing. The power of such ideological constructions to influence policies and actions in the water domain cannot be underestimated. Witness, for instance, the supply-augmenting policies in the water sector that are promoted globally through support for the creation of large water storage structures, such as dams, in spite of proven costs that far outweigh the projected benefits. (See Roy, 1999 for a compelling illustration of how the water-augmenting agenda is pushed for motivations other than provision of water security for all.) The rationale for such a one-sided emphasis on the need to create new 'water' potential is derived from an uncritical acceptance of scarcity as the basic malaise of water sector. Such misconceptions can often lend support to actions that go against mass interest. In the context of the relative roles of the ideational sphere and the material conditions for inducing social change, Marx had pointed out that '... an idea becomes a social force when it grips the masses ...'.[1]

I argue in this chapter that the notion of absolute water scarcity constitutes a powerful medium for legitimizing the social acceptance of several practical policy prescriptions. Arguments that focus on augmenting water supplies, say from large dams and infrastructure projects, receive strong impetus from such axiomatic positions of absolute water scarcity. These serve as an ideological legitimization for promoting supply augmentation strategies. I also demonstrate that the governance context of such policy implementation does not provide for reallocating water according to democratic norms and instead creates yet further scarcities. A large majority of the marginalized sections of the population have limited access to these augmented sources due to discriminatory access and appropriation of additional water resources by the politically strong.[2] This reinforces demand for 'more water' by the 'scarcity lobby' – and the cycle carries on.

The ideological promotion of the water scarcity thesis and its reinforcement through constant water jamborees such as the World Water Forum every three years and the annual World Water Week in Stockholm, the written word, the internet etc., drowns the (often) lone, scattered, isolated, sporadic voice that may attempt to question the notion of absolute scarcity. In this chapter I discuss and critique these various positions by drawing on examples from the Indian context and also critically discuss the emergence of Integrated Water Resources Management (IWRM) as a political agenda and way to mitigate scarcity. Challenging a politically dominant, financially popular and apparently reasonable viewpoint requires extraordinary courage and sometimes an element of innocence – like that of the child in 'The Emperor's New Clothes'. Going against the grain and weight of plausible populism carries costs – which not all can afford to pay. I write this chapter by drawing on several years of experience with research, advocacy, networking and capacity building in the water sector where I have focused on the social context of water to question technocratic and reductionist interpretations of mainstream water discourse. Along with other authors in this volume, I believe that positing a collective challenge that seeks a critical discourse on water scarcity is thus not just an option but is actually the only choice. This volume thus presents an opportunity to create a platform for articulating and strengthening such critical voices.

Statements of scarcity

The entire spectrum of water-related discussions begins with extended statements not only about current, but also about impending water scarcity. In this chapter I elaborate various positions and estimates of current and future water scarcity. These estimates are used to highlight the limited freshwater sources that are accessible to humans and their fast-approaching exhaustion at current rates of exploitation (see, for example, PAI, 2000; Gleick, 2000; SIWI, 2005). Declining per capita availability of water as an indicator of scarcity, with strong Malthusian undertones, is noted (PAI, 1993b). 'High' population is officially recognized as a major cause of water scarcity (see Chapter 3, this volume, for a critique of neo-Malthusian discourses and their links with scarcity).

The Public Information Bureau of the Government of India (GOI) has the following quote on its website:

> *Water scarcity is caused by population growth, environmental change and degradation and the unequal distribution of water resources. Water is getting scarce due to rising population, rapid urbanization and growing industrial demands.* (Nair, 2003)

Dr K. Kasturirangan, Director of the Indian Space Research Organisation (ISRO), aired similar views at the Sixth Vikram Sarabhai Memorial Lecture (Kasturirangan, 1996), carrying significant weight and authority from the scientific establishment of India. A strong sense of panic and alarm is thus generated – much like the Club of Rome report.[3] The *very real* adversities experienced due to water shortages in poorer regions and among poorer classes are cited to further reinforce the point. In the same vein, projections of severe social and economic stress warn of dire ecological and social consequences. A picture of excessive pressure on resources is sharply etched out – and correctly so. On the face of it, these positions are clearly difficult to contest and inspire a strong consensus among water professionals and practitioners – hence the *repetition, reassertion* and *universal recognition* of water scarcity. Based on such an absolutist articulation of 'scarcity', a call is sent out for putting water on the world agenda. The weight and focus of such a massive public projection of the problem, however, is asymmetrically on the *quantity* of water (and in some cases on its quality) – with relative silence regarding questions concerning *access and control* by different social agents. A recent Human Development Report of the United Nations Development Programme (UNDP), 2006, which focuses on water, clearly voices the latter concern. Lack of water, it is argued, is caused by lack of power, rather than by limited resources:

> *The scarcity at the heart of the global water crisis is rooted in* power, poverty and equality, not in physical availability. *There is more than enough water in the world for domestic purposes, for agriculture and for industry. The problem is that some people – notably the poor – are systematically excluded from access by their poverty, by their limited legal rights or by public policies.* (Thakkar, 2006 [emphasis added])

Concerns of equity are no doubt acknowledged in the mainstream discourse – but either as an 'add on' problematic issue considered in isolation or in terms of spatial and temporal inequity.

Social inequity based on *unequal power relations* that influence the technologies determining water resources development, efficiency and patterns of water usage as well as associated patterns of water deprivation, seldom constitutes an *essential* concern. Water-based inequity is thus considered more in its disconnected context and less as integrally emerging from practices of mainstream water resources development. Iniquitous access to water resources (existing and augmented) is usually based on overall iniquitous social structures in most developing economies and is in turn also constituted through water resource development policies and practices.

Positing the problem

There is a strong sense of *absolutism* that dominates the discourse on water scarcity. Much like the neoclassical paradigm in economics, the starting point of the discourse is the perceived imbalance between the supply and demand of water. Implicit in such conceptualization is seeking redress of this imbalance through various technical and managerial strategies. The problem is viewed as one of devising suitable strategies that impinge on 'creating water' (increasing supplies) or 'demand management' (reducing water demand) (Meinzen-Dick and Rosegrant, 2001). Ensuing discussions trap the options to be considered within the problem formulation stated above. Attention is thus diverted along supply augmentation or demand modulation tracks.[4] Further, the existing demand pattern and supply facilities are taken as given even if recognized as deviations or distortions. The fact that the latter have emerged *as a result* of past historical practices and policies gets submerged. Initiatives and interventions that are external to and independent of underlying causes (that generate this imbalance) are proposed to redress the situation. Such a presentation of the problem disconnects its understanding from its historical evolution and encourages its consideration in isolation from its social origin. Approaches that question the process/conditions that underlie the current state of water deprivations are neglected and marginalized. These include the following questions (Iyer, 2005):

- Who controls water resources?
- How much is water worth today?
- Who suffers as a result of water scarcity, and who gains?
- Is water a social good or an economic good?

A situation persists whereby the correction of a mismatch between the demand and supply of water is constantly sought through a stream of disconnected, random, ad hoc and often contradictory policies, practices and interventions. It is tantamount to *perennially chasing the problem without ever constricting its emergence.* Evidence often points to the aggravation of scarcities in certain areas despite heavy investment, with the explicit objective of enhancing the available water (see Mehta, 2005). For instance, it has been pointed out that the number of people without easy access to safe drinking water in India has increased as a result of water practices that have been encouraged by a host of water and agricultural policies – a conscious policy intervention, not a natural accident (WaterAid, 2005). In the case of rural drinking water Sharma (2003) notes that:

> ... despite massive resource allocation during the last nine Five-Year Plans, there were as many as 61,747 problem villages in the country towards the end of 1997. Interestingly, the country started out with a figure of 150,000 problem villages in 1972; this rose dramatically to 231,000 in 1980. (Sharma, 2003)

Mehta's (2005) research in Kutch, India, an area known for its water scarcity, highlights how decades of government interventions have failed to mitigate scarcity conditions. Instead, they have often exacerbated the 'scarcity' problem which is now considered to be 'universal' and 'natural' in the region.

Finally, water *inaccessibility* is often confused with water *scarcity*. This has serious implications for seeking solutions as the thought process is diverted towards ways of *increasing quantity* rather than examining reasons underlying *differential exclusion* from *existing* amounts of water. This is, however, not to disregard the imperative of increasing the total quantity of available water that *may well be required* for meeting the livelihood needs of the majority.

Scarcity as a 'relative' notion

As demonstrated by other authors in this volume, notions of scarcity (and surplus) are inherently relative concepts. Something is always scarce with respect to an assumed notion or understanding of what is sufficient. There is nothing inherently or absolutely scarce about any given quantum. Standards of scarcity therefore are contingent on subjectively acceptable standards of sufficiency. Hence a divergent and context-dependent interpretation of scarcity is essential for an assessment of scarcity-induced impacts. A clear articulation of the reference level of comparison with respect to which a quantum is 'scarce' is necessary for meaningful discussion. Discussions on water scarcity, however, seldom spell out such a reference point. The scarcity experienced by a poor person with reference to her basic livelihood needs is usually clubbed together with scarcity for a luxury consumer for whom water is scarce if it is not possible to water the garden, wash the car, bathe the dog or play golf. Such diverse 'scarcities' are collected together in a cauldron and the ideological broth of scarcity boils over to spread alarming fumes of 'absolutely less water available' across the globe.

Further, the *relational* aspect of scarcity also gets obscured by such fudging of specific scarcities. For instance, the fact that drinking water scarcity for the poor is often *related to* the water-intensive lifestyle of the affluent as discussed above is lost in the process of generalizing the scarcity thesis. A clear specification of the accepted/implicit requirements of each consuming constituency would expose the whole gamut of such causative interlinkages between different levels of scarcities experienced by equally different sets of potential water users. There is a possibility that, with effective regulation of water usage in line with socially prioritized *need*, there may well be no water scarcity – except for supporting indulgent production and consumption lifestyles.

However, the fudging of such diverse reference points for the assessment of water scarcity experienced by different segments of society is not accidental. Generating an absolute sense of water scarcity becomes politically expedient as it legitimizes the demand for augmentation of resources as opposed to reallocation of existing resources (Hildyard, Chapter 8 this volume, draws out similar parallels with respect to food). The concentration on supply-side interventions *excludes* considerations of access and control over consequently augmented water supplies. Efforts to enhance water supplies leaves intact the underlying power relations that enable discriminatory appropriation of water resources and end up reinforcing existing inequities by generating scarcities for *most* through the excessive use and control of water by the *few*.

A more socially just approach would be to contain the growth of water consumption over time and across sectors within the limits of feasible supply. This requires taking the total available water close at hand as the given point of departure. Socially equitable usage patterns then have to be contained within the available water supply and *not the other way round*. This is in contrast to the currently dominant view as noted above, where efforts are directed at realizing higher levels of water supplies to fulfil the demands of ever-increasing consumption. Given that the competing political interests of decision-makers in the water sector influence the ideologies governing their policy prescriptions, this methodological reorientation goes beyond intellectual conviction and debate. Thus, the struggle to get the concepts, method and action right is less a matter of intellectual or logical rigour. Instead, it is more a battle for political control over natural resources, including water.

Explanations of water scarcity

Most assessments of water scarcity are undertaken in terms of the per capita availability of water that is widely recognized as an index of water stress. This concept has been pioneered by Malin Falkenmark, a Swedish hydrologist and widely recognized authority in the field (see also Chapter 11, this volume). For instance, Malin Falkenmark's concept of a 'water stress index' is based on an approximate minimum level of water required per capita to maintain an adequate quality of life in a moderately developed country in an arid zone. Based upon her findings, Falkenmark suggests specific thresholds of water stress and water scarcity:

> When fresh water availability falls below 1000 cubic metres per person per year, countries experience chronic water scarcity, in which the lack of water begins to hamper economic development and human health and well-being. When renewable fresh water supplies fall below 500 cubic metres per person, countries experience absolute scarcity. (Falkenmark and Widstrand, 1992)

World Bank and other analysts have also accepted the 1000m^3 benchmark as a general indicator of water scarcity. It is also used by a host of national governments such as India and South Africa to calculate per capita water supply with regard to population numbers on a countrywide scale.

Witness further writings in a similar vein:

> Currently, more than 752 million people face water stress or scarcity ... While 36 countries currently experience either

> *water stress or scarcity, between 42 and 46 countries are now*
> *projected to face similar conditions by 2025.* (PAI, 2000)

> *... Given the high population growth rates of many of the most*
> *water-scarce developing nations, they are likely to suffer either*
> *limits on their use of water, hindering economic progress,*
> *or reliance on contaminated and untreated water, fostering*
> *disease.* (PAI, 1993a)

Similar linkages between population pressure and water scarcity are high-lighted in the mainstream and official water discourse (see KrishiWorld, undated; PAI, 1993a, b, c).

As Hartmann and Hildyard, Chapters 3 and 8 in this volume, have already discussed, the apparent plausibility of the thesis of population-induced water scarcity makes it imperative to unpack the bundle of arguments that submerge the political basis of water scarcity. Connection between *differential* consumption patterns across regions and classes and the argument that *large numbers cause scarcity* is seldom established. If the total population is growing, it begs the question as to whether it is the high-consumption segment or the low-consumption segment that is growing and by what proportion. Is it resource-deprived poor or high-end consumers who are responsible for creating the resource crunch? Disaggregated data are required to make more nuanced judgements.

A rather refreshing document published by United Nations Population Fund (UNFPA) strikes a different chord amidst the predominantly Malthusian music. Pointing to the linkages between population, poverty and resource depletion the report states:

> *Rural population growth does not necessarily damage the*
> *environment, but limited land availability often leads poor*
> *people to settle in fragile areas ... Despite soaring economic*
> *activity, now estimated at over $30 trillion annually, some 1.2*
> *billion people live on less than $1 a day ... A huge 'consump-*
> *tion gap' exists between industrialized and developing coun-*
> *tries. The world's richest countries, with 20 per cent of global*
> *population, account for 86 per cent of total private consump-*
> *tion, whereas the poorest 20 per cent of the world's people*
> *account for just 1.3 per cent ... The 'ecological footprint'[5] of*
> *the more affluent is far deeper than that of the poor and, in*
> *many cases, exceeds the regenerative capacity of the earth.*
> (UNFPA, 2001, pp5–6)

The 'State of the World' report of the World Watch Institute for 2004 also corroborates the above-noted asymmetries in consumption. The world's richest people, it points out, use on average 25 times more energy than the world's poorest and 12 per cent of the world's people living in North America and western Europe account for 60 per cent of this consumption, while the one-third living in South Asia and sub-Saharan Africa account for only 3.2 per cent (World Watch Institute, 2004).

Using calculations based on the ecological costs of consumption it has been found that at current rates of consumption, a person from Canada and the US would require roughly 4.3 and 5.1 hectares of land respectively to support his/her lifestyle, while corresponding figures would be 0.4 (India) and 1.8 (world) (D'Souza, 2003, p25).

The contrast is not only between countries but also between classes within countries. Further, the total consumption of water for domestic use – which is the main component of direct demand that may be imposed by large numbers of poor people – is barely 5 per cent of the total consumption of water in India and 8 per cent for the world (WWDR, 2003). Similarly, commenting on water crises, a World Water Council communication notes that water withdrawals for irrigation represent 66 per cent of the total withdrawals and up to 90 per cent in arid regions, the other 34 per cent being used by domestic households (10 per cent), industry (20 per cent), or evaporated from reservoirs (4 per cent) (WWC, 2009).

Most total consumption (90 per cent) is accounted for by industrial and agricultural use – both areas where the resource-poor are unlikely to contribute significant pressure. The asymmetric access to resources by the poor – who are typically deprived of their minimum livelihood requirements – is also hidden within these aggregate figures. This points to an anomaly in the argument that blames large numbers for creating water scarcities through their 'excessive' demand. Pressure on less than 10 per cent of total water use is presented as an explanatory variable for accounting for overall water scarcity. Therefore, the relationship between poverty, high population (and its growth) and environmental degradation is complex and cannot be reduced to a simplistic and reductionist mathematical juxtaposition of quantities.[6]

Lack of precipitation is also a prominent argument within this genre. What is open to question, however, is the translation of these variations into selective scarcities for the vulnerable that do not correlate with naturally ordained fluctuations in water supply. I shortly go on to discuss a few well-known illustrations of severe scarcities experienced amidst generous availability of water in various regions of India. In many of the areas worst affected by chronic droughts in recent decades – such as the Ananatpur and Mahabubnagar districts of Andhra Pradesh – official data for the last century do not point to any evidence of a corresponding decline in precipitation (Jairath, 2008a). The same is true for the Kutch district in India, an area known for its water scarcity. Mehta (2005) studied 120 years of rainfall in Kutch where the intensity of droughts has been increasing. She found that there has been no change in the volume of rainfall in this time period. Instead, the exacerbation of drought needs to be seen in conjunction with bad water management practices such as the damming of the grasslands, poor maintenance of reservoirs and excessive run-off.

Responses to water scarcity

Following on from the demand-supply mismatch point of departure, mainstream responses to the 'water problem' typically entail efforts at dealing with supply augmentation through direct interventions or indirectly through efforts to 'save' water through efficient technologies or to 'conserve' water through, for instance, the watershed programme implemented under the Ministry of Rural Development, India. The Desert Development Program (DDP) and Drought-Prone Areas Program (DPAP) are the major programmes that are implemented under this track of interventions with the objective of conserving groundwater and in situ moisture at the level of micro watersheds since the early 1990s. This excessive focus on water conservation in the recent water debates is based also on the myth of scarcities arising out of 'wastage in use' and not 'wasteful usage'.[7] Restoring water quality or preventing its further deterioration in order to conserve the quantum of freshwater supplies comprises another track of recommended actions in addition to possible supply augmentation through additional surface and groundwater exploitation.

The second typical approach is what is popularly referred to in the water literature as 'demand management'. Focus therein is on influencing 'demand' for water as reflected by extant use patterns through market/price and non-market measures. Emphasis is not based on 'need' in relation to the social norms of water requirements – but more on actually observed 'demand' based on economic capacity to command water resources. The latter may well have emerged as a net outcome of multiple contesting forces that reflect local political factors rather than a need-based demand necessary for survival. Distortions in such use patterns that may exist from a normative perspective are *de facto* accepted. The approach is not to question the evolution of use patterns (in other words, who *uses water for what purpose*) but to *accept* what is practiced and attempt to modulate it through efficient techniques, or volumetric controls, or reduce use through pricing strategies – all of which have demonstrated limited success (see Jairath, 2008b for a discussion of the issue).

Further, technological interventions and institutional reforms are suggested to facilitate a better match between water supply and demand – while leaving untouched the underlying social exclusions that are systemically reproduced and reinforced. The limited success of irrigation reforms (Jairath, 2001), and under use or inappropriate use of water technologies in a country like India, point to the weakness of such interventions. The formal institutional structure for self-management of localized water that is created through an administrative fiat under these reforms remains a stillborn child. Inadequate collection of water charges and failure to redress inequities in water sharing make the reforms relatively redundant and irrelevant. The strategy is cosmetic and symptomatic and problems continue while discourse and research support action that struggles to get a better fit of the quantum imbalances. Water allocation systems and water rights are documented but strategies for effective enforcement are missing. The fundamental malaise of political control over water by social elites remains beyond the domain of these reforms. They remain by and large managerial and administrative. The lack of assurance of access to water entitlements invites the disdain and indifference of socially weaker water users, as well as their reluctance to pay water charges.

A recent prominent reaction to the intractable issue of water control has been the shift from a focus on 'mitigation' of adversities to 'adaptation' (see for instance Burke and Moench, 2000 with reference to the challenge of declining groundwater). The logic is that since it is difficult to regulate groundwater extraction, the politically feasible alternative is to adjust to it. The argument, however, can be used to rationalize acceptance of all disasters as given, and shift the focus on adaptation. This also contains the possibility of diverting attention away from analysing underlying forces that caused the natural disaster. These forces could be geophysical as well as sociological. Ignoring the cause and highlighting strategies of how to adjust, adapt and mitigate its consequences could pre-empt challenging the emergence of such disasters. Such discourses blunt the need to unpack the trajectory that led to the disaster. This has implications for action and disaster management policies that may confine their attention to symptomatic handling of the situation. Such a myopic approach can serve to hide the linkages between policies/practices and physical/natural disasters – linkages that need to be unravelled and exposed in order to arrive at sustainable and structural solutions. This is critical as the magnitude of human-induced disasters is on the rise, not least due to human-induced climate change (WMO, 2004). Accepting a distortion as inevitable and encouraging adaptation may not only legitimize continued and unregulated groundwater mining for instance, but also blunt the need for resisting agendas of exploitation, with potentially dangerous ecological implications.

Scarcity amidst plenty: Examples from India

Data on extensive experience of water scarcity in the flood-hit and heavy rainfall areas abound, belying dominant naturalistic and absolutist arguments of water scarcity. Take the case of Bihar, which has one of the highest population densities and is the third most populous state in India with only about 11 per cent urban population (an indicator of backwardness and rural dependence). Dinesh Kumar Mishra (2004) notes:

> If Bihar suffers from too much water and floods, it is also a state that has regularly faced the specter of droughts ... Khagaria, one of the most flood-hit districts of North Bihar and which has acquired the dubious title of dooba zilla (submerged district) in the state, suffered drought conditions in seven of the 20 years! ... drought conditions occur not just in the hilly terrain of Jharkhand but also in the flood-prone districts of South and North Bihar. Indeed, sometimes these districts suffer drought and floods simultaneously because floods are mostly caused by

heavy rains in the upper catchment of the river basins even as the people face drought conditions at the local level because of deficient rainfall. (Mishra, 2004)

In contrast, Israel, a relatively prosperous country, is commonly cited for surviving on much less water – 461 cubic metres of fresh water per person annually (PAI, 1993d). Clearly, mere availability of natural water reserves cannot account for its accessibility. Cherapunji, a town in East Khasi Hills district in the Indian state of Meghalaya, is credited as being the wettest place on Earth. It has a yearly rainfall average of 11,430mm, the highest in the world, but suffers water scarcity during the pre-monsoon period. Ratnagiri district, located in the southwestern part of Maharashtra State on the Arabian Sea coast, gets 3500mm annual rainfall, yet still suffers from severe water shortage (Gadekar, undated).

The common response of planners to such situations is to argue for better 'water management through institutional and technical reforms'. That suitable managerial/technical interventions may well be necessary to regulate the naturally fluctuating water flows cannot be contested. However, the underlying asymmetry in access to and control of the resource persists despite various official reforms. No doubt changes are effected, but only to replace old mechanisms of exclusion with new ones. Instituting water user organizations in irrigated areas of rural Andhra Pradesh, for instance, consolidates dominance of the landowning class in rural areas. Caste oppression may be replaced by institutional exclusion or the two may be mutually reinforcing. (See Jairath, 2001 for a detailed discussion of the issue in the context of field evidence from canal-irrigated areas in Andhra Pradesh, India.)

The political agenda of scarcity and the rise of Integrated Water Resource Management (IWRM)

In recent years, Integrated Water Resource Management (IWRM) has been promoted as the new mantra for defining and dealing with issues of water policy, planning and practice particularly through global water bodies such as the Global Water Partnership (GWP)[8] and events such as the world water fora. For instance, it is argued by GWP (GWP, 2000) that previous sectoral approaches to water led to inefficiencies at the level of planning, execution and utilization of water facilities that were largely responsible for the current problems. Fundamentally, IWRM recognized the role of human-induced factors in explaining current water sector problems. Second, it is widely recognized that lack of coordination within the water sector as well as between water and non-water sectors led to wasteful and often contradictory actions. For example, conserving groundwater through the watershed development programme under the aegis of the Ministry of Rural Development, along with groundwater development through extensive installation of borewells in the same areas under the aegis of Ground Water Boards is a case in point. Integration in understanding, planning, implementing and utilizing water strategies, it is expected, will yield results that are more in tune with desired objectives. There is a strong underlying faith in alternative management strategies overcoming the problems of productivity and efficiency of water use. As a way to improve the situation, the World Water Vision Report (WWC, 2009) notes clearly, 'There is a water crisis today. But the crisis is not about having too little water to satisfy our needs. It is a crisis of managing water so badly that billions of people – and the environment – suffer badly'.[9]

That competitive demand for water has been increasing in recent decades cannot be denied. Various local struggles have emerged across the globe in response to acutely experienced water problems. There are also limits to further water augmentation imposed by closing basins. No longer is random and ad hoc water development possible through yet unexplored avenues. All these factors have necessitated looking at the whole gamut of water development in a comprehensive way – exploring the linkages of inter-sectoral water use, sources of new demand, wastages and, in particular, an assessment of cross-impacts. Due to the fragmented and sectoral nature of water knowledge and practice hitherto, integrated perspectives have rarely been advanced. IWRM as the relatively recent approach to understanding water resources within a developmental context has thus emerged at the present historical juncture as an inevitable response to the limitations of sectoral approaches that have failed to deliver sustainable WRD (water resource development) on the ground.[10]

The chaotic situation due to haphazard, sporadic, relatively localized and unregulated water harnessing under diffuse control by the select few has presented a serious challenge to control over water resources within recently emerged closed bounds. While a monopoly over water resources by the powerful in diverse localities could coexist alongside the availability of virgin spaces, the current situation has created the need for coordinated control. It is thus the need to manage water in light of recent constraints that has been the driving force underlying evolution of the new paradigm. It is the ideological response to the practical necessity of achieving more effective control through integrated approaches.

Conceptual weaknesses and the politics of IWRM

First, the IWRM paradigm acknowledges current water problems as socially induced; second, it recognizes the efficacy of alternative 'management strategies' to rectify the damage; and third, focus is on integration as a mechanism to achieve efficiency, productivity and equity. However, current inequity in access to and control over water resources is conceptualized as a management distortion and not as derived from an imbalance of power relations between those with differential access to water benefits. While productivity and efficiency gains are possible through better organized/coordinated activity, the same cannot be said about equal sharing of the benefits thus generated unless access to these benefits is ensured through rearrangements of political equations. Such political realignments require conscious processes that attempt to shift water-sharing norms – actions that will create conflict and invite resistance from those who have a vested interest in the status quo, usually those from socially powerful segments of society. The resolution of such conflicts depends on the political strength of respective constituencies. It would be naïve to expect such resolution to be achieved merely through different managerial rearrangements. Poor performance of water sector reforms in rural and urban areas bears witness to the ineffectiveness of top-down managerial interventions. Thus, while the IWRM paradigm is an improvement on earlier approaches, it does not go far enough in tackling the equity issue.

It is important to understand why this sort of idea has gained so much prominence at the present historical juncture and what purpose is served through the promotion of such ideological frameworks. Clearly the idea of integration is not new, neither can it be opposed (at face value) on any reasonable grounds. However, its resurgence in recent years, supported by very aggressive social marketing by various global agencies and fora, raises questions about the underlying rationale. Witness, for example: World Water Fora that are held every three years at a global level; establishment of the GWP in Stockholm in 1990s and its various activities, focused on establishing regional networks all across the globe with the agenda of promoting IWRM; production of literature, websites and promotional material; organization of conferences, water weeks, training, etc. – evidence for all of which is available on the web. Most of the above actions, it has been argued, have served to foster the agenda of control over water, by the powerful water lobby at every level: global, regional and local. IWRM has been the ideological ally in this process. Large corporate interests and multilateral banks have been part and parcel of this process through their patronage and endorsement of the process. There continue to be severe ambiguities within IWRM policy discourse (see Barlow and Clarke, 2002, p157). Barlow and Clarke maintain that the Global Water Partnership (GWP), the World Water Council (WWC) and the World Commission on Water (WCW) for the 21st century:

> ... *appear to be neutral because in theory, they exist to facilitate dialogue between the various stakeholders and to bring about a more sustainable management of water resources. But a closer look reveals that these agencies promote the privatization and export of water resources and services through close links with global water corporations and financial institutions. The Global Water Partnership was established in 1996 to 'support countries in the sustainable management of their water resources'. Its operating principle, however, is the recognition that water is 'an economic good' and 'has an economic value in all its competing uses'. This basic principle lies at the core of the GWP's main programmes to reform water utility systems and water resources management in countries around the world.* (Barlow and Clarke, 2002, p157; see also Barlow and Clarke, 2001; PSI, 2000)

It is also worth investigating the terms 'integrated' and 'integration'. IWRM promotes integrated conceptualization, study, policy, planning and practice in the field of water. Integration facilitates coordination and efficiency through more effective centralized control. On its own, integration is a politically neutral strategy. Organizations, countries, institutions etc. that are highly integrated can be associated with several different types of coordination, from democratic to autocratic, that have corresponding implications for equitable governance. Models of water planning that effectively integrate decentralized and socially peripheral interests and concerns within the macro plans and regulation strategies can expect to work towards creating a democratic water situation. It is thus necessary to specify the particular mode of integration that is implied while advocating IWRM. It is important to avoid the blanket usage of IWRM terminology and undifferentiated application of its strategies as it can have a range of implications for the water-starved which could either reinforce or counter the mechanisms of exclusion. Deliberate and conscious effort is required to integrate decentralization in a way that is politically tuned to the needs of the marginalized as distinct from bureaucratic or managerial decentralization. IWRM as a perspective is not likely to automatically entail democratic practices/consequences. Subjective inclusion of pro-poor policies in the current definitions of IWRM, for instance, does not constitute an element of operational necessity. See Maria Placht's comment on IWRM in this context:

> *Equity, another core tenet of IWRM, means all people must have access to water of adequate quantity and quality. The best way to ensure equity is participation in water management by all stakeholders (Jaspers, 2003; Giupponi et al, 2006). Ensuring that the poor, especially women, have a fair share of water means that they must be represented in the institutions that make water resource allocation decisions. Stakeholders must be involved in preparing and implementing IWRM for it to be sustainable. Their interests in, importance to, and influence over the proposed project cannot be overestimated.* (Placht, 2007)

This raises fundamental questions about modalities of ensuring democratic governance when the weak and strong are represented at a common table that brings together all stakeholders for deciding on water issues – as suggested above. The issue here is not one of intellectual definition, but one of on-the-ground practical and divergent strategies of integration with radically opposed consequences for the historically marginalized sections of society. Distinctions between alternative modes of integration need to be vocally articulated to forestall fudging and uncritical co-option of IWRM in policy documents. Integration, it may be noted, consolidates and facilitates control over planning. However, the questions that have been raised but are as yet unanswered are: who will integrate? What will they integrate? How will it take place? (Moench et al, 2003). In the case of water, while not many can dispute the wisdom of viewing through integrated lenses, the challenge is to ensure that the egalitarian mode of integration is adopted while dealing with the key water problem, namely the *exclusion of the majority from the resource* – which is what scarcity is all about.

Notes

1   Although the statement was made specifically with reference to mass social movements, it does emphasize the significance of populist perceptions for promoting certain social actions, which is the context for the present reference.

2   Once 'harnessed', access to water is conditioned by social/institutional structures that 'develop' water resources. These reflect and reproduce prevalent social discriminations in terms of access to the benefits of public resources. Ironically, therefore, 'more water' can lead to the reproduction of scarcity conditions although the stated intent was to do precisely the opposite.

3   The Club of Rome, founded in April 1968, raised considerable public attention with its report *Limits to Growth* (Meadows et al, 1972). It predicted that economic growth could not continue indefinitely because of the limited availability of natural resources, particularly oil. The emphasis on resource scarcity generated alarm bells about an impending doomsday, setting off a sense of panic in the discourse.

4   This includes water conservation or other waste reduction measures.

5   An accounting tool that is calculated as 'the flows of energy and matter to and from any defined economy. It then derives the value of the land/water area required from nature to support these flows' (see Wackernage and Rees, 1996, cited in Kothari et al, 2003, p35).

6   See Peluso and Watts (2001) for a comprehensive critique of the neo-Malthusian explanations of resource scarcity.

7   This is not to argue that waste reduction is not necessary, only to question its causative role.

8   GWP, Global Water Partnership, is a working partnership among all those involved in water management: government agencies, public institutions, private companies, professional organizations, multilateral development agencies and others committed to the Dublin-Rio principles. The World Bank, the United Nations Development Programme (UNDP) and the Swedish International Development Agency (Sida), created the GWP in 1996. This initiative was based on promoting and implementing integrated water resources management through the development of a worldwide network that could pull together financial, technical, policy and human resources to address the critical issues of sustainable water management.

9   However, asymmetric power relations, that influence allocation practices, remain a peripheral concern. Hence the weakness of most top-driven water programmes, something underscored in a recent report by Sule (2005) on the failure of the Hariyali Guidelines for Integrated Watershed Development.

10 See the presentation on IWRM issued by GWP for defining and rationalizing adoption of the IWRM approach (GWP, 2009). See also Biswas, 2004 for a critical assessment of the concept.

References

Barlow, M. and Clarke, A. (2001) *Blue Gold: The Battle against Corporate Theft of the World's Water*, Earthscan, London

Barlow, M. and Clarke, A. (2002) available at http://hydrousmantle.blogspot.com/2008/02/iwrm-relations-meaning-of-moniker.html (last accessed January 2009)

Biswas, A.K. (2004) 'Integrated water resources management: A reassessment', *Water International*, vol 29, no 2, pp248–256

Burke, J. and Moench, M. (2000) *Groundwater and Society: Resources Tensions and Opportunities*, UN Department for Social and Economic Affairs and Institute for Social and Environmental Transition, New York

D'Souza, R. (2003) 'Environmental discourses and environmental politics', in S. Kothari, I. Ahmad and H. Reifeld (eds) (2003) *The Value of Nature, Ecological Politics in India*, Rainbow Publishers, Delhi

Elkington, J. (2008) www.circleofblue.org/waternews/world/us-faces-era-of-water-scarcity/ (last accessed January 2009)

Falkenmark, M. and Widstrand, C. (1992) 'Population and water resources: A delicate balance', *Population Bulletin*, Population Reference Bureau, Washington, DC

Gadekar, M. (undated) 'Tracking the drought-II Ratnagiri: Water scarcity amidst plenty', available at www.infochangeindia.org/features106.jsp (last accessed January 2009)

Giupponi, C., Jakeman, A.J., Karssenberg, D. and Hare, M.P. (eds) (2006) *Sustainable Management of Water Resources: An Integrated Approach*, Elgar, Cheltenham

Gleick, P.H. (2000) *The World's Water 2000–2001*, Island Press, Washington, DC

GWP (2000) 'Integrated water resources management', GWP Technical Advisory Committee, Background Paper 4, Stockholm, Global Water Partnership Secretariat

GWP (2009) available at www.gdrc.org/uem/water/iwrm/slide-start.html (last accessed January 2009)

Iyer, R. (2005) 'The politicisation of water', in *The Political Agenda: The Politics of Water*, available at www.infochangeindia.org/agenda3.jsp

Jairath, J. (2001) *Participatory Irrigation Management – Water User Associations in Andhra Pradesh: Initial Feedback from the Field*, Concept Publishing Company, New Delhi on behalf of CESS, Hyderabad, India

Jairath, J. (2008a) 'Management of scarcity and scarcity of management: A case study of droughts in Mahabubnagar district in Andhra Pradesh', in J. Jairath and V. Ballabh (eds) *Droughts and Integrated Water Resource Management in South Asia: Issues, Alternatives and Futures*, Sage, New Delhi

Jairath, J. (2008b) 'Mis-governance of droughts in India' in V. Ballabh (ed) *Governance of Water – Institutional Alternatives and Political Economy*, Sage, Delhi

Jaspers, F. (2003) 'Institutional arrangements for integrated river basin management', *Water Policy*, vol 5, pp77–90

Kasturirangan, K. (1996) 'A space agenda for water: Challenges and perspectives', Sixth Vikram Sarabhai Memorial Lecture, available at www.isro.org/krangan/krangan_lecture-06.htm

Kothari, S., Ahmad I. and Reifeld, H. (eds) (2003) *The Value of Nature, Ecological Politics in India*, Rainbow Publishers, Delhi

KrishiWorld (undated) 'Pulse of Indian agriculture: Water resources', available at www.krishiworld.com/html/water_resources1.html (accessed January 2006)

Meadows, D.H., Meadows, D.L., Randers, J. and Behrens III, W.W. (1972) *The Limits to Growth*, Universe Books, available at http://en.wikipedia.org/wiki/Club_of_Rome (last accessed January 2009)

Mehta, L. (2005) *The Politics and Poetics of Water: Naturalising Scarcity in Western India*, Orient Longman, New Delhi

Meinzen-Dick, R. and Rosegrant, M.W. (2001) 'IFPRI overview: Overcoming water scarcity and quality constraints', 2020 Focus 9, Brief 9 of 14

Mishra, D.K. (2004) 'Bihar: Flooded and waterlogged', in *Disputes over The Ganga*, Panos Institute of South Asia, Kathmandu

Moench, M., Dixit, A., Janakarajan, S., Rathore, M.S. and Mudrakartha, S. (The Fluid Mosaic) (2003) 'Water Governance in the Context of Variability, Uncertainty and Change: A Synthesis Paper', Nepal Water Conservation Foundation, Kathmandu

Nair, R. (2003) 'Two billion people are dying for it', available at http://pib.nic.in/feature/feyr2003/foct2003/f091020031.html

Nepal Water Conservation Foundation (2003) *Fluid Mosaic*, Nepal Water Conservation Foundation, Kathmandu and The Institute of Social and Environmental Transition, Boulder, Colorado

PAI (1993a) 'Sustaining Water: Population and the Future of Renewable Water Supplies', Population Action International, Washington, DC

PAI (1993b) 'Population and water stress', excerpted from 'Sustaining Water: Population and the Future of Renewable Water Supplies', Population Action International, Washington, DC

PAI (1993c) 'Annual renewable fresh water available per person under three long-range United Nations population projections: India and China', excerpted from 'Sustaining Water: Population and the Future of Renewable Water Supplies', Population Action International, Washington, DC

PAI (1993d) 'Alternative Futures, excerpted from Sustaining Water: Population and the Future of Renewable Water Supplies', Population Action International, Washington, DC

PAI (2000) Engelman, R. with Cincotta, R.P., Dye, B., Gardner-Outlaw, T. and Wisnewski, J., 'People in the balance: Population and natural resources at the turn of the millennium', available at http://populationaction.org/resources/publications/peopleinthebalance/pages/index.php?results=1&searchType=countries&countries%5B%5D=72

Peluso, N.L. and Watts, M. (2001) *Violent Environments*, Cornell University Press, New York

Placht, M. (2007) 'Integrated water resource management: Incorporating integration, equity, and efficiency to achieve sustainability', The Fletcher School, MALD candidate, *Ideas*, October, available at http://fletcher.tufts.edu/ierp/ideas/default.html

PSI (2000) '"And Not a Drop to Drink!" – World Water Forum promotes privatization and deregulation of world's water', *Corporate Europe Observer*, Issue 7, October, Public Services International, available at www.world-psi.org/ (last accessed January 2009)

Rosegrant, M.W. (1995) 'Dealing with water scarcity in the next century', 2020 Vision Brief 21, available at www.ifpri.org/2020/welcome.htm

Roy, A. (1999) *The Greater Common Good*, India Book Distributors, Delhi, available at www.sandrp.in/pub/grcomgood.txt (last accessed January 2009)

Schneider, K. (2009) 'Era of Water Scarcity', www.circleofblue.org/waternews/world/us-faces-era-of-water-scarcity/ (last accessed January 2009)

Sharma, S. (2003) 'InfoChange News & Features', available at www.infochangeindia.org/WaterResourceIbp.jsp

Sule, S. (2005) 'Haryali: Not so green after all', available at www.indiatogether.org/2005/sep/env-haryali.html (last accessed January 2009)

SIWI Press Release (2005) 'Scientists call for action as global food demands threaten to outstrip world water supply', based on 'Let it Reign: The New Paradigm for Global Food Security', available at www.siwi.org

Thakkar, H. (2006) 'The powerful get water, the powerless don't', UNDP report, available at www.infochangeindia.org/analysis144.jsp

UNDP (2006) 'Human Development Report 1998', Oxford University Press, New York

UNFPA (2001) 'State of the world population, footprints and milestones: Population and environmental change', available at www.unfpa.org/upload/lib_pub_file/471_filename_swp2001_eng.pdf

Wackernage, M. and Rees, W. (1996) *Our Ecological Footprint: Reducing Human Impact on the Earth*, New Society Publishers, Philadelphia

WaterAid (2005) 'Drinking Water and Sanitation Status in India', Coverage Financing and Emerging Concerns, New Delhi

WMO (2004) 'Mitigating Risk and Coping with Uncertainty', Geneva, available at www.wmo.ch/pages/abut/index_en.html (last accessed January 2009)

World Watch Institute (2004) 'State of the world 2004: Richer, fatter and not much happier', quoted in *InfoChange News & Features*, available at www.infochangeindia.org/bookandreportsst58.jsp

WWC (2009) available at www.worldwatercouncil.org/index.php?id=25&I=0%22on focus%3D%22blurLink%28this%29%3Bti (last accessed January 2009)

WWDR (2003) *UNDP's World Water Development Report*, WWDR, Perugia

13

The Construction and Destruction of Scarcity in Development: Water and Power Experiences in Nepal

Dipak Gyawali and Ajaya Dixit

Developing the roadmap

The dominant ethos of development as propagated and practised by donors and planners implies that developing countries will necessarily undergo a fundamental shift from traditional energy sources (such as firewood, dung and agri-residues) to commercial ones mostly based on petroleum (such as liquefied petroleum gas, kerosene and electricity generated from coal, oil or in some fortuitous cases hydropower). This transition is neither as linear as national development planners have assumed, nor as altruistically beneficial as the evaluation reports of aid organizations suggest. Using examples from Nepal, which has been moving from traditional to commercial energy sources at breakneck speed over the last few decades (and only haltingly towards exploiting its alternative renewable resources), this chapter analyses the 'hijacking' of development that has occurred in this transition. Cases drawn from energy and transport as well as a large urban water supply scheme (which has a disputed hydropower component to it) show how various actors, including state bureaucracies, aid agencies, 'development merchants' and the ubiquitous politician–contractor nexus, have jockeyed for the prime spot, all trying to further their own agendas. Each is actively involved in suppressing the alternatives championed by the others, all the while believing that the silent consuming masses subscribe to only its version.

With the insights gleaned from these cases, lessons are drawn about the dynamics of demand creation and the politics of scarcity they entail. The three primary social solidarities at play – those of market individualism as well as the hierarchism of government hydrocrats and the egalitarianism of communitarian social and environmental activists – opt for dissimilar technologies and different development alternatives. We are both trained engineers (Gyawali is a hydropower engineer and Dixit is a water engineer) who have also engaged with social science debates. We have spent most of our professional and research lives focusing on Nepal's chronic dearth of water and energy and working towards economically and socially sustainable water and energy schemes. We conclude that scarcity is not an inherent characteristic of the natural resource in question, but that it is created and assiduously maintained by those making divergent technological choices to meet their specific socio-political ends.

Scarcity generation

Helena Norberg-Hodge, the first western scholar in Laddakh, describes an encounter that sheds light on the linkage between scarcity and development. When she first arrived in that Trans-Himalayan settlement to begin her research, as a good social scientist, she wanted to find out the economic class structure of the village. She asked her young research assistant, Tshewang, to take her to the house of the poorest person in the village. Once there, she found nothing distinctively 'poor' about it: it had just about the same level of amenities as all the other houses in the village. She was perplexed until she realized that the Laddakhis did not have a word for 'poor' in their language. The house that she had been taken to belonged, not to the 'poorest' as understood by modern development economics, but to the person least respected in the village, someone akin to a village idiot.

More than a decade later, when she was on her way to Laddakh again, she met Tshewang, now a tourism entrepreneur, at the foothills bus station. Glad to see her, he gushed to her and other western tourists that they were the only real friends 'poor' Laddakhis had and that they should do everything they could to help them. 'We Laddakhis are poor, and you should help us develop', was the essence of his plea. What Helena Norbert-Hodge found shocking was that a community that had not even known the concept of poverty had been so 'developmentalized' that it now believed it was intrinsically poor, even though it continues to have both cultural and natural resources in abundance.[1]

Development as practised in the second half of the 20th century has essentially meant a culture of moving toward a fossil-fuel (or non-renewable energy-dependent) lifestyle. Bringing development to a southern village has, in practical terms, meant bringing it a road and fossil-fuel vehicles along with it. Efforts to increase food production have resulted in an agricultural system dependent on petroleum-based tractors, chemical fertilizers and pesticides, which are often provided as tied aid 'commodity grants' by the producer countries of the north. Even domestic cooking in more affluent households that are seen as 'modern' or 'developed', primarily in urban areas but also, increasingly, in the villages, is shifting to kerosene or LPG (liquefied petroleum gas, or cooking gas) canisters. Since these are manufactured goods with complex production processes and long, transboundary supply chains – which require licences to produce, permits to establish factories, specialized professional knowledge to keep them going, market access to sell their products, statutorily defined rights to ensure payment etc. – scarcity is inherent in their very nature. Many things can go wrong in the complex delivery process outlined above, and surprises at each stage can disrupt the supply chain, creating a shortage in a system where these goods are not luxury items one can do without, but everyday necessities.[2]

The Indian cultural critic Ashish Nandy describes how ordinary needs (such as the need for a refreshing drink like lemonade) become debilitating commercial and socio-cultural dependencies due to the emergence of beverages mass produced through global capital. One cannot grow one's own soft drink. Instead, it has to be procured ready-made, on the global market. Scarcity is thus inherent in the industrialization process where consumerism – an ideology founded on the re-engineering of human values – requires the uprooting of traditional values and the fostering of individualization. Aggressive global marketing then targets the resultant lonely, narcissistic and alienated individual, promising to meet his or her artificial needs (Nandy, 2005).

Laxman Yapa defines scarcity as being created 'by expanding the demand for a commodity, which is done by contracting alternative sources of supply, and by expanding the use of that commodity beyond the original end use' (Yapa, 2005). Sanity, or lack thereof, in the end use of a commodity (especially of energy) is fundamental to Yapa's definition. Using high-quality electrical energy to heat a room in a poorly designed energy-inefficient house when alternatives such as better insulation or wood or coal would do just as well is one example of the absurdity behind scarcity. Often this inconsistency is the result of a careful social construction: it is made unfashionable to dry one's wet hands using a towel so that the demand for energy-squandering but modish hot air blowers will rise.

Yapa also includes political actions in his definition in two basic ways: first, consumerist advertising increases the demand for the use of a commodity beyond its original end use, and, second, alternatives are rendered unavailable. When a car is no longer a means of faster locomotion from point A to point B but has become a fashion or even a sex symbol, when shoes are no longer just comfortable for walking in but a way to display the right logo, when a watch no longer merely tells time but is an ornament, we are talking of the first type of political action. Examples of the second, which are more insidious, abound. The celebrated Gandhian march against the attempt of the British Raj to make it illegal for Indians to collect their own salt from the sea shore even though it was 'freely' available is an example of a power creating scarcity to perpetuate its stranglehold. Shutting out alternatives at various stages in the process of making development choices is another widespread method, one seen in the case of Nepal's energy infrastructure as well as transport as discussed below.

Yapa, in the same article quoted above, argues that 'unlimited wants and limited resources are not self-evident objective conditions of the world'. Rather, since scarcity is socially constructed, he outlines four steps in the study of scarcity:

- reconstruction of the commodity's history;
- identification of principal end uses;
- consideration of alternative ways of meeting those end uses;
- discussion of the reasons the demand for that commodity has expanded beyond its end use.

Hydropower development in Nepal is a case in point that substantiates the above line of reasoning. With 6000-odd rivers cascading down the Himalaya, the country boasts of being one of the richest in the world in hydroelectric potential. However, it is indeed ironic that, despite seeing the first hydroelectric plant as early as 1911 (earlier than most other Asian countries currently far higher in the 'development' hierarchy), the country has been reeling under severe power cuts at the time of finalizing this chapter, with 16 hours of load shedding[3] per day in April 2009. These officially announced and enforced power outages are not, however, new. They have, like the predictable seasons, regularly followed a few years after the commissioning of new hydroelectric plants. Since the 1970s, a few years of excess capacity in the national grid have inevitably been followed by several years of shortages, akin to a 'flood-drought' syndrome.

As a southern country that was not politically colonized, Nepal was a latecomer to development, a process that started in earnest only after World War II, the independence of India and the collapse of the international power base of the autocratic dynasty of Rana *shoguns* who maintained excellent relations with the British Raj in India. That they would only be interested in electricity as an item of luxury, one of the trappings of power for their stucco palaces and hence not just scarce but simply unavailable to the average Nepali, is understandable. But, after their dynastic rule collapsed in 1951, this seductive technology was in demand from one and all, as was piped domestic drinking water. Until the early 1970s, there were efforts to provide electricity through state-sponsored public corporations as well as through small private companies. However, with the increasing involvement of multilateral development agencies, the private power companies were nationalized by the 1970s and electricity became something supplied only by the government (Gyawali and Dixit, 1999).

It is from this point onwards that the story begins of the 'flood-drought' syndrome – periodic bouts of surplus followed by inevitable scarcities in a country propagandized in the media as having plentiful hydropower resources. Entwined with the government's monopoly over the supply of electricity was the role of international development financing institutions that bears equal responsibility for this syndrome. The government's hydroelectricity agencies (the hydrocracies) have tended to prefer larger, expertise-dependent technologies such as one large power project implemented by their in-house expertise (rather than by a host of smaller entrepreneurs and communes outside of their structure). Development agencies have found it more cost-effective to make one large sovereign loan to a single large dam than to many smaller projects. The first of such single large projects was the 60MW Kulekhani-1 – large because it was bigger than the total generating capacity within the existing power system – whose commissioning was preceded by massive system-wide power cuts in the early 1980s. It was followed by a period of surplus and exhortations by the electricity utility to the consumers to buy more electrical gadgets. The story of power cuts and load sheddings was repeated in the case of the 69MW Marsyangdi in 1989, again with the 144MW Kali Gandaki in the late 1990s and continues even today.

The only saving grace in this sad history has been the restoration of multi-party democracy in 1990, which was conducive to civic activism in the water and power sector. This democratic opening allowed activist groups such as the Alliance for Energy to question the economic, social and environmental viability of official hydrocratic plans, and led to the cancellation of the controversial 201MW Arun-3 hydropower project championed by the World Bank with the Nepal government (Gyawali, 2003). The sector was then opened to a mix of Nepali and private power developers, with the government agency still having a role through multilateral banks. This change allowed for the flowering of over a dozen Nepali power developers constructing small- and medium-scale schemes, which contributed significantly to providing electricity to areas that had never had it before, as well as to ameliorate scarcity in the national grid. It also heralded the entry of Nepali entrepreneurs and banks into the electricity policy terrain.

While this welcome shift in power development policy provided the national grid with almost a third more electricity at half the cost and half the time than would have been available with the Arun-3, the resistance from the power bureaucracy and its allies in the donor community has continued to be stiff. There is a telling reluctance to sign power purchase agreements with the small-scale developers who fund their projects with loans from Nepali banks in Nepali currency. Even though the country is reeling under daily load shedding, the push within the power bureaucracy continues to be to develop a single large project with international donors to meet the overall grid requirement through a 'generation expansion plan'. Because the official tendency is still to allow hydropower development through the hydrocracy and because the small- and medium-scale Nepali entrepreneurs continue to be sidelined, the story of scarcity amidst plenty is thus slated to repeat itself into the future. Is there a rational explanation, a method to this madness? The rest of this chapter hopes to answer this question.

Fork in the transport pathway

Nepal's development in general, and in particular its development of commercial energy, provides a window through which to view the manner in which scarcity is generated and destroyed. When Nepal entered the path of 'modernization' in 1951, except for a few kilometres of all-weather driveable roads in Kathmandu Valley and dirt roads in the Tarai, the country was basically road-less. Even today, there are districts in the northwest of the country that have no roads and have never seen a motor vehicle. The primary energy used for transport before 1951 was human muscle power. In fact, even the first few cars imported by the Rana rulers for their private luxury were carried to Kathmandu Valley on the backs of porters, about 40 of whom took three weeks to carry each partly-dismantled automobile from the piedmont across the Mahabharat passes.[4] For the Ranas, the automobile was a symbol of power and the flaunting of luxury, not a means of transport.

All that changed with the advent of modernization ushered in by the political changes of 1951 when Rana rule was overthrown. Vehicular transport became an item of mass consumption and the total length of all roads increased from 376km in 1951 to over 15,000km in 2001, by which time this sector's share of the national budget amounted to a sixth of the total (Shrestha, 2004). By the end of 2007, the total number of vehicles in Nepal was 617,305 of which 88,735 were automobiles.[5] Some 110,912 kilolitres of petrol and 306,667 kilolitres of high-speed diesel were imported to fuel this motorized movement (Kafle, 2007). Because Nepal's mountainous terrain is criss-crossed by high ranges and deep gorges, road construction is not only expensive but also difficult and only a fraction of the demand has been satisfied so far. Indeed, in any election, the primary vote-winning strategy is to promise to build roads to remote mountainous villages, even if no money can be found to do so after the winner moves to the capital city Kathmandu.

Everyday life in Nepal's mountain villages is a constant battle against enormous verticality. An apt comparison of Himalayan hamlets is with Pacific islands separated by wide expanses of ocean making them virtually inaccessible: a settlement on one ridge-top can often be reached from the next village on another ridge only by walking down a sharp valley and climbing back up for several hours. This physical constraint constricts not just social relations but also commerce and everyday life: it can take three hours to carry drinking water from a spring source below the village, and bumper harvests of fruits or vegetables have to be fed to cattle because of the near impossibility of carrying them to the market. Within such a context of back-breaking verticality, any energy technology that promised relief from human muscle-powered drudgery would have seductive appeal; and both the internal combustion engine (cars and trucks) as well as electricity (powering ropeways) can be seen as god-sent by those toiling up and down the mountain slopes to meet their daily needs.

Unfortunately, if the political power to decide on these aspects of development lies not with those engaged in actual production but with those at the upper realms of the hierarchy, technology can be desired and imported, not to increase productive efficiency, but to display wealth and power. In western Europe, the very birth of modern technology was due to the rise of capitalism and a host of social preconditions, ranging from the absence of a rent-extracting empire and of cheap labour from slavery to separation of church and state, Protestant work ethics and frugality in consumption (Stavrianos, 1981). The social carriers of steam, electricity and locomotive technologies of Europe and America were the productive industrial class entrepreneurs, not its feudal overlords.

In Nepal's case, however, the internal combustion engine technology, as well as electricity, was introduced into the country by the feudal Rana potentates, not as a means to increase production, as was originally the case, but as an element of luxury. As described above, a motorized vehicle was first a luxury for the Rana rulers with its trappings of power, but within a few decades it had become a mass consumption good for the public, one which was for the most part scarce. Piped water supply for private domestic use (as opposed to the *dhungey dharos*, communal stone water spouts that traditionally supplied water to core urban areas for the previous eight or more centuries, and still do) was also a Rana import for their palaces. Similarly, the primary function of the first 500kW hydroelectric power plant built in 1911 was to provide lighting for the chandeliers of Rana palaces. By 1924, the energy produced was also employed in a very limited way to operate a goods-carrying ropeway that connected Kathmandu to Bhainse, a town across the Mahabharat mountain range close to the Gangetic plains.[6] This aristocratic birthmark left by the original social carriers of modern technologies, such as electricity, drinking water or ropeways, continues to influence their planning and implementation even today, thus making scarcity a deeply ingrained feature of these artifacts.

When Nepal set out on the path of modern transportation, she stood at a fork: she could have opted to either construct more roads and increase importing petroleum-based vehicles or develop more ropeways that would run, in a demonstrably feasible manner, on indigenously generated hydropower. Ropeways (also called, in their various incarnations, cable cars, chair lifts or ski lifts) are a mode of transport where specially designed carriers holding goods or people are suspended and pulled along a steel cable strung across a valley or depression. Because these carriers do not have to roll on land as do trucks and buses on a serpentine mountain road, they move passengers and goods straight between two ridge points as the crow flies, the moving power often being an electric motor running on hydroelectricity generated from a mountain river. This option makes hill transport shorter, faster and in the end more economic than roads. The course of development politics, however, plunged Nepal headlong into the dependency path of imported petroleum-based roads and did not allow any space whatsoever for a mixed multi-modal transport that included main trunk roads with small ropeways extending from them to various hill hamlets. By 2001, the oldest ropeway that connected the capital city Kathmandu and the plains to the south, built in 1924 and upgraded in 1964, had withered away. And, despite the pronouncements of various political parties in their election manifestos that they would promote hydropower-based transport, government spending on ropeways had entirely ceased.

It required a different type of social carrier to resurrect this mountain-friendly technology. The case of Bhattedanda Milkway described below, which is a goods-carrying cable car (or ropeway) used to transport milk to the roadhead from remote villages, is widely regarded as a successful project. It has helped to significantly alleviate the poverty of marginalized farmers in Kathmandu Valley's southern Lalitpur. Initiated in 1994 with funding from the European Union (EU) as part of the larger Bagmati Watershed Project (BWP), it was implemented between 1986 and 1995. In its second phase, which ran from 1998 to 2003, the project's philosophy was enlarged to capture wider aspects of development through the concept of 'integrated management'. This new project, now called the Bagmati Integrated Watershed Management Project (BIWMP), strove to alleviate the chronic impoverishment in the middle hills of Nepal using innovative alternative technologies such as ropeways that would empower villagers to take advantage of the markets rather than letting the market – with its truck owners, petroleum suppliers and road maintenance crews – keep the villagers at its rent-seeking mercy. Unfortunately, because of lack of political will in the higher echelons of government, the political wrangling among parties forming unstable coalitions in the second half of the 1990s as well as the resulting institutional shortcomings, the European Union's project was terminated in 2003, and its remarkable contribution to 'sustainable development' died in the making.

Ropeway resurrection

The Milkway was never a part of the development ethos of either the Nepal government's Ministry of Forests and its Department of Soil and Water Conservation, which managed the BIWMP that built the ropeway, or the EU which provided the aid support. The BIWMP had been weaned on the technology of expensive check dams designed to prevent landslides together with what had proved to be ineffective afforestation.[7] The heavy monsoon cloudbursts with their roaring torrents in sharp gullies invariably washed away the check dams, and planting saplings without village community participation resulted in no forestation. The EU never internalized either ropeway technology or the institutional framework which linked the lack of market access with rural hill poverty because of the large gap between the thinking in aid headquarters such as in Brussels and the socio-political realities in the roadless deep rural hinterlands of Nepal (Gyawali, 2004). The idea for the ropeway grew out of the unconventional thinking of a few Nepali and European watershed managers and received support from several unusual institutional conditions between 1994 and 1998 which favoured the installation of this new technology.[8] These conditions that were amenable to sustainable development and rural poverty alleviation, however, subsequently proved to be ephemeral: they do not exist now, as political parties and donor agencies have gone back to their old ways of doing business.

What made this particular project a model of sustainable development? In the 18 months it operated between 1995 and 1996, the Milkway exported in Rupee terms one-and-a-half times more milk, vegetables and other rural products to the cities than it imported urban goods. It obviated the need for marginalized farmers to boil milk for many hours a day (cutting a lot of trees to fuel the process) in order to convert it into the thick *khuwa* paste that could be transported to the market without curdling but which sold for less than fresh milk. The Milkway earned money not only for farmers but also for itself (even with the low rates for transporting milk) and was even able to save some of the earnings after paying for its operating costs (something that cannot be said for some of Nepal's more prestigious irrigation projects in the country which are funded by major multilateral donors). These savings proved very useful after, as described further below, the EU withdrew its support. Local initiatives had to step in to revive the ropeway after it collapsed both institutionally and physically.

Because the institutional mechanism had not been correctly designed (the ropeway's beneficiaries were not its operators); because the marginal villagers had to make a quantum leap in technology from boiling milk on open-fire tripods to running precision-engineered mechanical cable cars with only learn-as-you-go training; because government and donor support had waned; and because a competing technology (a gravel road) favoured by truck-owning interests came into being nearby, the Milkway project could not be sustained and fell into disuse after January 2001. Eighteen months later, however, in July 2002, a massive cloudburst washed away a portion of the road (hardly a sustainable hill technology compared to a ropeway), leaving farmers cut off from the milk market.

Because their standard of living had increased considerably after the Milkway was built, farmers were not prepared to go back to their low-level subsistence economy. However, no help was forthcoming, because the EU was in the process of closing down the BIWMP, which finally happened in April 2003. The Ministry of Forests was more interested in conventional watershed management of check dams and forestation than unconventional ropeways for which there was no in-house expertise within its Department of Soil and Watershed Conservation. Indeed, from the perspective of the Nepal government bureaucracy, the Ministry of Forests was not supposed to be dabbling in transport, which was the turf of the Ministry of Transport and its all-powerful Department of Roads, even though the evidence on the ground indicated that the ropeway was far more effective in protecting the watershed from deforestation than conventional check dams and tree planting. Even though some Rs.30 million (approximately €3.4 million) had already been allocated to expand the ropeways, it lay idle for want of a social carrier to champion it. At least six, and possibly 10, studies were carried out (Upadhya, 2004) to examine the feasibility of extending the Bhattedanda Milkway but even after so much investment, neither the EU nor the government was able to disburse the money allocated from Brussels because, it seems, of purely bureaucratic accounting reasons, exacerbated by political instability in Nepal.

Even though the farmers had an urgent need to rehabilitate the Milkway after the road was washed away, they were unable to access the EU money. They tried numerous tactics, including sending delegations to various government agencies and lobbying with new sets of politicians, but to no avail: the EU money already allocated was not released despite EU Commissioner Chris Patten writing to the Minister of Forests. Eventually, the developmentally orphaned farmers decided to do something about their plight themselves. They used their savings to rehabilitate the Milkway, which has since then carried a million kilograms of goods (more from the village to the city than the other way around) and earned them more than half a million rupees gross income (roughly €57,000). The EU money allocated to expand the Bhattedanda Milkway remained frozen during this time and was eventually repatriated to Brussels.[9]

However, egalitarian advocacy for alternative, farmer- and environment-friendly technology continued with the farmers in the deeper hinterlands being galvanized into coming out of their structure-induced poverty trap. Rather than accept their fate passively, they were motivated to do something different: instead of continuing to destroy their forests to make *khuwa* when denied the opportunity to sell their milk directly, and to watch with envy their more fortunate neighbours able to transport their milk to the roadhead via the milkway and get richer, they decided to band together and put pressure on the government. The political changes of April 2006 in Nepal, which brought the rebel Maoists active in their villages to power, worked in their favour: they managed to rope in the Nepal government's Poverty Alleviation Fund to help them build a new scheme of ropeway expansion to their villages, and are currently engaged in implementing it.

Water-rich scarcity

Besides being examples of genuine rural development, the Bhattedanda Milkway and other cable cars in Nepal demonstrate in practice what is obvious in theory: in a mountainous terrain, hydroelectricity-based ropeways are more economical than petroleum-based road transport. Recent experiences in Nepal show that goods-carrying ropeways are three times cheaper to build than an equivalent road, eight times quicker to install and twice as energy-efficient (34 MegaJoules/ton of goods carried versus 53MJ/t for trucks running on imported petroleum, see Dhakal, 2004 for details). Furthermore, with the advent of 'communitized electricity'[10] in Nepal, the Bhattedanda Milk Cooperative has shelved its diesel generator and begun to use much cheaper grid-supplied hydroelectricity. The Cooperative used to spend Rs. 31,000 per month on diesel to run the ropeway, not counting the cost of transporting the diesel: with grid-supplied electricity, the cost of powering the ropeway has plummeted to just Rs. 7000! Why did ropeways not feature in policy planning or mass-scale implementation after 1924, when the first one was installed in Nepal? Why, with all this recent knowledge and experience, do they continue to be sidelined? Why is rural access still very 'scarce' in Nepal?

The answers to these intriguing questions seem to lie in the politics of development, the entrenched forces therein and the marginalization of both hinterland farmers and the social auditors who champion their cause. Before we deconstruct the energy and transport technologies and their different social carriers that perceive scarcity differently, it is instructive to also look at the better-studied situation of water supply scarcity in Kathmandu Valley for parallels.

Most people believe that the capital of Nepal is located in a valley surrounded by hills: in reality, it is located on a plateau surrounded by hills. This change in perspective is necessary if one is to understand Kathmandu's water supply problem: all major snow-fed rivers adjacent to the valley that could be tapped to meet the needs of the burgeoning city are located at least 400 to 700 metres below the valley floor, making these sources expensive, as pumping is required to make water available to the cities in Kathmandu Valley.

The Bagmati River that drains the valley is a much smaller, monsoon-fed river than the Trisuli and the Indrawati/Sun Kosi rivers to its west and east respectively. In the Himalaya, given the steep terrain and violent cloudbursts, the higher the flow volume in a river, the deeper the gorge it scours over geological time. Thus, the Kathmandu valley floor is higher than the river gorges in the east and west, ironically making it, so it would seem, a place of perennial water scarcity amidst Himalayan plenty.

However, is this really the case? As the capital of a developing country, Kathmandu invites a high level of in-migration due to the various facilities it offers. The influx of relatively well-to-do villagers fleeing Maoist extortion and terror in the rural hinterlands in the 1990s has increased the pressure of incoming numbers. This influx places a heavy burden on the city's infrastructure, including roads, sewerage and water supply systems. Four groups, the marginalized, the state, the market and civil society institutions have responded to the water stress differently (Dixit and Gyawali, 1999). Individuals and communities that fall outside the field of vision of development and government agencies continue to rely on the traditional wells and stone water spouts of antiquity. Despite their dilapidated condition, many of these sources continue to meet the needs of these individuals and communities. They may wish for modern amenities such as piped drinking water inside their homes, but they lack both the economic wherewithal to access a market solution as well as the political clout to be heard in policy circles.

Government and government-led corporations, the second group of actors, have taken upon themselves the responsibility of supplying water through modern piped systems. In partnership with international development agencies, they have opted for engineering solutions such as the trans-basin water transfer project known as Melamchi, whose 26.5km tunnel running through uncertain Himalayan geology is just one among several options. Melamchi and other such projects enhance the government's sense of control because only the management by their expertise-based bureaucracy can design, implement and operate such larger and complex schemes.

Since this option will not materialize for at least a decade or more, a bevy of street-smart operators have emerged as the third group of actors. They supply drinking water to Kathmandu denizens through a variety of means, which include tankers that draw water from spring sources in the valley outskirts, shallow groundwater-extracting 'rower pumps', as well as bottled water. The last item has suddenly appeared within the last decade or so as the poor level of municipal supply created incentives for the market to flourish.

The fourth group to respond has been activist NGOs and consumer forums of academics and journalists who question the solutions proposed by both government agencies and the private sector. They argue that there are alternative means of supply such as rainwater harvesting and reviving traditional ponds which, in their view, would be both cheaper and more equitable. The solution proffered by the state hydrocracy is the Melamchi project that requires trans-basin water transfer, which is expensive, large-scale and requires a long lead time as well as expertise-dependent management. It is based on the notion of scarcity that needs to be managed. The solution favoured by the market, either glamorized bottled water or the more humble tanker supply, stems from the belief that nature is bountiful, that resources are abundant and can easily be harnessed if suppliers are allowed to charge, and people are allowed to pay the proper price without government regulations blocking the way of innovation and progress. The egalitarian activists contest both these proffered solutions by the hierarchies and the market barons: they argue that the resource base is depleting through pollution, over-extraction of ground-water and scarcity is due to mismanagement, hence there is a need to look into alternatives. In other words, the market has unfairly exploited the situation of mismanagement by the state.

Structural change and social carriers

The question of scarcity of rural access in the ropeway case can be explained in a manner similar to the Kathmandu drinking water scarcity case described above. The traditional solution of Nepali villagers to scarcity was to gird their garments about their waists and carry their milk containers. The government did construct a ropeway in 1924, but by the 1950s this solution gave way to building of roads. The government was, of course, goaded into adopting this path by the market forces consisting of a coalition of aid agencies, vehicle and petroleum traders and road-building contractors. Not only did they start to have a major say in how government funds were allocated for the purpose of transport development but also in how important government positions were manned: the Ministry of Transport is completely dominated by the Depart-ment of Roads and its engineers. The alternative voices that defined the prob-lems of the Bhattedanda villagers as that of lack of access to market, which could be met by cheaper alternative technologies such as those of ropeways or motorized river rafts, were marginalized. The definition of the problem of development was hegemonized to mean 'lack of roads'.

It required the activism of those more committed to the ethos of the Kyoto concerns on climate change to put alternative transport possibilities back on the agenda. Many of them were active in reducing Kathmandu's air pollution by getting rid of diesel fume-spewing three-wheelers that have since been replaced by electric vehicles. The alliance between these activists and the alternative market has generated new perspectives and new policy initiatives.[11] Among the latter is the 'communitization' of electricity, an initiative that allows any organized rural group to buy electricity from the national grid at bulk rates and retail it among themselves at rates no higher than the national retail rates. This policy measure has alleviated rural electricity scarcity to some extent. The Bhattedanda Milkway, for example, was able to shift from diesel-supplied to the cheaper grid-supplied hydroelectricity when the local cooperative assumed the responsibility of local electricity distribution. Other proposed policy initia-tives have been to place a tax of at least 1 per cent on petroleum products and to collect the money so accrued into a fund for rural electrification and hydro-electricity-based transport access. Such initiatives are only possible when the policy environment acknowledges that the hierarchic state, the individualist market and egalitarian social activities profess differing perspectives.

It is argued by social scientists that 'goods do not fall into categories, they are captured into them, and at a later stage, liberated from them' (as antiques or rubbish).[12] (See Chapter 7, this volume, for a discussion of rubbish theory.) Because goods are also socially constructed and essentially contested, they are profoundly political. If one took two discriminators (see Table 13.1 below), *jointness of consumption* and *excludability of use*, one would generate four categories of goods. Those that have low excludability and low jointness would generate 'common pool goods' to which all have access, e.g. the atmosphere, large lake, groundwater, etc. At the other diagonal end, high excludability and high jointness result in 'club goods' that the poor are excluded from because they do not belong to the club. High excludability and low jointness result in 'private goods' preferred by the markets, and low excludability with high jointness are behind the production of 'public goods'.

In this classification, scarcity is built into the concept of 'public goods': with 'club goods', impossibility of access rather than scarcity is the norm, while with market-supplied 'private goods' it is paucity of wherewithal (money) that is the driving concern rather than scarcity in the stuff itself. Even in the heyday of Soviet hierarchism-dominated planned goods production, underground market individualism never found goods to be scarce: a *tolkach* (in Russian, literally a fixer 'who pushes') always found the right stuff if the desperate manager of the state-owned factory or construction work was willing to come up with the right price (Mars, 1982). Hierarchism-supplied 'public goods' are based on the principle of 'to each according to his/her rank': because it requires managing the allocation of a short-supply resource such as drinking water or electricity as per established procedures, it becomes necessary to first define it as scarce, and something that not everyone can have as much of as they like even if they have the money.

Table 13.1 *Four types of goods*

| | | Jointness of Consumption ⟶ | |
		Low	High
Excludability of Use ↕	Low	Low excludability and low jointness: *Common Pool Goods* championed by egalitarian social auditors ('civilizers')	Low excludability and high jointness: *Public Goods* championed by hierarchic bureaucracies ('regulators')
	High	High excludability and low jointness: *Private Goods* preferred by individualist markets ('privatizers')	High excludability and high jointness: *Club Goods* from which the fatalist masses are always excluded (those 'resigned' to their fate)

Note: The two discriminators more commonly used in cultural theory are, on the y-axis, symmetrical or asymmetrical transactions, and on the X-axis, competition fettered or unfettered as is shown in Figure 13.1 (see also Thompson, 2008). As cultural theory is a 'theory in making', for bringing forth more insights in explaining the social construction of goods (and to get away from Cartesian geometry), these discriminators have been rephrased as 'excludability of use' and 'jointness of consumption', the former referring to pre-ascribed rules imposing social order and the latter to group cohesion or lack thereof.

Kathmandu's water supply conundrums can be explained with this framework. The government framework of municipal piped water supply assures supply as per the established rules: who has the right to how many hours of supply, from which size of pipe and which day of the week. High government functionaries and places of national importance have high priority and better rations. Those on the lower scale get something much lower, either shorter hours of supply or tankers at fixed times during a drought. For the market, however, scarcity is an opportunity to exploit resources lying idle, in other words, spring sources 'flowing wastefully' or groundwater that 'no one is using'. These are converted to 'private goods' when the price is right. Rainwater harvesting, ponds and groundwater recharge fall within the 'common pool' category of goods accessible to all. Each of these categories of goods has different social carriers and champions, and they stem from a very different definition of what 'the problem' of Kathmandu Valley's water supply is.

Rural access and the energy associated with it can also be seen as any of the following four types of goods. The 'privatizers' (or individualists) would like to see a good as a commodity that they will always be able to provide to those who want it, if they can pay the price for it, that ensures it is worth the trouble (and profit) for the market player. The 'regulators' of the command-and-control bureaucracy want to see limited resources allocated according to hierarchical position and needs. The 'civilizers' (or egalitarians) see no scarcity: for them, whatever there is has to be shared equally among all with no privileged access, whether by governments or markets. The fatalists (or fatalized) feel that no matter what method is chosen, they are going to be left out, that all goods are club goods which they will have no access to because they do not belong to the club. (If they begin to organize and demand their share, however, they are no longer in the fatalist category; and it is the job as well as the eternal mission of the activists to so catalyse them away from their fatalism!) The first three groups actively try to strategize and get others to see things their way, while the fatalists absorb the strategies of the others. This process is the essence of political contestation.

Figure 13.1 below shows four different perceptions of electricity and water.[13] It is the hierarchical view (and the vertically integrated monopolistic public utilities that it favours), which is in the business of managing scarcity through regulation. When hierarchies are not challenged by a vibrant market providing many alternatives and by a civil society alert to inequities in both market and state solutions, they can quickly change from managers of scarcity to *creators* (and then only managers) of scarcity. The histories of load shedding in Nepal, drinking water scarcity in Kathmandu Valley or the scarcity in rural transport and access for poor marginalized farmers to the market to sell their products on their terms rather than that of truck-owners or middlemen, are prime examples of this phenomenon of hierarchism's scarcity managers creating and maintaining scarcity in order to more effectively manage them.

What we have earlier called the 'flood-drought syndrome' refers to the few years of power and energy glut in the Nepali power system upon the completion of a major hydropower project followed by years of loadshedding.

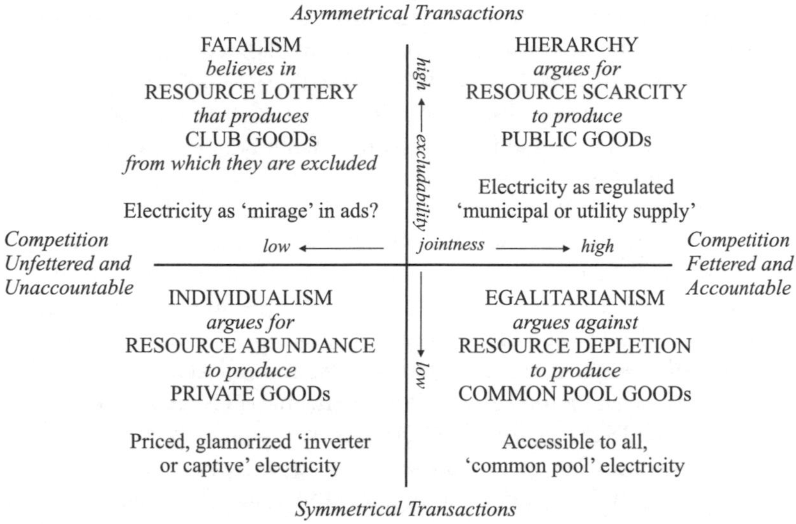

Asymmetrical Transactions

	FATALISM		HIERARCHY
	believes in		*argues for*

FATALISM
believes in
RESOURCE LOTTERY
that produces
CLUB GOODs
from which they are excluded

Electricity as 'mirage' in ads?

HIERARCHY
argues for
RESOURCE SCARCITY
to produce
PUBLIC GOODs

Electricity as regulated
'municipal or utility supply'

high ← excludability

jointness → high

low ←   → high

Competition
Unfettered and
Unaccountable

Competition
Fettered and
Accountable

INDIVIDUALISM
argues for
RESOURCE ABUNDANCE
to produce
PRIVATE GOODs

Priced, glamorized 'inverter
or captive' electricity

EGALITARIANISM
argues against
RESOURCE DEPLETION
to produce
COMMON POOL GOODs

Accessible to all,
'common pool' electricity

low

Symmetrical Transactions

Figure 13.1 *View from 'plural rationalities': Abundance,
scarcity or depletion?*

The state-owned electricity monopoly has completed two large hydroelectric projects in Nepal in the last decade with support from international aid agencies. The 144MW Kali Gandaki was completed in 2001 mainly with support from the Asian Development Bank, and the 70MW Middle Marsyangdi was completed in 2009 with support from the German government. Both projects, planned as the best-generation addition to the national grid, were preceded and eventually followed by inevitable shortages and load shedding; both were plagued with cost and time overruns as well as maintenance difficulties. Despite this 'planned scarcity', there is a tremendous reluctance within the state monopoly utility to allow small-scale Nepali power producers to enter the power supply market and meet the demand: the national utility has been reluctant to sign power purchase agreements with them. A recently constituted government study task force,[14] despite evidence to the contrary, has concluded that scarcity of electricity and load shedding will last till 2019!

The 'theory of plural rationalities' (or Cultural Theory[15]) argues that this state of affairs suits the bureaucratic solidarity just fine. Hierarchism is, after all, primarily concerned with control and its proclivity is for those technologies that allow it to control the overall process and consolidate its expertise-based structure. Large hydropower projects, often much larger than the capacity of the entire power system, are the natural choice of the hydrocrats. They shun a mixture of small and medium projects built by the private sector or local communities, which would 'follow the load curve', matching supply with demand, and favour the single large project path precisely because the structure is programmed to result in alternating cycles of electricity glut and scarcity, which need 'management'. This is true not only in Nepal but also in

India with its *dirigisme* of bureaucratic control over the provision of water and power services. The net result has been that state structures in both countries have maintained and managed scarcity, while the tedious commission agent politics of development merchants and donor agencies holds local market-led innovation hostage till the next major project is bagged by the right constellation of vested interests.

The 'roads versus ropeways' case shows that the transportation bureaucracy deliberately ignores alternatives and will not devolve control to villagers which would enable them to address the scarcity of access issue on their own. The bureaucracy would prefer to continue with its five-year and longer-term plans that give deserving villages road connections eventually, when their turn comes in the larger scheme of national planning and international donor consortium approved 'perspective plans'. The markets go with whoever is willing to pay, while the egalitarian activists, motivated by a sense of unfairness, look for solutions such as ropeways that give them a fair price for their products. Thus people's understanding of the concept of scarcity and its severity lies in the way they perceive what they see as fair or unfair. The logic is unequivocal in the case of energy scarcity. At every stage of the development game, there has been a hijacking of the definition of scarcity by more powerful actors, to suit the technology choices of their proclivities, a hijacking that can be reversed or rectified if there is sufficient plurality (in other words, genuine democracy) in the policy terrain.

Notes

1 Regent's Lecture at UC Berkeley in 1985 and also Norberg-Hodge, 1996.
2 Stavrianos, 1981. This history of the 'process of Third World-ization' argues that a debilitating (unfavourable or one-sided) dependence on traded necessities is what created Third World conditions since the 1500s, first in Eastern Europe, then in the Americas and then in Africa and Asia.
3 In this chapter 'load shedding' refers to officially scheduled power cuts to electricity consumers rolling across sections of the city or region at pre-announced hours of the day. Unlike power failures and sudden outages, this is a management tool used by electricity utilities facing power generation limitations due to unexpected droughts (for hydro) or fuel shortage (for thermal stations) or construction delays in the completion of new power plants.
4 See *Auto Nepal*, journal of transport and automobiles, vol 1 no 1, published by Surya Sundar Publications, Kathmandu, 2005.
5 The total number of vehicles is obtained from www.nepalpolice.gov.np/trafficpolice/ phq%20website.doc (last accessed September 2007). The number of automobiles is from Pradhan, 2007.
6 Its primary function was to haul flagstones and other construction material from the hills in the outskirts for the construction of opulent Rana palaces, hardly a productive use. Because the labour force had to be fed, the ropeway was also used to transport cheap lowland rice, a function that eventually benefitted the common people in the valley too as an afterthought.
7 In a rich, subtropical climate, forests do not need artificial forestation to grow: all they require is 'social fencing' that would prevent overgrazing, something now

proved beyond any doubt by the very successful community forestry efforts in the mid-hills of Nepal. That the aid industry led the forestation move from a paradigm based on self-serving ends has been documented in Thompson and Gyawali, 2007.

8   New-found democracy that gave some voice not only to villagers in far-off locales but also junior civil servants in the field. During the unstable, 'musical chair' governments of the 1990s, top bureaucrats in the forest ministry were too preoccupied with both their survival and furthering promotion interests, etc. to bother with a small project in a remote area. For details, see Upadhya, 2004.

9   Most of the information on Bhattedanda Milkway, in addition to what is described in Upadhya (2004), comes from personal communication with one of the authors (who was the Milkway's original implementer and project manager of BIWMP) as well as face-to-face interviews in 2007 and 2008 with lead farmer and community leader Surya Man Loh of Bhattedanda Milkway extension campaign. Loh describes how the Kathmandu central ministries were practically inaccessible and insensitive to village community groups such as his. Accessing EU aid decision-makers to appraise them of the village's needs was, in his words, as practicable as 'going to the moon'. Thus it was impossible to get the committed EU funding for the extension project released: it remained blocked for procedural reasons and lack of central political support. He and his villagers were subsequently able to lobby much more successfully with local governments at village and district levels to access alternative funding for the extension of the Milkway.

10 The 'communitization' of electricity in Nepal began in May 2003 with a change in electricity utility rules that allowed organized village groups to buy electricity in bulk and retail by themselves. This institutional freedom from the deadweight of large bureaucratic shackles allowed them to take innovative measures and exhibit entrepreneurial skills in the choice of local technologies as well as to seek and implement new ways of using electricity for productive ends. Running their Milkway with 'communitized' hydroelectricity from the Nepali national grid rather than imported diesel was only one of such community-level innovations. More details can be found in the magazine *Bidyut Khabar* (vol 2, no 7, April 2008), the mouthpiece of the National Association of Community Electricity Users Nepal (NACEUN) as well as on their website, www.naceun.org.np (last accessed 8 August 2010).

11 The 'alternative market' of small-scale businesses promoting photovoltaics, wind energy, bio-gas and small hydro, contrasts with the heavy market players in the petroleum-based industries. The contrast has been called the fight between the petroleum-based dinosaur industries and the small, quick and cheerful mammals championing alternatives and renewable energy.

12 This statement and the categories discussed below are from Thompson, 2004.

13 The fourfold typology of electricity – and that of four types of social water – are originally conceptualized in Verweij, 1999, pp27–42.

14 The task force – Task Force for Planning Ten-Year Hydroelectricity Development, 2065 – was created by the government of Nepal after the rebel Maoists won the elections and came to power in mid-2008. In one of their early pronouncements, the former rebels declared that they would build 10,000MW of hydropower in 10 years (the current total installed capacity of the country is only about 650MW). The task force, which has recently released its report, was mandated to suggest how this massive enterprise would be achieved, but has concluded that it is not possible without serious, almost impossible, preconditions. Admitting that Nepal's maximum requirements for the next 10 years would not exceed 5000MW in the most optimistic of scenarios, it concludes that power scarcity and load shedding would not fade away

but would have to be 'managed', in good hierarchic fashion, ignoring the challenge of curtailing massive power theft as well as the proven potential of Nepal's private sector to meet the challenge, if encouraged by the government.

15 The 'theory of plural rationalities', or Cultural Theory, is described and its implications discussed in Thompson et al, 1990; Thompson and Gyawali, 2007; Gyawali, 2003; Thompson, 2008.

References

Dhakal, R.R. (2004) 'Construction ropeways in Nepal', in D. Gyawali, A. Dixit and M. Upadhya, *Ropeways in Nepal: Contexts, Constraints and Co-Evolution*, Nepal Water Conservation Foundation, Kathmandu and Kathmandu Electric Vehicle Alliance

Dixit, A. and Gyawali, D. (1999) 'Social response to deficient drinking water supply, Kathmandu', in M. Moench, F. Caspari and A. Dixit (eds) *Rethinking the Mosaic: Investigations into Local Water Management*, Nepal Water Conservation Foundation, Kathmandu and Institute for Social and Environmental Transition, Boulder, Colorado, Box 13

Gyawali, D. (2003) *Rivers, Technology and Society: Learning the Lessons from Water Management in Nepal*, Zed Books, London

Gyawali, D. (2004) 'Governance, corruption and foreign aid', in S. Sharma, J. Koponen, D. Gyawali and A. Dixit (eds) *Aid Under Stress: Water, Forests and Finnish Support in Nepal*, published for the Institute of Development Studies, University of Helsinki and Interdisciplinary Analysts, Kathmandu, Himal Books, Kathmandu

Gyawali, D. and Dixit, A. (1999) 'Fractured institutions and physical interdependence: Challenges to local water management in the Tinau River Basin, Nepal', in M. Moench, E. Caspari and A. Dixit (eds) *Rethinking the Mosaic: Investigations into Local Water Management*, Nepal Water Conservation Foundation, Kathmandu and Institute for Social and Environmental Transition, Boulder, Colorado

Kafle, B.K. (2007) *Nepal Oil Nigam Ko Niyati* (Fate of the Nepal Oil Corporation), *Prabhat* (Journal of the Nepal Oil Corporation), Kathmandu

Lal, V. and Nandy, A. (eds) (2005) *The Future of Knowledge and Culture: A Dictionary for the 21st Century*, Penguin/Viking, India and USA

Mars, G. (1982) *Cheats at Work: The Anthropology of Workplace Crime*, Counterpoint and George Allen and Unwin, London

Nandy, A. (2005) 'Coca-Cola' and 'consumerism' in V. Lal and A. Nandy (eds) (2005) *The Future of Knowledge and Culture: A Dictionary for the 21st Century*, Penguin/Viking, India and USA

Norberg-Hodge, H. (1996) 'The Pressure to Modernise and Globalise', in J. Mander and E. Goldsmith (eds) *The Case Against the Global Economy*, Sierra Club Books, San Francisco

Pradhan, S. (2007) *Nepal ma automobile ko stithi* (State of the automobile in Nepal), *Kantipur*, 29 September

Shrestha, S.L. (2004) 'State Promotion of Ropeways: Moving from Stagnation to Change in Nepal's Policy Environment', in D. Gyawali, A. Dixit and M. Upadhya, (eds) *Ropeways in Nepal: Context Constraints and Co-Evolution*, Nepal Water Conservation Foundation and Kathmandu Electric Vehicle Alliance, Kathmandu

Stavrianos, L.S. (1981) *Global Rift: The Third World Comes of Age*, William Morrow and Company, Inc., New York

Thompson, M. (2004) 'Technology and democracy: A cultural theory approach', in F. Engelstad and O. Oseterud (eds) *Power and Democracy*, Ashgate, UK

Thompson, M. (2008) *Organising and Disorganising: A Dynamic and Non-Linear Theory of Institutional Emergence and its Implications*, Triarchy Press, Axminster, UK

Thompson, M., Ellis, R. and Wildavsky, A. (1990) *Cultural Theory*, Westview Publishers, Boulder, Colorado

Thompson, M. and Gyawali, D. (2007) 'Uncertainty revisited or the triumph of hype over experience', in M. Thompson, M. Warburton and T. Hatley, *Uncertainty on a Himalayan Scale*, Himal Books, Kathmandu, with the International Institute for Applied Systems Analysis, Austria and the James Martin Institute for Science and Civilization, Oxford University

Upadhya, M. (2004) 'Bhattedanda Milkway: Making markets accessible to marginalized farmers', in D. Gyawali, A. Dixit and M. Upadhya, *Ropeways in Nepal: Contexts, Constraints and Co-Evolution*, Nepal Water Conservation Foundation, Kathmandu and Kathmandu Electric Vehicle Alliance

Verweij, M. (1999) 'Whose behaviour is affected by international anarchy?', in M. Thompson, G. Grendstadt and P. Selle (eds) *Cultural Theory as Political Science*, Routledge, London

Yapa, L. (2005) 'Scarcity', in V. Lal and A. Nandy (eds) (2005) *The Future of Knowledge and Culture: A Dictionary for the 21st Century*, Penguin/Viking, India and USA

Afterword: Looking beyond Scarcity?[1]

Lyla Mehta

This volume has argued that scarcity is not merely a natural phenomenon that can be isolated from planning models, allocation and knowledge politics, policy choices, market forces and power, social and gender dynamics. Empirical and theoretical contributions have questioned the universal application of the scarcity postulate and *Homo economicus*. Examples from water, food/agriculture and energy have demonstrated that conventional visions of scarcity that focus on aggregate numbers and physical quantities are privileged over local knowledges and experiences of scarcity. Totalizing discourses of science and progress tend to support a universalizing notion of scarcity. These universal notions of scarcity often result in self-fulfilling prophesies around 'crises'. The 'scare' of scarcity has led to scarcity emerging as a political strategy for powerful groups, and problematic ideas about nature and society continue to be reproduced. These feed into simplistic and often inappropriate solutions that cause inaccessibility and perpetrate exclusions. Thus, the notion of scarcity often aggravates the problem of scarcity.

Are there ways forward for research, policy and practice? It is tempting to suggest that the word scarcity should be abandoned and replaced by something else such as finitude, finiteness or limitedness. While these terms do not have the same historical and disciplinary legacies that surround scarcity, getting rid of the term 'scarcity' will not eliminate the structures and power relations that promote scarcity politics and the accompanying processes of exclusion, control, neo-Malthusian slippages and so on. Nor will substitution eliminate the warrant of the term in the specific experiences of scarcity/scarcities in daily life (for example, the scarcity of time, attention, good health care, education and so on). Instead, we need to use new analytical tools, imaginaries and politics to recreate alternative visions of resources, scarcity and social justice. It is to these that I now turn.

There is a need to overcome existing strategic boundaries and erasures around scarcity and challenge the ways in which dominant instruments of power erase past and lived experiences of scarcity to create firm categories of what is to be valued and what is valueless. This means recreating what has been erased, while also interrogating the hidden assumptions behind the so-called neutral term scarcity. We thus need to be vigilant to focus constantly on the polyvalent nature of scarcity and the different ways that the problems of scarcity and the solutions to it can be contested and reconstrued.

In concrete terms, resource determinism and the dominant focus on the material characteristics of resources needs to be replaced by a lens that combines the discursive with the materialities of resources. The material nature of things gets rendered and fixed through ideas, knowledge, information and imagination, policies, rules, decisions and power. New conceptual tools that capture the diverse and dynamic aspects of resources must therefore inform high-level policy debate around water scarcity, energy and food politics. Issues concerning costs and benefits need to transcend mere monetary value to focus on non-quantifiable, non-monetary benefits and their wide ranging impacts on individuals in society (rich, poor, women, men, powerful and powerless).

More attention needs to be paid to the scarcities around knowledge. Conceptual enclosures allow live nature to become an economic resource and blanks out the realities of subsistence economies. Various domains of science and research policy are subjecting local people's knowledge to control, manipulation and exclusion. Elite narratives and institutions rarely allow the logic of the market to be questioned. Institutional responses towards scarcity and risk management and the drive to colonize and control the future, have led to epistemic, ontological and moral deletions. Monopolies over resources such as water also usually monopolize knowledge of how the resource should be managed. Thus constructions of scarcity and resource 'crises' need to be challenged, while local realities need to be a part of policy responses to resource management and allocation processes, ideally combined with more democratic decision-making. Also dominant policy frameworks need to focus much more on the 'good' and on human freedoms and capabilities where wealth and growth are not the ends but the means for providing the necessities of life leading to self-fulfilment and human flourishing. But as demonstrated in several chapters of this book, powerful global institutions, think tanks and individuals remain impervious to local level evidence and experiences. Therefore, it is important to tackle head on the mechanisms of power in shaping dominant knowledge about resources, markets and growth.

This would mean questioning the conventional role of communications, the media and formal education in erasing alternative perspectives and in sedimenting dominant discourses of scarcity. The corporate controlled media, be it North America or South Asia, have used their power to silence critical voices. We thus need to seek out alternative media to allow different views of the world to come into the public domain. In particular, we need a pedagogy of the powerful and new reflexivities that can question the role of institutions that colonize the future in simplistic ways without drawing lessons from the past and without bringing complexity into our understandings.

Wider socio-political and economic issues must stay in the frame of analysis. It is thus important to make links between notions of resource scarcity, the politics of aid and donors, the role of the private sector, transnational corporations and the military-industrial complex. In particular, this needs to be done in so-called fragile and weak states where rich nations, individuals and corporations carve out and distribute 'scarce' resources among themselves as a way of sustaining economic and military interests.

Challenging dominant models must start at the personal level. As concerned scholars, activists, practitioners and policy-makers we need to be upfront and reflexive about our own role in the creation and sustenance of *Homo economicus* and the contradictions in our own lifestyles and consumption patterns. Most of all, this book urges us to recover alternative realities. Since notions of scarcity often lead to an erasure of issues of equity, scale, embeddedness and locality, there may be the need to recover different notions – for instance of the 'good' and the 'commons'. This must not be done in a utilitarian way to justify problematic macro-level programmes, or in an overly romantic way that wipes out deliberation, diversity and heterogeneity. Regaining the commons is also about promoting just decision-making processes and curtailing those who unseeingly and overbearingly exercise power over the weak and marginalized.

With the global system in a financial crisis and our planet in peril due to global warming, it is a good time to think bold and big and use fantasy and imagination to conceive of the possibilities of a fairer world. Efficiency can be replaced by sufficiency. Trickle down growth (where scarcity is the norm) can be replaced by a growth that bubbles more equitably. The fixation with commodities, credit, markets and growth has delivered a development model where almost 4 out of 6.7 billion people live without basic entitlements and where the economic system may soon accumulate more 'illth' than wealth. Such gross deprivation of both humans and nature should no longer be naturalized or tolerated and we need to draw on new politics and imaginaries to create a more just world where resources are distributed equitably. Debunking scarcity myths is one place to start.

Notes

1 Some of the ideas presented in this afterword were expressed by several participants at the scarcity workshop to whom I'm most grateful. I also draw on Princen (2005), Sachs et al (2007), Jackson (2009), Nussbaum (1987), UNDP (2006) and the Casablanca Dreamers (2010).

References

Casablanca Dreamers (2010) *Vision for A Better World: From Economic Crisis to Equality*, UNDP, available at www.casablanca-dream.net/ (last accessed May 2010)

Jackson, T. (2009) *Prosperity without Growth: Economics for a Finite Planet*, Earthscan, London

Nussbaum, M. (1987) *Nature, Function, and Capability: Aristotle on Political Distribution*, World Institute for Development Economics Research, Helsinki

Princen, T. (2005) *The Logic of Sufficiency*, MIT, Cambridge, MA

Sachs, W., Santarius, T. and Camiller, P. (2007) *Fair Future: Resource Conflicts, Security and Global Justice*, Zed Books, London

United Nations Development Programme (2006) *Human Development Report 2006: Beyond Scarcity: Power, Poverty and the Global Water Crisis*, Palgrave Macmillan, New York, available at http://hdr.undp.org/en/reports/global/hdr2006/ (last accessed December 2009)

Appendix: Institute of Development Studies Conference Statement on Scarcity

Scarcity is considered to be the ubiquitous feature of the modern condition and is widely used as an explanation for social organization, social conflict and the resource crunch confronting humanity's survival on the planet. Scarcity is made out to be an all-pervasive fact of our lives – be it around housing, food, water or oil. The scarcity of these essential commodities and resources is used as an explanation for growing environmental conflicts and human insecurity. In order to mitigate scarcity, there have been calls for further scientific and technological innovation, and science and technology are evoked as the appropriate 'solutions'.

We, however, believe that scarcity is not a natural condition. It is not something that is inherently in the nature of things. It does not arise because there is too little water, food and so on to go around. Instead, the problem lies in how we see scarcity and the ways in which it is socially generated.

Often conventional visions of scarcity that focus on aggregate numbers and physical quantities are privileged over local knowledges and experiences of scarcity that identify problems in very different ways. Universal theories are privileged, and problematic ideas of nature and society continue to get reproduced. These feed into simplistic and often inappropriate solutions. Thus, the scarcity problem gets aggravated.

Studies now highlight that the universal notion of scarcity emerged in affluent societies. Scarcity justifies the dynamic of spiralling needs, wants and desires and the resultant scarcity legitimizes market domains and property regimes. Not all of these have favourable outcomes for the poor and marginalized. Detailed sociological and political attention to what is actually happening on the ground has almost always located the causes of pressing social problems such as hunger or water shortage not in an *absolute* scarcity but in *socially generated* scarcity arising from imbalances of power that deny people access to food or water. These include: unequal gender relations, ethnic and racial discrimination, unfair terms of trade, biased markets, and unequal access to land and resources. Moreover, the 'scare' of scarcity has led to scarcity emerging as a political strategy for powerful groups. It is used to make problematic linkages between the so-called population explosion in the Third World and global environmental degradation to justify controversial water and agricultural projects under the guise of TINA (there is no alternative) and to legitimize resource capture. It is also used to provide simplistic solutions rather than focusing on the social and political reasons that cause inaccessibility and perpetrate exclusions.

Therefore, it is necessary to understand the different ways through which notions of scarcity are contested and created and how they are being perpetuated by the media, donors, politicians and through formal educational processes. We also believe there is a need to be vigilant when the notion of resource scarcity is invoked to justify the politics of aid, and the role of the private sector, multinational corporations (MNCs) and the military-industrial complex.

We must develop alternative ways of regarding the use and allocation of resources, if we are to prevent powerful groups from presenting scarcity as a 'natural condition' and then using this theoretical construct to capture resources at the expense of the weak. For this, democratic debate that embraces deliberation, diversity and heterogeneity must be allowed to take place. There is also the need to regain the notion of the 'good' or the 'commons' – in a way that avoids resource capture by the powerful and is sensitive to local social and power relations.

Tony Allan, King's College London
Franck Amalric, University of Zürich
P.B. Anand, Bradford Centre for International Development
Nurit Bodemann-Ostow, MA Student, IDS
Sue Branford, journalist
Vinita Damodaran, University of Sussex
Ajaya Dixit, Nepal Water Conservation Foundation
James Fairhead, University of Sussex
Tim Forsyth, London School of Economics and Political Science
James Fraser, Dphil candidate, University of Sussex
Martin Greeley, IDS
Richard Grove, University of Sussex
Dipak Gyawali, Institute for Social and Environmental Transition
Lawrence Haddad, IDS
Betsy Hartmann, Hampshire College
Nicholas Hildyard, The Corner House
Jasveen Jairath, CAPNET South Asia
Sheila Jasanoff, Harvard University
Bruce Lankford, University of East Anglia
Melissa Leach, IDS
Fred Luks, University of Hamburg
Gordon MacKerron, University of Sussex
Lyla Mehta, IDS
Erik Millstone, University of Sussex
Synne Movik, IDS

Sobona Mtisi, DPhil candidate, University of Manchester
Peter Newborne, Overseas Development Institute
Alan Nicol, Overseas Development Institute
Paul Nightingale, University of Sussex
Oga Steve Abah, Theatre for Development Centre, Ahmadu Bello University
Christian Poirier, MA Candidate University of Sussex
Steve Rayner, Director, ESRC Science in Society Programme
Jean Robert, Universidad del Estado de Morelos
Catherine Setchell, MA Candidate, IDS
Ian Scoones, IDS
Jan Selby, University of Sussex
Andy Stirling, University of Sussex
Vanessa Taylor, Cultures of Consumption Programme, Birkbeck College
Jaisel Vadgama, MA Student, University of Sussex
Barbara van Koppen, International Water Management Institute
Shiv Visvanathan, Dhirubhai Ambani Institute for Information and Communication Technology
Nick von Tunzelmann, University of Sussex
Linda Waldman, IDS
Will Wolmer, IDS

June 2005

Index

Note: page numbers followed by *n* refer to the end of chapter notes